Aurora G. Morcillo
(In)visible Acts of Resistance in the Twilight of the Franco Regime

Historical Gender Studies | Volume 2

Aurora G. Morcillo (PhD) is a professor of history at Florida International University. She is a cultural historian and a gender studies specialist of modern Spain and Post-1945 European history.

Aurora G. Morcillo
(In)visible Acts of Resistance in the Twilight of the Franco Regime
A Historical Narration

Bibliographic information published by the Deutsche Nationalbibliothek
The Deutsche Nationalbibliothek lists this publication in the Deutsche Nationalbibliografie; detailed bibliographic data are available in the Internet at http://dnb.d-nb.de

This work is licensed under the Creative Commons Attribution-NonCommercial-NoDerivatives 4.0 (BY-NC-ND) which means that the text may be used for non-commercial purposes, provided credit is given to the author. For details go to http://creativecommons.org/licenses/by-nc-nd/4.0/
To create an adaptation, translation, or derivative of the original work and for commercial use, further permission is required and can be obtained by contacting rights@transcript-publishing.com
Creative Commons license terms for re-use do not apply to any content (such as graphs, figures, photos, excerpts, etc.) not original to the Open Access publication and further permission may be required from the rights holder. The obligation to research and clear permission lies solely with the party re-using the material.

© 2022 transcript Verlag, Bielefeld

Cover layout: Maria Arndt, Bielefeld
Printed by Majuskel Medienproduktion GmbH, Wetzlar
Print-ISBN 978-3-8376-5257-4
PDF-ISBN 978-3-8394-5257-8
https://doi.org/10.14361/9783839452578
ISSN of series: 2627-1907
eISSN of series: 2703-0512

Printed on permanent acid-free text paper.

Contents

Acknowledgements 9

Foreword
By Jo Labanyi 13

PART 1

Introduction
Space and Time or the Poetics of Oral History 17

Chapter 1
Concha & Amalias's Kaloskeagathos 41

Chapter 2
Revolutionary Mystique: Socorro and Jesús 55

Chapter 3
Claros del Bosque: Joaquín and Arturo's Stories... 73

Chapter 4
Al Amparo de Fecun 89

Chapter 5
Julia's Prosody.. 105

Chapter 6
Marga's Dos Orillas 115

Intermezzo:
In-visible: Aurora's Trinity 123

PART 2

Intro Part II
Time and Invisible Things: Working Class Narratives 139

Chapter 7
Patrocinio 101 165

Chapter 8
Pura's Rashomon Effect (1926-2013) 179

Chapter 9
In Antigone's Shadow: Valentina 207

Chapter 10
Esperanza's and Adoración's Cartographies of Mercy 233

Chapter 11
Luz Invisible 263

Coda 287

Bibliography 289

Glossary 307

Appendix I
For A History of Mercy by María Zambrano (1989) 309

Appendix II
DIOTIMA DE MANTINEA by Maria Zambrano (1987) 317

Appendix III 327

This book is dedicated to my mother, Aurora, and all the strong and valiant women of Spain.

Acknowledgements

In the course of writing this book, Aurora[1] suffered a tragic accident. She passed away on March 3rd, 2020. This book is the culmination of many years of hard effort. It is in many ways the defining work of her illustrious career and the natural follow-up to her previous two books on women under Franco: *True Catholic Womanhood: Gender Ideology in Franco's Spain*, and *The Seduction of Modern Spain: The Female Body and the Francoist Body Politic*. This third part of the trilogy was especially important to Aurora because it involved women she knew personally—mentors, aunts, her mother, neighbors—who had had a profound effect on her development as a person and a scholar. This work also allowed Aurora to delve into the areas of philosophy and literature which she deeply loved, and to expand the discipline of history to include, not just those previously outside the grand narrative, but different ways of doing history.

It falls to me, her husband, to write the acknowledgements to the many people who were instrumental in the making of this work. Aurora used to say that a book has one mother but many relatives. There may be some "relatives" I do not acknowledge because of my ignorance, but for those who are left out, know that Aurora appreciated your contributions nevertheless.

First, thank you to all the women who agreed to open up their hearts and memory vaults to give us their insight into the turbulent times of the late Franco era. Reliving these difficult times could not have been easy. Thanks also goes out to the women who were interviewed for this project but were not included in this volume, and to a larger generation of women who keep this history alive by passing down their own stories.

While writing this book, Aurora had the opportunity to spend a term at Exeter College, Oxford, as a visiting scholar. While there, she was able to present early versions of these chapters and learn from colleagues in the Oxford Centre for Life Writing and the History Department. The three months she spent at Oxford were

---

1   Aurora Morcillo Memorial Fellowship: https://history.fiu.edu/graduate/fellowship-opportunities/aurora-morcillo-memorial-scholarship/

some of the happiest in her life. Thanks go out to all her colleagues and friends there who made this such a rewarding and productive period.

Aurora grew into the internationally known scholar she was thanks in large part to her university, Florida International University in Miami. She thrived in the competitive but supportive environment of the history department in the Steven J. Green School of International and Public Affairs. Thanks go to Department Chair Victor Uribe and the rest of Aurora's history colleagues for their support of Aurora and this work. A special thanks to Dean John Stack and his office. Dean Stack was an early supporter of Aurora and her scholarship, and was there for her always.

Aurora was deeply committed to her students. Many of the ideas for this book came from discussions with them as she put forth a different approach to thinking about history. Thank you all for being a big reason she worked so hard on scholarship like this.

Aurora was able to present widely many of the ideas for this book thanks to invitations from a supportive network of scholars in both America and abroad. She truly valued your intellectual fellowship, but more importantly your friendship.

Transcript Verlag had the courage to publish this unconventional work of scholarship when others wouldn't. Thanks go to Jakob Horstmann and all those at transcript Verlag for working with Aurora and me to get this important work into print.

Family always came first for Aurora. She may have left Spain physically, but emotionally she remained in Granada. Thanks go to her mother and father, Aurora and Manuel, who always encouraged her to study, to take risks, and to never set limits on what she could accomplish. Her brother Jose and sister Emilia were constantly in her thoughts and provided important feedback on this very personal work. Her niece and nephews in Spain were a source of never-ending pride.

For their help in editing the manuscript, I would like to thank my chief copy-editor Angélica Sánchez-Clark who labored many hours getting this manuscript ready to print. Also, thanks to Cayce Wicks, and June Pilsitz for all your help in editing different versions along the way. This was truly a team effort, and all made this a better manuscript. A special thanks goes out to Aurora's great friend and colleague Jo Labanyi, who agreed to write the forward to this book and gave me much needed feedback and support as I put together the final draft.

And finally, I would like to thank our son Carlos who knew, first-hand, how valiant and strong are Spanish women. Carlos has been my greatest support over these difficult months and was his mother's inspiration always.

Carlos and I would like to further Aurora's legacy. We have set up a fellowship at Florida International University to support young women scholars studying abroad. We encourage everyone who reads this book to visit the fellowship webpage to learn more about Aurora and to support the next generation of Spanish Historians.

Charles Bleiker

Foreword
By Jo Labanyi

I write with a complicated mix of feelings: sorrow at Aurora's tragic loss but gratitude to her husband Charles Bleiker—who has finalized the preparation of Aurora's manuscript for publication—for inviting me to write this foreword. This project was very dear to Aurora's heart. She talked about it when we met in her hometown of Granada during several summers, and she gave a wonderful paper on it at the panel I organized on "Alternative Histories" for the 2014 MLA Convention in Chicago. In that memorable paper, she declared that her aim was to condense each life story of the various women she had interviewed in a haiku—she offered a few examples. The point of the haiku was to appreciate the silence around the words.

The most original feature of Aurora's book is her intercalation of poems in her analysis of the life stories that comprise each chapter. One poem comes near to the brevity of the haiku—an evocation of the hunger that marked her mother's postwar childhood, which Aurora read at the 2014 MLA convention. In addition to the poetic chapter titles, each interview is prefaced by one or more poems, taken from an impressively international range of authors, with several by Aurora herself. The manuscript was to have ended with a concluding poem by Aurora, which sadly we do not have. Aurora talks of "the poetics of oral history," for oral history is a medium, like poetry, that conveys its meaning through what lies in between, behind, and beneath the words. And all poetry, even when it is considerably wordier than a haiku, makes us aware of the blank space around the text, just as oral histories—especially when recalling lives that have not been given their due, as is the case here—are also a mesh of what is said and what was not or could not be said before, and may remain unsaid even now because of the difficulty of acknowledging it (something that Aurora is particularly sensitive to). Hence the book's title, *(In)visible Acts of Resistance*.

Above all, poetry conveys emotions whereas prose is, for the most part, a vehicle of information. Aurora acknowledges her debt to Spanish Republican exile philosopher María Zambrano's concept of "poetic reason." There is a noticeable difference between the interviews analyzed in Part I—conducted in 1989 with former anti-Franco student activists, subsequently professors at the University of

Granada—when Aurora was a history student about to take up a doctoral fellowship at the University of New Mexico, and those analyzed in Part II—conducted after the year 2000, by which time the history of the emotions had become a burgeoning field of inquiry, emerging out of memory studies in which oral history has been so important. Interest in the emotional textures revealed by oral history is what inspired Aurora to return to those early interviews and to conduct further interviews with working-class women in Granada, several from her own family. By the time of the second batch of interviews, Aurora's interest had shifted to lives that are marked not by overt political activism but by everyday acts of resilience which, Aurora argues, should also be seen as acts of defiance. While the interviews in Part I are important for their information content, reminding us of the risks involved in being a student activist under the late Franco dictatorship, it is the emotional content of the working-class life stories in Part II that clearly engages Aurora's poetic imagination.

The majority—but not all—of the life stories presented here are of women. Aurora's career as a scholar, as everyone familiar with her work knows, was devoted to documenting the ways in which the Franco dictatorship constrained the lives of Spanish women. This volume is an important complement to her earlier books in that it does not focus on what the regime did to women, but on how women resisted the imposition of power through daily acts of micro-resistance—by refusing to play the role of victim, by surviving and fighting for their loved ones. It is also an exploration of Aurora's own subjectivity via the emotions and memories that the interviews awoke in Aurora herself. The book is an explicit homage to women—her professors in Part I, family members and acquaintances in Part II—who shaped her life and made her the feminist historian that she became. The final chapter was to have analyzed the interview that Aurora conducted with her parents, Aurora and Manuel; sadly, this chapter remains unwritten. However, her tribute to her family is present in the Intermezzo "Aurora's Trinity" that narrates the story of the three Auroras in her family—her grandmother, her mother, herself—as the basis of a theorization of experience as becoming.

This book is an account not only of the becoming of the individuals interviewed by Aurora, but also of the becoming of Aurora herself as a creative and caring historian.

Jo Labanyi

New York University

PART 1

Introduction
Space and Time or the Poetics of Oral History

> Movement must be at the very heart of listening.
> Eudora Welty[1]

Time passes, moves through us, conferring an evanescent quality to our lives. Listening to each other is "stirring" for the heart, as time and space converge. The oral historian turned illusionist embarks on a journey to past unseen things, transforming them, through language, into visible transubstantiations. The space where historian and informant meet is filled with a tempo, a rhythm, a revelation. Movement is at the heart of it all.

Since the beginning of my career some thirty years ago, my historical analysis has been informed by an exploration of the shadows. Using the lens of gender to identify and illuminate the dark interstices of time and place, I began by exploring gendered official discourses as expressed in the laws and decrees of both the Francoist state apparatus and the Catholic Church. In my first book, *True Catholic Womanhood: Gender Ideology in Franco's Spain*,[2] I focused on the Francoist university and the various Catholic women's organizations that represented the ideal notion of what I called "True Catholic Womanhood." Building on this ideal in my second book, *The Seduction of Modern Spain: The Female Body and the Francoist Body Politic*,[3] I sought to further understand how gender ideology informed the state's tight control of public morality through the censorship and repression of popular culture. This work delved into the somatic metaphors used in National Catholic rhetoric to better understand the correlation between the gendered human body and the Francoist bio-power. In this new book I paint the third panel in the tryptic by focusing, not on official state discourses or mass communication, but on the counter discourses articulated by ordinary people experiencing the twilight of Franco's regime.

---

1 Eudora Welty, *One Writer's Beginnings* (Cambridge, MA: Harvard University Press, 1995), 11.
2 Aurora G. Morcillo, *True Catholic Womanhood: Gender Ideology in Franco's Spain* (Dekalb: Northern Illinois University Press, 2000, 2008).
3 Aurora G. Morcillo, *The Seduction of Modern Spain: The Female Body and the Francoist Body Politic* (Lewisburg: Bucknell University Press, 2010).

In Part 1, I focus on the stories of middle class, well-educated college student activists in the 1960s and 1970s. In Part 2, I shift to the narratives of women from working class families with little or no formal schooling. Together, these two perspectives form a more complete, balanced picture of everyday resistance to the regime's control. I title this work *(In)visible Acts of Resistance* to highlight the pervasiveness of the struggle to break through the strictures imposed by Franco's regime, and the heroic acts of ordinary people made in the name of survival. The weight of so many individual acts of resistance by those portrayed in this work, and the many more just like them, helped break down the regime's control, and set the tone for the successful transition to democracy that was to come.

The interviewees are individuals outside of mainstream history. Their *stories* represent the substratum of what Miguel de Unamuno, in his work *En torno al casticismo* (1902), called intra-history:[4]

> The newspapers say nothing about the silent life of millions of men without a history who, at all times and in all parts of the world, get up with the sun and go about their obscure, silent, eternal daily work in the fields, the work upon which, much like the sub-oceanic reefs, the islets of history are erected.[5]

As Javier Krauel points out, Unamuno's concept of the intra-history affords us a new sense of personhood, which downplays political and economic aspects of the superficial historical narrative in favor of an intra-historical exploration of a more authentic being in time.

Therefore, this study aspires to shed light on ordinary acts of resistance rather than headline-grabbing events that typically serve historical narrative. As Howard Eiland and Kevin McLaughlin point out, Walter Benjamin's intent in *The Arcades Project* was to show a "primal history" only possible to realize through "cunning":

> [I]t was not the great men and celebrated events of traditional historiography but rather the "refused" and "detritus" of history, the half-concealed, variegated traces of the daily life of "the collective;" that was to be the object of study.[6]

Oral history is the tool of choice in this study to aid in the "cunning" process of unveiling the visible and invisible strategies of self-empowerment utilized by ordinary people in spite of the Francoist regime's attempts at control in the late 1960s and early 1970s. The theoretical and methodological rationale used to examine the informants' narratives draws from philosophy, but also includes urban, literary, and

---

4 Peggy Watson, *Intra-historia in Miguel de Unamuno's Novel: A Continual Presence* (Potomac, Maryland: Scripta Humanistica, 1993).
5 Miguel de Unamuno, *En torno al casticismo* (Madrid: Alianza Editorial, 2000), 40.
6 Eiland and Kevin McLaughlin, "Translators' Foreword," in *The Arcades Project*, by Walter Benjamin (Cambridge, MA: Harvard University Press, 1999), ix.

gender studies. The notes that follow address oral historiography from the perspective of autobiographical and memory studies, utilizing the vectors of time and space. Oral history represents an apt instrument of analysis to better understand how space and time collide in the construction of historical narration.

I draw from urban theory as proposed in the work of Henri Lefebvre's (1901-1991) *Critique of Everyday Life* to analyze the lives of citizens affected by the changes in demographics following the Spanish Civil War (1936-1939). Spain's rapid urbanization led to the proliferation of shanty towns on the edges of major cities such as Madrid, Barcelona, and Bilbao. Neighborhood associations with their ad-hoc governing councils sprang up and would later become legitimate political voices for the labor movement. Urbanization was also a response to the transition from post-war economic isolation (autarky) to an open consumer economy fed by American dollars (The Pact of Madrid in 1953). Mass migration after the civil war, both inside and outside the country, added to the growth of Spain's urban centers and the dislocation of its people. The examination of the layout of the city of Granada in the late 1960s and early 1970s is used to show the meaning of space as conceived and experienced over time.

The stories should be read as creative non-fiction, or ficto-critical narrations, following María Zambrano's focus on emotions and the invisible connections they articulate among us, which guides the analysis of the narration.[7] The stories are not just told plainly, but "poeticized." Ficto-criticism is particularly fruitful in the realm of autobiography within cultural studies. As Anna Gibbs explains:

> Fictocriticism does not illustrate an already existing argument, does not simply formulate philosophy (or anything else) in fictional terms. It is not translation or transposition: it says something which can't be said in any other way: because it is not reducible to propositional content. It is, in essence, per-formative, a meta-discourse in which the strategies of the telling are part of the point of the tale.[8]

The goal is to prioritize a lyrical narrative to better capture the emotional landscape of late Francoism. The interviews uncover how people creatively resisted and trespassed figurative and physical boundaries set up by Franco's Cold War, a technocratic, modernizing project.

---

7   Anna Gibbs, "Bodies of Words: Feminism and Fictocriticism- Explanation and Demonstration," Text 1, no. 2 (1997). See also on art-based research: Thomas Barone and Eliot Eisner, *Arts Based Research*, 1st ed. (Thousand Oaks, CA: SAGE Publications, 2011); Heather Kerr and Amanda Nettelbeck, *The Space Between - Australian Women Writing Fictocriticism* (Perth, AU: UWA Publishing, 1998); Elizabeth Pattinson, "Discovering the Self: Fictocriticism, Flux and Authorial Identity" http://www.aawp.dreamhosters.com/wp-content/uploads/2015/03/Pattinson2013.pdf.

8   Gibbs, "Bodies of Words."

Finally, the last aspect to consider when reading the narratives is my own autobiographical narrative, placed strategically throughout the book.[9] These provoked memories, rooted in the spatial and temporal remembrances of the informants, transported me back to the point in time in which they occurred. Time and space, like a fresh water river meeting salty ocean in a brackish delta, mix and merge in my writing. When shaping each individual's story, I was unable to avoid my own presence as a young girl, bearing silent witness to their struggles.

In the final analysis, the oral history practice opens the door to a new historical pursuit, one that leads to a creative historical ontology in which the history we learn is a history of becoming rather than being. The collected interviews expose how both college students and homemakers articulated their resistance in the comings and goings of daily life. Identifying the tactics and practices ordinary Spanish women used to survive the regime makes visible their micro-transgressions of conventional norms. But these women did more than just survive; they also calculatingly worked to better the odds of their daughters overcoming limited expectations and opportunities. They did this by instilling in them a sense of independence, desire, and even defiance.

There are three methodological lenses applied to the analysis of the narratives in this book: 1) Henri Lefebvre's *Critique of Everyday Life* through what he called Rhythmanalysis of the urban space; 2) María Zambrano's "Poetic reason" through creative non-fiction or ficto-criticism; and 3) Auto-biography/life writing as intrinsic to the oral history process. The ultimate goal is the exploration of oral history as a valuable, humanistic tool to better understand the role of time and space in historical writing when the primary sources at hand are oral interviews and our own DNA.

The Purpose of History: A Creative Historical Ontology

In his book *The End of History*, Lefebvre questions history's master narratives or *les grands récits*. He instead speaks of *le sens de l'histoire*. The term "sense" in French implies both directional and semantic connotations. The directional connotation is

---

9   Ronald Grele calls it "conversational narrative," as it is the result of the exchange between the interviewer and the informant in which both shape the outcome of the conversation. While the informant provides the story, the ultimate author of the narrative resulting from the interview is the interviewer. See Ronald Grele, "Private Memories and Public Presentation: The Art of Oral History," in *Envelopes of Sound: The Art of Oral History*, ed. Ronald Grele (New York, London: Praeger, 1991), 257-58. See also: Lynn Abrams, *Oral History Theory* (London: Routledge, 2010); Miren Llona, ed., *Entreverse: Teoría y metodología practica de las fuentes orales* (Bilbao: UPV, 2012); Pilar Domínguez, Rina Benmayor, and María Eugenia Cardinal de la Nuez, eds., *Memory, Subjectivities, and Representation: Approaches to Oral History in Latin America, Portugal, and Spain* (New York: Palgrave Macmillan, 2016).

understood as the "end of" or "purpose of" history, while the semantic connotation is understood as the meaning or signification of the historical process. History is chaos without a purpose or meaning.[10]

Turning the historian's task into a pursuit of understanding of our human condition endows it with a "sense," a "purpose." The traditional positivistic History might hence be overcome and radically altered. In other words, the sense of history (directional and semantic) resides in an exercise of cunning interrogation towards introspection and empathy.[11] The historical importance of ordinary actions carried out by "insignificant" people is what this book is all about. Therefore, in searching for historical signification, this book puts oral history in conversation with philosophy (Gilles Deleuze, Maurice Merleau-Ponty, Henri Bergson, María Zambrano), and cultural, literary, and urban studies from a gender perspective. Intersecting all these vectors brings to light issues of periodization and location—time and space—entangled in the historical unfolding as becoming rather than being in time.

I propose to dwell in the "moment" when time and space traverse each other. To freeze a moment in time through narrative retelling allows us to gain insight into the actions and choices made by people living unspectacular lives. Spanish historian Miren Llona proposes the notion of "memory's enclaves" or anchors as privileged mental sites (moments) to which individuals return to peek down and *feel* past emotions. These memory enclaves act as mental repositories of images that over the individual's lifetime have merged with their sense of self in relation to particular personal past experiences. Llona further explains how the memories stored in those enclaves are recurring and resilient to oblivion. No doubt, forgetting is intrinsic to remembrance,[12] an essential element in organizing fragmentary

---

10   As Stuart Elden explains: "There is a plurality of times, of physical, biological, social, cyclical and linear times, which overlap and conflict in various ways. [...] If there is nothing fundamental about time then history is a *fiction* [my emphasis] or an abstraction." Lefebvre bases his argument on Nietzsche's understanding of the modern world and his notion of "civilization" which would imply a radical break with "historicity, the historic, the past and its knowledge as useless excess, burdens on the memory, more and more sterile inventories of the accomplished. The birth of this civilization implies a radical break, a total discontinuity, a renewal of methods of knowledge, and a repudiation of historical thought." Stuart Elden, *Understanding Henri Lefebvre: Theory and the Possible* (London: Continuum, 2004), 176-77.

11   The discipline of history emerges simultaneously with the rise of nationalism at the end of the nineteenth century. But Lefebvre actually identifies its origins in Ancient Greece, just as the city-state is born. History develops from "insignificant tales, [du récit anecdotique] annals, and epic poems to talk about the constitution to tell of the struggles of the city state." Therefore, he suggests that "history did not just emerge to tell any story, but a particular one, that of the state" and its power. Elden, *Understanding Henri Lefebvre*, 177-78.

12   On forgetting and the importance of oblivion see: Harald Weinrich, *Lethe: The Art and Critique of Forgetting* (Ithaca: Cornell University Press, 2004); Paul Ricoeur, *Memory, History, Forgetting*

recollections into a coherent narrative. Therefore, it seems imperative to apply an analysis of those repetitions, of those (eternal) returns to the "memory enclaves" (or moments), both linear and cyclical rhythmic returns, which in the moment of the interview come alive. But I would further propose that the way the informant revisits the enclave is also in every instance unique.[13] We construct our life stories anew every time we retell them because their meaning is always chasing the context in which they are told.

The individual reconstructs her life's story from the social and collective parameters in place at each historical juncture; however, the meaning of the collective story can only gain depth through an analysis of the individual *récit anecdoques*. As Max van Manen points out, "what makes anecdotes so effective is that they seem to tell something noteworthy or important" about the quotidian. The anecdote serves as an example of a concrete moment in place when the agency of the informant is revealed.

What everyday practices allowed women to sustain and fulfill individuality and agency under dictatorial rule? Were these women able to have an impact on the opportunities and self-esteem of their daughters? Listening to their evaluation of their own lives reveals subtle truths. Instead of just passively going along with the regime, they calculatingly taught their daughters to have greater expectations than they would dare allow themselves. Instead of indoctrinating them in the limiting role of the true Catholic woman, they were inoculating them against its harmful effects.

The Visible: Space's Rhythmanalysis

> The rhythmanalyst [...] will be attentive, but not only to the words or pieces of information, the confessions and confidences of a partner or client. He will listen to the world, and above all to what are disdainfully called noises, which are said without meaning, and to murmurs [rumeurs], full of meaning -and finally he will listen to silences.
> Henri Lefebvre, *Elements of Rhythmanalysis* (2004)[14]

(Chicago: Chicago University Press, 2006); Marc Auge, *Oblivion* (Minneapolis: University of Minnesota Press, 2004); Svetlana Boym, *The Future of Nostalgia* (New York: Basic Books, 2002).
13   Gilles Deleuze, *Difference and Repetition* (London: Bloomsbury, 2017).

The Francoist regime's longevity is inextricably tied to the economic developments of the 1960s. Therefore, it makes sense to study the social and political dynamics emerging from that modernizing moment. The industrialization and urbanization unleashed a radicalization of the opposition to the dictatorship, coalescing around the labor and student movements. The study of these movements in the Spanish context provides a deeper understanding of the global social unrest that unfolded in what has been called the long 1960s.

Henri Lefebvre's multidisciplinary work puts in conversation a variety of disciplines: geography, history, sociology, literary criticism, urban studies, and philosophy. Regarded as one of the godfathers of the 1968 French student movement, he was at the time a professor in Nanterre and had developed a close relationship with avant-garde groups like Cobra, *Situationists International*, and *Letterist International*. Ultimately, Lefebvre's critique of everyday life in post-World War II European cities offers us methodological tools to help uncover the workings of capitalism. Lefebvre identified the urban environment as the site of both control and resistance to alienation. Therefore, Lefebvre's framework will help illuminate the means used by the Francoist regime to maintain power. By pivoting to the West in the aftermath of the Second World War, Franco ensured his relevancy to the outside world and protected his regime's power from outside meddling. His new role as benign dictator opening his country up to the West and fighting the common Communist enemy helped satisfy the conscience of his new American partners, who saw Spain as having democratic possibilities. Authoritarianism replaced fascism, as the American dollars and military aid flowed in. Although Spain was originally excluded from the Marshall Plan, or the European Recovery Program, in 1948, its strategic importance to Cold War anti-Communist policies made it a natural partner. Only five years later, in 1953, the Pact of Madrid was signed by the two new allies. This newfound friendship was further consecrated by an embrace between President Eisenhower and dictator Francisco Franco when the US president visited Spain in 1959.

Industrialization and its ensuing urbanization, helped by United States economic aid, was at the heart of the regime's international rehabilitation but also central to understanding the dynamics of social interaction in the urban environment. The urban transformation came with problems of overcrowding, as rural mass migration to the developed industrial urban poles (Barcelona, Bilbao, and Madrid) exploded. The Ministry of Housing and the Instituto Nacional de Industria (INI) became key agencies in the deployment of the capitalist economy orchestrated by the Opus Dei's skilled technocratic planning. Space turned into a crucial site of power for the regime. As Lefebvre makes clear, space is crucial to understanding the transition from a "use-value city" to one where the priority is exchange and

---

14 Henri Lefebvre, *Elements of Rhythmanalysis* (London, Oxford: Continuum, 2004), loc 301 of 1306, Kindle.

consumption—what he calls "exchange-value city." That change is clearly manifest in the Francoist transition from autarky (self-sufficient post-war economic isolation) to capitalist consumerism, and from pseudo fascist to National Catholic to better fit the international propagandist image of "Sentinel of the West." Lefebvre points out how "capitalist leaders treat everyday life as they once treated colonized territories: massive trading posts (supermarkets and shopping centers);[15] absolute predominance of exchange over use; dual exploitation of the population in their capacity as producers and consumers."[16] Technocracy turned out to be the new means to create a rationalized conformity, representing modernization without compromising state control of space(s), both symbolic and physical. While Franco reluctantly agreed to the Americanization of the economy, his tight technocratic urban planning offered the promise of continuity of order, conformity, and ultimate authoritarian control.

In *The Production of Space* (1991), Lefebvre elaborates a dialectical triad of space to understand its fluid nature: first, what he calls "conceived space" or representational space produced by urban planners and economic technocrats; second, "lived space" or spaces of representation involving hidden symbolism; and third "perceived space" or spatial practices where individuals implement their own autonomous movements in between reestablished zones. College students would trespass physical and symbolic boundaries in their daily comings and goings, as they moved from their middle-class enclaves to working-class neighborhoods to recruit and educate, and in and out of their symbolic roles as students and activists. Female students more specifically would be in the university and at the same time be "out of."[17] Even the spaces and hours of the day were gendered, male or female, friendly or threatening.

---

15   Alejandro Gómez del Moral's dissertation entitled "Buying into Change: Consumer Culture and the Department Store in the Transformation(s) of Spain, 1939–1982" (PhD diss., Rutgers University, 2014) is a ground-breaking study that intersects gender, consumption, and modernization during the Francisco Franco dictatorship.

16   Henri Lefebvre, *Critique of Everyday Life: From Modernity to Modernism (Towards a Metaphilosophy of Everyday Life)*, Vol. 3 (London, New York: Verso, 2005), 26.

17   The Francoist university was ruled by the *Ley de Ordenación Universitaria* (LOU, Regulatory University Law) issued in 1943, which was replaced with the enactment of the General Law of Education in 1970. As I have explained in my previous work the Francoist National Catholic rhetoric forged an ideal "True Catholic Womanhood" based on the revival of the counter-reformation values of purity and subordination of the 1500s as proposed in Luis Vives' *The Instruction of the Christian Woman* (1523) and Fray Luis de Leon's *The Perfect Wife* (1583). This ideal womanhood was inimical to the intellectual subjectivity constructed by the letter of the LOU. See: Aurora Morcillo, "Gendered Activism: The Anti Francoist Student Movement in the University of Granada in the 1960s and 1970s," *Gendered Education in History, Theory and Practice-Case-Studies on Women's Education, Gendered Spaces and Performativity of Knowledge, Encounters in Theory and History of Education*, 19 (2018): 90-109, and *True Catholic Womanhood*.

The rich literature on feminist geography emerging in the 1980s gives form to the social relations in space and time. The works of feminist geographers like Gillian Rose and Doreen Massey are crucial to our more sophisticated understanding of how gender, space, and time are inseparable.[18] The informants in the narratives made self-conscious choices to transgress those urban zones and bio-political (gendered) limitations. As women, they entered the male-centered space of the university where they were implicitly excluded or "out of place"[19] as the Regulatory Law of the University—in place from 1943 to 1970—defined them. Being a university student was seen as an affront to the official discourse on true Catholic womanhood.[20] In many instances, the university students interviewed for this study asserted themselves by becoming "one more of the guys."[21] The small transgressive choices each informant revealed in the interviews are illuminating as a historical account of invisible acts of resistance and empowerment. While the urban landscape was their visible space of action, the impetus behind their decision to move from one zone to another is only revealed through a new understanding of spatiality and temporality, placing time and space in a dialectical, continuous engagement.

Implicit in this conceived, lived, perceived spatial triad is Lefebvre's critique of alienation—particularly relevant for our understanding of the student and labor movements' historical agency in late Francoism. According to Lefebvre, alienation is encountered, suffered, and negotiated in every aspect of everyday life and administered through the spatial triad he establishes for the urban environment. In the process of negotiating these alienating dynamics we are actually able to discern the atomized nature (Foucauldian) of power relations. In accordance with the "theory of the moment," our ability to transgress socio-political expectations in different alienating encounters through sometimes invisible tactics and strategies is at the heart of people's agency and self-empowerment. According to Lefebvre, in the words of Stuart Elden, "moments are significant times when existing orthodoxies are open to challenge, when things have the potential to be overturned or radically altered, moments of crisis in the original sense of the term."[22] This inter-

---

18 Gillian Rose, *Feminism and Geography: The Limits of Geographical Knowledge* (Oxford: Polity Press, 1993); Doreen Massey, *Space, Place and Gender* (Cambridge: Polity Press, 1994); Linda McDowell and Joanne P. Sharp, *A Feminist Glossary of Human Geography* (London: Arnold, 1999); Lise Nelson and Joni Seager, *A Companion to Feminist Geography* (Oxford: Blackwell, 2005); and Geraldine Pratt, "Feminist Geographies: Spatialising Feminist Politics," in *Envisioning Human Geographies*, ed. Paul Cloke, Philip Crang, and Mark Goodwin (London: Arnold, 2004), 128–45.
19 See Massey, *Space, Place and Gender*, 130-34.
20 See Morcillo, *True Catholic Womanhood*.
21 See Socorro and Marga stories.
22 Elden further points out how the moment has a long tradition in Western thought from Kierkegaard and Nietzsche. The latter is particularly relevant to Lefebvre. "In Nietzsche's *Thus*

est in the moment explains Lefebvre's close, though ephemeral, collaboration with the *Situationists International* movement. A member of a radical group of artists located in Paris, known as Letterists International, Guy Debord (1931-1994) founded the Situationist movement, which gathered interest in the *First World Congress of Free Artists* celebrated in Alba, Italy, in 1956. A year later, several avant-garde actions launched the movement.[23] The movement criticized the capitalist consumer society as profoundly alienating and fanned by spectacle. Their name "Situationist" referred to their strategies to raise consciousness by creating "situations" or "moments" in the public space to provoke a shift in behavior by using the shock factor, with the intention to reignite true meaning and purpose in life. The students at the Spanish universities enacted "critical trials" against their professors in lecture halls, where they challenged academic authority and demanded a radical change in the content of their studies. It was precisely around the synergy between the theory of the moment, elaborated by Lefebvre, and the "construction of Situations" by the Situationists, that the collaboration between the two started.[24]

The situation, as a created, organized moment—Lefebvre expresses this desire as "the free act defined as the capacity . . . to change a 'moment' in metamorphosis, and perhaps to create one"—includes perishable instants, ephemeral and unique.

Spoke Zarathustra," Stuart Elden points out, "the moment, the *Augenblick*, the blink of an eye, is a gateway where past and future collide." Stuart Elden, "Rhythmanalysis: An Introduction," in *Rhythmanalysis: Space, Time and Everyday Life*, by Henri Lefebvre (London, New York: Continuum, 2004), loc. 52 of 1306, Kindle.

23 Some of the groups included: Letterist International, the International Movement for an Imaginist Bauhaus, and the London Psychogeographical Association.

24 In an interview Lefebvre pointed out the origins of the movement and his connection with them: "During the postwar years, the figure of Stalin was dominant. And the Communist movement was *the* revolutionary movement. Then, after '56 or '57, revolutionary movements moved outside the organized parties, especially with Fidel Castro. In this sense, Situationism wasn't at all isolated. Its point of origin was Holland—Paris, too—but Holland especially, and it was linked to many events on the world stage, especially the fact that Fidel Castro succeeded in a revolutionary victory completely outside of the Communist movement and the workers' movement. This *was* an event. And I remember that in 1957 I published a kind of manifesto, *Le romantisme révolutionnaire*, which was linked to the Castro story and to all the movements happening a little bit everywhere that were outside of the parties. This was when I left the Communist Party myself. I felt that there were going to be a lot of things happening outside the established parties and organized movements like syndicates. There was going to be a spontaneity outside of organizations and institutions—that's what this text from 1957 was about. It was this text that put me into contact with the Situationists because they attached a certain importance to it—before attacking it later on. They had their critiques to make, of course; we were never completely in agreement, but the article was the basis for a certain understanding that lasted for four or five years —we kept coming back to it." Henri Lefebvre, "Henri Lefebvre on the Situationist International," interview by Kristin Ross, 1983. http://www.notbored.org/lefebvre-interview.html.

[...]
The "moment" is mainly temporal, forming part of a zone of temporality, not pure but dominant. Articulated in relation to a given place, the situation is completely spatio-temporal [...] Moments constructed into "situations" might be thought of as moments of rupture, of acceleration, *revolutions in individual everyday life*. On a more extended—more social—spatial level, an urbanism that almost exactly corresponds to Lefebvre's moments, and to his idea of choosing these and leaving them behind at will, has been proposed in the "states-of-the-soul quarters."[25]

Guy Debord published *The Society of the Spectacle* in 1967, and Belgian philosopher Raoul Vaneigem published *The Revolution of Everyday Life* the following year. These texts had a profound impact on university protests originating in Nanterre and later spreading to Paris in May 1968. Raoul Vaneigem was fascinated by Lefevbre's critique of everyday life and sent an essay on "poetry and revolution" to his professor who in turn put him in contact with Debord. Both Lefevbre and Vaneigem would leave the Situationists and dissociate themselves from Debord by 1960. According to Lefebvre, "Debord's dogmatism was exactly like Breton's. And, what's more, it was a dogmatism without a dogma, since the theory of situations, of the creation of situations, disappeared very quickly, leaving behind only the critique of the existing world, which is where it all started, with the *Critique of Everyday Life*."[26]

While the classroom "critical trials" represented a visible example of the construction of a Situationist moment, the less theatrical trials of homemakers, working class individuals who raised their daughters and sons in quiet opposition, represented invisible Situationist moments. They existed, certainly, but like ultraviolet light, they were unnoticed, hiding past the limits of human perception. The second part of this book focuses on these unseen, daily acts of defiance deployed by working class women and how these acts had a profound impact on the next generation.

In *The Revolution of Everyday Life* (1967), Vaneigem sought to explain how to give significance to the insignificant, to the instance that transforms repetition in order to enrich the monotonous routine of the quotidian.[27] "The enrichment of life calls inexorably," he wrote, "*for the analysis of the new forms taken by poverty, and the perfection of the old weapons of refusal.*" The path to enrichment is, in Vaneigem's view, a creative one deeply rooted in imagination. It is taken consciously to escape an alienation derived from the obsession with comfort and the implicit happiness wrought by the modern, affluent capitalist society:

---

25 "The Theory of Moments and the Construction of Situations," *Internationale Situationniste* #4, (1960) http://www.notbored.org/moments.html.
26 Lefebvre, interview.
27 Raoul Vaneigem, "The Insignificant Signified," in *The Revolution of Everyday Life* (London: Rebel Press, 2006), 21-29. See also a 2009 interview with Vaneigem in http://www.e-flux.com/journal/06/61400/in-conversation-with-raoul-vaneigem/.

> People without imagination are beginning to tire of the importance attached to comfort, to culture, to leisure, to all that destroys imagination. This means that people are not really tired of comfort, culture and leisure, but of the use to which they are put, which is precisely what stops us enjoying them.
>
> The affluent society is a society of voyeurs. To each his own kaleidoscope: two fridges, a VW, TV, a promotion, time to kill.... But then the monotony of the images we consume gets the upper hand, reflecting the monotony of the action which produces them, the slow rotation of finger and thumb that in turn rotates the kaleidoscope. [...]
>
> People who talk about revolution and class struggle without referring to everyday life, without understanding what is subversive about love and what is positive in the refusal of constraints—such people have a corpse in their mouth.[28]

Urban alienation, according to Vaneigem, trumps all other forms of alienation and therefore offers us the ideal site to observe the conflicting urges to embrace and at the same time reject the rising consumerism in Spain during the 1960s and 1970s. It is not surprising that many Spanish youth turned from the alienation and empty promise of consumer culture by joining either the radical Christian movements such as FECUN (Federación Española de Comunidades Universitarias) or the Communist Party of Spain (PCE). It is also not surprising that working class mothers turned toward consumerism and its modernizing force as an escape from their alienation, and as a way for their daughters to break through the confining carapace of "True Catholic Womanhood."

The city is situated, according to Lefebvre, halfway between "near order" or face-to-face individual and group relations, and "far order" or society regulated by institutions like the Church, the State, the University, the Army, etc. The materialization in the urban landscape is a matter of "scale" assigned to zones (neighborhoods, shanty towns, institutional buildings such as colleges or police stations) and groups (civil, university, and religious authorities versus the student and workers organizations) which reveal different levels of influence and power as each city zone was allotted to a specific group. The scale here is understood as a social construction rather than simply a matter of a space's size, which is also always in flux. Doreen Massey addresses the issue of scale when considering the embodied/gendered nature of space. It is necessary to distinguish between space and place within the space, and to think of social space in terms of a site where social relations play out. Therefore, "one way of thinking of place," Massey argues, "is as particular moments

---

28   Vaneigem, *The Revolution of Everyday Life*, 25.

in such intersecting relationships."²⁹ Male and female spaces are so by virtue of the embodied experience of those spaces, and each space constructs gender specific places. "Thinking of places in this way implies that they are not so much bounded areas, as open and porous networks of social relations."³⁰ According to Kate Driscoll Derickson, Lorraine Dowler, and Nicole Laliberte, Massey's

> "analysis of 'sense of place' adds another dimension to feminist understandings of space, that of scale. She argues that the connection of the everyday practices of women can be linked to societal relationships, at which point these experiences can be 'stretched out' and understood in a local, regional, and sometimes global context."³¹

This is ultimately a rethinking of the historian's task and brings to the fore the fruitful use of oral history. According to Massey, "The past is not more authentic than the present; there will be no one reading of it. And 'traditions' are frequently invented or, if they are not, the question of which traditions will predominate cannot be answered in advance. *It is people, not places themselves, which are reactionary or progressive.*"³² In her essay, "A Woman's Place?" Massey looks at the realignment of gender relations in four different geographical locations in the UK in the mid 1960s as a result of government economic reorganization. The development plans launched by the Francoist regime in the 1960s created similar economic poles of development that led to the realignment of gender relations in Spain. There was a redefinition of the construction of masculinity and femininity as urbanization, migration, and tourism re-signify multiple spaces, both physical and symbolic. The different development poles during Francoism led to challenges in the way patriarchy had to be realigned. The poor regions (Andalusia or Galicia) saw their men leave to find work in the urban areas or to other European countries. Wives, in many cases left behind, had to raise children alone. However, the men continued to maintain economic dominance as the sole breadwinners. When women migrated, they experienced new mores and had to adjust to them accordingly. I am echoing here Massey's argument: "The contrasting forms of economic development in different parts of the country [she is referring to the UK, but it fits Spain in this analysis] presented distinct conditions for the maintenance of male dominance [...] capitalism presented patriarchy with different challenges in different parts of the

---

29   Massey, *Space, Place and Gender*, 119.
30   Massey, *Space, Place and Gender*, 120.
31   Kate Driscoll Derickson, Lorraine Dowler, and Nicole Laliberte, "Advances in Feminist Geography," in *The International Studies Encyclopedia*, ed. Robert A. Denemark and Renée Marlin-Bennett (Hoboken: NJ, Wiley-Blackwell, 2017), 5.
32   Massey, *Space, Place and Gender*, 140-41.

country."[33] Massey is referring to 1960s and 1970s economic developments in different regions in the UK, but obliquely she highlights the historical experience of the working class in all of Europe during that period. It is important to point out that the economic transformations described by Massey were carried out by the Labor Party while the development plans in Spain were the work of an authoritarian regime led by Opus Dei technocrats. These circumstances become more apparent when we introduce the variable of gender into the examination of time and space. Interestingly, Spain surfaces in Massey's work when she notes how Henri Lefebvre himself pointed out the sexualization of the space in his work *The Production of Space*:

> Picasso's space *heralded* [sic] the space of modernity...What we find in Picasso is an unreservedly visualized space, a dictatorship of the eye—and of the phallus; an aggressive virility, the bull, the Mediterranean male, a *machismo* [sic] (unquestionable genius in the service of genitality) carried to the point of self-parody—and even on occasion to the point of self-criticism. Picasso's cruelty towards the body, particularly the female body, which he tortures in a thousand ways and caricatures without mercy, is dictated by the dominant form of space, by the eye and by the phallus—in short by violence.[34]

Lefebvre's analysis of everyday life allows us to delve into his reconceptualization of the assumptions behind history and his understanding of historicity, temporality, and their spatiality. For Lefebvre, time and space must be thought of together, and in no other instance are both intertwined better than in the practice of oral history.

Historians and economists examine the rhythms of eras, their cycles, their slowness or rapidity. They are not, however, able to measure the tiny repetitions of daily life, the repetitions that fill the majority of our lives. History focuses not so much on the repetition but the break from routine. It is the unusual that wakes us from our slumber. The truth is that the rhythm, or repetition, is the fact and truth of most lives. "What is repetition?" Lefebvre askes, "What is meaning? How, when and why are there micro and macro re-starts, return to the past in works and time? Therefore, 'not only does repetition not exclude differences, *it also gives birth to them*.'"[35] Sooner or later, the formulaic "once upon a time" happens and introduces a variable into the monotonous, mechanical repetition; such is the moment, the difference. Those differences constitute the thread of time and in the moment of the interview, the invisible resistance to routine and everyday life becomes visible.

---

33 Massey, *Space, Place and Gender*, 191.
34 Henri Lefebvre, *The Production of Space* (Oxford, UK: Blackwell Publishing, 1991), quoted in Massey, *Space, Place and Gender*, 82.
35 Lefebvre, *Rhythmanalysis*, loc. 155 of 1306, Kindle.

The oral history process brings to life the cyclical and linear repetitions. The former originating on the natural unfolding of days, months, seasons, etc.; the latter more the result of the social practices and structural impositions in the conversation between informant and oral historian's time and space. The cyclical and the linear collide and measure themselves against each other. Measure is key here as it is consubstantial to rhythm. The duration of a particular act of self-assertiveness, concealed over decades and unearthed in the interview, discloses the rhythm, the measure of invisibility, the calculated project (both in spatial and temporal dimensions) that is agency. Duration is quantified and qualified by measure like a song's melody or the meter of a poem. Rhythm must be analyzed.

The Invisible: Time's Poetic Reason

> Because poetry will not accept what already has "number, weight and measure," [...] but will find the number, weight and measure that corresponds to what still does not have it.
> María Zambrano, *Filosofía y poesía*[36]

Rhythmanalysis is of great value for the practice of oral history. It works as a conduit into a history of emotions through an attentive study of signification. Lefebvre posed the question: "What makes the measurable and the non-measurable?" I pose a similar question: what makes the visible and the invisible? Under the construct of measurement exist several sub-constructs: repetition and difference; mechanical and organic; discovery and creation; cyclical and linear; continuous and discontinuous; and quantitative and qualitative. It is my hunch that the answer to what makes the invisible visible can be found in the human ability to construct meaning based on the context of time and place. In oral history as life writing, what individuals say about their history is determined not just by past events but also the present. The narrative is a negotiated account agreed upon by past and present selves. What emerges is of necessity, a dialogic compromise between the younger and the older versions of the informant. This introspection leads to an understanding of not just the individual but the very human condition that is the purpose of history.

How best to uncover the humanity of history? I propose an alternative understanding of oral history writing informed by the concept of poetic reason afforded

---

36 "Porque la poesía no va a captar lo que ya tiene 'número, peso y medida,' [...] sino que va a encontrar el número, peso y medida que corresponde a lo que todavia no lo tiene." María Zambrano, *Filosofía y Poesía* (Mexico: Fondo de Cultura Económica, 1996), 88-89. My translation.

by Spanish philosopher María Zambrano (1904-1991). History in general and oral history in particular is a system of signification,[37] which is gendered, racialized, and quantified through the collaborative process of the (inter)view. Making the world intelligible is the common purpose of history and language. Such purpose is fulfilled in narration. The mode of writing warns the reader of the message the author wants to express beyond just language. When we see a poem on a page, we read it differently than when we are presented with an account of facts. Writing contains signs that indicate its relation to society and history.[38] Historical writing claims to be neutral and transparent, but the rejection of any literariness in historians' craft confers to it a recognizable historical *écriture*.

The analysis of the interviews contained in this book allows me to create a distance from historical *écriture*. Each narrative inspired a free verse poem, most selected from known poets; some I ventured to write myself. These poems intend to capture the self-empowering moment revealed by each informant. Each story's poem exposes in simple words a profound signification. They are the poetic rendition of the eternal return to the memory enclaves that Miren Llona warned us about. The simplicity and impressionistic nature of the poems encapsulates what I, as a historian, am in search of: revealing what feminist/gender historians advanced theoretically, what we called "becoming visible"[39]—poetizing these stories has the power to transform something invisible into something luminous. Walter Benjamin tells us, "The true image of the past flits by. The past can be seized only as an image which flashes up at the instant when it can be recognized and is never

---

37 The concept of signification Roland Barthes proposed is applied in the examination of these interviews to decipher the historical meaning of insignificant actions carried out by ordinary people. Roland Barthes in his 1968 work entitled *Elements of Semiology* explains his concept of "systems signification." "There is at present a kind of demand for semiology, stemming not from the fads of a few scholars, but from the very history of the modern world...Now it is far from certain that in the social life of today there are to be found any extensive systems of signs outside human language." Roland Barthes, *Elements of Semiology* (New York: Hill and Wang, 1977), 9. For Barthes, there is no meaning outside of language. "Working with no linguistic substances," he writes, "semiology requires, sooner or later, to find language." Thus, Barthes' semiology is that part of linguistics that covers the great signifying unities of discourse. In this way, semiology helps us understand the significance of the narratives sought in oral histories.

38 Jonathan Culler points out how "no prose is transparent, as Sartre would wish. Even the simplest language of novels—Hemingway, for example or Camus—signifies by indirection a relationship to literature and to the world. A stripped-down language is not natural or neutral or transparent but a deliberate engagement with the institution of Literature; its apparent rejection of literariness will itself become a new mode of literary writing, a recognizable *écriture* as Barthes calls it." Jonathan Culler, *Roland Barthes: A Very Short Introduction* (Oxford: Oxford University Press, 1983), loc. 428 of 2267, Kindle.

39 Renate Bridenthal, Susan Stuard, and Merry E. Wiesner-Hanks, *Becoming Visible: Women in European History*, 3rd ed. (Belmont, CA: Wadsworth Publishing,1997).

seen again. [...] For every image of the past that is not recognized in the present as one of its own concerns threatens to disappear irretrievably."[40]

The exploration and analysis of these narratives utilizing Zambrano's poetic reason may help us map a piece of the history of emotions under the Franco dictatorship. Moreover, this analytical approach promises to shed some light on feminist historiographical concerns: periodization, agency, and authenticity versus truth in the utilization of gender as a category of analysis. To make intelligible the symbolism behind these women's experiences is to pursue a creative historical ontology—a poetics of history.

Poetizing the stories into short verses slows time, allowing for more leisurely contemplation. Since writing history is about the conceptualization of time and periodization, it is also gendered. As Walter Benjamin wrote: "History is the subject of a structure whose site is not homogeneous, empty time, but time filled by the presence of the now *[Jetztzeit]*" and declares that "a historical materialist cannot do without the notion of a present which is not a transition, but in which time stands still and has come to a stop. For this notion defines the present in which he himself is writing history."[41]

Lefebvre points out that starting with the conceptual brings with it a series of risks: "speculation in place of analysis, the arbitrarily subjective in place of facts."[42] And yet, it is incumbent upon us to take this risk, as Zambrano proposes, to be able to "find the number, weight, and measure" that correspond to those things which "still does not have it"—our emotions:

> Pleasure and joy demand a re-commencement. They await it; yet it escapes. Pain returns. It repeats itself since the repetition of pleasure gives rise to pain(s). However, joy and pleasure have a presence, whereas pain results from an absence (that of a function, an organ, a person, an object, a *being*). Joy and pleasure *are*, they are *being*; not so suffering. Pessimists used to affirm the opposite: only suffering *is*, or *exists*. The propositions that precede ground an optimism, *in spite of everything*.[43]

The same optimism inspires the examination of these narratives, as I choose to dwell, poetically, in the joyful assertive moments that gave hope to these women trapped in the bleak landscape of Francoism.

---

40 Walter Benjamin, "Theses on the Philosophy of History," in *Illuminations* (New York: Schocken Books, 2007), 254, eBook.
41 Benjamin, "Theses on the Philosophy of History," 61-262.
42 Lefebvre, *Elements of Rhythmanalysis*, loc. 134 of 1306, Kindle.
43 Lefebvre, *Elements of Rhythmanalysis*, loc. 218 of 1306, Kindle. Italics in the original.

Oral History as Life Writing or The Making of the Self

> Oral sources are generated in a dialogic exchange – an interview—literally a looking at each other, an exchange of gazes.
> Alessandro Portelli[44]

Lynn Abrams reminds us how the oral history interview "is an event of communication, which demands that we find ways of comprehending not just *what is said, why it is said and what it means.*"[45] Because the interview is a communicative process, it is also, as Abrams points out, a "means to access information but also signification, interpretation and meaning." Therefore, the practice of oral history is intrinsically bound up with theorizing and reinterpreting historical narrative. Moreover, the narrative is in constant flux since the meaning or signification of what is told acquires the category of historical source.[46] The result is a life story/history which does not seek objective rendition of facts but rather the meaning, the signification, built in the process of exchange product of the so-called inter-subjectivity of the (auto)biographical story.[47]

Lynn Abrams indicates that the theorist adds "performativity" and "mutability" because s/he is part of a much larger process known as inter-subjectivity and/or collaboration. Therefore, as the historian is drawn into the story, "objectivity" is

---

44 Alessandro Portelli, "A Dialogical Relationship: An Approach to Oral History," (1985) http://www.swaraj.org/shikshantar/expressions_portelli.pdf.
45 Abrams, *Oral History Theory*, 1.
46 For Ronald Grele's theory of "conversational narrative," see Grele, "Private Memories and Public Presentation," 257-58.
47 Llona, *Entreverse*; Domínguez, Benmayor, and Cardinal de la Nuez, *Memory, Subjectivities, and Representation*.

impossible.[48] There is an autobiographical component that I embrace in the narratives that follows what Portelli calls a "composite genre":

Oral sources are generated in a dialogic exchange—an interview—literally a looking at each other, an exchange of gazes [my emphasis]. In this exchange questions and answers do not necessarily go in one direction only. The historian's agenda must meet the agenda of the narrator; what the historian wishes to know may not

---

48   Cited in Abrams, *Oral History*, 19. Some of the oral history seminal works include: Luisa Passerini, *Autobiography of a Generation: Italy, 1968* (Middletown, CT: Wesleyan, 1996); *Fascism in Popular Memory: The Cultural Experience of the Turin Working Class (Studies in Modern Capitalism)* (Cambridge, UK: Cambridge University Press, 2009); Alessandro Portelli, *The Death of Luigi Trastulli and Other Stories Form and Meaning in Oral History* (Albany, NY: State University of New York Press, 1990); Donald Ritchie, *Doing Oral History (Oxford Oral History Series)*, 3rd ed. (Oxford: Oxford University Press, 2014); Paul Thompson, *The Voice of the Past: Oral History* (Oxford: Oxford University Press, 1988); Alistair Thomson, *Anzac Memories: Living with the Legend* (Manchester: Manchester University Press, 2011), as well as Thomson and Anisa Puri, *Australian Lives: An Intimate History* (Victoria, AU: Monash University Publishing, 2017); and more recently Paula Hamilton's work on the role of the senses in oral histories: Paula Hamilton, "The Oral Historian as Memorist," *The Oral History Review* 32, no. 1 (Winter - Spring, 2005): 11-18; and Graham Smith's current work on food and family relations and doctor-patient memory narratives. Some works on Spanish historiography include: Pilar Folguera, *Cómo se hace historia oral* (Madrid: Eudema, 1994); Miren Llona, *Entre señorita y garçonne. Historia oral de las mujeres bilbaínas de clase media (1919-1939)* (Málaga: Universidad de Málaga, 2002); Mercedes Vilanova, "El combate en España por una historia sin adjetivos con fuentes orales," *Historia Antropología y Fuentes Orales*, 14 (1995); Cristina Borderías, "La historia oral en España a mediados de los noventa," *Historia Antropología y Fuentes Orales*, 13 (1995); Miren Llona, "Memoria e identidades: Balance y perspectivas de un nuevo enfoque historiográfico," in *La historia de las mujeres: Perspectivas actuales*, by Cristina Borderías (Barcelona: Icaria, 2008), as well as Miren Llona, "Archivar la memoria, escribir la historia: Reflexiones en torno a la creación de un Archivo de Historia Oral. AHOA, Ahozco Historiaren Artxiboa," in *Historia Oral. Fundamentos metodológicos para reconstruir el pasado desde la diversidad*, ed. Laura Benadiva (Rosario: Suramérica Ediciones, 2010); Elena Hernández Sandoica, *Tendencias historiográficas actuales* (Madrid: Akal, 2004). It is impossible to do justice to the voluminous oral history literature, today a truly global interdisciplinary field across cultures. Some of the best information is available online at the Columbia Center for Oral History (CCOHR) http://www.incite.columbia.edu/ccohr/; the Oral History Association http://www.oralhistory.org/resources/; and the International Oral History Association provides a good bibliography http://www.ioha.org/useful-readings/ . In Spain see the following archives: In Madrid late Professor Carmen García Nieto from the Universidad Complutense de Madrid established in 1981 the Seminario de Fuentes Orales http://www.seminariofuentesorales.es/somos/somos.php to explore the experiences of women during the Spanish Civil War; in the Basque Country professor Miren Llona from the Universidad del Pais Vasco leads the establishment of the Archivo de Historia Oral. AHOA, Ahozco Historiaren Artxiboa http://www.ahoaweb.org/.

necessarily coincide with what the narrator wishes to tell. As a consequence, the whole agenda of the research may be radically revised.[49]

It is a composite genre, the narrative resulting from the collaborative process between interviewer and interviewee, a process Miren Llona calls "entreverse" (to see each other). Far from being a mere declaration from the informant, it is a two-directional exercise that reveals through the production of that composite narrative the inter-subjectivity involved in the historical becoming. Likewise, autobiographical information provides insights into hidden aspects of mainstream historical narratives and how the actors negotiate their understanding of their "selves" in the context and in response to the master narratives or ideological parameters of the time and place discussed.[50] The individuals that I interviewed told their stories within the parameters of the gender ideology of Francoism, which articulated what I have called "True Catholic Womanhood." Some elaborated a sense of self in opposition to the conventions of the time, while others tried to take advantage of those same parameters (piety, modesty, motherhood) to assert themselves. The narratives constructed respond to each person's gender, class, political and subjective appraisals of the past events, and experience of the political and social events. The oral historian, therefore, must incorporate into his/her methodology the cultural and communicative memories that frame the narrative.

As we will examine in the narratives that follow, the city of Granada becomes the site of encounter between the repressive forces of the Francoist state apparatus against the students and workers and, simultaneously, the site where individuals reclaimed their sense of individuality and group consciousness. They trespassed physical and symbolic boundaries laid out, with technocratic precision, by urban planners. Within the city they moved from the middle-class urban center to the newly established marginal developments and shanty towns, and from the learned

---

49   Portelli, "A Dialogical Relationship."
50   Portelli identifies three narrative models: institutional, communal, and personal. The first is told in the first person and refers to political and economic themes; the second utilizes the "we" to tell the collective actions and is located in the workplace and neighborhood; finally, the third is the personal that reveals intimate, family, and domestic events. All three interact and inform each model. This process is known as the "theory of composure," which puts in contact on the one hand, the format of the narration (epic, romantic, heroic) proper of the time period the memories are produced, and on the other hand, the way the informant constructs his/her self in an effort to reconcile personal and collective themes. On the theory on composure see: Abrams, *Oral History Theory*, 66-67. Penny Summerfield has further problematized the concept of composure by proposing the process of "de-composure" when some of the informants depart from community conventions rather than reconcile their personal and collective identities. See Penny Summerfield, "Discomposing the Subject: Intersubjectivities in Oral History," in *Feminism and Autobiography: Texts Theories, Methods*, ed. Tess Cosslett, Celia Lury, and Penny Summerfield (London, New York: Routledge, 2000), 91-94.

male-centered university space to the working-class suburbs. These perambulations generated a rhythm, a pulse of the city we retrieved and relived through the interview process, turning the spatial into a doorway to the temporal as well. As the informants recall and retell their experiences in prison, at neighborhood associations, or as members of the Communist party cells, I, the author, turn into a *Flâneur,* not of concrete streets but rather of the memory lanes those spaces evoke in our conversations. In a poetic fashion, my "self" is part of the story. Their stories were/are my story. Like Alice in Wonderland, I alternate between becoming big, as adult writer/historian, or small, as I go back in time to involuntary memories triggered by the narratives. The universal and the individual reconcile in this microspace of Granada where I came of age. I can taste, smell, and hear the Granada of my childhood in their recounting. In our conversations is a communion—a historical transubstantiation. Authenticity trumps old-fashioned clinical "objectivity," turning the quest for truth into emotional authenticity.

The two groups of women (college and working class) I interviewed, over a span of more than twenty years, told me stories that might be retold in a different fashion now. I was not the same interlocutor in 1989 as in 2004, and my interaction and collaboration in the creation of these primary sources has evolved as well. Therefore, the resulting study is not only a collection of oral histories to voice the voiceless, but rather an attempt at signification. Passerini made clear in her study of fascism in 1979 that oral sources, rather than telling us about historical facts, provide insights into the subjectivity of the informant and the context in which the communicative process of the interview takes place. Passerini made us appreciate and pay attention to silence and the seemingly irrelevant responses of her interviewees when she asked them about fascism. My Spanish interviews came to fruition (or not), depending on what the informants might have sensed about where my sympathies to Francoism lay. In some instances, they declined my request to interview them because the book had a feminist approach. Unavoidably, I am part of the narrations that follow.

Both Henri Lefebvre and María Zambrano insert their living selves into their intellectual pursuits. In both cases, we encounter a reference to the new beginning, a point of inflexion and change that utilizes the symbol of the crucified sun in the case of Lefebvre and the poetic notion of the dawning thought (*pensamiento auroral*) in Zambrano. Both thinkers resort to light, the sun, and sunrise as an opportunity to criticize modernity, capitalism, and the discarding of humanness from Western thought.

In his autobiographical book *La somme et le reste* (1959), Lefebvre recounts a vision of the "crucified sun" he had in his youth in the 1920s when he was visiting the Pyrenean countryside. While on a walk, he saw a cross with a circle surrounding it. "They had crucified the sun!" Lefebvre asserts:

I no longer saw the cross of Christ wreathed in solar glory or surrounded by the crown of thorns, as had been explained to me, but the darkened sun, marked by a black sign, nailed to the Christian cross. The sun was youth, brilliant [*l'éclarite*] my own, but overcast, pinned down by mental, sexual, and social misery. It was the heat of vitality the ardor of energies fallen into the coldness of the void and its sign. Even in the research bearing the name which had appeared so beautiful to me for a long time: Philosophy.[51]

La somme et le reste was written in 1959, two years after Lefebvre had been expelled from the French Communist Party. He had joined the party not to enter politics but because he felt it was the answer to the end of politics. The symbol of the crucified sun reappears in other writings, and it becomes Lefebvre's metaphor of choice to criticize modernity and the alienation of the urban masses. While the sun represents all that is vital and full of life, the cross embodies repression and alienation in life. The metaphor also made him sensitive to the significance of what that moment of realization had in his life and his thinking. Moreover, it made him aware that certain moments themselves were important turning points in the human experience.[52] A singular moment is full of potential, transcendent, when the individual is radically free to make a decision that will affect his/her destiny.

Since oral history and memory intertwine in Maria Zambrano's exploration of the dictum "I am I and my circumstance" that her teacher Ortega y Gasset articulated through his ratio-vitalism, we can explore the historiographical mandate of truth and objectivity. Zambrano carries further the radical view "I am I and my circumstance" by contemplating the emotional nerve in human thinking processes. She puts it this way: "In the deepest realm of the howling, the weeping, and the groaning resides the core, the insoluble seed of our being, of the word itself."[53] That emotional element only emerges through poetry, revealing an authentic universal being rather than simply a factual objective representation. Zambrano reinterpreted "I am I and my circumstance" and the radical reality of historicity by appealing to the emotions of the human condition. The human subject, the "I," is conscious of his/her self in the measure s/he embraces his/her temporality and its context; it is up to the individual to shape his/her destiny in the face of conventional conditions of a particular time and place. In other words, "I" only becomes "I" in interaction with an "Other." The practice of oral history turns into the most useful tool to achieve historical authenticity—variations of being in the world in time.

---

51   Henri Lefebvre, *La somme et le reste*, quoted in Elden, *Understanding Henri Lefebvre*, 170-71.
52   Elden, *Understanding Henri Lefebvre*, 171.
53   En el interior más hondo del reino del sollozo y del llanto y del gemido habita tal vez el núcleo, semilla indisoluble ha de ser, de la palabra misma [...]." [my translation], in María Zambrano, *De la Aurora* (Madrid: Tabula Rasa, 2004), 124.

Out of this communicative experience arises the "Thinker/Historian as Poet." The historian turned thinker does as the poet: *poetiza, compone, articula* (poeticizes, composes, articulates).[54] Poetic reasoning maintains rigor and critical insight while making the symbolic nature of language work in its favor, opening the door to the emotions and malleable nature of the human condition. Zambrano suggests that the purpose of thinking is "to open up and take true measure of the dimension of our existence."[55] Such introspection is what will make possible the unveiling of the authentic gendered being I am pursuing in the analysis of these interviews. Such thinking is a recalling, remembering, memorization, but also a responding and an autobiographical immersion into the analysis. Past and present meet in the moment informant and historian talk to each other.

---

54   Martin Heidegger, *Poetry, Language, and Thought* (New York: Harper Perennial Modern Classics, 2013), xi.
55   Ana Bundgaard, "Ser, palabra y arte: El pensar originario de Martin Heidegger y María Zambrano," in *Aurora: Papeles del "Seminario María Zambrano,"* 12 (2011): 7-12.

Chapter 1
Concha & Amalias's Kaloskeagathos

> Quien de admirarte no se torna cisne,
> recoge en sí el más suave tacto,
> temeroso ante el enigma,
> al abordar las formas de esa triple ecuación,
> entre Keats y Platón entretejida?
> Pues si en ti verdad y belleza son bondad
> Su despojada esencia es tan humilde,
> Que por sencilla y pura se hace altiva,
> Más, !ay!, por entregada libre
> Y a la par cautiva.
> Clara Janés, "Leda cautiva" (1983)[1]

Like any other Saturday, Amalia was looking forward to having lunch with her neighbor Concha. They had been friends since the late 1960s when they were both students at the University of Granada. Now they lived in adjoining apartments C and D, on Melchor Almagro Street by the Colegio de Ciencias.

Their lunches were ritualistic rather than routine, reflecting the reverence with which they treated their long friendship. Concha had lived alone for three years after suffering through a traumatic divorce. Amalia, still married and a mother of

---

1   *Who from admiring you would not turn into a swam*
    gather within herself the softest touch
    afraid of the enigma
    posed by the contours of that triple equation
    interwoven from Keats to Plato?
    Because within you, truth and beauty are goodness
    their generous essence so humble
    that being so simple it is really lofty
    but, Oh! so faithful and free
    while at the same time enslaved.
    Clara Janés, *Vivir* (Madrid: Hiperión, 1983), 55. [My translation intends to capture the meaning of this beautiful poem by Clara Janés.]

two, extended her family in offering. Concha accepted and became one of Amalia's family.

Figure 1: Concha with Amalia's family watching TV after lunch for the last time (1990)

When Concha did not call that Saturday, Amalia was not particularly worried. She knew that Concha was making last-minute edits to her new book on renaissance art in Granada and assumed she had lost track of time. When she saw her the next day, Concha would tell her all about it. But that next time never came.

Work had always been Concha's safe harbor. It had sustained her after her infant daughter died suddenly. It nurtured her after her divorce. And now it kept her going when other areas of her life seemed to fail her. Instead of wearing her struggles on the outside, though, Concha kept them tucked away. On the surface she was all business, with a wry, some would say sardonic, sense of humor. Underneath, a sense of world-weariness occasionally seeped through.

Concha was an Associate Professor of Art History at the University of Granada. As well as being a noted Art Historian, she was well known in Granada's political circles—part of the clandestine student movement of the late 1960s and later, during the transition, a proud candidate for the newly legalized Communist Party.

Despite her well-known public persona, Concha was an enigma for many. Coming from a background of privilege, she became an ardent Communist. Raised as a true believing Catholic, she shed her religious carapace without losing her Christian zeal to serve the less fortunate. She had risked everything—career, family, relationships—many times for her political beliefs, and would do it all again.

A year before the missed lunch date, I met Concha in her apartment, with Amalia joining us. It was May 3, 1989, the Day of the Cross. Outside, a multitude of carnation covered crosses—monumental, large, medium, and small—festooned every park and plaza. Manila shawls hung from balconies while children, looking like miniature adults in their colorful flamenco dress, paraded through the streets.

This year, I was not focused on the colorful celebrations but on my interview. I was leaving for the University of New Mexico (in the United States) in a few weeks, and I had to finish my research beforehand. As an overly earnest graduate student, lucky enough to come of age during the transition, I had the freedom to study abroad and to critically investigate what had been until recently a taboo topic—women under Franco. My fellow female students and I saw ourselves as a generation of change in the recently liberated Spain. Concha and Amalia were from the generation before mine. During their college years they did not enjoy the same freedoms. In fact, they had to fight a clandestine resistance that made my studies even possible. They were my spiritual godmothers.

Concha and Amalia had belonged to "Mujeres Universitarias" (University Women Association) established in 1976 at the University of Granada.[2] The Association provided legal cover for women of different ideological backgrounds to press a liberal feminist agenda, before the political parties were given official approval. Catalan professor Montserrat Rubio Lois took the lead in establishing a chapter of the Association and was the president. Some of the executive board members included: Mari Luz Escribano Pueo and Concha Félez as vice- presidents and Julia García Leal, Carmen Guerrero Villalba, and Angela Olalla Real. In the beginning the Association formed several committees: urban planning, education and teaching, women's legal counsel, and health. An important focus was on the struggle against discrimination of women within academia. Another was the increase in tuition that was a hardship for working class women. The Association also fought for daycare at the university, access to birth control, the legalization of divorce, and the need to reform the still extant Francoist civil and penal codes that discriminated against women. In addition, the Association focused on urban and cultural reform. Creating welcoming public spaces for women was considered important in the feminist agenda, as was promoting a more inclusive cultural and artistic agenda that went beyond the religious laden, anachronistic one imposed by Franco's regime. The University Women supported a 40th anniversary tribute in honor of poet Federico García Lorca, a symbol of anti-fascist sentiment who

---

2   Founded in Oviedo and Madrid in 1953, the Asociación de Mujeres Universitarias replaced the former Asociación Española de Mujeres Universitarias, founded by Clara Campoamor and María de Maeztu during the Second Republic (1931-1936) with members such as Soledad Ortega Spottorno, daughter of philosopher José Ortega y Gasset, and the Granadina Isabel García Lorca, sister of poet Federico García Lorca. The 1930s association soon had a presence all over the country and joined the International Federation of University Women, founded after World War I with the mission to improve women's access to higher education. The Spanish Civil War (1936-1939) meant the end to their activism, understood in feminist terms until 1953, when the new Asociación de Mujeres Universitarias was established.

was assassinated by the regime in August 1936 in Fuente Vaqueros, just outside Granada. They fought to rename streets honoring Franco-era stalwarts, and to preserve the stately trees lining the then named Boulevard Calvo Sotelo (named after a fascist MP assassinated in Madrid before the Spanish Civil War). The crowning glory of their many achievements, though, was uncovering a plot in 1977 to turn the historic Carmen de los Mártires into a private hotel.

The three of us sat in plush armchairs around a coffee table in a small living room lined with bookcases full of Concha's art books. As Carmen spoke, a cloud of cigarette smoke hung over her head, punctuating her sardonic speech like a diaphanous diacritical mark.

Concha remembered the profound emotional blow she felt when she moved to Granada: "I cried for three months. Granada was very different from Málaga where I was born, and from Madrid where I grew up in the bourgeois Barrio de Salamanca." At that time, in the early 1950s, Madrid projected a cosmopolitan air, while Granada held fast to its provincialism. In Madrid, Concha attended the Colegio de la Asunción on Velázquez Street, an elite nunnery school that sent most of its girls to college. That was not the case in the high schools of Granada, where the daughters of the bourgeois had to fight to be able to attend college. "There existed a great isolation in Granada... You need to take into consideration that this was a closed city both geographically and historically. I was invited by a Señorita Granadina to spend the day in her country home. I made sure to dress very prim and proper. Her brother drove me back to my dorm afterword and remarked, 'I am so pleased to have met you, because, although you are from Málaga and a college girl, you are still very nice and proper.' I was so offended. What did he expect, that I was going to eat the soup with my fingers? You, Amalia, deserve a lot of credit coming from this town...."

"Perhaps because in my family," reflected Amalia, "we never went without but did not have extra either. We were seven brothers and sisters, and I was the oldest girl. This meant that my mother relied on my help, and my studies were always secondary. Nobody seemed to understand that I needed time to read and study for exams. It was a constant battle. I went to the Regina Mundi nunnery school run by the Daughters of Charity," Amalia said with ironic emphasis on the word "charity." "I saw so much prejudice in that school against the so-called 'gratuitous' girls, in comparison to ones like me whose families could pay tuition," she recalled. "While we entered through one door, in our wool uniforms with starched white collars, the 'gratuitous' girls had to come in through a separate door in the basement where they were sequestered and taught. We were not allowed to mix."

This blatant discrimination made a big impression on Amalia that carried over into her later years. "I would have preferred attending the public Ganivet Institute, but my parents refused to even listen to my pleading. My mother thought that the girls from the public schools were not, in her words, properly protected. This from a woman who was not particularly right wing. That was a difficult time for me and had a profound impact on my life."

Concha was forced to compromise as well over the course of her studies. "I had wanted to study law but there was little professional future for women in the field, until the law of Political and Professional Rights for Women was approved in 1961, one year after I began college. I decided to continue in Philosophy and Letters rather than start over."

From 1961 to 1965 Concha lived in the Residence Hall of Jesús María where she enjoyed a rich extracurricular life of *tertulias*, poetry readings, and theater. This was a time of transformation for the university. Beside a richer cultural life on campus, the out-of-town students were allowed to rent private flats, fostering even more independence and autonomy.

"I was so jealous of the out-of-town girls," Amalia remarked. "I missed out on so many college experiences because I lived under the control of my family. This was a big difference between us, the local students, and those from outside Granada."

Concha acknowledged her friend's frustration and added, "In the dormitories you met people from different backgrounds and parts of Spain. There was an excitement being away from home for the first time as women and having some of the freedoms that only men used to have. It wasn't just the freedom to come and go as we pleased, but to think for ourselves as women and imagine a different future. And it wasn't just an island of women. Our Residence was located across from the male Loyola Residence, and both dorms organized co-ed activities. This is where I met some of the future politicians of the democratic transition. I lived in the dorms eight years, first as a student and then as an instructor, until I married in 1969."

"One of the most frustrating things of my college years," Amalia lamented, "was the lack of autonomy and access to all the things Concha is describing…. I did not even have my own room at home…. Those College Dorms were a separate world, physically and culturally. I studied classical philology, Greek and Latin, and immediately after graduation got a job in Málaga. I couldn't wait to leave home…."

"You had so much fun," Concha muttered. "You got a boyfriend right away." Amalia ignored the last comment and continued reminiscing: "I remember fondly going to the movies. That was so much fun…cinema, cinema, cinema. Reading film magazines like *Fotograma* or *Cahiers du Cinema*. The wonderful films of Antonioni or Truffaut."

"I could not stand the French ones… the American comedy was fabulously light—" interjected Concha. "You know, my husband, Juan Carlos, had not met me yet, and he used to tell the story that one day while visiting the dorm he had heard me entering the lobby yelling, 'Girls, I just saw a fabulous movie! Scaramouche!' He always remembered that anecdote warmly"—Concha sounded nostalgic, longing—"because, you see, he had enjoyed it too and was pleased to hear me say I had liked a popular film.... He would say, 'Wow! I could not believe it, because you had a reputation for being very studious.'"

Admitting any kind of frivolity was not something university girls could afford to do. They had to prove they were bona fide intellectuals, fully committed to their studies.

"Panties-ville, remember?" said Concha, looking at Amalia. "That's how the guys used to refer to our Philosophy and Letters College."

"Yes, of course, because our college was almost all women. It was even more obvious once we moved from Puentezuelas in the city center to the Cartuja campus on the outskirts of town."[3]

"It was also a way to put the agitators outside of the urban center where the police could easily contain us," Concha pointed out.

"By that time the Women's Section girls (the state sanctioned women's group) were losing popularity," continued Amalia. "They cultivated a very austere style."

"Remember those cheap uniforms? ...blue blouses and grey skirt suits. Their demeanor was kind of mannish," said Concha.

"Yes, I thought they looked a little butch," murmured Amalia.

"We called them *marimachos* (tomboys, butch)," added Concha. "You would never see them wearing makeup or flowery dresses. By the 1950s and 1960s they were mostly from lower middle-class families, in contrast to the aristocratic elite that founded the Women's Section with Pilar Primo de Rivera and her university friends earlier in the regime. The Women's Section was often the only way they could afford to go to college."

"There were also the religious organizations. Concha, you were very active in the Congregaciones Marianas,[4] right?" asked Amalia.

"Yes," Concha replied. "I had been a Daughter of María in school and continued my commitment to the Congregation in college until I joined the Communist Party. My family was very religious." After admitting this, Concha paused for a moment,

---

3   In the summer of 1936, shortly before the civil war erupted, the University of Granada announced that due to lack of space its goal was to move its facilities to the environs of the monastery of Cartuja in the northern part of the city. The war, and later the reluctance of the faculty to move away from the urban center, made the process extremely slow. Closer to the center of town was the area called Fuentenueva, where in 1962 the Faculty of Sciences, designed by Cruz López Müller, was built. The Philosophy and Letters building, inaugurated in 1976-77, was a 1971 design of Francisco Prieto-Moreno Pardo in the period's brutalist architectonic style: massive concrete structure on pillars, floor to ceiling windows.

4   Established in Rome in 1563, the Marian Congregations arrived in Spain in 1586 while female congregations were founded in 1751. By the end of the 19th the century, the Marian movement reached beyond the Jesuits' schools: the *Daughters of María* had significant membership, along with the male congregations for secondary education students called the *Kostkas*, and the university associations known as *Luises*.

as if in reflection. She then began talking about her family's religious devotion. "My father used to collaborate with Málaga's noted bishop Angel Herrera Oria,[5] ...I remember as a little girl going with him to the countryside where he helped build schools for the poor. My mother also was pious, but in a different way. Going to mass every Sunday was an unavoidable family ritual.... For me, actually, it was the most natural thing to do.... Sundays we went to mass and afterwards had cakes...you know, you picked up some cakes to take home... Therefore, at a very early age I joined the Congregaciones Mariana as the most natural thing for a girl from a respectable conservative family. I carried my father's religious commitment into my college years. These university religious groups paradoxically became seedbeds of leftist politics because our pledge to fix social problems sprang from our profound Catholic beliefs. We read the journals of the Christian organizations such as the French La Croix or Concilium...where you learned about not just the divine but also the human condition...all those thinkers and theologians that today remain a problematic crowd for John Paul II. Within the Congregaciones Mariana there were two positions; those who thought the purpose was to organize rosaries and communal prayers to the Virgin, and others, like myself, who spent our free time trying to solve the problems of poor gypsies in the Sacromonte. We wanted to transform the world. In that space and frame of mind, a leftist Christian discourse emerged, which led naturally to Marxist activism. For us, a commitment to social change was a mix of existentialism and Vatican II ecumenical principles. We were known as Federación de Congregacionaes Universitarias Marianas (FECUM, Spanish Federation of University Marian Congregations)."[6]

"All that came about," interrupted Amalia, "because 1968-1969 was a year of division, of rupture, of separations. For me it was a significant moment because I was graduating and starting a job, taking off. It meant emancipation from my family. To be able to do whatever I pleased, read whatever I wanted, carve my own space...everything I had never enjoyed at home. I had not experienced any privacy at home and therefore my story is different from that of Concha...that is a big difference between us. The first year after graduating I got a teaching position in Málaga. As

---

5 Ángel Herrera Oria (Santander, 1886-Madrid, 1968) founder of, along with the priest Ángel Ayala, the Association of National Catholic Propagandist (ACNP) in 1910 and a year later launched the Editorial Católica with the daily paper *El Debate*. In 1936, just before the beginning of the civil war, he moved to Switzerland and entered the San Carlos Seminary and was ordained in 1940. Herrera Oria returned to Spain in 1943 to manage the parish of Saint Lucia in Santander. Through the ACNP he collaborated closely with the Francoist regime, becoming a broker in the discussions between the Holy See and the regime. In October 1947, he was appointed bishop of Málaga where he worked for a social Catholic program inspired by Leo XIII doctrine. He created over 200 hundred schools and led a literacy campaign.

6 Javier Alberdi Alonso SJ and Juan Luis Pintos SJ, *Actitud religiosa del universitario español: Encuesta FECUM 1967* (Madrid: Editorial Razón y Fe S.A., 1967).

I was commuting back and forth, the PCE used me as a messenger to bring party documents between the two cities."

Amalia spoke with pride when she talked about becoming an agent for the PCE. She would not officially join the party until 1975 but was sympathetic to its aim long before. She readily agreed to ferry parcels back and forth between Málaga and Granada. She explained the routine, the repetition, the rhythm that filled her first year of emancipation: "I traveled by bus every Monday from Granada to Málaga and returned every Saturday afternoon. Someone would give me a package, wrapped in brown paper, and tied with thin twine. They did not tell me about the contents, and I did not ask questions. There was always someone waiting at the bus station who would take the package from me. I never saw the same person, and I never knew how they identified me. At the time this felt like a small transgression. Now I realize how dangerous it all was."

"Well...yes, of course, for you it was a complete departure," admitted Concha after listening to Amalia's rendition of those events. Concha then explained: "Really, for me the last couple of years of college were all about destroying the SEU.[7] When I graduated in 1965, I was still a member of FECUM and later on...it must have been 1974...I spearheaded Mujeres Universitarias because we felt we had to organize ourselves for action. It was a global political approach, which meant the creation of a platform where women could have a visible impact in society and current affairs.... We organized working committees and were part of a national network linked to the Institución Libre de Enseñanza (Free Institution of Learning)."[8]

"We were criticized by several women's groups from the left because they found us to be too elitist," Amalia pointed out.

"We created this platform when there were no sanctioned political parties," continued Concha, "and it was precisely when the political parties started organizing

---

7 SEU (Sindicato Español Universitario), established in 1939 and dissolved in 1965, was the only state-sponsored student organization and part of the Falange. All students were mandated to join this organization, which served as a political means of control and socialization of the college youth. See Miguel Ángel Ruiz Carnicer, *El Sindicato Español Universitario (SEU) 1939-1965: La socialización política de la juventud universitaria en el franquismo* (Madrid: Siglo XXI, 1996).

8 ILE (Institución Libre de Enzeñanza) was established in 1876, based on the ideas of obscure German philosopher Frederick Krause. It aspired to academic freedom and lay instruction, with one of its most important elements being the commitment to co-education of the sexes. Founded by Julián Sanz del Río, along with a small circle of Madrid University professors, it had a profound impact on Spanish politics and the educational system during the Second Republic (1931-1936). The Francoist regime committed itself to the eradication of all educational principles espoused by the ILE, declaring them to be anti-Catholic and thus, by definition, anti-Spanish.

themselves for the first democratic elections in 1979 that our initiative dissolved. Most of us in the leading roles belonged to the Communist Party."

The Communist Party had been deeply entrenched among the student movement with an extensive clandestine network able to lead the anti-Francoist resistance rather than the almost nonexistent PSOE (Partido Socialista Obrero Español).[9]

"With Mujeres Universitarias our goal was to have an impact at the cultural and intellectual level because that was our setting, our place of action. That was where we were and where we spent most of our time," explained Concha. "One of the most relevant actions that we undertook concerned the Carmen de Los Mártires,[10] which turned into a national scandal." The town hall closed down the historic site to begin construction of a hotel. The Carmen, a nineteenth-century palace and gardens built next to the iconic Alhambra, had long been a part of Granada's history.

"The site was very special for all Granadinos...we used to go there almost every day...to enjoy the sunny afternoons, to study...and...without warning the authorities closed it down," remarked Amalia.

"We broke into the property with two Dobermans that belonged to a wonderful woman, Mari Luz,...remember her?" asked Concha. "A journalist married to one of the Marins, a very important family in town.... Well, she came with her dogs. The Alhambra Board of Trustees was involved in everything, you know. Scandalous. And even my boss, Dr. Pita Andrade, head of the Art History department at the University of Granada, was involved. We organized a series of lectures with slides to show the public the horrible destruction going on at the site. We received a downpouring of attacks...calling us leftist radicals etc., ...but it was a bombshell! We uncovered a real estate speculation scandal in which the Town Hall and the Alhambra Board of Trustees were deeply entangled."

"Now, there it is! We preserved Los Mártires," asserted Amalia proudly.

---

9   The Socialist Workers Party (PSOE) was founded in 1889 by Pablo Iglesias. They also had a trade union UGT (Unión General de Trabajadores). For more information, visit http://www.fpabloiglesias.es/.

10 Carmen is the name of a typical Granadina estate house. The name derives from the Roman term "Karmen," meaning vines, which were commonly used in the gardens of these houses. The Carmen de los Mártires sits on a hill in the proximity of the Alhambra overlooking the fertile valley countryside and Sierra Nevada, as well as a Moorish castle. A Carmen follows a topographical design in several levels that expands from the interior of the house to the surrounding lavish gardens. The Carmen de los Mártires was built on a site that was previously occupied by a Franciscan monastery until the disentitlement process that led to General don Carlos Calderón's purchase in 1845. In 1957, Granada's Town Hall purchased the property, and in 1972 the city opened a public contest to demolish the Carmen and build in its place a hotel. It is during this time that Mujeres Universitarias engaged in a campaign to save the estate. For more on this monument see: http://www.granada.org/inet/palacios.nsf/xedbynombre/58475794CDC857ECC1257188003A3DA0.

These women claimed the right to the city space for the people of Granada. The Carmen de los Mártires remains today a valuable historical site and beloved public space where couples celebrate civil marriages, families stroll through the gardens, and elderly couples sit in the sun. Concha and Amalia never thought they were waging a feminist fight, but simply a fight for justice. This simple ideal captured so much about what the determined band of university women fought for. When women win, everyone wins.

Ultimately what drove both Concha and Amalia was a struggle for their own autonomy. They were tired of having to ask permission from men, or even from women's organizations controlled by men. They wanted to make their own decisions, not only as individuals, but as part of a larger collective who shared their history of oppression and their longing for a more equitable Spain. At the heart of this struggle was the economic discrimination that women had for so long been the target.

"Our generation was very clear on what was our main objective from a feminist perspective, and that was economic independence...everything else was secondary," stated Concha.

"Well...yes, that is a feminist issue obviously, but I am not sure we were aware of it or even called it feminism at that time...were you?" asked Amalia.

"Yes, yes, yes I am convinced," affirmed Concha.

"I am not!" declared Amalia.

"I am, I am convinced," emphatically asserted Concha. "Because, as I have told you many times...my parents had a very conventional marriage and yet, since I was a little girl, I hated when my mother had to ask my father for money...I don't know...I saw her every October beg my father: 'Andrés, I have run out of money this month because I had to buy winter shoes for them,'" Concha enacted her mother's voice with visible indignation. "That was something that made my skin crawl.... And I remember I used to tell myself...this is a society for both men and women...I saw it from a very young age...I knew that situation was utter stupidity, and I was determined not to follow that path."

"We were feminist without knowing it," concluded Amalia.

"In my case, I had been raised like a boy," continued Concha heatedly, "with all the perks and possibilities, and then I saw the contradiction so clearly.... So, I was like a boy until I turned twenty and then I had to explain myself to a man so he would give me a thousand *pesetas*...? Oh no, never...that does not make any sense whatsoever!"

The context of the university also offered a different set of challenges when it came to their relationships with male colleagues. As students, intellectually, they often were superior to their male counterparts, performing better on examinations and receiving higher grades. But this did not translate into more opportunities once they graduated. Concha did get hired as an instructor at the University of Granada but was denied promotion to full professor.

"When they denied me the promotion to full professor, one male colleague told me, 'Well, Concha, don't worry, you are married anyway....' When referring to a male candidate competing with you, they would say something like, 'See, you need to understand that he has a family...' and then when I separated from my husband they would tell me, 'obviously you don't feel like competing again for promotion, right? You must be so upset....' Nobody would say anything like that to a man!" Concha continued with indignation. "This was already the late 1970s and the early 1980s.... So, sexism might not be as blatant at first sight, but shows up as soon as you try to step outside of the conventional space assigned to you.... I wanted to punch them," remarked Concha, laughing. "I decided not to put myself through any more of those grueling promotion committees.... Why should I become a full professor, anyway?"

* * *

We concluded the interview that day with high spirits. I left shortly after for the University of New Mexico where I had been awarded a doctoral student assistantship. My dissertation topic morphed into studying the official Catholic discourses of the regime (the basis for my first book, *True Catholic Women*), and the interviews I had made shortly before my departure languished in their plastic cassette cases until thirty years later, when I awoke them from their slumber. After listening to them, I decided it was time to catch up with my old friends. We had lost touch after I left for the United States. My research had gone in different directions, and I had not taken up the topic of university women again. I was no longer a wide-eyed graduate student interviewing my heroes, but a battle tested senior scholar with my own past to deconstruct. Amalia was only a phone call away. One morning, sitting in my office in Florida, I decided to make the call and transport myself back to that afternoon thirty years ago.

Amalia is a grandmother now. She retired as soon as she turned sixty and is enjoying her new role as matriarch. I reminded her of what we discussed so long ago and took up the conversation as if it were yesterday. I asked her to elaborate on what was said. On April 14, 1977, she was arrested along with fifteen other university professors for putting up posters on the streets demanding the legalization of all left-wing political parties, including the PCE. While they were plastering posters on the walls in the San Agustín Public Market in the downtown area, a strange man wearing a trench coat pulled a gun on them and led them to the Plaza de los Lobos police precinct. "I was terrified because I thought this was a fascist fanatic ready to shoot us," Amalia recalled. "Once we reached the police station, I felt we might be alright."

The undercover policeman had taken it upon himself to catch some Communists, even though the party was on the verge of being legalized. Amalia spent the night in jail and had to go before a judge the next morning in the sixteenth-century building, The Chancillería. She remembered how the authorities were not sure what to do with them. It was Holy Week, and by Sábado de Gloria, in three days, the government would legalize the PCE. "When we left the courthouse and came out into Plaza Nueva," Amalia smiled, "a large crowd was there hailing our bravery, throwing carnations and making us feel like heroes."

Amalia is proud of her activism in the PCE, which she believes was the result of her Catholic upbringing. For her, Christian values were her moral compass: "Nothing to do with the institutional Catholic Church that was always on the side of the powerful rather than coming to the aid of the poor. Therefore, the PCE provided the means to put into action those moral values they had inculcated us with in nunnery school. The Party," she remembered, "reminded us to be always coherent with our principles and preserve our integrity. If we wanted to truly change society's injustices, we had to be exemplary in our conduct everywhere we went: in the workplace, our home, our studies. So, my work has always been for me a very serious facet of my life and self-esteem. I was never interested in parliamentary appointments or the big political game but rather in being the best Communist, the best person I could be in my immediate circle. That's why I left the party as soon as I saw the internal power struggles and backstabbing. This resonated with me as a classicist, and I highlight it to my students when discussing ancient Greek and Roman culture. During Homeric times the oral tradition promoted the notion of *Kalóskeagathós* for the hero, the perfect fusion of beauty and goodness. As Plato would further elaborate, goodness is always beautiful. I am not talking about a physical beauty. Goodness and beauty are inseparable qualities and perfectly squared with my Christian upbringing. Therefore, the best Communist person must necessarily be the best worker, the best friend, the best human being." Amalia was quiet for a moment and then with tears in her eyes, said, "That was Concha. She was an extraordinary human being, *'bellísima persona.'*"

She takes me back to that Saturday in the spring of 1991 when she did not know why Concha had not shown up for lunch. "On Friday we dined at my place, and I was looking forward to seeing her the following day. By night, I became really worried. She had not answered the phone all day. When I went to the balcony that separated both of our apartments and saw the lights and her television on, my heart sank. I opened her door with the spare key I kept and went in. There I found her on her bathroom floor, dead. The clothes she was wearing the day before for dinner were on top of the bed. She had had a massive heart attack." Amalia is silent. "This is the first time in many years," she uttered, "that I have spoken of this day." Amalia lost her *Kalóskeagathós* friend when Concha died in 1991.

After the legalization of the PCE, Concha ran for office on the Party's ballot to be an MP in the general election in June 1977. She was the only woman who participated in the first PCE rally in Granada on April 20, speaking alongside General Secretary Santiago Carrillo, among other local male comrades. Between 1978 and 1981, Concha was one of six women who were part of the PCE's Provincial Committee (a total of forty-four members) and a delegate of the PCE First Regional Congress in 1979. Her name appeared on a list of 3,000 Spaniards (fifty-one from Granada, seven of them women) who probably would have been jailed—if not shot—if the February 23, 1981, coup d'état had been successful.[11]

Amalia remembers Concha's heroism. She remembers how difficult it had been for Concha to overcome the shunning of her conservative family. The day she was to speak at the rally with Santiago Carrillo on April 20, 1977, she had a fainting spell as a result of a fight with her sister, eleven years older than her and a member of the ultra-conservative Opus Dei. Amalia was standing by Concha as she engaged in a heated conversation over the phone. No sooner had Concha hung up, she passed out. Amalia and her husband picked Concha up from the floor and helped her regain her bearings. They were running late to the rally. "She was so strong," Amalia remarked. "Her speech was inspiring that day, and after the rally we went to celebrate over a beer at a local bar. She then confided in me what had happened. She had received a call from her sister because in a week's time Concha's goddaughter would make her First Communion. This was their brother's little daughter, Vanesa, who Concha called 'mi Vane.'" Her sister was furious because Concha was running for office with the Communists. She told her that the family was ashamed of her and that she was not welcome at the First Communion in Málaga. Amalia remembers how Concha started sobbing as she retold the episode in the dark corner of the small, packed tavern.

Concha remained committed to social justice her entire life. She was also a paradox—a privileged woman professing such a fervent belief in communism. She unselfconsciously used to wear her mink coat to distribute the Communist newspaper in the main street in town, La Gran Vía. Amalia tried to explain: "She was a cultivated person, very educated, who realized how the true great minds in our history always sought to make the world a better place." Amalia continued, "She believed in the Christian principles of justice, just not in the Church itself. We saw the PCE as the best means of action at that particular moment in time."

The religious upbringing of the two women ironically radicalized them. The blatant unfairness of the regime toward women was clear to everyone, but it took the clandestine student organizations to turn resentment into action. The feminists

---

11 Alfonso Martínez Foronda and Pedro Sánchez Rodrigo, *Mujeres en Granada por las libertades democráticas: Resistencia y represión (1960-1981)* (Granada: Fundación de Estudios y Cooperación de CCOO de Andalucía Unión Provincial de CCOO de Granada, 2017), 102.

were a natural fit with the Communists. Both groups were seeking to break out of the Francoist straight jacket and saw each other as natural allies. The experience in clandestine politics helped turn the radicals of Franco's final years, like Concha and Amalia, into savvy politicians during the transition. Their life-long friendship was a testament to the strength of those bonds and the lasting effect they had on creating a better place for women in a modern Spain.

Chapter 2[1]
Revolutionary Mystique: Socorro and Jesús

Figure 2: Socorro and Jesús as college students

1   Interview by author, Audio recording, Granada, May 29, 1989.

Tú no puedes volver atrás
porque la vida ya te empuja
como un aullido interminable.

Hija mía es mejor vivir
con la alegría de los hombres
que llorar ante el muro ciego.

José Agustín Goytisolo, *Palabras para Julia*[2]

Every morning on my way to school, my little brother and sister tagging along behind me, I would walk by the remains of the old tannery across the street from Granada's provincial prison. Only years later, on a sunny spring afternoon in 1989, over a cup of strong coffee, did I learn that Socorro had been inside that very same prison in September 1971. The jail had been built on the outskirts of town, but over the years, a lack of common-sense urban planning had swallowed it up. It now stood incongruously in the middle of a city neighborhood, my neighborhood. Its unadorned red brick facade concealed its sinister history like an aging mass murderer hiding behind the visage of an old man. The ruins of the tannery still gave off a fetid, organic smell. Built during the Second Republic (1931-1936), Granada's provincial jail was inaugurated in 1933 as part of the modernization plan led by then General Director of Prisons, Victoria Kent (Málaga 1891- New York 1987), a socialist and a feminist. The architect, Felipe Jiménez Lacal, found inspiration in the mudejar style, with a floor plan organized in renaissance revival fashion around four interior patios. The prison emulated, in humble economical red brick, the design of the ostentatious sixteenth-century Hospital Real, a jewel of gothic, renaissance, mudejar, and baroque style that today is the home of the University of Granada's central administration.

While the modest prison, originally built for 500 inmates, aspired to be a model of rehabilitation in the modernizing project of the Second Republic, it would ultimately hold ten times that number during the dictatorship—mostly political dissidents. Demolished in 2010, only the main entrance survives, protected as a historical monument to the Second Republic, whose shield still greets visitors.

---

2   *Tú no puedes volver atrás/ You cannot go back*
    porque la vida ya te empuja/ because life is already pushing you
    como un aullido interminable./ like an endless howl.
    Hija mía es mejor vivir/ My daughter, it is better to live
    con la alegría de los hombres/ with the joy of men
    que llorar ante el muro ciego. / than to cry before the blind wall.
    José Agustín Goytisolo, *Words for Julia* (Barcelona: Lumen Editorial, 1990). [My translation].

For me, as a nine-year-old girl, that time does not stand out in my memory. Each morning walking to school, I was unaware of the Art History student, a senior in college, taking her final exams behind the red brick walls, after being on the run from the police for eight months straight, her only crime a devotion to Communism. Her passion for knowledge had led her on a search for truth and love. The first she found in her faith and studies, the second in her boyfriend Jesús.

> Jesusito de mi vida
> Tu eres niño como yo
> Por eso te quiero tanto
> Y te doy mi corazón[3]

Just sixteen, they met at a party and fell in love.[4] Jesús, the son of a strict father who was a teacher and head of the Falange, was born in Calahonda, a tiny coastal city in the province of Granada. Socorro, born in the city of Granada, was the daughter of a post office employee and a stay-at-home mom. She had only one brother, four years older than her, an anomaly in a country of pro-natalist policies where many families typically had seven, eight, or nine children. Socorro worried about her parents' piety and their irregularity in attending mass. As a child she would pray, "Please make them more religious, I'm afraid they'll be damned." Things changed after her father took some catechism courses, making him—not her mother—the religious one in the family. "My mother was emotionally fragile," Socorro explained. A woman from a small village who grew up fatherless—her father had left for Cuba—Socorro's mother suffered from periodic depression. "My mother, while she belonged to a conservative family, felt a visceral anticlericalism and would express herself like a Lorquian character: 'don't bring me flowers, those are for the dead' or 'I need to be close to the soil because it is my shroud' she used to say."

Socorro's father served with the Nationalists during the civil war. He was only seventeen years old when he was forced to serve with the Francoist troops, even though his family's sentiments were for the other side. His brother joined the Republicans and was later imprisoned in a concentration camp. He did not directly espouse his leftist beliefs—probably as a way to survive as a mutilated war veteran whose brother served with the other side—but in secret listened to the clandestine radio station known as "la Pirenáica."[5]

---

3   Popular children's prayer before going to bed.
4   Jesús Carreño Tenorio, phone interview by author, September 18, 2017.
5   Established as *Radio España Independiente* (July 22, 1941- July 14, 1977), known also as *La Pirenáica*, created by Dolores Ibarruri after the civil war by the Communist Party of Spain in exile to reach the population inside the country. This was the most important clandestine radio station in opposition to the regime and its location was never disclosed. The first broadcast took

Socorro received a Catholic education, attending first the Adoratrices nunnery school, then one run by Cristo Rey. Always a good student, she was given scholarships meant for lower income families like hers. Her intelligence and hard work would eventually lead her to the university, despite the resistance of a father who considered education wasted on a girl. Being leftist did not preclude her father from being sexist. He imagined her working in a perfume boutique, "something elegant," she laughs. Her persistence led him to consent to her entering the Normal School for teachers in 1965, a "proper and feminine" career for a girl. Socorro had other ideas. Once she received her teaching credential in 1968, she transferred to the University of Granada to pursue a degree in Art History. At the University she made friends with students who shared her commitment to social justice. Her relationship with Jesús, who was on a similar path, blossomed. His family, unlike Socorro's, was unapologetically pro-Nationalist.

Jesús attended the Escuela del Ave María in the historic neighborhood of the Albayzin in Granada. Though conservative in their teachings, his teachers taught the students to have compassion for those in need. Delivered in religious rather than political terms, the message, instead of bolstering the right's moral authority, undermined its position in impressionable idealists like Jesús. Gradually he began to reject the right-wing politics of his family in favor of leftist beliefs that fit more with his direct observations of the crippling poverty and lack of opportunity in Granada during the 1960s.

Socorro's conviction was strengthened when she joined a Granada youth group working with the poor in neighborhoods like La Virgencica,[6] El Chinarral, and La Chana. One hundred and seventy-three families were forcefully evacuated in trucks from the Sacromonte after the disastrous flooding and landslides in the winter of 1963. A total of 7,000 people were resettled to the outskirts of the city. The Sacromonte[7] (Sacred Hill) was historically occupied by the Gypsies who made their homes in the hilltop caves. A twenty-four-year-old man and his toddler son died in one of the collapsed caves. Franco visited the devastated region, and his Ministry of Housing, working with the Town Hall, developed the temporary housing project of La Virgencica. The design of the temporary housing was an innovative beehive of hexagonal 37m^2 (scarcely 400 square feet) apartments. The small dwellings, though

---

place on July 22, 1941, from Moscow. On January 5, 1955, the station was moved permanently to Bucharest, Romania.

6   On the urban development of La Virgencica and other marginal neighborhoods in Granada see: Tomás Andreo Sánchez, "La Virgencica, una intervención de urgencia para un urbanismo vivo" (PhD diss., Universidad de Granada, Facultad de Bellas Artes Alonso Cano, Departamento de Dibujo, 2015); Teresa Ortega López, "Obreros y vecinos en el tardofranquismo y la transición política (1966-1977): Una 'lucha' conjunta para un mismo fin," *Espacio, Tiempo y Forma, Serie V. Historia Contemporánea* 16 (2004): 351-69.

7   Álvaro Calleja, "La lluvia que silenció el Sacromonte," *GranadaiMedia*, October 29, 2018,

praised for their design, were not equipped to handle the large families of ten and fifteen they typically sheltered. The resulting overcrowding overwhelmed the basic infrastructure, water, electricity, and sanitation, making the striking buildings no better than any other urban slum.

As Socorro talked about La Virgencica, I flash back to 1968 when I was six years old. My uncle Miguel, a young construction worker who had recently moved to the city, was relocated there with his new wife and her family. Among my parents' old black-and-white photos is one of my sister and me sitting outside in the tiny front patio.[8] It occurs to me that my family's history and my own are held together by these small coincidences. They, like the threads in a finely woven cloth, become visible only upon close inspection.

It was in La Virgencica that the first neighborhood association[9] was established in 1969, with the encouragement of the parish priest, Antonio Quitián González. Father Quitián inspired and worked with young students like Socorro and Jesús. With his encouragement, Socorro joined a project to teach reading and writing in La Virgencica in 1969, her first academic year in college. Father Quitián's reward for all his good deeds was to be arrested and imprisoned like other priests who were sympathetic to the Communist party.[10]

---

8   By the mid-1970s, many of the residents of La Virgencica relocated to the new district in the north of the city limits called Polígono de Cartuja where they resettled in tiny cheap single-story homes sponsored by the regime's *Obra Sindical del Hogar*. City Hall was determined to move the families in La Virgencica by force to the northern district by 1981. They came with bulldozers and forced the remaining families to evacuate. The Gypsy clan "Los Jaros" refused to leave, as they claimed to have received death threats from other clans now settled in the Polígono.

9   On the important work of the neighborhood associations as seedbeds of democratization in late Francoism, see: Inbal Ofer, *Claiming the City/Contesting the State: Squatting, Community Formation and Democratization in Spain (1955–1986)*, The Cañada Blanch Series: Studies on Contemporary Spain, LSE (London: Routledge, 2017). Also by the same author, see: "*My Shack, My Home*: Identity Formation and Home-Making on the Outskirts of the City of Madrid," Special issue in *Homes & Homecomings, Gender and History*. On women's participation in the neighborhood association movement, see Pamela Radcliff, "Ciudadanas: Las mujeres en las asociaciones de vecinos y la identidad de género en los años setenta," in *Memoria ciudadana y movimiento vecinal*, ed. Vicente Pérez Quintana y Pablo Sánchez León (Madrid: La Catarata, 2008), 54-78.

10 Father Quitián was arrested and sent to prison in 1975, but Cardinal Enrique Tarancón was able to intercede on his behalf under the provisions of the 1953 Concordat between the regime and the Vatican. Quitián was released from the prison of Carabanchel in Madrid with bail. See Alfonso Martínez Foronda and Isabel Rueda Castaño, eds., *La cara al viento: Estudiantes por las libertades democráticas en la Universidad de Granada (1965-1981)* vol. II (Sevilla: Fundación de Estudios Sindicales CCOO-A, 2012), 772. See also: Antonio Quitián González et al., *Curas obreros en Granada* (Alcalá la Real: Asociación Cultural Enrique Toral y Pilar Soler, 2005).

Socorro quickly discovered that distributing a bag of chickpeas among the indigent families did not address the fundamental problems of inequality. It only heightened the contrast between the young "señoritas" like herself and those they were helping. She realized that sometimes they were of little help in the face of so much hardship, as was the case when a young pregnant mother calmly told her that the baby she was still carrying was already dead. Her feelings of helplessness and of self-conscious privilege led her on a more radical course. During her second year of college, she left behind the religious-based groups to join the Communist Party.

College enabled her to transition from religious charity to political activism. She wanted to be one with the people she worked with, not an outside savior. The "revolutionary mystique" of being one of only five young women who joined the Party appealed to her daring side as she felt like a historical actor in a great drama about to unfold. From her perspective, only the Communists in the university were seeking true solutions to the socio-political problems facing the people. Organizations like FECUM, openly Catholic and more accommodating to the regime's status quo, were only offering band-aids.

The youthful idealism of Socorro and Jesús cast them in a heroic light. "We were not physically violent," Jesús remarked, "but were violent with our words. That is why the regime feared us. We were also fearless, almost welcoming the repression that we provoked. I remember saying to myself, 'I won't live in a country with this state of affairs and will do everything in my power to change it.' The Communist Party was truly the only effective political organization at that time. The Spanish Socialist Workers' Party, Partido Socialista Obrero España (PSOE) existed in name only. We were the ones who mobilized, fought the regime and marshaled the opposition on the street, in the university, and in the factories."

The propaganda used to recruit other students did not emphasize Stalinism but rather a pragmatic agenda to bring democracy and civil liberties back to Spain. The party was critical of the Soviet's Prague Spring repression in 1968 and distanced itself from Soviet Communism in general. The student Communists were more in line with the international wave of student and labor movements bubbling up from the layers of colonial and imperialistic subjugation.

Socorro and Jesús had independently come to the same conclusions about the need to oppose the regime. When they fell in love in college, their commitment only grew stronger. Joining the Communist party did not at first seem like a dangerous decision. Having lived mostly sheltered lives, they could not imagine the extent to which the regime would go to suppress a group of idealistic students. Soon enough Socorro and Jesús would learn how naive they were.

The first time Jesús was arrested was in mid-June of 1969, charged with instigating the PCE, protest against the showing of *The Green Berets*, a propagandistic American film in which John Wayne leads a team of patriotic special forces against godless, un-American, Viet Cong. Vietnam represented a very important issue to the student resistance movement in Spain, one that gave them solidarity with their counterparts in the US. Socorro was also arrested a few days later, but both she and Jesús were released after a few days. Their arrests seemed more like a warning than a true punishment. This warning, though, did little to deter them from continuing their activism, and if anything made them more determined.

Marxism, for the two young radicals, was not just a series of field operations but an intellectual pursuit. They studied it as a way to understand what was happening in Spain and in the larger world. Although the mass social media platforms of today did not exist then, foreign newspapers, the BBC or Parisian radio stations, along with the Pirenaica, kept them informed about the larger world

The act of studying Marxism was itself a subversive act. The censorship of certain books and literature led the student Communists to smuggle prohibited titles from France or London. From Paris, they would bring back Ruedo Ibérico and works by Althusser, Sartre, and Camus. Socorro and Jesús hid those readings at home from the Brigada Político Social (BPS) who would search the students' homes when they came to arrest them. Finding prohibited books could lead to arrest and prison. In the eyes of the Political Police, banned books were rhetorical fuses that lit the bombs of incitement.

Jesús was also incensed by the regime's whitewashing of the Spanish Civil War. When he began reading about the causes of the war in college, he discovered that those who presented themselves as victims, the Nationalists, had been, in reality, the aggressors. This realization was, in Jesús' words, "like Saint Paul's conversion after falling from his horse." The betrayal was so profound that Jesús threw himself into the resistance.

Marxism became almost an obsession for the two young radicals, especially when they discovered that almost anything could be given a Marxist reading. Like many of those in the student movement, they often let their biases cloud their rationality. Everything the government did was seen as a nefarious plot against working people. This anti-intellectualism, the reluctance to consider counter arguments, was regrettable but understandable, given the desperate urgency of Spain's political circumstances at the time.

Jesús remarked, "Our cell structure allowed us to hold discussions and we tried to maintain a certain discipline as comrades, utilizing our 'combat names' in an attempt to forget for that brief moment that we were all friends." They read Gramsci, Althusser, and Lukacs. Jesús remembered how Marta Harnecker's book on Materialism was rather basic and read like a catechism rather than a philosophical text.

He read the Marxist tracts to prepare for recruiting other students and creating propaganda. Recruiting went beyond the University walls. Jesús and Socorro taught workers and peasants to read. They used cinema and poetry to help the workers understand the unfairness of their circumstances. Many of the workers were the same age as the college students but had grown up without the same advantages. Converting the workers felt like a fulfillment of Jesus' and Socorro's life's mission. Their zeal to convert, however, could be off-putting to many, who equated the students' dogmatism with that of Franco's regime.

The Communist Party created the Women's Democratic Movement (Movimiento Democrático de Mujeres)[11] to enlist other women. Socorro was put in charge of political militancy and the recruitment of women. At the same time, she was a course delegate and a representative of the College of Arts and Letters in the university's governing assembly. As part of their Party duties, Socorro and her comrades would visit different villages around Granada (Fuentevaqueros, Pinos, Atarfe) to meet rural women married to Communist party members. They spoke to them about feminism, contraception, and women's role in the Communist struggle. Most of the women who attended the meetings did so as a favor to their husbands and boyfriends, rather than as a sincere commitment to Communism, Socorro recalled. She called their commitment a "vaginal political consciousness." The main goal was really to make sure these women would not interfere with their husbands' and boyfriends' political activism. The task to rein them in was given to the university's young women, whose knowledge of party doctrine and infectious commitment to the cause could be effective. The men in the party did not see a disconnect between the rhetoric of equality and the deeply held sexist views that they continued to practice.

In hindsight, Socorro never felt like an equal within the party, in spite of the many well-intentioned manifestos and theoretical discussions on women's important role in the struggle. Joining as a woman was a conscientious effort to prove to "ourselves," Socorro reflected, "that as women we had self-determination." But the women were only called upon during elections in the transition period, she emphasized, when they were needed on the lists for the ballot. Real change began in 1977, when the electoral campaigning made it necessary to incorporate more explicit feminist agendas that would later become policy.

---

11   In the early 1960s, the Communist Party of Spain (PCE) launched a platform to mobilize women. The first goal was to connect prisoners' wives with each other through the organization of Communist female party members. The two leaders were Carmen Rodríguez and Dulcinea Bellido, wives of Simón Sánchez Montero and Luis Lucio Lobato respectively, both imprisoned in 1959. Carmen and Dulcinea worked with the intellectual group of women in the party to protest the repression inflicted upon the wives of miners arrested as a result of the 1962 strike in Asturias and called for a rally in Puerta del Sol in Madrid. Two years later, the Movimiento Democrático de Mujeres was born with a dual objective: first, to establish a wide anti-Francoist women's front and second, to expand the influence of the PCE to continue the solidarity activism with political prisoners and work towards amnesty. The Party had to confront the cultural sexism within the rank and file. See Francisco Arriero Ranz, *El movimiento democrático de mujeres: De la Lucha contra Franco al feminismo* (Madrid: Catarata, 2017).

Jesús admitted, "We all had a very sexist upbringing. Eventually I saw the transition as an opportunity to reevaluate my attitudes toward women." Working for equality for all meant giving up some of the power and influence to women. This, the men did only reluctantly. "That was a challenge for all of us," Jesús recognized in hindsight, "especially our working-class comrades."

The men from the village were used to having control over their girlfriends, wives, and even sisters. Spanish men, traditionally, were the protectors of women's virtue. This was not going to work in a modern, liberated society. The university men themselves were not exactly paragons of feminism, but they did understand, deep down, that not listening to half the population was unjust and untenable.

For Socorro, activism as an anti-Francoist student increased after the State of Emergency was declared by the government on the 14th of December 1970. The academic year began with a tense political crisis at the University of Granada. In July of that year, the construction workers went on strike and took to the streets. This led to a brutal police crackdown, resulting in the death of five workers and large-scale arrests.[12] The Communist Party mobilized students to join the protests. A number of students, including Jesús, were arrested during an assembly in October.

In addition to the workers' crisis that summer, the national political landscape in 1970 was heating up. Sixteen members (including three women and two priests) of the Basque terrorist organization ETA were court martialed for the assassination of three people: in June 1968, José Pardines Arcay, a Civil Guard officer, was killed when he intercepted two ETA members at a road control point; Melitón Manzanas, Chief of the Political Brigade of the Police, was killed in August the same year in San Sebastian, Basque Country; and finally, Fermín Monasterio Pérez, a taxi driver, was killed in April 1969.[13] By the fall of 1969, all the accused were awaiting trial, with the prosecution seeking six death penalties and a total of 752 years of imprisonment in what became known as the "Burgos Trial."

The Basque independentists and the opposition to the regime beyond Euzkadi (Basque Country) appealed to the international press to denounce the regime's repression and demanded a civil trial rather than a military one. The Burgos Trial process revealed the lengths the regime was willing to go to quell any resistance and the increasing violence with which it was met from groups such as ETA.

The trade unions and the PCE benefited from the popular rejection of the regime's repression, swapping the roles of maligned villains to sympathetic and virtuous defenders of freedom. The trial of Burgos ignited student and faculty mobilization in universities, joining an international trend that mirrored other protests in Europe (Prague and Paris, 1968), Mexico (Mexico City, 1968), and the

---

12 See Josefina's story, wife of one of the construction workers arrested that summer.
13 The regime declared the State of Emergency in 1969, first in Guipuzcoa and then throughout the entire country.

United States (anti-war Vietnam protests at Kent State University in Ohio in 1970). Finally, the Catholic Church's rejection of the regime's crackdown signaled a profound generational rupture among Catholics exemplified by the case of Father Antonio Quitián, who was imprisoned for his involvement in Granada's labor strike.

Figure 3: Socorro as a college student

"I had been successfully concealing my political activities from my father, who I feared even more than the police. I would sneak out of the house at night to place pamphlets into home mailboxes. The thrill of escaping was part of what drove me. It was the only place in my life I felt truly liberated. I also wanted to gain the respect of the men. That meant taking chances. When I fled Granada, I was the only woman in the group, but in a sense, we were all men," Socorro asserted.

Knowing the BPS (Brigada Político Social, the name of Spain's secret police) would soon come for her and Jesús, Socorro, early one morning, packed a change of underwear and her hair curlers and fled. "I met up with some of the other students in my party's cell. My heart was pounding. I was scared but also excited." She and her comrades first hid out in a house in El Barrichuelo belonging to Maria del Carmen Sanmillán, one of their sympathetic professors. For an entire week they waited, passing the time with mundane chores punctuated by intense debates about the movement.

Socorro kept expecting the doorbell to ring with Jesús on the other side. When it finally did ring, it was not Jesús but the police. "All of us froze. I tiptoed to the door and looked through the peephole. All I could see was a red tie. None of our comrades wore ties. We scurried up the stairs and through a second-floor window onto the rooftop. My mouth tasted like metal and my feet moved as if being controlled by their own power." Socorro and the others hopped from one rooftop to the next, not even thinking about the danger. A strong flight instinct carried them until they were safely on the ground. Once there they fled in different directions, as they had practiced, only to rendezvous later that night.

"It was clear we could not stay in Granada. What I did not realize at the time was that I was about to embark on a six-month-long game of hide and seek with the authorities. The plan was to go to Málaga, to the district of El Palo after hiding in another safe house belonging to Juan de Dios Luque and María Izquierdo Rojo. María agreed to drive us early the next morning, to avoid any checkpoints the police might try to set up. I was surprisingly upbeat, focusing on my grand adventure and not on the pain I might be causing my parents. I spent the two-hour drive talking to María, this marvelous woman who was risking everything for us. The conversation was surprisingly normal—about ordinary things like where I grew up, and what I liked and disliked about Granada. It wasn't like in the movies where every moment is filled with tense anticipation. When I got to Málaga, I decided to choose a pseudonym, Laura Izquierdo."

Jesús had not been so lucky. He was arrested on December 14, 1970, as soon as he set foot on the street. This was not the first time Jesús had been in police custody. After being detained for the protest against the *Green Berets* film in 1969, Jesús was arrested a second time, along with Berta Ausín Momblana, for distributing propaganda at a construction site. After his arrest this time, he was taken to the main police precinct in Plaza de los Lobos. Because he had been arrested previously, he would not be let off so easily. In the eyes of the regime, this time he was not a misguided student but rather a hardened dissident.

During eight days of interrogations Jesús was beaten, threatened, and deprived of sleep. The authorities wanted him to give the names and addresses of the other party members. They also wanted to know how the group was organized, where they met, and who was in charge. While the regime had not been as harsh on the student movement during the first State of Emergency, declared in 1969, this time the regime was not playing around. The government detained and tortured many students from the PCE who were suspected of militancy. This lasted for six months during the time of martial law.

Jesús' ordeal did not end after the eight days of imprisonment and torture. Once the regime felt there was no more information to get from him, they moved him from the precinct in the Plaza de los Lobos to the prison outside of town. It was December 24, Christmas Eve. With temperatures below zero, Jesús recalled, "They gave us some filthy blankets, stained with dry feces, to keep us from freezing." The students demanded to be placed apart from the other, non-political inmates. They refused to eat what they were fed and were granted permission to receive outside food from their families. Federico Mayor Zaragoza, Rector of the University of Granada at the time, negotiated some leniency from the Civil Governor who allowed the academic authorities to administer exams in the prison. Jesús took his exams in February 1971 and would remain in jail until the 24th of May 1971. Eventually the TOP (Tribunal de Orden Público) released him for lack of evidence. The whole episode was an act of terror and retribution. To add insult to injury, students or their families had to pay bail of between 15,000 to 25,000 *pesetas* before they were released.

While Jesús was well into his sixth month of confinement, Socorro and her other comrades had resettled in an apartment in the El Palo beach district of Málaga. With all the interrogations going on, they knew that it was only a matter of time before the police came knocking again. "My father and my brother came to El Palo to make sure I was all right. Our encounter was emotional, tense, angry. My father gave me an envelope and told me to open it when I was by myself. We parted a little bit calmer but uncertain of when we would see each other again. When I opened the envelope that night, I found a stack of bills, 10,000 *pesetas*!"

As the group started to make plans about where to go next, they decided to split up. Some of the men wanted to go to Zaragoza to hide out at the house of another comrade. Socorro thought that would be dangerous since the BPS was surely keeping watch over the party's members. In the end, after the festivity of the Epiphany on January 6, Socorro went by bus with another Comrade, Miguel Ángel, to Alicante where they rented an apartment for a month, pretending to be a married couple relocating for work. Alicante was only a rest stop on their journey. After a tense month playing house and avoiding questions, they went their separate ways.

Socorro made her way to Barcelona where she could more easily disappear. The money her father had given her lasted only a couple of more months, prompting her to look for work. Her teaching credential was useful for finding a position at a small private school. There was still the risk of being found out. She couldn't stop looking over her shoulder or feel like the police were closing in. She moved three times in Barcelona, making sure never to stay too long in any one place. The romance of life on the run soon wore off as she shuffled from one cheap *pensión* to another. Her companions in the *pensiones* were women who lived desperate lives, not from political repression but the repression of poverty. Many had to sell themselves for money just to keep themselves, or in some cases, their children, from starving. She saw the bruises from the beatings they took from boyfriends, customers, and even family members. The evils of capitalism did not exist simply in books, she thought, but also in the faces and bodies of the women with whom she shared her temporary existence.

Even though she was hiding out, Socorro was still in touch with the Communist Party. She would be handed an address or given a place and a time to meet. No names were used, and the less information exchanged the better. During one meeting her contact told her to drive with another comrade to Madrid to seek the counsel of a Party lawyer. "That was the lowest point in my escape," Socorro recalled. "The comrade who drove me dropped me in the center of Madrid at three in the morning. I had no place to go and wandered the city scared and alone. I had been on the run for four months. The lawyer to whom I was to speak was Manuela Carmena. Her office was located in a tough part of the city. After listening to my concerns, she advised me to remain in Barcelona but to keep changing my address every few weeks."

By June 13, 1971, the State of Emergency had been lifted, and Socorro decided to return home to Granada. "I might have left with just a pair of underwear and my curlers, but I came back with two suitcases full of books and some borrowed clothes. Even though I was going to jail, I was still determined to finish my education." In her interrogation she denied "absolutely everything and they surprisingly did not touch me. I had been outsmarting 'Don Paco,' known as 'El Jirafa,' the policeman noted for his violent treatment of prisoners." She was charged with the usual crime of illicit association. They tried to pin on her the throwing of a Molotov cocktail at the Bilbao Bank in the Telefónica building, but they did not have any evidence. "The jail in Granada for women was filthy. They put me in a small cell with a rickety bed and a latrine in the corner. The only ventilation was a small opening high above the wall that barely let light in. Moldy food, that I at first refused, came on a metal plate shoved through a slot in the door."

The women activists were imprisoned in the same jail as the men, but, unlike their male counterparts, they had to share cells with common inmates. "There was the whore abandoned by her man," recalled Socorro, "illiterate, whose letters to her family I had to write; or that other poor soul, always pregnant, who survived by committing petty crimes. The ghastly conditions in the Granada jail made the *pensiones* seem like four-star hotels. I remember the celebration of the Patron Day of Prisons, the Virgen de la Merced. The guards gave everyone cake as a special treat. What irony! Let them eat cake! The cake turned out to be spoiled and caused serious dysentery among the children housed in jail with their mothers. Some treat! There were about twenty women, a small enough number for us to get to know each other."

"Eventually they moved me to a separate area called the Brigada on the second floor, but only after I made a big fuss about wanting to be treated as a political prisoner. In the Brigada the political prisoners were housed together in one large room instead of individual cells. The windows were broken, and although I was there in September and the weather was not bad, many comrades who stayed there in the winter of 1970-1971 during the State of Emergency suffered through one of the coldest winters in Granada's history. I could put up with the weather, but I could not stand to see children, from infants to about three years old, suffer."

"It was September 1971, and I demanded that I be allowed to take my final exams. After complaining loud enough, they acquiesced. Professor Pita brought the slides for the art history exam to an empty room in the jail. It was a three-hour exam. The beautiful art, projected on a dreary concrete wall, was a nourishing mental tonic, but also a surreal reminder of the strange journey I had been on. It gave me hope that I would get out someday and that there would be a better world waiting for me." Socorro stayed in prison for another month, freed as a result of the pardon decree issued on 27 September 1971.

"I was a fanatic. My commitment and conviction to the cause bordered on religious. I never hesitated in sacrificing for the movement or my fellow members. Only later did I feel guilty about deserting my family, abandoning my mother. I paid dearly throughout my young adult life for my political commitment and prison record. I could not work in the public school system or obtain a passport, or even get a driver's license. Fortunately, the father of Joaquin, a fellow imprisoned student, helped some of us out. After we graduated, he started a private school where many of us "disgraced" radicals could find work. This was a lifeline for both Jesús and me as we had only recently been married in 1972 and were struggling to survive."

Franco's death in 1975 and the legalization of the PCE in 1977 created other challenges for the Communist Party and for those who had been part of the resistance. With the legalization of the Party "there was a moment of euphoria," said Jesús. "In that moment, we felt that the sacrifices had all been worth it; the suffering, the prison, the beatings in the police precincts. It had been a great political, economic, and above all emotional risk that seemed to have actually paid off." The moment of celebration, however, was short-lived. Jesús and Socorro quickly became disillusioned with what ensued. Instead of coming together in solidarity, the members began to fight over the small number of political appointments allotted to the party. Jesús, embittered, began to disengage. His loss of enthusiasm and revolutionary spirit recalled Ortega y Gasset, who would declare during the Second Republic, "No es esto, no es esto." It was not what they had in mind or were hoping for. Now that the party was sanctioned, it was supposed to operate like all the other parties. What was the fun in that? The leadership of the Party became more authoritative and dogmatic. This was something that Jesús and Socorro had been fighting against for so many years. They had not joined the resistance to gain power over others but to liberate them from those in control. True to their ideals, they turned their efforts to what they saw as more genuine causes.

Socorro and Jesús found an outlet for their activism by joining the trade union CCOO (Comisiones Obreras) as part of the Education sector. By now both of them were high school teachers. In the CCOO, dissent was still possible, with much work needed to improve labor conditions. Socorro was asked to lead the women's office. "I have to confess, the gender politics and the misogyny within the union were profound. My taking charge of the women's office was regarded almost like a demotion, something beneath my talent," she explained. "Every time I had to report to the executive committee, I could see the disregard and impatience in my male comrades' faces. That did not stop me. I have joined several feminist groups along the way: the Asamblea de Mujeres de Granada, the Mujeres Universitarias platform, and within my working environment I spearheaded a high school curriculum initiative to infuse our teaching with gender awareness and content."

The prison no longer exists today, torn down and replaced by new construction. A big supermarket chain and fancy gym are just down the street. You would be hard pressed to find anyone in the neighborhood who still remembers the tannery. That Granada does not exist anymore. Amid the hypermodern world of today, with students staring into ever-present cell phones, it is hard to imagine that a small group of university activists risked everything for their ideals. It is hard to imagine, for that matter, that for over forty years Spain was one of the few Western European countries ruled by a dictator. But that too happened. In order to see the history in the present, you have to be able to transcend it.

Today Socorro and Jesús look nothing like the Marxist student rebels they once were. They are grey-haired grandparents succumbing to the weight of time like the rest of us. Socorro is retired. She and Jesús divorced in 2015 after fifty-years together. They still remain good friends. How could they not? "Our two daughters have given us grandchildren, and I continue to be involved in trying to make life better for others. I am still just as much a feminist and just as radical in my politics," she asserted with a proud grin.

Jesús is more nostalgic. "I was fortunate to be part of a brotherhood. I never was interested in paid political appointments. I always considered myself a citizen politician rather than a professional one." He is still active in the PSOE (the socialist party) and is just as passionate as ever about the problems of the poor and working class. He is still teaching high school and uses his experience to inspire his students.

"I would not be the same teacher without my political experiences. Ironically, I draw from my father, a teacher in La Calahorra, a poor village in the 1950s, who once said to me, 'They live in utter poverty and their only way out is education.' Imagine, my father, a right-wing Falangist, inspiring me, a socialist, to do the same thing. My generation had to struggle with these contradictions, contradictions that still exist in Spain. We are very good at 'othering' each other which prevents us from making progress," said the once firebrand radical turned thoughtful intellectual.

The fact that neither Socorro nor Jesús went on to become one of the new national leaders to emerge during the transition does not diminish their contributions nor lessen the importance of their story. In many ways it makes it more authentic. It was not the possibility of glory that drew them to the resistance but the chance to do what was right. Once the Communist Party became just another official government entity, they moved on. The difference was that after the transition they could fight battles as concerned citizens, not outlawed dissidents. This was a privilege that was not given to them but one they had earned.

Figure 4: Socorro and Jesús' wedding photo

Chapter 3
Claros del Bosque: Joaquín and Arturo's Stories

> El claro del bosque es un centro en el que no siempre es possible entrar;
> Es otro reino que un alma habita y guarda.
> Es la lección inmediata de los claros del bosque:
> no hay que ir a buscarlos, ni tampoco a buscar nada de ellos.
> [U]n instante de lucidez que está más allá de la conciencia y que la inunda.
> Y se recorren tambien los claros del bosque
> [C]omo se han recorrido las aulas. Cómo los claros, las aulas son lugares vacíos,
> Lugares de la voz donde se va a aprender de oido.
> la llaga que de todo ello queda en el claro del bosque.
> Y el silencio.
> María Zambrano, *Claros del Bosque* (1977)[1]

---

1   "The clearing of the forest is a place where it is not always possible to enter;
(It is) another kingdom that a soul inhabits and keeps.
(It is) the immediate lesson of the clearings of the forest: you do not have to look for them, nor look for anything from them
[A]n instantaneous lucidity beyond consciousness which floods it.
We go through the clearings of the forest
Like we have gone through the classrooms. Like the clearings, the classrooms are also empty places,
Places of the voice where you will learn by hearing.
the wound that all this inflicts upon us remains in the forest's opening.
As well as silence." (My translation)
These lines are extracted from Zambrano's poetic prose in this essay entitled "Claros del Bosque." Written in 1977 while she was still in exile, the metaphor of the clearing in the forest speaks of the nonlocality of the exiled existence. María Zambrano, *Claros del Bosque*

The clearings in a forest may be likened to a space of refuge, an oasis bathed in sunlight or domed with stars. These clearings can also represent the mental spaces, pockets of repose, that the young, imprisoned dissidents stumbled upon in the midst of the dark and violent forces at work in the tangled forest of a prison system under the regime.

Joaquín and Arturo were both Philosophy and Letters students. The former was the head of the Communist cell in Granada, the latter a leading member of the Jesuit university organization FECUN. Their lives crossed daily in the halls and classrooms of the university, and they met in the Sindicato Democrático de Estudiantes de la Universidad de Granada (SDEUG, The Student Assembly) where different opposition factions convened in the wake of the SEU's (the right-wing Falangist Student Union) closure in 1965.

Joaquín was born in 1948 to a middle-class family from Zaragoza. The family only moved when his father found a position as a geography professor at the University of Granada. While his father taught, Joaquín's mother stayed at home and raised four children, two boys and two girls. His liberal leaning family had no sympathy for the regime, which had executed two of his uncles during the civil war, but they were not outwardly rebellious. Not particularly religious, Joaquín remembers going to mass as a matter of custom more than devotion. From early in his life, he felt sympathy for those less advantaged and understood the relative privilege he enjoyed as the son of a university professor. Granada during the 1950s was slow to recover from the effects of the civil war, and poverty and deprivation were everywhere.

In his first year of college, during the academic year 1965-1966, Joaquín joined the Juventud Estudiantil Católica (JEC). This is when he began to gain his political bearings, informed by a lifelong love of reading. "I remember being exposed to Benito Pérez Galdós's *Episodios Nacionales* and feeling transformed," he related.

If his reading of philosophy laid the groundwork for his activism, it was his experience working in a mine that called him to action. "In 1967, I was working in a coal mine in Turón, in the northern Spanish region of Asturias, for a month...as part of the Servicio Universitario del Trabajo (SUT) University Working Service.[2]

(Barcelona: Biblioteca de Bolsillo, 1986); see electronic version: http://files.bibliotecadepoesiacontemporanea.webnode.es/200000188-12de013d42/Mar%C3%ADa%20Zambrano.pdf.

2   The SUT was an initiative spearheaded in the early 1950s by José María de Llanos, a Jesuit priest identified as one of the so-called priest workers (*curas obreros*). The goal was to facilitate the encounter between university students preoccupied with the inequality and poor conditions of the working class and workers. The students would spend time working side by side with their worker counterparts in the mine, the factory, or the construction site. However, the Falangist Student Union, the only and mandatory university student association, ended up taking hold of it until its dissolution in 1965. Nonetheless, many of those college students who participated in the SUT ended up gaining insight into the oppressive labor

On August 14, a terrible accident took place on level 12 of the Santo Tomás pit, a neighboring mine. Eleven miners were killed."[3] Joaquín recalled how he and the rest of the student workers, along with the full-time miners, took to the streets to protest for safer working conditions. The police broke up the march and detained many, including Joaquín. The funeral for the miners was held a few days later, attracting more than 20,000 people, according to the newspapers of the time.[4]

"The Turón events were a shock to me," he reflected, "and reinforced my anti-Francoist beliefs. This would eventually lead me to join the Communist Party. It was the first time I had been arrested, and, as a result, I became a target every time there was a political raid against the PCE."

---

policies of the regime and joined the opposition Catholic organizations, JOC, HOAC as well as the Communist Party, as in the case of Joaquín. The SUT was inspired by the experience in the German universities in the 1950s, where workers and college students shared classroom and workshop experiences, an initiative regarded as beneficial by the Vatican. For more on the SUT history, see: Ruiz Carnicer, *El Sindicato Español Universitario*, 437-45; and Jordi Gracia, *Estado y cultura: El despertar de una conciencia crítica bajo el franquismo, 1940-1962* (Barcelona: Anagrama, 2006), 85-91.

3   Eleven miners died as a result of a gas explosion in the mine of Saint Tomás on August 14, 1967. Joaquín remembers instead the twelfth. The families of those who died that tragic day congregated to remember the 50th anniversary of their loss on August 14, 2017. See: CM Basteiro, "Flores por los once de la mina Santo Tomás" *Nueva España*, August 15, 2017. http://www.lne.es/cuencas/2017/08/15/flores-once-mina-santo-tomas/2149847.html.

4   On August 14, 1967, when Joaquín was spending a month working within the SUT at the Valley of Turón, the dead included: Celestino González Pulgar (Tino Tuiza), 38 years old; Manuel Vázquez Prieto, 40 years old; José Antonio López García, 19 years old; Francisco Lobeto Dacal, 26 years old; Juan Díaz Fernández, 46 years old; Manuel Grandas López, 26 years old; Rafael Alonso García, 38 years old; Adriano Augusto Teixeira, 17 years old; Félix González López, 42 years old; José Martínez Faro, 18 years old; and Luis Flórez Lavín, 45 years old. Previously that year on February 13, there had been another accident in the Santa Bárbara Pit. Jesús Martínez Miranda, 48 years old, fell down the pit mouth while working on its deepening between the 6th to the 7th levels. On July 20, there was a coal mine collapse on the 4th level that killed 4 miners: Víctor Agustín García Fernández, 33 years old; José Antonio Álvarez Menéndez, 24 years old; Ceferino Argimiro González, 29 years old; and José María Sánchez Suárez, 46 years old. See: http://www.elvalledeturon.net/prensa/1961-1970/1967.

Figure 5: Funeral of the eleven miners killed in the Santo Tomás mine in the Valley of Turón, Asturias, August 1967

Upon his return from SUT service to the University of Zaragoza, Joaquín chose to major in Physics—since he was a young boy, astronomy had been his passion. However, his political activism made it impossible for him to pass his courses that year and led him to move to the Universidad de Granada in 1968 to pursue a degree in geography, his father's field. Juggling both politics and studies was difficult, but Joaquín felt that both were important for his future. His commitment was "to achieve a representative democracy and political freedom in Spain," he asserted, "and also lessen social inequalities." These objectives were neither simple nor easy to achieve.

"The large majority of the population was not aware of the extent of the anti-Franco sentiment. We had to struggle to make our cause known. There were a large number of people who were sympathetic to our cause, and a smaller fraction who provided actual support without directly getting involved. On the other side, many people supported the regime because they benefited and profited from it, not because they agreed with its ideology." To be part of the opposition required a greater commitment because there was a potential greater cost. Anyone caught supporting the Communists could lose his job, be socially shunned, and potentially be arrested.

"The entire population endured censorship, lack of labor protections, and constant surveillance," Joaquín continued. "Those of us who actively resisted were treated worse as a cautionary tale of what would happen if you did stand up to the regime." The college students, mostly the sons and daughters of the middle and upper classes, were spared the worst punishment in the beginning but eventually received the same beatings as the workers in the Party.

Joaquín took a leadership role in the student resistance at the University of Granada in 1968. His involvement in the Turón events and subsequent student activism at the University of Zaragoza made him a natural leader of a Communist cell in Philosophy and Letters in Granada. For the next ten years, he helped expand recruitment and consolidate a Communist inner circle before moving to the University of Alcalá de Henares as a professor of geography in 1977.[5]

The cell originally consisted of only students from Philosophy and Letters, but after the State of Emergency in 1970 it welcomed students from Medical, Science, and Law schools. The most challenging task for the young, idealistic university Communists was to join forces with the labor movement. The year 1968 was a critical one in the Spanish student movement, as it was for student movements in the rest of Europe, the United States, and Latin America. The shift to consolidating forces for mass activism led to the predictable government backlash. This can be seen in the July 1970 construction strike in Granada and the resulting deaths of three workers at the hands of the police.

The Communists' organizing benefited from a national clandestine network as well as the more open Catholic grassroots groups like Catholic Action and the Jesuits' FECUN. These different factions came together after the dissolution of the Falangist SEU (Sindicato Español Universitario, Spanish University Union) in 1965. The regime sponsored the RCP (Reuniones Coordindoras Profesionales, Professional Coordinating Conventions) to monitor the self-government push from within the student movement. Students were supposed to enlist in the new official RCP through elections of representatives, but the opposition within the student movement created new and autonomous student associations conceived as multi-faction platforms known as Sindicatos Democráticos de Estudiantes or SDE (Democratic University Syndicate). Both moderate and radical elements found a forum to articulate their academic and political demands. Inspired by the University of California, Berkeley, student movement in 1964 and the 1968 French student protests, Spanish university students actively challenged the authority of conservative professors through the so-called classroom "critical trials." Groups of students would disrupt a professor's lecture and demand a more participatory pedagogy as well as the introduction of some alternative (mostly Marxist) academic readings. Joaquín remembered these "happenings" more like "negotiation" exercises rather

---

5   Some of the members included: Joaquín Bosque Sendra, Jesús Carreño and Socorro Robles, all of them included in this study. See also Martinez Foronda et al., *La cara al viento*, 239. This is the most exhaustive study on the student movement at the university of Granada. It is the result of ten years of research by numerous scholars who conducted archival research and 50 interviews of the participants in the anti-Francoist resistance in Granada.

than confrontational challenges. "We would propose changes to the course content," he said. "Many professors did not reject it directly, because we were neither excessively critical nor ill-intentioned. Our goal was to raise consciousness among our fellow students."[6]

They also raised awareness among the student body through a newsletter/newspaper called *Nuestra Lucha*, launched in September 1968. That same year, following other university districts across the country, the University of Granada students formed the SDEUG. Being part of the SDE provided access to printing facilities and materials supplied for the RCP. Through the SDEUG, students increasingly became more defiant, which led the regime to declare two States of Emergency (Estados de Excepción) in 1969 and 1970-71. The Francoist Supreme Court declared the Democratic Students Associations' activities illegal, making it possible for the state to crack down. The Court further declared the students' dissent as a threat to national security and authorized the police to infiltrate the previously protected sanctuary of the university.[7]

Caught up in the maelstrom of protest and backlash was another socially conscious student. Arturo was born in 1948 in the Cuesta de Gomérez, the ascending street to the Alhambra. His parents had moved to Granada from the coastal city of Motril after the civil war, fleeing persecution for being Republican. In Granada he worked many different jobs—truck driver, insurance agent, "a thousand things," Arturo remembered poignantly. He tried to hide the fact that he was a Republican and a Communist by never talking about the civil war.[8] This, in many ways, made the war even more horrible in the mind of Arturo.

Like Joaquín, Arturo initially focused on science but later moved to Philosophy and Letters. "When I enrolled, 66/67, in Pharmacy there was little [political] activity. Some SDE and RCP delegates came from Pharmacy, Sciences, Medicine...but Pharmacy lacked the student leadership of Philosophy and Letters.[9] The core group in Philosophy and Letters were: Bernabé López García;[10] Chavique, a big guy from

---

6   Foronda et al., *La cara al viento*, 232.
7   In January 1967 the first RCP national meeting took place in Valencia. Students from the districts of Madrid, Barcelona, Granada, Málaga, Oviedo, Salamanca, Bilbao, Zaragoza, Navarra, and Valencia signed a critical letter against the regime's repression, denouncing the persecution of the student movement and its demands for a democratic reform of the university system. Foronda et al., *La cara al viento*, 590-91.
8   Arturo González Arcas, interview transcript, July 2, 2007, provided by Alfonso Martínez Foronda, Oral Interviews Collection, Archivo Histórico de Comisiones Obreras de Andalucía, AHCCOO-A.
9   Arturo González Arcas, interview transcript, July 2, 2007.
10 He was referring to Bernabé López García, a member of the university communist cell the political police was after. Bernabé's maternal grandfather and Federico García Lorca's father were brothers.

Almería, who I think was Bernabé's classmate in Semitic Studies; Paulino; and a militant of the PCE from Murcia. These students organized and ran assemblies in which even known Falangists like Francisco G. and Antonio L. participated. We had a lot of heated debates."

Arturo transferred to Philosophy and Letters after his father died and money became tight. "After my father died, I could not continue studying without a scholarship. I found out I was eligible for the so-called 'salary-scholarships' from the Ministry of Labor and decided to apply. Because these funds were only for freshmen, I had to start a new major to qualify. That is why I quit Pharmacy, enrolled in Philosophy and Letters, and received the scholarship in 1968."

Arturo's first encounter with student activism was with FECUN, the Jesuit student organization.[11] According to Arturo, "the liberal wing of the [Catholic] Church tried to change with the times. They were often at odds with the more established ecclesiastical hierarchy which remained committed to the regime's national-Catholic agenda. The generational gap between the young Catholic Action Movements like JEC and the old guard led to their dissolution by Monsignor José Guerra Campos. As a result, many of us found our way into FECUN."[12] The Catholic Action organizations like HOAC (Hermandad Obrera de Acción Católica, or Catholic Action Labor Fraternity), JOC (Juventud Obrera Católica, or Catholic Workers' Union), and JEC were committed to grassroots Christian activism, following the principles of liberation theology. Many in the organizations regarded themselves as Christian socialists. All of these movements were closely associated with the workers' oppo-

---

11   Arturo González Arcas, interview transcript, July 2, 2007.

12   José Guerra Campos (1920-1997) was ordained in 1944 and became head in 1946 of the Catholic Action University Youth. "On June 15, 1964, he was appointed titular bishop of Mutia and auxiliary to the archbishop of Madrid-Alcalá. That same year he took charge of the secretariat of the Spanish episcopate upon the constitution of the Episcopal Conference. In 1973 he was appointed bishop of the Diocese of Cuenca, where he remained until June 26, 1996. In 1967, Franco appointed him *procurador* in Cortes. In 1972 he supported priests gathering in Zaragoza with a clear right-wing nuance, but Pope Paul VI prohibited him from attending. Between 1966 and 1974 he was president of the advisory commission of religious programs of Spanish Television TVE. As *procurador* of the Francoist Cortes, he opposed the political reform after the dictator's death. He was also against the divorce law, against which he published a pastoral in 1978. In 1980 he denounced the progressive 'Protestantization' of the Spanish Catholic Church in an article entitled 'Strange Things in the Spanish Church.' In 1983 he attacked the decree of decriminalization of abortion. See "José Guerro Campos, obispo emérito de Cuenca," *El País*, July 16, 1997 https://elpais.com/diario/1997/07/16/agenda/869004001_850 215.html.

sition movement within the Communist trade union, CCOO,[13] and many priests and their followers in these Catholic movements later became union leaders.

The students within the Christian student movements became more radicalized once they joined up with the Communists. "We ended up joining different political factions," Arturo explained. "Some enlisted in the FLP, others in the PCE and others, especially in Granada, joined FECUN. Father Arrupe promoted the Latin American theology of liberation, and almost all Jesuit seminars focused on following a path of social engagement with the poor. A number of democratic and radical students found these principles appealing, while others used the Christian organizations as a legal front for dissension."[14] Many young priests helped to produce and hide propaganda in their own priory cells. "We had a duplicating machine in one storage room with a small window in the College of Theology. On many occasions we would enter through that window at night to make copies."[15]

The relationship between FECUN and the Communist Party was cordial but distant. "We were always careful...," said Arturo. "We all were working together in the SDE, so, obviously, we knew who was who, but we never acknowledged it openly. I was in charge of academic activities while another guy from the PCE ran the cinema club and organized various cultural events. We were acutely aware of our competing loyalties. This meant that we would not ask sensitive questions to avoid possible betrayal in case we were arrested."

---

13 The CCOO started in the 1950s as a spontaneous movement. These first spontaneous Workers Commissions were promoted by the PCE, Christian workers movements, and other collectives opposed to the regime. One of the first Workers' Commissions to be remembered is the one formed in Asturias at the La Camocha mine (Gijón), in 1957, on the occasion of a strike. It was in 1964 when CCOO turned into an organized movement of the Spanish workers under the Franco's regime. CCOO achieved a great triumph in the union elections of 1966, which represented a serious blow to the regime's corporatist union and allowed the consolidation of CCOO. The first national meeting of the CCOO took place in June 1967, in Madrid. The Supreme Court, in November 1967, declared the organization subversive and illicit. Therefore, CCOO went from a semi-legal movement to being persecuted systematically. The repression against CCOO was brutal: an immense majority of 9,000 convicted between 1963 and 1977 by the Court of Public Order (TOP), which replaced the Military Courts as a repressive instrument, were militants of CCOO. In 1968, Marcelino Camacho, Julián Ariza, and other union leaders were imprisoned and prosecuted for belonging to CCOO. The regime responded to the rise of the workers' movement by declaring successive states of emergency, highlighting the one of 1969 and the one of 1970-71, which caused numerous detentions and torture of labor leaders. See: "Historia de CCOO," https://www.uv.es/ccoo/documents/historia_de_ccoo.html.
14 Arturo González Arcas, interview transcript, July 2, 2007.
15 Arturo González Arcas, interview transcript, July 2, 2007.

Figure 6: College of Theology today houses the Odontology and Library of Sciences colleges at the University of Granada Campus in the district of Cartuja. From right to left: Façade, and two views of the main Chapel in 1968 (from the entrance and from the altar)

The University of Granada's unrest was part of the national outcry brought on by the tragic news of Enrique Ruano's death while in police custody. Ruano, a 21-year-old law student at the University of Madrid, had been arrested for handing out anti-Francoist leaflets. The regime's version was that Ruano had committed suicide, jumping from a second story window,[16] a claim no reasonable person believed. In addition to the disturbing news of Ruano's death, there were incidents of the police trespassing onto the supposedly autonomous university to confiscate personal and academic files on student activists. The student leadership in Philosophy and Letters demanded action from Dean Gallego Morell but only received excuses. Things took an even darker turn in January 1969 when the regime, facing mounting labor and student protests throughout Spain, declared a State of Emergency.

Joaquín was arrested on February 4 and taken to his hometown of Zaragoza. "They gave me a couple of good beatings while in custody to push me to name my comrades in the PCE. Then they sent me to the prison in Torrero, all on the charge of distributing propaganda," Joaquin remembered. He remained in Torrero until May 1969, after which he was transferred to the Carabanchel Prison in Madrid, known for holding political prisoners. The experience did not lessen his rebelliousness as he joined his fellow inmates protesting their conditions. "Those of us who

---

16 The case re-opened in 1996 and a second autopsy revealed Ruano was tortured for four days and then shot; from his corpse the bone of the clavicle was sawed to hide the hole of the bullet. Miguel Angel Marfull, "La muerte que levantó a los estudiantes contra la dictadura," Público, January 18, 2009. http://www.publico.es/espana/muerte-levanto-estudiantes-dictadura.html.

did not attend mass," he recalled, "had to go to a classroom of sorts where we had to read aloud a book of the warden's choosing. We refused to read one day and were put in solitary confinement. That led to a hunger strike." The hunger strike lasted only a week, ending when the government lifted the State of Emergency. Those arrested from Zaragoza were released under "provisional freedom." The Public Order Tribunal later absolved Joaquín of all charges in a trial held that September.

Arturo also remembers vividly 1969's State of Emergency. "On December 10, 1968, the student movement in Granada reached its high point. From SDE we called an assembly to commemorate the 20th anniversary of the United Nation's declaration of Universal Human Rights. We decided that we would invite the public to attend the assembly at the College of Medicine and spread the word through leaflets to the various neighborhoods. The celebration was a thinly disguised protest of the lack of human rights in Spain. The police, having learned of our plan, arrested two medical students, Antonio Nadal and Mohamed Abdelkáder. Nadal and Abdelkáder gave the police my name under interrogation, so I was picked up as well."

At the time of his arrest Arturo was living with his mother and brothers. The family was having lunch at his home in Cuesta de Gomérez when the telephone rang. "There was no answer on the other end, but I could hear someone breathing. Telephones were tapped very clumsily back then. I hung up and tried calling other people, but the line had been cut. I made the decision not to flee. After all, I had done nothing wrong. I wasn't even a member of the Communist Party. I would explain all this to the authorities when they brought me in, I told myself. So, we sat wordlessly around the dining table, my mother crying and holding her head in her hands, while I pretended to be calm. After about half an hour, there was a loud knock at the door. As I slowly opened it, I saw Don Paco, El Jirafa, the notorious captain of the secret police, grinning at me from the other side."

Everyone in the movement knew Don Paco, as much for his tall, gangly physique as for his reputation for cruelty. "He said 'Hey pretty boy! We're coming for you, and we also have a search warrant.' I went into the kitchen to tell my mother, and she immediately started pulling her hair and slapping her face. She mumbled something like 'again, again,' probably remembering the arrest of my father and his brothers during the civil war. They searched the desks and the bookcases, throwing things everywhere, and putting some random papers in boxes. It was all a show. I had already taken any compromising papers to the young Jesuits' priory in the Colegio Máximo."

Although they did not find anything in the search, Arturo was arrested and walked, handcuffed, down the street. They took him down Gomérez Hill, where a Z car, a FIAT 124 with its little blue light on top, waited for them in Cuchilleros

Square.[17] From the Niño hostel across the street, Antonio Nadal and some other students watched as the car drove away. Word quickly got out that they had arrested Arturo.

The police took him directly to the infamous Plaza de los Lobos police station on Duquesa street. He was alone in the Z car but had plenty of company once he got to his jail cell. "It was like a reunion for the SDE, but we were not there to plan our next march. A policeman punched me with his finger, and laughed, 'You think you're pretty smart. What a disgrace you are to your parents.' More students were brought in during the night. José María L., Antonio D; Abdelkáder, Miguel Ángel who was from Cartagena, José María, we were all together in the same leaky boat."

"One student started to have a panic attack. Miguel Ángel, a medical student, called for a doctor. After a long wait, Dr. Francisco Morata arrived, gave the panicking student a cursory look and pronounced him healthy. Then he warned Miguel Ángel not to diagnose any more patients."[18]

They crammed the students into one small cell. It was the middle of winter, but they didn't bother to heat the basement where they kept the prisoners. "As you entered the police station in Duquesa street," Arturo recalled, "you went down the stairs into a rectangular anteroom, no more than 2 meters square. At one end there was a WC without a toilet, only a hole on the ground and a place to put your feet. There were two or three cells with tiled walls and a cold tiled bench to sleep on. There must have been twelve of us in a space no bigger than two and half by three meters. We stayed there all night, leaving the cell only when we were taken for interrogation. The next-door cell was occupied by a gypsy woman who kept screaming, 'Tell the *payo*[19] to come and fuck me.' An officer came down from time to time to tell her to shut up or they would beat her. In hindsight, we were treated better than most because we were students and had some social standing.... Certainly we were treated better than Joaquín in Zaragoza. I don't remember how long we were there...one or maybe two nights. I do remember vividly the shock of that first night. We all had thoughts of Enrique Ruano flying out the window...."[20]

The interrogations took place in a small, bare room. The police confronted each student one by one, hoping to catch them in a lie. At the time, Arturo recalled, "I had a fractured tibia because of a car accident, so I walked with a limp. The policeman began by taking his gun out of his holster and putting it on the table. He then left the room for a few minutes before coming back. This was common practice at the time,

---

17   The urban police car was known as Z vehicle in the 1960s. Z was the initial that referred to the name of the vehicle "zonal" or urban district vehicle. The particular model FIAT 124 Berlina that Arturo remembers here was utilized between 1963 and 1973.
18   Arturo González Arcas, interview transcript, July 2, 2007.
19   *Payo* is the term used by the Roma people to refer to those racially outside their culture.
20   Arturo González Arcas, interview transcript, July 2, 2007.

a form of psychological terror. The gun must have been unloaded, but you were alone with it. After one officer threatened you, they would send in another one, a good cop who assured you he was on your side. They were not very sophisticated, but still managed to break some of the students, many of whom had never in their lives been in trouble with the law."

"We never revealed anything that the police did not already know. They had every piece of information about us." Arturo remembered one offhand remark he made that almost led to disaster. "Don Paco, El Jirafa, said, 'You know that Bernabé is a faggot?' 'No, I do not know anything,' I replied. 'Well, he's a faggot,' El Jirafa repeated as he was about to leave the room. 'If you say so…you would know,' I blurted out, not realizing until too late how the remark must have sounded. Suddenly, he turned around and threatened, 'Are you calling me a faggot?' Then shoved me against a metal cabinet, took out his gun, and started pressing the mouth of the gun into my neck while screaming 'Are you saying I am a faggot?!' I could have easily been the next Enrique Ruano."[21]

After a couple of days in the precinct, the students were sent to the Granada prison. "They put us in the infirmary. I remember vaguely having been photographed and my fingerprints taken. At the reception, they removed our shoelaces, watches, everything that could serve to injure ourselves. The place was disgustingly filthy: the mattresses smelled of urine; the pillows were covered in yellowish sweat circles. They gave us some torn sheets, and we threw them on top of the mattresses. Imagine, the infirmary was the 'good' part of the jail. As political prisoners we had certain privileges that the general population lacked. We could buy food from the commissary and got our own dining room."[22]

Arturo remained in jail for approximately one month. "Not all of us were released the same day. When we got out, we were relocated, what was called 'destierro' or exile." The authorities sent the prisoners to live with relatives outside of Granada. "When I got out of jail, they took me back to the Duquesa Street precinct. There, I met with Don Ángel Mestanza, the chief of police. I was being sent to Sevilla to be under the supervision of my oldest brother, Antonio. Antonio was then second lieutenant in the Air Force. He had agreed to take me in and make sure I reported daily to the police station in Sevilla. I got the not-so-subtle message that my brother's career opportunities were tied to my continued good behavior." The regime often used the students' families to pressure them into leaving the movement.

After the meeting, Arturo returned home, packed his suitcase, and took the bus to Sevilla where his brother Antonio was waiting for him. "The next day at the Tablada air base, my brother introduced me to his superior officers, explaining to them why I was there. From the first day we didn't hide my situation. I think my

---

21   Arturo González Arcas, interview transcript, July 2, 2007.
22   Arturo González Arcas, interview transcript, July 2, 2007.

brother was somewhat sympathetic to me, even though I had put him in a tough spot. Every day, I walked from Tablada to the police station, limping in my dirty cast the whole way."

The police station was behind the Duque Square. It was the site of some of the worst abuses of the secret police. "I remember hearing horrible screams from the interrogation rooms down the hall from the registration desk where I had to report. They didn't make the least effort to hide what was going on. I had to stay in Sevilla until the Civil Governor lifted the deportation order in February.[23] After that I returned to Granada. The city was all abuzz with the announcement that the city of Granada had been picked by the regime as one of the 'development poles' in the new technocratic economic plans."[24] The festive mood of the city contrasted with the somber reality of the university students.

Arturo quietly resumed his studies. He did not, however, stop his political activism. It would have been like telling him to stop eating. The repression slowed down after the 1969 State of Emergency was lifted in June, and there was hope among the students that the worst had passed. But it was not to be. A second State of Emergency was declared in December 1970.

Upon his return to Granada from Carabanchel, Joaquín resumed his political activities in the Philosophy and Letters Communist cell. During the next year, 1969-1970, he steered the student group toward a close synchronization with the labor movement in Granada. Some of the activities organized under his leadership included a protest in solidarity with the construction workers' strike in July 1970 that ended in the tragic assassination of three workers and massive arrests in the following months. More demonstrations followed to protest the detention of the student opposition. The regime responded with the second State of Emergency on 14 December 1970. While some members of the cell fled, many were detained for the six months of martial law.

---

23   Arturo González Arcas, interview transcript, July 2, 2007.
24   In February of 1969, Granada joyfully received the decree that granted the creation of a "Development Pole" that would help stimulate the stunted industrial sector in the town. The project consisted of the construction of a designated industrial area called "polígono" and the granting of important aid (such as tax reduction) to companies that wanted to settle in it. On January 14, 1972, the first company protected by this business plan was inaugurated in Maracena. It was a factory of fishing rods and sporting goods jointly founded by a company with French capital and the Bank of Granada. The propaganda machinery of the Franco regime was launched, and the factory was opened in style, with the presence of the most important provincial authorities and the Falange Movement. The Caudillo, Franco himself, received the directors of the factory in the Palace of El Pardo in Madrid. Stateurop S.A., the name of the company, was the first of a few. But the Development Pole failed. Professor Gil Bracero points out that only 665 of the 3,288 planned jobs were created and that, in 1974, only nine companies had been created under the Development Pole. "Se inaugura la primera industria del Polo de Desarrollo," 9 January 2012. http://granadablogs.com/terecuerdo?s=gil+bracero.

Joaquín remained in hiding for the next two weeks, moving to different safe houses to avoid capture. Tired of being inside, though, he and some of the others got careless. One of the few times they ventured outside, an undercover vehicle of the Political Brigade recognized them. They ducked into the narrow, maze-like streets of the Albaycin, Granada's historic old neighborhood. While his companions narrowly escaped, an exhausted Joaquín tripped on the stairs leading to the San Ildefonso church on the Calle Real de Cartuja near the Barriocuelo and was captured. It was back to the precinct of the Zaidín district where his old friend, Don Paco, supervised a fresh round of beatings with rubber hoses. "They made me do what was called the bicycle, which consisted in making you walk while handcuffed with your arms behind your knees, sort of half seating," he recounted. The beatings were so severe this time that when he was finally transferred to Granada Provincial prison, the doctor had to write up his bruises in the admission's medical report.[25] "This report allowed my father to seek legal support from a Madrid lawyer, José Jiménez de Parga,[26] who filed a complaint for ill-treatment under police custody. But people were so afraid of the police that no lawyer would take my case. The case was filed and closed without anyone ever being charged."[27]

After suffering beatings and torture in the various police station cellars around town, the students were almost relieved to be transferred to the prison. Once in the prison, their lives settled down into a more benign monotony where they could carve out space for contemplation. Joaquín pointed out, "The second worst thing that happened to me was being put in isolation. While depressing and lonely, it was better than getting beaten with rubber hoses."[28]

"Life in prison was very monotonous. To pass the time we organized activities: readings, classes, sports etc." These were their clearings in the forest. "We even studied, and I passed several exams that spring. The prison food was terrible, but we supplemented it with what our families brought to us from outside. You could not drink wine or beer; you could not read newspapers, not even the regime's; the director and the teacher authorized books and sometimes in a very arbitrary and absurd way they did allow certain works. Diversion had to be concealed from the eyes of the wardens. Any communication with our families was carried out in booths under officials' surveillance." This went on for months, until Martial Law

---

25   Joaquín Bosque Sendra interview, June 1989 (transcript provided by Joaquín Bosque Sendra himself), Oral Histories Collection, Archivo Histórico de Comisiones Obreras de Andalucía, AHCCOO-A.
26   Born in Granada in 1929, José Jiménez de Parga was a prestigious jurist, Minister of Labor (1977-78) and President of the Tribunal Constitucional (2001-2004). He defended many political prisoners before the TOP. Jiménez de Parga died in Madrid in 2014.
27   Joaquín Bosque Sendra, interview, June 1989.
28   Joaquín Bosque Sendra, interview, June 1989.

ended. The regime's crackdown had fragmented the student opposition and suppressed much of its most public resistance, but it did not end it. Much of the organizing went on, unseen by the public. The crackdown and the transparent attempts by the regime to distract the public with bogus economic initiatives turned public sentiment against the regime. The valiant young students confronting the decrepit old regime were ultimately seen as sympathetic underdogs. After the second State of Emergency, the regime had lost its taste for blood. The students and all the other opposition factions would ultimately declare victory with the death of Franco and the transition to democracy signaled by the ratification of the new constitution on December 6, 1978.

Joaquín left the Communist party in 1980 as a result of the internal struggle between *renovadores* and *oficialistas*,[29] precipitated by a series of unfortunate circumstances: a severe criticism of General Secretary Santiago Carrillo's centralizing leadership style, the economic crisis in the second half of the 1970s, and the political miscalculations derived from the failure in Spain's transition of the Euro-Communist formula and the PSOE's political move towards the moderate left, which resulted in its absolute parliamentary majority in the 1982 elections.

Arturo joined the more moderate Partido Socialista de Andalucía, one of the many political parties that emerged after the Constitution of 1978 established the new autonomous regional system. This particular development negatively affected the PCE at the national level and its rigid "democratic centralization" structure as each region saw the opportunity to implement policies closer to the needs of their constituencies without renouncing their mass activism in the labor, intellectual, and neighborhood realms.

In the end, both Joaquín and Arturo found their clearings in the forest but were still not out of the woods. There is always the danger that the canopy might reclaim that one sunny aperture. You can still sense wariness in both men, a hypersensitivity to the political swaying in the air, when they talk about the past. Like soldiers returning from combat, they are forever tied to the battlefield.

> You make time stand still
> You make time stand still
> And I can deal with that
> 'Cause I got time to kill
> I'll breathe when I have to
> And I'll leave when you say so
> I'll burn in the meantime
> But only on the inside

---

29   Carme Molinero and Pere Ysàs, "La Crisis," in *De la Hegemonía a la autodestrucción: El Partido Comunista de España (1956-1982)* (Barcelona: Editorial Planeta, 2017).

We have an oath to keep
And we rise while the rest sleep
There's no going back
At least not for me
I'm dying for answers
Things that I used to know
But that was years ago
I'm biting my tongue now
Some things can't be said aloud
From my lips to your ears
You'd only see through me
See into the true me
Yeah!
You know that time's a wheel
And if we stand right here
You can see for miles
You could even see for years
I'll bleed if I have to
But I'm never letting go
Oh no!
I'm biting my tongue now
Some things can't be said aloud
From my lips to your ears
You'd only hear screaming
While I whisper the meaning
To you [30]

---

30 Iron Chic, "Spooky Action at a Distance," 2013, track 1, on *Spooky Action*, digital album.

Chapter 4
Al Amparo de Fecun

> Hail, holy Queen,
> Mother of Mercy!
> our life, our sweetness, and our hope!
> To thee do we cry, poor banished children of Eve;
> to thee do we send up our sighs,
> mourning and weeping in this valley of tears.
> Turn, then, most gracious Advocate,
> thine eyes of mercy toward us;
> and after this our exile
> show unto us the blessed fruit of thy womb, Jesus;
> O clement,
> O loving,
> O sweet Virgin Mary.

When I first interviewed Amparo in 1989, she was in her late thirties and already tenured and chair of the Geography department at the University of Granada. Never before had there been a woman chair and there has not been one since. She had intimidated me when I was one of her students in 1983 and still did. I remember her, a petite young professor commanding a crowded two hundred-seat auditorium, delivering succinct lectures on climatology and physical geography in a soft-spoken but firm voice. Her formidableness came, not from her stature or from an outsized personality (she is quite reserved), but from a sense of bedrock convictions rooted in faith.

Her name, popular for Spanish women of her generation, means protection. She was born in 1950 in a small village located in the Almanzora Valley in Almería. Her religiously conservative family moved to Granada when she was in high school, settling in the centrally located Realejo district on Calle Molinos. Her mother, against custom, continued to work as a teacher, even after she married and had a family—six children in all, Amparo the next to last. Her mother's not-so-small act of independence made a big impression on Amparo. She felt free to pursue her education without the typical resistance most of the girls in her class faced from home. In her house, the expectation for both the boys and the girls was that they would study and eventually have a career. "My mother worked as a teacher from the age of eighteen, and she thought that her children, both sons and daughters, must study, follow a career, and carve out a future for themselves," Amparo recalled. "Never was I told that my goal in life should be to find a boyfriend and marry. That was one thing that was totally eliminated from my household. What we were told was that we had to be independent, whether male or female."[1]

This egalitarian attitude in her family only went so far, though. With regard to housework, the females were expected to do the bulk of the work. "In the daily practice at home, there was this unwritten obligation for me to clean my brothers' room," shared Amparo. "I refused. I said I would not clean anyone's room. My parents and I used to fight about this. Growing up I was always the most rebellious, the one who caused problems. Even now my children ask me 'Mom, where did you come from?' With regard to social justice, I carried that same rebellious attitude."[2]

Her mother's rebellions carried over into the family's religious practices. Amparo remembers a very private, family-centered devotion. They never participated in the popular rotation of the Virgin effigies from home to home, and they did not attend the annual Holy Week processions on the city streets. Instead, the family observed an austere and private piety with the daily rosary prayer as their cohesive ritual.

The rosary prayer dedicated to the Virgin Mary represents the quintessential Catholic devotion to the Mother of God. The rosary diagram itself resembles the schema of the female symbol.

Amparo prayed the rosary every day at home, surrounded by her parents and five siblings: a Hail Mary for each of the ten beads that make up the so-called decade, repeated five times to complete a set of three mysteries dedicated to the life and Passion of Christ. Annunciation and birth constitute the Joyful mysteries to be prayed on Mondays and Saturdays. Christ's Resurrection and the crowning of the Virgin compose the Glorious mysteries prayed on Wednesdays and Sundays. Finally, the Sorrowful mysteries cover Christ's arrest and crucifixion were prayed on Tuesdays and Fridays.[3]

---

1 Amparo, phone interview with author, January 8, 2018 (recording 1 hour and 34 minutes).
2 Amparo, phone interview, 2018.
3 The fourth are the Luminous mysteries instituted by Pope John Paul II (1978-2005) and dedicated to the miraculous adult life of Jesus Christ from his baptism until his consecration of the Eucharist.

Figure 7 (left): Rosary
Figure 8 (right): Prayers of the Rosary

The Rosary Prayer was a meditative communal prayer with a long Catholic tradition rooted in medieval times and particularly promoted during the pontificate of Leo XIII (1878–1903), known as the Rosary Pope. It established the Mariology tradition within the Catholic Church, making the Virgin Mary *Mediatrix* through her intercession between the faithful and Jesus Christ. The veneration to the Virgin Mary also provided young girls with a female divinity who nurtured their spiritual self-worth.

Amparo's mother would not allow her children to leave the house until this family ritual was completed. For her mother, the fifteen promises[4] derived from the rosary prayer represented a means to deploy protection over her family in the fraught times of totalitarian rule and persecution.

The family's religious fervor influenced Amparo's social consciousness in the mid-1960s. "I found my Christian beliefs supported completely in my student activism. That Christian combative attitude gave me the moral upper ground I was looking for. Unfortunately, my parents did not see the connection between opposing the government and Christian devotion the same way I did. My mother would say 'Where did my daughter learn these ways?' On occasion they went to talk with the Jesuit in charge of our FECUN community to figure out what was going on; what was I doing?"

---

4   "The Fifteen Promises Granted to Those Who Recite the Rosary," *The Most Holy Rosary*. http://themostholyrosary.com/15promises.htm.

Figure 9: Mysteries of the Rosary

——— **Mysteries of the Rosary** ———

Joyful (Monday & Saturday)
1. Annunciation
2. Visitation
3. Birth of Jesus
4. Presentation of Jesus in the Temple
5. Finding of the Child Jesus in the Temple

Sorrowful (Tuesday & Friday)
1. Agony in the Garden
2. Scourging at the Pillar
3. Crowning with Thorns
4. Carrying of the Cross
5. Crucifixion

Glorious (Wednesday & Sunday)
1. Resurrection of Jesus from the Tomb
2. Ascension of Jesus into Heaven
3. Descent of Holy Spirit at Pentecost
4. Assumption of Mary, Body and Soul, into Heaven
5. Coronation of Mary as Queen of Heaven and Earth

Luminous (Thursday)
1. Baptism of Jesus in the Jordan
2. Wedding at Cana
3. Proclamation of the Kingdom of God
4. Transfiguration
5. Institution of the Holy Eucharist

——— Feast of Our Lady of the Most Holy Rosary · 7 October ———

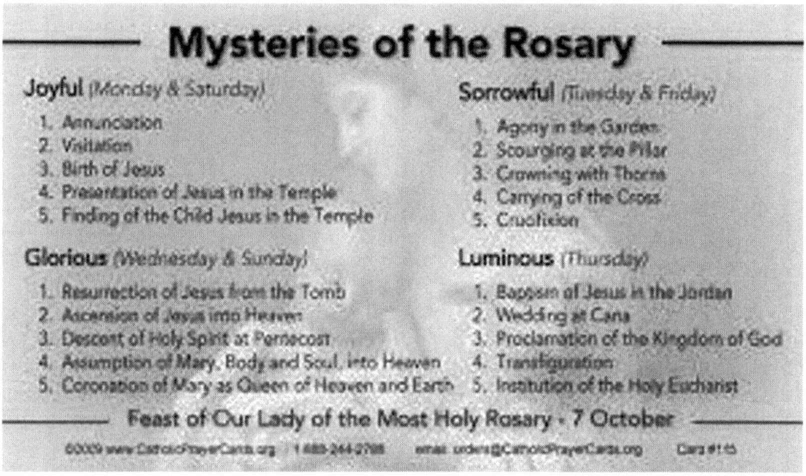

As they grew up, each of Amparo's siblings opted for their own particular religious understanding and commitment. While the oldest sister joined the ultraconservative Opus Dei, one of her brothers became an ardent militant in the labor movement through his membership in the HOAC and later joined the Brotherhood of Foucauld or Brotherhood of Jesus to live among the poor.[5] As demonstrated by the various religious paths taken by Amparo and her siblings, the Church's social doctrine inspired different movements from right to left ideologically. The increasing radicalization of the labor and student movements after World War II included many Catholics, particularly in Mediterranean Europe.[6] The Second Vatican Coun-

---

5   The Brotherhood of Jesus was founded after Carlos de Foucauld (1858-1916), a French missionary who dedicated his life to live among the poor in the Algerian Sahara Desert. The communities live among the poor in urban areas and non-Christian countries and observe vows of poverty, obedience, and contemplative prayer.

6   Gerd-Rainer Horn accurately points out the "general state of myopia within the historical profession," as there is little attention paid to the religious dimension of the social movements in the narrative of the "global 1968." What he defines as the Second Wave of Left Catholicism in Western Europe reached its peak from 1968-1975. Spain is key to understanding the Catholic left and the Liberation Theology better studied in the Latin American case. As Horn says: "The Spanish Left Catholicism, virtually unknown to the north of the Pyrenees to this day, was not only a pioneering venture, but it might stand as a powerful reminder that, in the last analysis, it is material conditions which gave rise to social movements, new theologies, and apostolic experiments, rather than new theologies spawning grassroots action as if by spontaneous generation." Gerd-Rainer Horn, *The Spirit of the Vatican II: Western European Progressive Catholicism in the Long Sixties* (Oxford: Oxford University Press, 2015), 3.

cil unleashed a wave of leftist Catholicism[7] in the Western Hemisphere that has been better studied in the Latin American continent as Liberation Theology. Europe had its own leftist, Catholic theology starting as early as the 1910s, largely in response to increasing industrialization and the problems it wrought for poor and working-class families.[8] Founded in 1946 by the conservative curia, the HOAC[9] (Catholic Action) was the most important Catholic trade union in the Spanish labor movement. In Spain, Catholic Action received the impetus from the conservative pontificate of Pius XII (1939-1958); however, the so-called specialized groups among the youth in the labor and student movements became radicalized under the aegis of the new pope, John XXIII (1958-1963), after his launching of the Second Vatican Council in 1962.

A number of leftist Catholic organizations emerged in Spain in the 1950s. The Spanish New Left was represented by the Frente de Liberación Popular (FLP),[10] colloquially called "*Felipe*," with Madrid and Barcelona as epicenters. The *Felipes* read broadly beyond Catholic sacred texts, including philosophy, new sociology, and radical renditions of theology. They held small seminars outside their classrooms to educate themselves with diverse writings, from Mao to Lenin and to philosophers like Sartre and Simone de Beauvoir. In addition to the FLP there were other organizations including the largely Catholic UDE (Unión Democrática de Estudiantes) founded in 1957 and the FUDE (Federación Universitaria Democrática Española)

---

7   I am utilizing here the terminology put forward by Gerd-Rainer Horn who establishes the first wave as 1924-1959 in his book, *Western European Liberation Theology: The First Wave 1924-1959* (Oxford: Oxford University Press, 2008).

8   In 1924 Joseph Cardijn established the Jeunesse Ouvrière Chrètienne (JOC) which expanded rapidly to Spain and Italy. The Belgian priest Cardijn moved to the northern suburb of Laken in 1912 where, during his six years of residence there, he established a *sui generis* Catholic organization. The area had a population of 25,000, predominantly from working-class families who lived under precarious economic conditions. He first launched a local needlework trade union for young seamstresses in his parish. His goal was to strengthen the Christian trade unions. By 1917 he established a trade union organization specifically for young people, the Jeunesse Syndicaliste, acknowledging the needs of youth in the labor force. Horn, *Western European Liberation Theology*.

9   The head of HOAC was Guillermo Rovirosa who had worked as an engineer during the Spanish Civil War on the Republican side and who had gained some consciousness about the dismal conditions of the workers in Madrid. Also important was Tomás Malagón, a former priest who joined the Communist Party during the Spanish Civil War. For more on the history of the HOAC see: Basilisa López García, *Aproximación a la historia de la HOAC, 1946-1981* (Madrid: HOAC, 1995), cited in Horn, *The Spirit of the Vatican II*, note 36, 230.

10 Gerd-Rainer Horn points out that that the inspiration for the FLP acronym came from two organizations: the Algerian FLN (Front de Libèration National) and the French MLP (Mouvement de Libèration Populaire). The Felipe thus was "Locating its intellectual and activist traditions within Third World liberation movements and European Left Catholicism." Horn, *The Spirit of the Vatican II*, 190-91.

founded in 1961. All of them competed with the regime's Falangist Student Union SEU until its extinction in 1965. Especially important in the UDE was Catholic Action's JEC, which was dissolved in 1968 by the Church's conservative hierarchy due to its increasing radicalization. This empty space became occupied by FECUN, a student group sponsored by the Jesuits.

Amparo joined FECUN in 1967 and fell in love with Arturo, a fellow student. Just like everything in her character, her love was devotional. She saw in Arturo a kindred spirit fighting society's ills with the same righteous indignation she had felt when she refused to clean her brothers' room. Their love was heated by the religious home fires of their upbringings but also by the idealistic fervor that their faith engendered. FECUN implied not only a religious but also a "political and social engagement," she recalled, "understood in diverse ways by the many individuals who came together under its guidance."

The Society of Jesus founded the Marian Congregations to promote the devotion to the Virgin Mary in the mid-1500s, and FECUM experienced a global expansion. By the mid-1960s FECUM was no longer just a religious organization but also a political one.

The transformation towards a social and political outlook brought FECUN closer to the JEC[11] objectives but with the added benefit of the Jesuits' know-how for turning faith into action.[12] FECUM, meanwhile, transitioned into what was called Comunidades de Vida Cristiana (Christian Life Communities).

Amparo's devotion to the Virgin Mary and her growing self-confidence as a young woman made her a great fit within the FECUN community. Encouraged by a young friend, Fermina, who was active in the HOAC labor movement, Amparo joined the FECUN community during her last year in high school, along with Pili, a schoolmate. There they met Pedro, who had just left the priesthood and entered the student movement along with Arturo, who proved to be the most radical of them all. "He [Arturo] was singularly intelligent," remembered Pedro, "brilliant in his oratory, well read in political and social matters, but very funny and extremely mischievous in everyday life. He also played the guitar, always singing Raimon and Serrat's songs in Catalan. He taught me the ins and outs of anti-Franco politics and, above all, the intricacies of the university movement."[13]

FECUN's meeting facility was located at the corner of Marqués de Falces and Elvira Streets in "a five-story building in which the top three floors were reserved

---

11   Aurora Morcillo, "In their Own Words: Women in Higher Education," in *True Catholic Womanhood: Gender Ideology in Franco's Spain* (Dekalb: Northern Illinois University Press, 2000), 129-61.
12   Amparo Ferrer, interview by author, Granada, May 15, 1989.
13   Pedro Ruiz Morcillo, "Con la FECUN y contra Franco en los pasillos de Puentezuelas (1968-1973)" [unpublished mss.; pdf essay provided], 10.

for the Jesuits," described Pedro. "FECUN occupied the first floor which was divided into several meeting rooms. On the ground floor there was a room large enough for assemblies. The spacious basement spread the entire length of the upper level[14] There the students printed different pamphlets and anti-establishment propaganda materials. On many occasions they had to move the printer and propaganda for safekeeping to the Colegio Máximo in the Cartuja.

The Jesuits established the Colegio Máximo in the late nineteenth century. The Colegio, a College and Novitiate of the Society of Jesus, was built between 1891 and 1894, following the design of the architect Francisco Rabanal Fariña. The design called for a central courtyard and four interior patios with a cross structure of galleries on three floors. The building's style featured elements of Granada's Hispano-Muslim tradition, what could be described as Arabic revival. Between 1916 and 1917, an allegory of the Eucharist was added to the top half of the front façade. The peaceful and ordered monastery proved to be an oasis in the hectic, modernizing city of Granada at the time and a good hiding place for the student activists.

This architectural treasure is part of my childhood memories as well. In the spring of 1969, when the FECUM students were hiding contraband documents in the priory, I was making my First Communion in the church's chapel. All through the winter my classmates and I had prepared for this rite of passage. The nuns of Jesús María measured our little bodies and ordered for each girl a plain white tunic and matching head cover.

The Jesuits ran the boys' school adjacent to ours and supplied the grooms to our brides. Every afternoon for months we marched up the hill towards the Colegio through the elaborate English gardens and into the chapel. Our thoughts were turned to our eternal salvation, not to the young priests on the premises risking their mortal selves.

The lives of the student activists followed a circular rhythm, like the rosary prayer—daily circuits of sorrowful, glorious, and joyful mysteries. The students spent their days at the College of the Arts (or Philosophy and Letters, as it is referred to in Spanish) attending classes and their evenings meeting in the Jesuit facilities on Marqués de Falces Street.

The college was located in a small palace on Puentezuelas street, on the corner of Obispo Hurtado, in front of Carril del Picón and Tablas Street.[15] Built at the beginning of the nineteenth century by the Conte de Luque, and acquired by the Ministry of Education in 1946 to house the Faculty of Arts, its neo-classical style alternates brick wall flanks with stone in the corners. Imposing classical columns announce the main entrance. The two-story building contains a large interior patio

---

14 Ruiz Morcillo, "Con la FECUN," 21.
15 The Puentezuelas site was what Concha and Amalia remembered as called "panties-ville."

with tall trees and manicured gardens where the students spent time hanging out between classes.

Figure 10: The College of the Arts. The College of the Arts was located in the magnificent nineteenth-century palace of the Counts of Luque on Puentezuelas Street. This was the site of student activism from in the 1960s until the mid-1970s, when the college was relocated to a new facility built outside the city center in the northern part district of Cartuja.

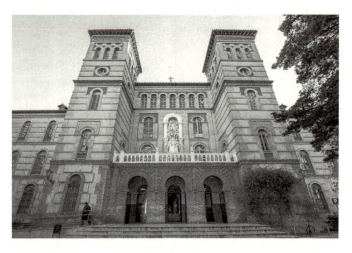

The patio is also where students gathered for assemblies. This did not go unnoticed by the local authorities, whose Plaza de los Lobos police station was located close by. The police also had their informants, like the lowly administrator the students derided as "El Foca" (seal), keeping an eye on what the students were up to.

Amparo vividly takes us back into the building in her retelling. "The stairs were on the right side. They led down to the basement and up to the upper floor into the galleries through a big iron double door, almost always adorned with political posters. The halls ran around the patio where the classrooms and the library were located. Going down the staircase we accessed the basement. On the patio level, the stairs consisted of two sections divided by a wide landing where a huge corkboard displayed hundreds of advertisements of all kinds, including subversive posters against the regime, some erotic poems by Sabina[16] and the occasional

---

16   She refers to Joaquín Sabina, today an internationally renowned songwriter, singer, and poet, who was one of the fellow students in the College of Arts. Sabina exiled himself to England when the State of Emergency was enacted in 1970-1971.

crudely drawn cartoon. The lower section faced the cafeteria, a small rectangular space with the bar on one side and a bench with tables on the other."

Granada's FECUN community had almost a hundred members, most of whom had been recruited during their high school years. Some joined the mountain club *El Sadday* and the Congregation of the Stanislaus that one of the Jesuits, Father Ferrer, directed from the upper floors of the house on Marqués de Falces street, the so-called Intercollegiate Center.

In 1968, FECUN experienced a profound radicalization. Many of the members came from the city's lower middle classes and many others from rural areas who had gained access to the university through scholarships, as in Arturo's case. They were acutely aware of the plight of the poor and working classes. They also had roots in the communities where unrest with the regime was percolating.

FECUN students came from different colleges but Philosophy and Letters contributed the greatest number and the most active members. Known as "the Christians," in the resistance against the regime FECUN represented a counterweight to the Communist Party among the students at the University. For those who were not ready or able to identify with the socially ostracized Communist Party, FECUN offered a more palatable alternative.

FECUN's tactics and strategies drew inspiration from the HOAC Brotherhood of Christian Workers, but they made their distance from the anti-Franco political opposition parties explicit. Some of the members were more radical than others. Those less engaged in the collective fight found inspiration in French theologian Emmanuel Mounier's (1905-1950) personalist movement that took a stand midway between liberalism and Marxism and focused on the cultivation of self-affirmation rather than collective action. Still, there were others within FECUN who Amparo considered more radical because of their socialist and anti-fascist feelings. Her boyfriend Arturo was one of them. Though she was not as outwardly radical as Arturo, Amparo, in her own way, was just as steadfast in her opposition to the regime. Her opposition was more tied to her gender and the indignities she felt at being told what she could and couldn't do. Though fighting against the regime was the stated goal, many of the women in the movement were also fighting for themselves.

It wasn't all "sturm und drang" in the student movement. The FECUN students also enjoyed a rich social life. Amparo described the FECUN headquarters at Marqués de Falces Street as "a boisterous hotbed" all year round, except during the summer academic break. Some of their activities included courses on religious or political matters, book discussions, and debates on social, political, or cultural issues. Once a week they celebrated a "very simple" mass, participating with authentic fervor, without sacred vestments (perhaps only the stole), and with ordinary bread and wine. The meetings followed a prearranged agenda. The debates and decisions on the fundamental issues were adopted in a monthly assembly. Mass on Sundays ended with a party in the basement with music, dancing, flamenco, singing, and poetry readings.[17]

FECUN was organized around small "Life Revision" teams, which met weekly. Larger committees, in which members of those different groups participated, were in charge of putting into practice the community activities: studies, training, organization, treasury, information, external relations, publications. Elected democratically, representatives of each of the committees formed FECUN's Board of Directors. The Board of Directors elected a secretariat, president, vice president, secretary, and treasurer. The secretariat represented the group in national assemblies. The *Comunitas*, a newsletter written by the militants themselves, was their official mouthpiece.

At the beginning of each academic year, FECUN held a retreat in Fuente Grande in the Alfaguara Mountains, seven kilometers north of Granada. The purpose of the retreat was to prepare their academic year activities. In the retreat of 1968/69, Pedro and Arturo shared sleeping quarters and soon became fast friends. Pedro remembered, "As always, we began the meeting with a presentation on some important issues to later discuss with our Life Revision teams. Ours was composed of Luis, Mayte, Arturo, Amparo, Pili and me."[18] The six members, three men and three women, became a tight group of friends who, in a form of social mitosis, split into three couples: Luis and Mayte, Arturo and Amparo, and Pedro and Pili. What began as a largely Christian commitment to fight the regime's injustices turned into a very personal commitment to each other.

The three couples went everywhere together. On one beautiful November day, they borrowed a van from Juan F., the leader of the HOAC, and took off to visit another FECUN member, Felipe, who was serving his mandatory military service in Cadiz. Pedro related, "We took the old road from Andalucía to Cadiz. The weather was good, so we had no reason to worry, but on one of the open lanes around Aguadulce the car hit a muddy patch and flew off the road into an olive grove. Everyone had some bruises and a few small scratches on our hands and faces, but Arturo got the worst of it. He fractured both his tibia and fibula. We quickly buried a bunch of pamphlets that we had hidden inside a guitar case. I don't know why we were carrying a guitar case full of propaganda on that trip, but in those years we were like that. The Civil Guard took us to an emergency room where they put Arturo's leg in a cast. We left the van in a garage for repairs and returned to Granada on a bus. In the following weeks we had to borrow money from friends and family to pay for the repairs. Arturo spent a month with his leg in a cast after a few days of surgery and hospitalization."[19]

---

17   Ruiz Morcillo, "Con la FECUN," 40-41.
18   Ruiz Morcillo, "Con la FECUN," 52.
19   Ruiz Morcillo, "Con la FECUN," 40-41.

The Spanish student movement, which had its beginnings in the crisis of 1956,[20] when it helped oust the Minister of Education Joaquín Ruiz Giménez (1913-2009), gained strength and momentum in the mid-1960s. With the disappearance of the SEU in 1965, university students founded autonomous democratic unions, first in Madrid and Barcelona, and then in the rest of the universities. These new student platforms operated outside the control of the regime, which inevitably led to friction with authorities and later repression. The Professional Students Associations (APE), which replaced the SEU, lasted only a short time and was used mainly as a cover for the clandestine unions. The PCE, which dominated the student anti-Franco movement, used the student groups to promote its Pact for Freedom.

The student resistance groups throughout Spain wanted to unify through a Democratic Student Congress (Reuniones Coordinadoras Preparatorias). This was a tactic that had already been carried out by the CCOO in the labor movement. Their members might have come from different factions, like Catholic Action and the outlawed Communist Party, but they were united in opposing the government.

The University of Granada joined the national student movement in 1968. "The atmosphere of camaraderie and 'coffee talks,'" as Amparo recalled, "intensified with the founding of the Democratic Union of the University of Granada."[21] The electricity was palpable in the dark cafés and dingy bars where students gathered. The Bimbela, the Natalio, the Síbari, the Enguix, and the bodegas de Puentezuelas, located on the side streets of the Bibarrambla Plaza, gave silent witness, in the words of Pedro, "to the secret accumulation of many hopes and utopian dreams of the precociously anti-Franco youth of those years."

In January 1968 the SDEUG was formally constituted and the first District Assembly took place. The Declaration of Principles, the Statutes, and a manifesto of solidarity with repressed students at other universities and protest against government repression, were approved.

The union structure was straightforward: division by Colleges, and within them assemblies per year cohort, cohorts' council, branch council, Faculty Chamber, functional departments, and delegates at different academic levels. The appointment in the summer of 1968 of a thirty-four-year-old Biochemistry professor, Federico Mayor Zaragoza (1934), as the new Rector, was received by FECUN members with hope. Zaragoza was a young and open-minded professor willing to entertain reforms. But the appointment of Antonio Gallego Morrell (1923-2009), a regime figure, as Dean of Philosophy and Letters was a disappointment.

The two appointments were made by the new Minister of Education, José Luis Villar Palasí (1922-2012), who was trying to walk the tightrope between the demands

---

20 See Morcillo, *True Catholic Womanhood*, 77-101.
21 Ruiz Morcillo, "Con la FECUN," 40-41.

of the students and the dictates of the regime. The new minister was an unimaginative technocrat whose goal was to adapt the educational structure to the government's new economic plan, "desarrollismo" (economic development policies).

In Philosophy and Letters, FECUN's group had a natural leader in Arturo. Amparo was also very involved in activism, although she did not hold a leading office in the SDEUG.

Figure 11: Amparo, 1968

Even though she was not visibly out in front, Amparo worked tirelessly behind the scenes. That is the way she liked it. When Arturo was arrested, she went to the rector to lobby for his release. Later, during the transition, Amparo was one of the founders of the Socialist Party of Andalucía (PSA).[22] She was always the first to comfort the other students or organize their Christian community to help out where they were needed. Pedro remembers her as someone with "fortitude," who was undaunted by the challenges facing the movement. "She would confront anyone, the police or Dean, if she thought she was right," remarked Arturo. It was that unflappable demeanor that had intimidated me as an undergraduate in her class. I now understood what made this tiny woman such a force of nature. When I interviewed Amparo in 1989, she talked about Arturo's arrest more in depth. She rec-

---

22 The PA was founded in 1976 when the Socialist Alliance of Andalusia, created in 1971, adopted the name Socialist Party of Andalusia (PSA). Later, in January of 1979, during the course of the II PSA Congress, the name of the Andalusian Socialist Party-Andalusian Party (PSA-PA) was adopted. In February of 1984 it adopted its current name: Andalusian Party. Historically, the PA has held the office of mayor in important urban centers of Andalusia such as Sevilla, Jerez de la Frontera, or Algeciras.

ognized the radicalization of some of the members of FECUN, like Arturo himself, who accepted Marxism as a form of Christian praxis. That was difficult to accept for her and her conservative family. "There were many shifts in our beliefs that caused us serious moral dilemmas. My now husband,[23] was arrested twice...and well, one of the things I...remember with horror, was that...they were accusing him of being a Communist! That was really hard for me, for anyone...." She spoke in the third person, as if trying to gain some distance from the events she had brought to mind: "One could understand that it was not so bad, but even socially, if it was bad enough that they had arrested him, the fact that they could also accuse him of being a Communist became the gravest of charges against a person."

To the members of the opposition, the differences between Christian militancy and Communism were mostly semantic, but to the larger world they were profound. Pedro explained the tension between the Communist and Christian militants in the student movement as follows: "Certainly, there were people who criticized Marxist-Leninist strategies, the Marxist theoretical principles as a whole or in part, and/or the tactics of the PCE, but not because of our Christian principles, but because some among us had other theoretical foundations and considered other strategies and political tactics more effective or better, or at least as legitimate as those of the PCE. The FECUN community as such was not anti-Marxist or anti-Communist. And, I am fully convinced that those who left FECUN did so because of a crisis of faith, not because those of us who stayed in it might have been anti-Communists. The 'reds'[24] did not go leaving the rightists behind; at least some of us who stayed in the community continued being 'red.'"[25]

Women endured greater social shame when they were publicly recognized as leftists, and for many it cost them in their professional and personal lives. That was the case for Concha, or Mari Carmen Sanmillan, the Latin professor who lent her home to hide the young Communist students during the State of Exception in 1970-71. Amparo remembered Mari Carmen with affection but also great sadness: "She was a serious person but was socially ostracized after it was found out she helped the student movement. She was one of those women who I have always believed was mistreated in the University. Imagine, the University, being a place where supposedly there is a progressive community, right? And I think she was misunderstood, and serious obstacles to professional advancement were put in her way. She was an excellent person. Few people, in truth, were like her. She nurtured all the students, regardless of their belonging to one faction or another. For example, we, FECUN I mean, got along with her perfectly, and she got along

---

23 Arturo and Amparo separated in 1998. These are Amparo's remarks in 1989.
24 "Red" is the term used to refer to communists.
25 Ruiz Morcillo, "Con la FECUN," 118.

with PCE militant students as well. Harassed and abused by her department, she left academia to become a high school teacher...."[26]

Mari Carmen Sanmillan died in the mid-1980s, and Amparo recalled the tribute that the University organized to her: "Last year [1988] they organized an homage to her at the university. I kept thinking of her, and telling myself 'Look at this, a tribute to her by the university, how ironic....'"[27]

Amparo was no stranger to gender discrimination herself. She recalls her memories of the male-centered university on my second interview with her thirty years after the first one. She passionately conveyed over the phone how she still subscribed to everything said in 1989, though she had some revealing insight into her journey. "I do not consider myself a leader of the feminist movement in the University," she remarked emphatically. "I was a person, involved in all the political and professional actions, but not a leader. I remember sometimes arguing with feminists...sometimes I thought they were confused in their approaches. For example, I often argued with some of the leaders like Marga B...Maribel L., or Candida M. especially in the adjunct's assemblies...because they would propose to include in our demands things like...'recognition of divorce,' and I said, 'But let's see...let's focus...divorce? This is not the place to demand such a thing, this is an adjunct professor's labor meeting.'"[28]

Even after the transition, the male-centered university took advantage of many of the academic women. They were cheap labor who did the bulk of the work. For all their struggle they had to accept a lesser prize than their male counterparts. While the men in the movement transitioned into the more highly paid and respected tenure lines, the women became less well compensated adjuncts with heavy teaching loads. "It was not until 1984 that I became a permanent professor," Amparo recalled. "I had started in 1974 with a research fellowship. Note that I had been working as an adjunct for ten years. By 1976, I was in charge of at least three prep course assignments. Most of the faculty who taught you [in the early 1980s] for sure were non-permanent faculty or adjuncts. We were the sole teaching body. There were no opportunities for permanent contracts with better pay for women...."

Even though Amparo was relegated to adjunct professor, she didn't stop fighting for what was right. "Remember Villegas, the catedrático? ...He frequently asked adjuncts to teach his class with no notice, out of the blue. So, I told him one day that I was not going to do it...and I was not going to do it, I said, because I considered that it was not my responsibility, and I had no obligation to do so. I said, if the rector wrote me a letter saying that I had the obligation to replace him [Professor

---

26   Amparo Ferrer, interview, 1989.
27   Amparo Ferrer, interview, 1989.
28   Amparo, phone interview, 2018.

Villegas] then I would do it. But it would have to be by an order of the rector himself. That.... Well! That was...! Imagine!! ...From that day onwards...Villegas hated me to death!! Standing up for myself may have hindered my advancement, but in the end, I was recognized as a consequential, independent person, who never sold myself short to anyone."[29]

One of the most difficult times in Amparo's career came when she had her three children. In hindsight, she regretted not having had access to maternity leave. "That's one of the things that at this point in my life I blame myself for, because I did not ask for maternity leave in any of the pregnancies. I kept on working. And I reproach myself for putting myself through such an ordeal.... My oldest daughter was born in 1974 when I was still teaching high school in Montefrío.[30] So it happened that she was born on a Palm Sunday and I started classes the following week on Monday after Resurrection Sunday. That is to say, within eight days of giving birth I went back to work. But it also just so happened that I received a university research grant, which meant I had to teach some classes at the University of Granada as well. I will never forget, for example, the first class I taught at the university on cartographic projections, which is a very difficult lecture! So...I profoundly dreaded all of it. As a new mother, of course, I breastfed my baby and since we lived nearby Montefrío's high school, I brought her with me and had a young girl babysit while I was teaching. So, you see, I tried to combine everything, at a great cost to me personally. The men did not have to do that."[31]

Amparo was never afraid of working extra hard and certainly never used her condition as a woman in academia to gain advantage. Like most of the other women at the university, she endured extra burdens and struggled against a male-dominated hierarchy. "As years go by, I am conscious of the fact that there was a lot more gender discrimination than I was ready to admit or acknowledge," she concluded.

Certainly, the self-worth and defiance in Amparo's professional life found its roots in the Catholic leftist community within FECUN. Her radical sense of justice derived also from her profound Christian beliefs. Her praying of the rosary and veneration of a female divinity, the Queen of Heaven, impressed in young girls this sense of being equal in the eyes of God. Amparo may not think of herself as a leader in the feminist movement of the University of Granada, but in many ways, she was. It is not only the one who holds the banner or the megaphone who leads, but also

---

29 Amparo, phone interview, 2018.
30 Montefrío is a municipality located to the northwest of the province of Granada, bordering to the north with Priego and Almedinilla (Córdoba) and with Alcalá La Real (Jaén); and on the south with Illora, Villanueva de Mesía and Loja (Granada); on the east with Illora; and on the west with Loja and Algarinejo (Granada). It is part of the region of Poniente Granadino, occupying much of the north of the area.
31 Amparo, phone interview, 2018.

individuals like Amparo, who thoughtfully and methodically direct the action from the rear. Amparo was a leader who showed a younger generation like mine the possibilities in our own lives.

Chapter 5
Julia's Prosody

The antiquated Radio Shack cassette player, rummaged from the bottom of a storage box of long discarded electronics, emits the high-pitched timbre of Julia's voice from 1989, as I, now a middle-aged woman, am transported back to when a wide-eyed history student listened with rapt attention to tales of heroic women casting aside caution and convention, to tear at the fabric of a regime woven from lies. Julia's voice reverberates in her story—her prosody:

I was just a kid, only 17. I still cannot believe I was able to pull through it all, the way I did. The police did not know my name, but Berta[1] betrayed me after a serious beating while she was being interrogated. I don't blame her. No. She ended up being the Party's scapegoat when many others opened their mouths too. Berta and I spent our time together in jail. No. I do not hold it against her.

---

1   Berta was from Tolosa, Guipúzcoa, a 20-year-old student of Biological Sciences and militant of the PCE cataloged by the police as someone who "had created volatile subversive situations violating article 28." She had been first arrested on October 16, 1970, for distributing illegal propaganda pamphlets together with Jesús Carreño Tenorio in the Camino de Ronda area of Granada. The leaflets supported the construction general strike in July that same year and protested the police assassination of three workers. Berta was the first detainee during the 1970-71 State of Emergency, on December 15, 1970. Spending the mandatory 72 hours in a cell in the Plaza de los Lobos police station, she was interrogated and severely beaten and then transferred to the Provincial Prison of Granada. Passed to the TOP, and convicted for the crime of sedition and provocation, she was sentenced to three months imprisonment. She remained in prison by order of the Civil Governor who did not let her out even after posting the required bail of 10,000 pesetas. Her behavior was classified as "bad." The proceedings for her freedom were unsuccessful until the month of May. She was accused by the Public Prosecutor of terrorism, illicit association, and illegal propaganda. Martínez Foronda and Sánchez Rodrigo, *Mujeres en Granada por las libertades democráticas*, 48. On the bail payment irregularities, see Informe del Departamento de Información del Distrito de Granada, "Situación de los presos políticos en Granada," 14 de abril de 1971, in Archivo Universidad de Granada, Secretaría General del Rectorado, Asociaciones de Estudiantes, 69/71, leg. 23-272.

The State of Emergency ruined our Christmas of 1970 for sure. There were no "noches buenas"[2] but rather many rotten nights from December 14 on. Carols and fear do not syncopate. I should have known, having been raised by a father who is a musician. Though, when you think about it, my dad being in the army may have furnished some intuition on how to harmonize terror and tone. I must say, he was a sweet man to my sister and me, always. He had a sweet spirit like the sound of the oboe he played so artfully. I know how much pain I caused my family. I was very sheltered, and they had no idea how deeply involved I was. They only saw their 17-year-old daughter still living at home, excelling in her studies as a student of Geography and History at the University of Granada.

The morning after Christmas, I woke up with a premonition. I knew of the arrests of my comrades and worried that my parents would find the large stacks of pamphlets I was hiding at home. I figured I should contact another comrade to dispose of the propaganda, so after breakfast I told my father I had to run an errand. For some strange reason, he insisted on coming with me. The police were already waiting for me as we stepped out onto the street.

No doubt my arrest shocked my family. We were so ordinary, you know. I never felt the need to rebel against a tyrannical father like other friends did. No, that was not what led me to the Communist Party. I was very naïve, confused, eager to make my mark on the world. My adolescent curiosity had led me to read José's[3] work and even turn into a pious daily communion churchgoer for an entire summer. At home, religion was always pro-forma, never felt. I am proud to say my parents never sent me to a nunnery school. My parents did not think deeply about anything. Both were compliant with religious rituals, never politically engaged. My father had to fight on the "Nationalist" side, though never was a committed fascist. He was someone without strong beliefs, unwilling to think things through.

---

2   Julia Cabrera, interview by author, tape recording in Granada, June 1989.

3   José Antonio Primo de Rivera (1903-1936), son of former dictator General Miguel Primo de Rivera (1870-1930) and founder of Falange Española in 1933. He had been a deputy to the Republican parliament. In 1936 he was executed in Alicante by the Republican Government as the Spanish Civil War erupted. José Antonio became mythologized by the regime. His sister Pilar Primo de Rivera (1907-1991) was the head of the Falangist Female Section (Sección Femenina de Falange) founded by a select elite of university women in 1934. The Female Section became the only official women's organization in charge of indoctrinating Spanish women in national duties for the regime until it was dissolved in 1977. The bibliography on these topics is extensive. A few key readings include: Stanley Payne, *Falange: A History of Spanish Fascism* (Redwood City, CA: Stanford University Press, 1961); *A History of Fascism, 1914-1945* (Madison: University of Wisconsin, 1995); and *Fascism in Spain 1923-1977* (Madison: University of Wisconsin, 1999). The bibliography on Sección Femenina's history is exhaustive. Some recent publications include: Inbal Ofer, *Señoritas in Blue: The Making of a Female Political Elite in Franco's Spain* (Brighton: Sussex Academic Press, 2009); Sofía Rodríguez López, *El patio de la carcel: La Sección Femenina de FET-JONS en Almería (1937-1977)* (Sevilla: Centro de Estudios Andaluces, 2010).

Dad had briefly been a carpenter in Baeza, his hometown.[4] Since a few men in his family played in the village band, they encouraged his interest in music. My mother was from the same town. They belonged to the lower middle class but had aspirations to climb up the social ladder. Just married, my father was stationed in Segovia, where my sister and I were born. We lived there until I was nine or ten years old, when we moved to Granada because my father wanted to bring his family closer to his hometown.

I truly feel like I'm from "Graná!"[5] They may have delivered me in Segovia, but I identify as Andalusian in spite of the Castilian remnants in my speech. I am southern most definitely. I suffered the teasing from other children when we moved here. First, I attended a public, or as they called it then, "national" school in Plaza Nueva as we settled in the historic district of Paseo de los Tristes at the foot of the Alhambra. I missed my teacher, Doña Visi, from Segovia. It was she who opened my mind to learning. She was brilliant, one of the many teachers from the Republic ostracized by the regime after the war, making it impossible for her to find a job in the school system. A group of children attended her home school instead, and we received the gift of knowledge. Then in Granada I was punished severely in my new school by a mean, sanctimonious teacher who ridiculed me in front of my classmates when she discovered I had taken communion without keeping the mandatory fast. The daily anxiety I faced at school made me sick. I developed an ugly rash on my face from some of the stress that comes back every time I get anxious. My torture ended when our family moved to the newly minted working-class neighborhood of Los Pajaritos near the train station. There I finished my prep to enter the baccalaureate at a private school where I was able to assist the teacher with the geography lessons. Doña Visi's teachings still carried me through after all those years.

I attended Instituto Ganivet, the girls-only high school located next to the boys' school, Padre Suárez in Gran Via. While in high school I started to engage with other students in certain minimal activism in solidarity with the college students who were on strike the year I was finishing my entrance exams for the university. I remember we organized a twenty-minute protest, refused to enter the mathematics class until twenty minutes into the lecture, all to show our solidarity with the college students whose cause we would join within a year. I, only 17 years old, was eager to fight for a cause by the time I enrolled in October 1969, my freshman year.

I knew nothing about politics, and yet within a couple of months I had joined the Communist Party. It was by happenstance rather than by design. That was the first year the university opened a new building for the Philosophy and Letters students, the monumental sixteenth-

---

4   The ancient town of Baeza is located about 48 km northeast of the provincial capital of Jaen in Andalucia. It borders on the east with the municipality of Úbeda, with which it shares the capital of the historic Comarca de La Loma. In 1960 the total population was 15,461, decreasing slightly to 14,834 in 1970. The rich history and monumental Renaissance architecture led UNESCO to declare it a World Heritage site in 2003. Today it hosts one of the headquarters of the International University of Andalusia.
5   Traditional way local *granadinos* refer to their city. Accentuating the middle syllable and dropping the last one in the manner of the Andalucian dialect: Graná(da).

century Hospital Real by the Triunfo Gardens. Magnificent! There were so many people and obviously most of us were women, as you know. The SDEUG had been established a year earlier in 1968,[6] and there were delegate elections in different classes. I could not believe only guys were nominated in a class where women were the majority, so I instinctively volunteered to be a delegate. Obviously, the candidates were all members of political organizations, mainly the PCE.[7] And in January 1969 there had been a State of Emergency that led to several arrests among them.[8] But I just jumped to the front, a total unknown. I suddenly was terrified, con-

---

[6] In October 1967, delegates from the universities of Barcelona, Madrid, Oviedo, Santiago, Seville, Valencia, Valladolid, Zaragoza, Bilbao, and Málaga met in Madrid, and in the academic year 1967-1968 democratic student unions were created in most of the universities. Two factors were definitive for their short existence, although in different ways: the repression and the radicalization of a part of the student militancy.

[7] As Carme Molinero and Pere Ysàs point out: "At the universities in the mid-sixties students' representatives in the SEU were chosen by the students themselves. This situation allowed them to call assemblies to deal with certain academic or cultural issues, where it could be disguised as formally 'of the SEU.' For other matters (meaning political matters), the assemblies were held outside the official channels. By 1965 these other assemblies were already more and more frequent than the meetings of the Falangist SEU, particularly in the case of Barcelona. The agenda included: first, students' self-organization outside the SEU; second, solidarity with social sectors the dictatorship repressed; and third, the configuration of alternative university and culture to Franco's university and culture. This third aspect included the organization of cultural (or political-cultural) activities that clashed with the strict censorship imposed by the regime. The communist militants played a fundamental role between 1965 and 1966 culminating in the process of student rejection of the Franco regime that began in 1956. The PCE called its university militants to try to advance in the process of self-organization that it presented as parallel to the push of Workers' Commissions. Aware of the different conditions of the various university districts, the call was to promote the elections, although adapting to local circumstances. In some university districts free elections could be called, which would serve to consolidate the structures of the Student Democratic Union (SDEUG, Sindicato Democrático de Estudiantes, UG stands for University of Granada); in most cases, it would only be possible to present candidates in the official elections to win spaces of action." Pere Ysàs Solanes and Carme Molinero, *De la hegemonía a la autodestrucción: El Partido Comunista de España (1956-1982)* (Barcelona: Editorial Crítica, 2017), loc. 879 of 10995, Kindle.

[8] According to Carme Molinero and Pere Ysàs, "[t]he repressive threat was effective, and many opponents fled their homes. The classified information kept in the Ministry of Information and Tourism indicates that on March 18, 1969, after successive police operations, 735 people were detained or under house arrest, of which 315 were students and 420 had other professions. Of the 735, there appeared as 'domiciled' 159, while of the rest, 196 were at the disposal of the military authority, 212 of the civil jurisdiction, and 168 of the governmental authority. The most affected organization was the Communist party and, particularly, the PSUC (The Partit Socialista Unificat de Catalunya or Socialist Unified Party of Catalonia). More than seventy militants were arrested, and fifty others had to leave work and home. [...] The militant overexertion had to be very important. To gauge what the term 'overexertion' could mean, it must be borne in mind that a large part of the communist force depended on the character and fortitude of the base: men and women with a deep sense of personal sacrifice materialized

scious of my move, having to prepare a little speech for my classmates. I was saying to myself, "What do I say now?" I came up with some sort of spiel on the value of cultural matters or something like that. Surprisingly, I was elected by my fellow women in the classroom. Then and there the PCE came to recruit me, and before the end of the academic year I had joined them.

I did not know a thing about Marxism. Everything I learned about it, I learned inside the Party. I remember that time with great affection. We owe the Communist militants all the gratitude in the world because they devoted their lives to change the course of our nation. They convinced me of the worthy cause in which I was embarking. Along with the Christians in FECUN, the PCE carried the resistance[9] in the university and led the collaboration with the labor movement. I realize now how hard the collaboration with FECUN was, but at the same time we all found ways to overcome those differences.

The most stimulating aspect of my militancy was the high-level theoretical discourse that sustained our political action. I admired Socorro and Jesús, as well as Joaquín, who taught me so much in the Party seminars. In those seminars we discussed policy and strategies as well as texts by Marx, Lenin, etc. All these activities were prohibited, of course, and kept secret through a network of contacts that linked the various cells.[10] It was in hindsight comical but

---

in the form of renunciation in their professional career, in private life, and personal freedom in the form of years of imprisonment. Their militancy completely conditioned their life, becoming the axis of their existence. Until the 1970s, underground activism forced militants to a double life, as only those closest to them (and not always those) knew of their militancy. Fear was their most intimate companion and, almost from the moment of entering the party, that individual had to prepare psychologically for detention. In addition, repression had more consequences than the detention and torture of the militants on the one hand, and the need to rebuild the collective organization on the other. It affected the self-esteem of the militants. When there was a 'fall,' the control system of the situation on the part of management was based on analyzing who had been the first detainee and what had been disclosed; from here the 'responsibilities' were refined. This meant placing all 'responsibility' on the detainees themselves." Ysàs Solanes and Molinero, *De la hegemonía a la autodestrucción*, loc. 1307 of 10995, 1321 of 10995, 1335 of 10995, Kindle.

9   Carme Molinero and Pere Ysàs Solanes point out that in the mid-sixties, the communist militants were the axis of the student movement focused on the goal of self-organization. Students formulated clear objectives of alternative learning spaces to the Francoist university while developing a method of action that was supported by concrete demands and by the full involvement of students in the organization, but that design, while appropriate and adapted in the working world, was not able to take hold and expand in the university context. Fundamentally, the university was a very specific framework that was easily isolated from the general context, where the student movement had managed to put an end to the APE before they were born. Ysàs Solanes and Molinero, *De la hegemonía a la autodestrucción*, loc. 1014 of 10995, Kindle.

10 In his memoirs *Autobiografía de Federico Sánchez*, Jorge Semprún characterized as problematic and ineffective the PCE system of contacts in the clandestine operations inside Spain. Federico Sánchez was one of Semprún's clandestine aliases during his communist militancy. This

necessary for our safety. We Communists were a relatively small group, but at the same time, we had a large impact on the University, mainly due to the reluctance of other groups to step up and oppose the regime. Our organization was very hierarchical, authoritarian really. I myself was rather undemocratic, even harsh, when I was in charge of a cell, but at the time it had to be that way.

I did not have a record, but Berta turned me in. I don't blame her. There were others who were rats, and nothing came of their disloyalties. Many things went wrong. We got careless. Many times, we would continue our secret meetings over a beer in a bar, even though we weren't

---

work is Semprún's bitter criticism of the PCE after his expulsion, along with Fernando Claudín, in 1964 upon disagreements with Santiago Carrillo and the older generation of Communists (those who fought during the Spanish Civil War), who he characterized as having authoritarian and personalist (read Stalinist) tendencies. In March 1960, Semprún published an essay in the Party's journal *Nuestra Bandera* about his concerns regarding the clandestine methods and the so-called "contacts system": "In recent years, the most widespread method of organization and direction has been the one that you will allow me to define now as a *contact system*. Around a small group of leading comrades, many of whom, if not all of them, were obliged to carry out their work in conditions of the most rigorous secrecy, a whole network of individual contacts was established, with comrades of such and such a company, of this or that neighborhood, of that town, of that village. This network of contacts forced the communist leaders to maintain a real chain of appointments and interviews. [...] The drawbacks and negative features of this *contact system* do not seem to be difficult to point out. It is evocative that in a contact, deep political problems cannot seriously be discussed. Things are limited to a mere exchange of information and opinions, to a simple transmission of general orientations, and precisely because of this, abstract information most of the time. In the second place, the *system of contacts* constitutes, independently of the will of the comrades, a brake on the development of the organization and on the elevation of the political level. And this is due to several reasons. Because it hinders the incorporation to the Party of the revolutionary worker youth, of the young unorganized communists that today are counted by dozens in our country. Because the contacts are established logically, with the comrades already known, who are usually those with a police record, who have been in jail, which objectively and subjectively restricts their mobility, their capacity to accelerate the massive entry into the party of the new revolutionary forces. Because the *contact system* also divides the real possibilities of action of the base organizations, it is not rare the cases in which we have had in a certain company, or in a certain place, a half dozen contacts, even more, which means that we do not have a real organization. And above all, because the *contact system* makes the political life of the party groups precarious, both in the aspect of political discussion and the elaboration of concrete issues and in the continuity of the work. The *system of contacts* does not stimulate the initiative of the comrades of the grassroots organizations, of the leading business or local cadres; it hinders the essential vivifying current, that must occur from the bottom up in the Party; it makes this current almost always one-sided: to a contact one usually goes with the spirit of informing and knowing that 'the comrade' is bringing from 'above;' now, this comrade from 'above,' however capable, can only bring general orientations, possibly abstract, because he does not know the concrete issues, because he does not dominate them." Jorge Semprún, *Autobiografía de Federico Sánchez* (Barcelona: Editorial Planeta, 1977), 190-92.

supposed to fraternize in public. Ours was not a very well-kept secret! And so, I think there was a certain level of negligence or complacency on our part...mistakes we paid for dearly. For me, personally, the worst experience that fall happened in the police precinct. I pretended I knew nothing for as long as I could endure. You know how they approach women, right? We are whores to start off with. Then they are screaming in your ear how worthless you are. I was only seventeen, my life had just begun. It was in the precinct that my biological condition as a woman became a source of humiliation at the hands of the police. Because of the panic, I got my period. Bleeding down my legs in the cell of the precinct added another layer of vulnerability and a blow to my dignity, as I had to ask the guards for a pad. The latrines were revoltingly filthy. Of course, our male comrades did not know the half of it. An annoyance, a pest, a girl in jail. Precisely in those moments, your body turns into another enemy. But then, in spite of it all, I took advantage of the fact that they did not know me, so I played dumb. A girl in jail, a pest, an annoyance. Playing dumb turned into my weapon of choice. I saw others carried out of the interrogation and into the cell, bleeding from the beatings as I bled too, from my period, as if my body, my entrails, had already been crushed by an invisible torturer.[11]

11   The brutal police treatment in the precinct of Los Lobos did not discriminate between men and women. The repression against women students intensified between 1972 and 1977. One of the most dramatic incidents took place in the precinct in 1975 and involved Carmen, two years younger than Julia and a member of the Communist Party, like the latter. Carmen became head of the Philosophy and Letter's College party's cell and soon after became part of the executive provincial committee. Her marked activism placed her on the police most wanted list. And so, in a campaign to encourage participation in the student elections and after placing a poster in the Royal Hospital with another comrade, Encarnación, they were arrested on Santa Bárbara street at 9 o'clock in the morning on November 13, 1975 (only a week later Franco was dead). "We were walking down towards Sciences' College keeping on the left of the sidewalk away from the street traffic when suddenly some individuals got out of a car and identified themselves as policemen and told us we were arrested. From there, without further explanation, they took us to Duquesa Street, two of them behind and two others in front of us." Once they arrived at the precinct in Plaza de los Lobos, they were booked and taken to their respective homes, where, before their parents and a couple of neighbors as witnesses, the police searched their homes but did not find or take anything. After the search they returned to the police station to give their statement. During their interrogation, a policeman put a gun to Carmen's temple and threatened to go after her father. Under the newly approved Antiterrorist law, Carmen feared the possibility of ten days of solitary confinement and new violent interrogations. Such grim prospects led her to hurt herself by violently hitting her head several times against the stone bench in her solitary cell. She immediately started convulsing and lost consciousness. First, they took her in a police car rather than an ambulance to the Hospital of San Juan de Dios, where the doctor on duty refused to treat her. In the same car, they then drove her to the Psychiatric Hospital where she was admitted and treated. The following day, Judge Terrón met with a court clerk and a forensic doctor to take a statement and informed her that she was accused of illicit association and distribution of illegal propaganda. Meanwhile, the students placed a poster denouncing her situation which was promptly removed by the authorities, as it stated that "on Saturday, the 15th, she was admitted to the Psychiatric Hospital, victim of a nervous breakdown, the student of Stories,

As a member of the Communist party I was charged with illegal association and distribution of subversive propaganda. I accepted it, recognized my sins, confessed, "yes I was illegal!" to end it all. ENOUGH! On my transfer from the precinct to the trial court something unexpected, almost poignant happened. It snowed. That drew me back in time to a cherished childhood memory.

> Del cielo gris, en silencio, /From the gray sky, in silence,
> los copos de nieve bajan:/ snowflakes come down:
> son petalos de azucena, / Like lily petals,
> plumas de palomas blancas. / or feathers of white doves[12]

I remembered my winters in Segovia when the snow used to freeze the ground, and we did not go to school. The joy as we woke up in the morning and ran to get in bed with our parents. One of those divine memories from my childhood. I loved the snow, even more in Granada where it was so rare. But somehow something wonderful happened in the midst of this particular 1970 ugly Christmas season. I said to myself with an ironic smile, "Is this for real? Now that it starts snowing, they decide to lock me up!" The first snowfall since we moved to Granada, nine winters waiting for it and when it came, I was inside the police van.

Jarring as was my entry into prison, it turned into a forced gynaecium for the next four months. The very few women—five, maybe six, political prisoners—already were sitting around what every sitting room in every Spanish home has in winter: a warm round table we call "mesa Camilla" with its brazier underneath the table and its flowing skirt covering the legs of the women. That was New Year's Eve. On this occasion, the five or six prisoners, along with the women guards, were enjoying some shrimp.

We had certain advantages over the common inmates, mostly whores and petty thieves. I remember one of the guards with special affection. She treated us with maternal interest. Berta, who had turned me in, was among the women. After a couple of days, Arantxa arrived as well, and the guards arranged a common space for us upstairs called the "brigade," where they gave us some bookshelves for our books and a small desk for studying...it was our own private space, our apartment of sorts! Only we were under lock and key and could not leave. We were able to write letters to our male comrades imprisoned on the other side of the facility. I remember the love letters between Arantxa and one of the guys. Our families brought us food, and we cooked and shared it with every inmate. Yes, definitely an experience I remember as not too traumatic, yet one that stays with you for the rest of your life. The psychological scars show

---

Carmen M., had enough bruises on her body to demonstrate the mistreatment received during 48 hours that she had remained in police custody." On November 26, 1975, she finally left the Psychiatric Hospital, released from police custody and receiving a general pardon after Franco's death. Entry record in GC 064098 of November 14, 1975, in AHGCG, File 1325 A, quoted in Martínez Foronda and Sánchez, *Mujeres en Granada*, 159-61.

12 Angela Figuera Aymerich, "Invierno," in *Obras Completas* (Madrid: Ediciones Hiperión, 1986), 432 [my translation].

up from time to time as a bad temper unexpectedly surfacing in the idleness of daily nothings. Things I never experienced before being imprisoned suddenly became regular occurrences. I never suffered from painful menstruation cycles before my arrest, but in jail every month I agonized in pain and started taking Buscapina.[13] *You think everything is fine but no, there is something within yourself and in my case, it was through my period that it manifested itself over and over again.*

My family suffered as well. They put up with it, my mother much better than my father. As an army officer, he had an especially hard time even though there were so many army families whose children had joined the anti-Francoist resistance. My parents considered the whole affair a youthful indiscretion. They believed I had been deceived into joining the wrong cause. As a result, when I was released and sent home, they tried to confine me to the house.

This led to a terrible fight. At one point I took a small suitcase and left. I told them, "Look, I've been locked up for months.... You're locking me up again? NO! This I will not stand.... You must change your attitude." They had to accept it. "I must be free, be able to go out, interact with people." I assured them no one had fooled me or forced me to think or act against my will, that my convictions guided my actions and not only that, I intended to remain a Communist and keep fighting.

In reality, it was not possible to go back to the way it was. For security reasons, the party ostracized those of us who were imprisoned. They knew the police were watching us. This helped me to assure my parents that I would not get into any more trouble. I made my parents see the absurdity of their qualms, made them see how I must be loyal to those very people I had been in jail with, while at the same time not be able to acknowledge my old comrades on the street. This was not only bizarre but also painful because they were more than friends to me. So, I confronted my parents that day in despair as I readied myself to leave the house. Our own home turned into a mini civil war, one that was being fought all over Spain between parents, who had long ago accepted their fate, and their children who did not. No, I did not surrender nor was I about to allow my parents to lock me up again. My five months imprisonment had been long enough.[14]

---

13 For more than fifty years Buscopan® has been used to treat abdominal spasms. It relaxes the contracted muscles of the digestive tract and relieves pain caused by spasms.

14 Julia's experience highlights the significance of space as an active entity in the repressive mechanisms of control and discipline, which extended beyond the prison walls to the everyday life under Franco. These repressive technologies are certainly mediated by the gender distinctions deployed by the regime as well. For more on the experience of women in the Francoist prisons see: Ricard Vinyes, *Irredentas* (Madrid: Temas de Hoy, 2009); M. Edurne Portela, "Writing (in) Prison: The Discourse of Confinement in Lidia Falcón's *En el infierno*" *Arizona Journal of Hispanic Cultural Studies* 11 (2007): 121-36; Carme Molinero and Margarida Sala, *Una inmensa prisión: Los campos de concentración y las prisiones durante la Guerra Civil y el Franquismo* (Barcelona: Crítica, 2003); Rodolfo Serrano, *Toda España era una carcel: Memoria de los presos del Franquismo* (Madrid: Aguilar, 2002); Tomasa Cuevas and Mary E. Gilles, *Prison of Women: Testimonies of War and Resistance in Spain, 1939-1975* (Albany: State University of New York Press, 1998); Janet Pérez and Genaro J. Pérez, "Prison Literature: Introduction," *Monographic Review/*

I won't lie to you. Those years of my youth were so precious to me. I do not mean to say that the next generation lacked political and social consciousness. However, I don't find my students today are willing to challenge me in the classroom. Since I became a professor in the ancient history department at the University of Granada, I have witnessed a wave of disinterest. When I lecture nobody raises a hand to question anything but only to ask me to repeat whatever I just said. They write and write, page after page, uncritically, and memorize and memorize like automatons. So different from my experience as a student when we organized the critical trials for the professors and questioned their content and the bibliographies they made available to us. Our Geography and History majors organized an assembly to discuss the purpose of the disciplines, and the meaning of history and how to create a critical inclusive understanding of human experience.[15] *The university has undergone a transformation, from being a space of contestation and critical thinking to just becoming a site of conformity and competition for grades. The social and political drive we had is not there in my students' reality.*

Revista Monográfica 11 (1995): 9-25; Ángel Suárez, *Libro blanco sobre las cárceles franquistas: 1939-1976* (Paris: Ruedo Iberico, 1976); Nancy Vosburg, "Prisons with/out Walls: Women's Prison Writings in Franco's Spain," *Monographic Review/Revista Monográfica* 11 (1995): 121-36; Lidia Falcón, *En el infierno: Ser mujer en las cárceles de España* (Barcelona: Ediciones de Feminismo, 1977); Eva Forest, *From a Spanish Jail* (New York: Penguin, 1975). Eva Forest and Lidia Falcón were involved in a bitter fight as the former implicated Falcón in the proceedings following the ETA terrorist attack in a cafeteria in the Calle del Cirreo in Madrid. Eva Forest managed to secure a number of hiding flats for ETA operatives from around 200 intellectuals like Falcón and artists in Madrid. Forest spent three years in prison and Lidia Falcón eight months. Both women wrote of their prison experience in testimonies.

15   The practice of critical trials was an extended tactic among the 1968 generation who appreciated the *Situationist International* language and strategies. As Gerd-Rainer Horn points out, "They began to create situations, brief moments in time and space, which pointed out to anyone willing to look and listen the absurdity of life as currently organized and the possibility of a radical shake-up, if only people were willing to jump out of their own shadows. 'So far philosophers and artists have only interpreted situations; the point now is to transform them. Since man is the product of situations he goes through, it is essential to create human situations.' And so, they did." Horn, *The Spirit of '68*, Kindle. *Situationist International* operatives were invested in the urban environment, seeking hidden meanings in the quotidian and producing poetic and artistic situations to induce a non-alienating environment they felt the cities created. There was a close collaboration between the leading figure of the Situationists, Guy Debord, and Henri Lefevbre. The shift towards a mostly political rather than artistic outlook caused some Situationist artists to distance themselves from the movement. Again, Horn explains: "This paradigm shift from cultural to political action engendered the increasing distance of several leading Situationist artists from the International's project, most notably Asger Jorn and Constant Nieuwenhuys. Their central role in the Situationist universe was taken over by Raoul Vaneigem instead, a student of the poetry of Lautreamont, introduced to Debord by their mutual acquaintance, the Marxist sociologist of everyday life and urban encounters, Henri Lefebvre." Horn, *The Spirit of '68*, loc. 246 of 4087, Kindle.

Chapter 6
Marga's Dos Orillas[1]

Time,
like a cartographer,
Heartbreaking
Charts
The painful journey.

If one could 'know' from outside
the beatings of the heart of such and such person (the speaker),
one would learn much of the exact meaning of his words.
Henri Lefebvre, *Rhythmanalysis: Space, Time and Everyday Life* (2004)

The cult of the Sacred Heart as we know it is based on a series of apparitions St. Margaret Mary Alacoque (1647–1690), a French nun from the Holy Mary Visitation Order, received in which Jesus offered her His heart and instructed her to spread the cult.[2] The first apparition took place on the Feast of St. John the Evangelist on December 27, 1673. The nun tells of her exchange with Jesus as follows:

> He said to me: 'My Divine Heart is so passionately inflamed with love for mankind, and for you in particular, that, not being able any longer to contain within itself the flames of its ardent charity, it must needs spread them abroad through your means, and manifest itself to men, that they may be enriched with its precious treasures which I unfold to you, and which contain the sanctifying and salutary graces that are necessary to hold them back from the abyss of ruin.'[3]

---

1 Marga, interview by author, Miami, August 4, 2010.
2 On the Cult of the Sacred Heart in France see: Raymond Jonas, *France and the Cult of the Sacred Heart: An Epic Tale for Modern Times* (Berkeley: The University of California Press, 2000).
3 "Devotion to the Sacred Heart of Jesus: Historical Origin," October 2, 2020. http://www.salvemariaregina.info/Reference/Sacred%20Heart.html.

Baptized in honor of St. Margaret Mary Alacoque, Marga, a professor of Early Modern Spanish History, knows the story well. Like her namesake saint, she spread the message of the heart in a life filled with love and charity for others. It is her giving spirit that marks her remarkable journey from one shore of the Atlantic to the other.

To Puerto Rico and Back (infancia y años formativos)

Marga was born on a cold January morning in Madrid in 1953. Her parents met in Madrid where her father, Tomás, a Puerto Rican, was studying medicine at the Universidad Complutense and her mother, Esperanza, was a secretary in the INI. Esperanza had grown up in Asturias, in a well-to-do family. Her grandfather had been the Consul of Brazil but fell into trouble with the Francoist authorities after issuing passports for those escaping the civil war.

After marrying, the couple spent the first decade of their marriage starting a family and moving them back and forth between Puerto Rico and Spain before finally settling in the coastal town of Almuñécar on the Costa Tropical in the province of Granada. With her parents estranged by this time, and her father back in Puerto Rico, Marga would make the province of Granada her permanent home.

Almuñécar was a sleepy fishing village that experienced an economic boom from sugar cane production in the 1950s. The first time Tomás and Esperanza visited the seaside town was in response to an invitation from some friends they had met in Madrid. That summer of 1952, early in her pregnancy with Marga, Esperanza packed her Jantzen bathing suit, anticipating some swimming in the Mediterranean. It did not take long before she noticed how the local men started to sit close by and stare. To the locals, a woman showing her thighs on the beach represented an immoral display. Back then women wore knee length skirts over their bathing suits. Esperanza always made a point to reminisce about the prudish mores of the town and how she had to comply with the swimming skirt herself.

By the 1960s, when Marga was coming of age, much had changed in the coastal town and in Spain itself. Gone were the bathing skirts, replaced by formfitting modern one-piece suits and even bikinis, worn by an invasion of northern European tourists lured to the coast by the regime's economic development initiatives. By encouraging the waves of tourism to splash upon its shores, Spain was also inadvertently allowing a more progressive view of women to roll across a new generation of young girls.

When it came time for Marga to enter middle school, her mother decided that more educational opportunities were available inland in the region's capital of Granada. Marga attended the Teresian Institute middle school, founded in 1911 by Father Pedro Poveda (1874-1936).[4] The Teresians were an all-female secular order created to train women as teachers and fulfill the ideal union between faith and knowledge.[5] The school was a good fit for the studious young girl who was already thinking about college. The Catholicism imparted in the Teresian school was deeply rooted in the Vatican Council II and led Marga to a better understanding of injustice. This was a theme that was to stay with her when she entered the Instituto Padre Manjón, a lay magnet high school under the purview of the University of Granada. Marga remembers the Instituto as the place where she became interested in leftist politics and feminism. She read Durkheim, Margaret Mead, Lucy Mair, Betty Friedan, Caro Baroja, the Informes FOESSA, and a new research journal, *Cuadernos Para el Diálogo*.[6] From her readings and discussions with like-minded students, her nascent curiosity about feminism was born, a curiosity that would lead to a lifelong passion for female justice and fairness.

When Marga entered college, she joined FECUM[7] because the Jesuits matched her political and social outlook at the time. FECUM was also a social network for the young students who became a close-knit group of friends. They went to the movies together, discussed the works of Julio Cortázar and Mario Vargas Llosa, hiked in the mountains, and shared many late nights discussing their futures. "We felt so alive," she reminisced. "We read a lot of Marxism. It was the theory that made sense to us because it explained so many things, lent coherence to many religious precepts we had internalized since childhood." Even though the goals of FECUM and the Communist party were aligned, the Communist party was more forceful in its stance against the regime's treatment of the poor and working class. Whereas the Catholic group was content with gradual, long-term change, the Communists wanted revolution. Marga, like many of the students, was being gradually pulled leftward. "Marxism put at our disposal the instruments to build a more just social order," she explained. "We read Lenin alongside Paulo Freire, Marcuse, and Wilhelm Reich. We demanded that our professors include these extracurricular readings in our classroom discussions."

Marga eventually joined the Communist party but did not abandon her friends in FECUM. Always the mediator, she was helpful in negotiations between the two

---

4   Canonized in 2003 by Pope John Paul II.
5   See Morcillo, *True Catholic Womanhood*.
6   *Cuadernos* was the first current affairs magazine of Spain established in October 1963 until 1978. Originally it was a Christian democratic publication that evolved to become center-left and later socialist. This publication, along with *Triunfo*, were the two political journals that advocated for democratic reforms during the transition to democracy.
7   Federación Española de Congregaciones Marianas Universitarias (Spanish Federation of University Marian Congregations) founded by the Jesuits in the 1960s. See Juan Carlos Sainz Martínez, "De FECUM a FECUN: Política y Religión entre los Congregantes Marianos (1965—1977)," *Política y Sociedad*, 22 (1996): 103-21.

groups. She had grown up partly in a democratic system, the United States territory of Puerto Rico, which gave her a perspective that many of her fellow students did not have. She understood especially how messy democratic systems were, and that absolutism was not something that worked in an open society.

Even though she was fighting for a better society for all, she felt that she had a special role to fight for the emancipation of women. Many of her male comrades felt that women's struggles were secondary and needed to be set aside for the good of the larger cause, the dissolution of the Franco regime. This underlying sexism in the movement led her to seek out other women in the party. Socorro and Amparo, women a couple of years older than Marga, were her heroes and role models. They had endured the worst of the government's repression and had shown that women could fight and endure every bit as well as men.

Transformative Journey of the Heart (abortion & feminism)

The women Marga admired had put aside many of their reservations about the male-dominated student movement in order to achieve the larger objective of transforming Spain into a more democratic nation. Once that goal was achieved, women like Marga, following in their wake, were not going to be as accommodating. Marga belonged to a new generation of young women faculty under contract to teach at the university. She and others were given low salaries and occupied the lowest rank of faculty at the university. They were expected to be satisfied that they had been given a seat at the academic table, while the men still sat at its head.

Despite the ongoing struggles, the early 1980s were promising years for women in many ways. The socialists won control of parliament in the 1982 election and quickly established the post of Secretary of Women (Instituto de la Mujer), appointing the feminist Carlota Bustelo to lead it. For the first time since the Second Republic, leftist women occupied positions of power in the Spanish government. More women than ever were filling seats in colleges and imagining careers that were previously blocked to them. Social mores were changing, reflected in the depiction of women in movies and television. The "Madrid Movida" (la Movida Madrileña) was in full bloom, and in 1986, Pedro Almodóvar's *Women on the Verge of a Nervous Breakdown* won the Academy Award Oscar for best foreign film.

Not every change after the transition was necessarily advantageous to women, even if advertised that way. The "destape" (literally meaning "uncovering") of women's bodies became a metaphor to discuss the opening of the political system and women's role in the new democracy. The wave of eroticism and sexual freedom that followed the transition was advertised as a liberation for women as well as men. Feminists like Marga, in hindsight, see it as often less liberating than promised.

The new narrative of sexual freedom, ironically, felt to many newly emancipated women like another form of subjugation. Being free to have sex without care or commitment might have fit the male fantasy of female liberation, but it presented a whole other host of other dilemmas for women. Sexual harassment by men, even men in the resistance movement, was allowed to flourish under the guise of sexual freedom. Now women were free to be harassed by both friend and foe with little of the protections built into the more conservative norms of earlier times. Reproductive issues also remained largely a female problem, with newly liberated men often using sexual liberation to avoid responsibility for their actions.

At the university, the men were not in a hurry to open up the academy to a more female-centered curriculum or pedagogy. They might have made radical changes to the curriculum in their view, but from a woman's perspective, it looked a lot like swapping out one group of male thinkers for another. Marga remarked, "Our male peers questioned the intellectual value of writing about gender issues, about women's experiences. When we would bring it up in meetings, they acted like we were throwing a tantrum. Sometimes they would deign to let us 'pretend' to be scholars, leaving them access to the plum professorships and administrative positions."

Marga's feminist consciousness did not suddenly emerge during the liberal 1980s but had been growing since she was a teenager. She remembers reading Betty Friedan's *The Feminine Mystique* (1963) and Simone de Beauvoir's *The Second Sex* (1949) in high school and becoming aware on an intellectual level of the different experiences women faced in society. She remembers being cognizant of the double standard for behavior when she got her first boyfriend. "My first real kiss was experienced while walking in the gardens of Los Mártires, where lovers used to stroll and steal caresses and kisses under the protection of trees and manicured shrubs," she remembered. Afterward, she was worried about her reputation and then became angry when she realized that women were the only ones who had to worry about their "reputation." "Men never faced the same scrutiny and were even looked up to for their sexual conquests," she remarked. Women in traditional Spanish culture were placed into two camps, whores and virgins. There was no middle ground to explore your sexuality as a woman in this bipolar world. Many women patiently endured years of long courtships before having sex, often awkward and painful, on their wedding night. Further, the regime's prohibition of birth control and abortion made sex seem more like a game of Russian Roulette than a consummation of desire. This virginal straitjacket might have been acceptable to earlier generations of Spanish women, but for a college-educated woman, raised on second-wave feminist writings and exposure to more liberal western European mores, this was untenable.

Being part of a self-identified coterie of feminists came with challenges for Marga and her colleagues. There were a series of unwritten codes to follow to fit into the mold of the "feminist." "We hid our bodies," Marga said, "learning to dress not so much to seduce but to please. We dressed and carried ourselves in a more stereotypically masculine way in order to be taken more seriously by the men." The women of Marga's generation also had much more agency in their relationships with men. "I could not understand how couples in Granada could last in courtships for seven, eight, or even ten years without having sex. I decided when and with whom to lose my virginity. I picked the guy and regarded the entire experience as a transactional act. I must say, it was a pretty disappointing experience as he was not very skilled. But I later had other relationships and enjoyed my sexuality completely, never considering it linked with marriage or love. I never thought that monogamy and exclusivity was essential for a relationship to last but rather open communication and commitment to not hurting each other." This type of thinking would have been reputational suicide for a woman under the regime but was widely becoming the norm in cosmopolitan Spain in the 1980s.

Marga's first true love was Lalo. She was already in her senior year of college, and he was a freshman, a free spirit with an artist's soul who was pursuing an Art History degree. She recruited him to join the Plataformas Universitarias de Estudiantes (University Student Platforms). Lalo and Marga were drawn to each other by their shared political activism. This led them to move in together in one of the poorer neighborhoods in Granada, El Polígono, where they could live and work to improve the conditions from the inside as true members of the neighborhood association. Even though they did not believe strongly in the institution of marriage, the practicality of it made sense to them. They would be married in 1980 only to separate eighteen months later. "We had had problems for a while because we had diametrically different life goals. We grew apart. I was more practical, needed to finish my dissertation, had to fight to find a space in the university and wanted to grow academically. Lalo was a bohemian spirit, disillusioned after he finished Art History, lost and not knowing where to go." Marga's deteriorating marriage led her to make another difficult decision. She became pregnant at a time when the relationship was past salvaging and decided to have an abortion.

Having access to safe and legal abortions was something that feminists throughout Europe and the United States had fought for since the beginning of the student movement. Abortion and birth control were essential to removing the biological handcuffs that had been restraining women. Birth control allowed women to uncouple sex from reproduction, and abortion gave them the power to decide their fate if they inadvertently got pregnant. If women were to have equal opportunities and some semblance of parity with men, both needed to be freely available. In Spain, abortion was still illegal when Marga made the decision to not carry her pregnancy to term. This meant that she, like many other Spanish women of her generation, had to go outside the country to have a safe and legal abortion.

Marga opened up about her experience: "I traveled to Holland and had an abortion: the most difficult decision of my life. I did not have the freedom to have or not to have children...to put it somehow in words...and to this day it hurts. My relationship with Lalo was finished, and I believed I could not raise a child alone nor was I willing to be a single mother. I was convinced. And later over the years some women my age had babies and I reconsidered it, but I came to the realization that I was not willing to have a child to fill the emotional void of not having a partner in my life. So, I have never regretted my decision, although it was extremely painful."

"That trip was devastating, painful, frightening. I went to Holland because the abortion providers were part of a feminist network, while in London it was just a business. I don't remember exactly who gave me the information, but there were channels like the feminist group around the bookstore Librería de Mujeres, and within the MC I also assisted in counseling some girls and on some occasions, colleagues. Having an abortion abroad was very expensive and only those with means could afford it. I paid 65,000 or 70,000 pts in 1981. That included a roundtrip flight, hotel, and the procedure. It was a little odyssey, you know. I always forget something when I travel. I left so sad because I had to go alone. I didn't have money to pay for someone to go along with me. Through the MC party I arranged to stay with a comrade in Madrid. This particular person was a wonderful guy who worked in a travel agency and found me a very affordable flight and hotel. He really helped and gave me a referral to a tour called 'Amsterdam en vaqueros' (Amsterdam in jeans), the best guided tour in the world, and also he recommended a *pensión* across from the Central Train Station that served the most wonderful breakfast. I did not speak a word of Dutch and only some broken English. When I arrived, I took a nap and then started unpacking when I realized I had forgotten the address of the abortion clinic. I called Lalo at his father's home and asked him to look for the address, but he could not find it. Disastrous! Back in the hotel I looked in the travel guidebook. Flipping through the pages I found a women's center in Amsterdam. I decided they might be able to help me, so I took a taxi there. I was so worried about spending too much money that when I entered the center, so upset, I could not explain what I needed to the receptionist. After a little while I was able to tell them in broken English what my circumstances were. It so happened that this Women's Center was part of the same network and was able to tell me the address where I had to go the next day. I took a train and a taxi because the clinic was very far from my hotel. They were excellent professionals and treated me so well. The nurse who assisted me spoke Spanish. She told me she was Catholic and felt it was important for women to have choices. I was supposed to be in the clinic only a few hours, but they kept me there longer to make sure that I was not hemorrhaging. After a time, they let me go. I cried disconsolately...I was profoundly distraught, so lonely. I will never forget it happened in early September, on Saturday the 11th. The morning after, I was bleeding heavily but got out of bed and went out on the street where

I ran into a rally led by Chilean exiles in remembrance of the ten-year anniversary of the Pinochet coup d'état. I joined the march and screamed with them against that aborted revolution of theirs that we from Spain had hoped would succeed. I felt enraged, bleeding inside and out and so profoundly defeated."

The experience of her failed marriage and subsequent abortion only strengthened Marga's resolve to fight for women's rights. She, like a lot of women of her generation, had been disappointed that the transition did not bring about the radical changes to women's lives that were promised. Access to birth control and abortion, taken for granted in most Western European countries, was still illegal in Spain in the early 1980s. Violence against women was commonplace. Discrimination and harassment in the job market was tolerated.

It was in this atmosphere that Marga brought together some graduate students in 1984-85 and established the Seminario de Estudios de la Mujer and later organized the First Symposium on Women's Studies at the University of Granada in 1987 with international keynote speakers such as economist Lourdes Benería from Cornell University and historian Paola Di Cori from the University of Urbino. It is because of what she had seen and experienced that Marga continued to fight for women's rights at the university and beyond.

Intermezzo:
In-visible: Aurora's Trinity

The Life of the Nomad is the Intermezzo[1]

Holy and blessed Three,
glorious Trinity,
Wisdom, Love, Might;
boundless as ocean's tide
rolling in fullest pride,
through the earth far and wide
let there be light.[2]

Figure 12: Hymn #466

---

1 Gilles Deleuze and Félix Guattari, *A Thousand Plateaus* (London: Bloomsbury, 2016), 443.
2 The New English Hymnal, Hymn # 466: "Thou, Whose Almighty Word," by John Marriott, 1813. https://hymnary.org/text/thou_whose_almighty_word.

This chapter serves as an intermezzo, or in-between space, to address the personal and autobiographical in pursuit of revelation. As has been expressed earlier, poetry, or rather a poetics of history, is the instrument I use in my analysis of oral histories rendered in the book's two parts. The first set of interviews examines space and the visible, while the second half explores time and the invisible. To illustrate the relation between the visible and the invisible, as well as space and time, I tell in this intermediate chapter the story of three generations of women, grandmother, mother, and daughter, using the metaphor of the Trinity to explain how we can construct a historical narrative centered on the Deleuzian "becoming" rather than the traditional historical "being." The fusion of time and space through the practice of oral history facilitates a representational shift in historicizing. Poetry is the language which makes intelligible the symbolism behind three generations of women and reveals an ontological conception of history informed by gender. This is the story of three Auroras, my grandmother, my mother, and me, respectively, characterized as "Wisdom, Love, and Might." We are an entangled triune, sharing our names but also the mystery of a sacrificial history of small renunciations driven, as Spanish philosopher María Zambrano proposed in her work, towards a poetic reason:

> And the most elemental human experience has revelation qualities, although it only reiterates what is often known. History and tradition need to be reborn, to reappear; which will happen more intensely in the personal history, without the need for it to be specially woven as the history of all.[3]

The result is historical meaning infused with a sort of religious transcendence, an agapeic historical narrative filled with the ultimate force of life, according to both Hannah Arendt and María Zambrano, the force of love and compassion. "For love," says Arendt, "although it is one of the rarest occurrences in human lives, indeed possesses an unequaled power of self-revelation. ...Love, by reason of its passion, destroys the in-between which relates us to and separates us from others."[4] While Zambrano reminds us that the connecting link between life and truth is love: "the love that bears his name, that prepares and leads life toward truth. The nature of that love is to become all the more impassioned because truth is all the most universal and unmoved, distant and pure."[5]

The language to unveil this ontological history, this becoming, employs metaphor and analogy best expressed in poetry (verse or prose). Metaphorical is the quality of scientific language as well. Metaphor from the Greek etymologically

---

3   María Zambrano, *Notas de un método* (Madrid: Tecnos, 2011), 66.
4   Hannah Arendt, *The Human Condition* (Chicago: The University of Chicago Press, 1998), 242.
5   Noël Valis and Carol Maier, *Two Confessions: María Zambrano and Rosa Chacel* (Albany: State University of New York Press, 2015), loc. 265 of 4386, Kindle.

means "to take further." Therefore, explains poet and philosopher Chantal Maillard, it is an instrument to reach beyond the literal form of language, allowing our mind to establish associations between two distinct realities for the purpose of explaining or developing new ideas and/or abstract arguments.[6] "It means that human reasoning," says Zambrano, "must embrace the movement and flow of history, and even when it seems unlikely doable, it must acquire a dynamic structure replacing thus the static structure in place until now."[7] Movement, rhythm, and music are all important for rendering faithfully the act of history. In *La creación por la metáfora: Introducción a la razón-poética*, Maillard explains how Zambrano establishes the foundations of a "relativist method." Such method only procures models rather than absolute truths.

I resort to metaphor to explain the in-visible history of the three Auroras of this story in order to illuminate a new historical insight from the practice of oral history, which I argue offers us a path to a history understood as becoming in Deleuzian terms. This approach affords us a more dynamic narrative structure such as Zambrano proposed and aspires to highlight relativism in method and outcome.

My argument is that oral history allows for the elaboration of a history as becoming because in the practice of the interviewing and subsequent writing and construction of life narratives, time and space collide in the act of remembrance. In the following pages I develop the argument in four parts. First, I explain the historical notion of history as becoming in light of Gilles Deleuze and Félix Guattari's work in *A Thousand Plateaus* (1987). Second, I focus on the notion of the in-visible as put forth by Maurice Merleau-Ponty in his posthumous work entitled *The Visible and the Invisible* (1968) to reach into the emotional fabric (or the sentient being, as Zambrano following Zubiri would call it) of historical unfolding while making the flesh (gender) its conduit. Third, I put in conversation two metaphors, the theological Holy Trinity and the quantum theory of entanglement, to escape, on the one hand, time linearity in traditional historical discourse, which privileges being over becoming and, on the other hand, spatial deterministic locality fragmentation resulting from notions of embodiment and its life to death temporal segmentations. Finally, I illustrate my argument with fragments, vignettes, memories of each Aurora utilizing the poetic form of Haibun as the medium to explore Zambrano's poetic reasoning to render an agapeic historical narrative.

---

6   Chantal Maillard, *La creación por la metáfora: Introducción a la razón poética* (Barcelona: Anthropos, 1992), 97-113. See also, George Lakoff and Mark Johnson, *Metaphors We Live By* (Chicago: University of Chicago Press, 2008).

7   María Zambrano, "La reforma del entendimiento español" (1937), quoted in Maillard, *La creación por la metáfora*, 157 n. 8.

1. History as Becoming

María Zambrano speaks of multiple temporalities in line with the Bergsonian conceptualization of the past not as a linear series of bygone events but rather a virtual whole. This conceptualization of the past as a virtual repository of multiple potentials and the present as one (of many possible) actualizations of such potentials is also developed further by Gilles Deleuze in *Difference and Repetition* and with Félix Guattari's *A Thousand Plateaus*. Eugene Holland explains how Deleuze developed a philosophical concept that "combined instinct (from Hume and Jung), *élan vital* (from Bergson) and will to power (from Nietzsche) with the insistence that the unconscious is accessible only in and through its contingent expression in historical institutions and archetypes."[8] For Deleuze, it is fundamental to privilege that fluid becoming rather than the fixed being. Becoming as creative repetition promotes difference rather than sameness as being and identity unfold. These notions are present in the relativist method that Zambrano proposes, rather than a static structure of being necessary to transverse temporalities across history and unveil the fluid repetitions leading to unknown realizations in the present after multiple permutations. This line of thought connects Zambrano's poetic reason with Deleuze's history as becoming, showing how profoundly liberating and fertile a line of enquiry it is because the outcome of creative differential repetition is always unknown, unpredictable. In *A Thousand Plateaus*, Deleuze and Guattari, following Bergson, propose the past as an "a-temporal bloc where each and every past event co-exists with all the others."[9] This virtual whole is the precondition for the realization of the present. Deleuze and Guattari explain how this understanding of the past as the potential of the realization of the present privileges their notion of history as becoming rather than being in time. They see being as only a momentary, subsidiary contraction of becoming while the latter is always fundamental. This means that everything **is its history** rather than everything has a history.

This view, Holland points out, aligns with contemporary science informed by non-linear mathematics and complexity theory. Things' present being is understood as a more or less temporary and unstable contraction of becoming(s). As Deleuze says, "Death is what never ceases and never finishes."[10] Life is manifest in historical stratification (generations) and death is only a stage in becoming, rather than a firm ending.

---

8   Eugene W. Holland, *Deleuze and Guattari's 'A Thaousand Plateaus': A Readers Guide* (London: Bloomsbury, 2013), loc. 150 of 3787, Kindle. This is an excellent guide to understanding Deleuze and Guattari's dense text.
9   Holland, *Deleuze and Guattari's*, loc. 346 of 3787, Kindle.
10 Gilles Deleuze and Félix Guattari, *Anti-Oedipus* (London: Athlone, 1983), 330, quoted in Russell West-Pavlov, *Temporalities* (London: Routledge, 2013), 51.

For María Zambrano, time and being construct and sustain each other. She distinguishes a variety of temporalities: succession, duration, and a-temporality, which correspond with three different activities: vigil (succession), sleep (duration), and dreaming (a-temporality).[11] Time for Zambrano is a mixed reality, primarily a felt reality which intersects the biological and the emotive states. The most basic form of temporality for her is duration. For duration to exist it must suffer interruptions, so we can inhabit time. For her, Pythagorean philosophy numbers in conjunction with their musical expression provided the means to interrupt the primal time continuum into measurable and habitable extensions: "The simple feeling of time is hellish. The number reduces it, rationalizes it. When we are prisoners of the feeling of time, counting is a placating activity, a kind of rite. The horror of time is placated first by monotony. The time simply numbered is the first victory over Cronos, over the primary time that does not account for rendering any explanations."[12] The narration or counting of the three generations of Aurora(s) is understood as habitable extensions of the perpetual becoming.

2. The Visible and the Invisible

Through the act of remembering we engage with a metaphysical exploration of Being in the world, which is nothing more than the engagement between the visible and the invisible. It is important to define the visible and the invisible argument, which informs this book's structure. Maurice Merleau-Ponty's unfinished and posthumously published work entitled *The Visible and the Invisible* (1968) allows me to articulate the important crux upon which I build my analysis of a creative ontological gendered history, a history which is more about becoming than about factual linearities.

For Merleau-Ponty, the visible contains the invisible and vice versa:

> When I say that every visible is invisible, that perception is imperception, that consciousness has a *punctum caecum*, that to see is always to see more than one sees—this must not be understood in the sense of contradiction—it must not be imagined that I add to the visible perfectly defined as in Itself a non-visible

---

11 Gabriel Astey, "La forma de la temporalidad," in *Nacer desde el sueño: Fenomenología del onirismo en el pensamiento de María Zambrano* (Oxford: Peter Lang, 2017), 5-29.

12 "El simple sentir del tiempo es infernal. El número lo reduce, lo racionaliza, Cuando estamos presos del sentir del tiempo, contar es una actividad aplacadora, una especie de rito. El horror del tiempo se placa primeramente por la monotonía. El tiempo simplemente numerado es la primera Victoria sobre Cronos, el tiempo primario que no da cuentas ni razones." María Zambrano, "La condenación aristotélica de los pitagóricos" (1955), quoted in Astey, *Nacer desde el sueño*, 8.

(which would be only objective absence) that is objective presence elsewhere, in an elsewhere in Itself. *One needs to understand that it is the visibility itself that involves a non-visibility* [my emphasis].[13]

For Merleau-Ponty, the world is a "system of equivalencies" and not a collection of spatio-temporal individuals. The story that follows intends to be read in this light. Each of the three women represent an equivalency in a "system of equivalencies," a unity in multiplicity with an inner logic that does not follow the Cartesian path but rather is predicated on a philosophy of intuition, interrogation, and at the end, revelation. Revelation sparks in the blindness point [punctum caecum] of the consciousness. "What it does not see," says Merleau-Ponty, "is what makes it see, it is tied to Being, it is corporeity. The existentialities by which the world becomes visible is the flesh wherein the object is born."[14] Disoriented consciousness grasps the indirect. The inverted, what Merleau-Ponty calls "the Being of the far offs," is usually ignored or non-visible. "The Being of the far offs" is also our being in a vertical (rather than horizontal) temporal arrangement, which in this narrative constitutes the Trinity of the three generations of women.

This means an understanding of history as becoming.[15] This new historical approach is possible through the interviewing process in oral history, which reveals the *in*-visible sentient Being. I embrace Merleau-Ponty's explanation: "What I [Merleau-Ponty] want to do is to restore the world as a meaning of Being absolutely different from the 'represented' that is, as the vertical Being which none of the 'representations' exhaust and which all reach the wild [meaning natural] Being. This is to be applied not only to the perception, but to the universe of the predicative truths and significations as well."[16] The predicative truth at hand in this study is patriarchy and the different generations of women's invisible transgressions of the customary social practices. Moreover, Merleau-Ponty highlights how the distinction between cultural and natural is abstract as everything is both cultural and natural in us (such as gendered roles) and our perception of those two planes is culturally and historically determined:

> Being is the "place" where the "modes of consciousness" are inscribed as structurations [sic] of Being (a way of thinking of oneself within a society is implied

---

13   Maurice Merleau-Ponty, *The Visible and the Invisible* (Evanston: Northwestern University Press, 1968), 247.
14   "The experience I have of myself perceiving does not go beyond a sort of imminence, it terminates in the invisible, simply this invisible, i.e., the reverse of its specular perception, of the concrete vision I have of my body in the mirror." Merleau-Ponty, *The Visible and the Invisible*, 248-49.
15   Deleuze and Guattari, *A Thousand Plateaus*.
16   Merleau-Ponty, *The Visible and the Invisible*, 253.

in its social structure) and where the structurations of Being are modes of consciousness. ...The perception of the world is formed in the world, the test for truth takes place in Being.[17]

Therefore, the writing of history will be of a history understood as "immanent geology" in which time and space collide—"this very time that is space, this very space that is time."[18]

The three generations rendered here represent an attempt to demonstrate the "immanent geology" which turns into a historical landscape, a cartography of becoming, which reveals the sedimentations of each generation and a reactivation of the vertical temporal system of equivalencies rather than separate experiences with a beginning (birth) and an end (death). This continuity follows the understanding of the mind-flesh relation. Merleau-Ponty defines mind "as the other side of the body." He points out, "We have no idea of a mind that would not be doubled with a body."[19] He explains there is a "body of the mind and a mind of the body." Rather than understanding those as separate entities, the other side is understood as depth, dimensionality, that is, not that of extension, and a transcendence of the negative toward the sensible. It resonates with the quantum entanglement notion of non-locality. The relation of the three generations reveals a sort of historical "spooky action at a distance."[20]

3. Entanglement Theory as Metaphor: Aurora's Trinity

What is number? Number may be defined in general as a collection of units, or, speaking more exactly, *as the synthesis of the one and the many*.[21]

Number. Trinity. Mystery. I present here the three Auroras' continuity through the metaphor of the Holy Trinity, a narrative of difference and repetition of "three individualities but one unity," to unveil the invisible in the visible. A loving legacy of empowerment and self-determination is built upon the multiple acts of renunciation and words of encouragement and the gift of love passed from one generation to the next. This is a triune generational story, which intends to deploy María

---

17 Merleau-Ponty, *The Visible and the Invisible*, 253.
18 Merleau-Ponty, *The Visible and the Invisible*, 258.
19 Merleau-Ponty, *The Visible and the Invisible*, 259.
20 George Musser, *Spooky Action at a Distance: The Phenomenon that Reimagines Space and Time-- and What It Means for Black Holes, The Big Bang, and Theories of Everything* (New York: Scientific American/Farrar, Straus and Giroux, 2015).
21 Henri Bergson, *Time and Free Will: An Essay on the Immediate Data of Consciousness* (New York: Dover Publications, INC., 2001), 75 [my emphasis in italics].

Zambrano's sacrificial agapeic history and poetic reason through non-fictional creative language.[22] It follows Zambrano's intuition methodology facilitated through remembrance, metaphorical evocation, and unexpected disclosure of self-renunciations.

Why Trinity as metaphor? First, because it is illustrative of an understanding of history as becoming as it deals with concepts that encompass the notions of the one and the many, the visible and the invisible, and the entanglement of the different personas through vertical time. Second, it is a useful metaphor to explore the multiplicity of temporalities discussed above—time as a virtual whole in which all the potentialities of becoming co-exist and provide latent multiple outcomes in the present. And finally, the metaphor resonates with María Zambrano's poetic reason and pursuit of the auroral origin. She points out how a philosophy informed by poetic reason is the path to follow beyond pre-established historical periodization(s):

> If philosophy exists as something characteristic of man, it must be able to cross historical distances, it must be able to travel through history; and even above it, in a sort of supra-temporality, without which, otherwise, the human being would not be one, neither in Him/herself ... nor in the unity of their kind.[23]

Zambrano proposes to reach into the revelation of all forgotten and invisible past experiences through the path of love, to theology and the mystical poetry of Saint John of the Cross: "Saint John of the Cross's poetry shows the fertile approach possible only through the love."[24] It is the manifestation of the love of life and its intrinsic mystery as Zambrano exposes it in her essay, "For a History of Mercy," impossible to grasp through only conventional rationalism:

> Won't there be, away from distinct and clear knowledge, the necessity of other knowledge that is less distinct and clear, but equally indispensable? *Aren't there things and relationships so subtle, hidden and indiscernible that they can only be apprehended by feeling or intuition?* Will we be able to dispense with inspiration? In sum, let's say the dreaded word that we have been concealing so far. *Will it not be a bedrock of mystery supporting everything that is clear and visible, everything that can be enumerated?*[25]

---

22 See María Zambrano, *Persona y democracia: La historia sacrificial* (Madrid: Anthropos, 1988); María Zambrano, "Para una historia de la Piedad," in *Aurora: Papeles del "Seminario de María Zambrano"* (2012): 64-72. https://www.raco.cat/index.php/Aurora/issue/view/19528/showToc.
23 Zambrano, *Notas de un método*, 66.
24 Zambrano, *Notas de un método*, 67.
25 María Zambrano, "Para una historia de la piedad," in *The Modern Spain Sourcebook: A Cultural History from 1600 to the Present*, ed. Aurora G. Morcillo et al. (London: Bloomsbury Press, 2018), 40.

Therefore, to reach into the past experiences of anonymous women in Francoism through their memories is to set out on an excavation into their feelings as they reveal their acts of renunciation.

As Ernest L. Simmons[26] demonstrates, the Holy Trinity shares much with entanglement theory and non-locality. He constructs a new theological understanding of the Trinity through the Trinity as metaphor in conjunction with quantum entanglement and superposition. As he points out, "Entanglement is simply another way of addressing the fact that physical reality is interconnected at the deepest levels."[27] The two aspects in common between quantum systems[28] and the Trinity include: nonlocal relational holism (entanglement) and complementarity (superposition). According to holism, the part derives from the whole and the whole is more than the sum of its parts; everything is interconnected in the subatomic level: "together in separation."[29] Once a pair of particles or a divided one are entangled, they remain connected no matter where in the universe they go. There is a certain "veiled reality"[30] inaccessible (mysterious in Zambrano's terms or invisible in Merleau-Ponty's) to human understanding. Metaphor and analogy provide us the means to reach into the inaccessible. The appropriation of metaphorical concepts in quantum mechanics, side by side with Trinity, allows us here in this study to test a historicizing focused on Becoming rather than Being. Simmons explains how science and theology "struggle with the problem of reconciling unity with diversity."[31] In examining the narratives resulting from the oral histories, I also need to explain

---

26   Ernest L. Simmons, *The Entangled Trinity: Quantum Physics and Theology* (Minneapolis, MN: Augsburg Fortress, Publishers, 2014). See also: John Polkinghorne, *Quantum Theory: A Very Short Introduction* (Oxford: OUP, 2002); Kirk Wegter-McNelly, *The Entangled God: Divine Relationality and Quantum Physics* (London: Routledge, 2011); F. LeRon Shults and Lindsay Powell-Jones, eds., *Deleuze and the Schizoanalysis of Religion (Schizoanalytic Applications)* (London: Bloomsbury, 2016).
27   Simmons, *The Entangled Trinity*, 145.
28   "Quantum mechanics is the name given to the field of physics that studies the very small: the forces and structures below the atomic level. Quantum comes from the work of Max Planck who very early hypothesized that energy does not exist in an incremental continuum but rather exists in packets, which he named 'quanta' to indicate discrete energy levels rather than continuum. It all began with the discovery of the dual nature of light as both wave and particle, what is now known as 'wave-particle duality...The term mechanics is inherited from Newton and refers to the regular nature of rationally discernible and mathematically expressible physical processes.'" Simmons, *The Entangled Trinity*, 130.
29   Simmons explains how non-lineal relativity has been proven by scientists like Anton Zeilinger at the University of Vienna which carries with it some form of "action at a distance" or connectedness (entanglement). Simmons, *The Entangled Trinity*, 148.
30   Philosopher and physicist Bernard d'Espagnat's terminology. Simmons, *The Entangled Trinity*, 140.
31   Simmons, *The Entangled Trinity*, 141.

the intersection of individuality with generational connections. The Trinity's concept of perichoresis is key to sorting out the connection in separation I am after. Perichoresis is the Greek word that describes the inner relationship in the Trinity: three persons but only one substance. It could be translated as "indwelling." The three indwell with one another and yet are distinct from each other. The triquetra image that represents this concept is like a "trifold Möbius strip" in the words of Simmons. So, the three persons of the Trinity flow in and out of one another in a continuous dynamic energy exchange of Becoming.³²

Figure 13: Trifold Mobius Strip

There is an affinity between Deleuze's concept of difference as life and the Christian doctrine of the Holy Trinity. Both Deleuzian difference and the Trinity are propelled by perpetual movement, a "creative force" (potentia). This turns the divine absolute (God in the Trinity) into life as pure dynamism, which, in the words of Christopher Ben Simpson, "is the affirmative force or power of repetition and differentiation."³³ Life manifests itself in individuals. Life is the invisible virtual force incarnating ceaselessly in infinite visible forms. Simpson points out how "Deleuze's axiomatic decision to think difference," in this light, "is a decision for that which is invisible, imperceptible, immensurable, and not thinkable."³⁴ The autogenic power springs from the dark bottomless (unground) chaos, the *infernos* (suffering and renunciation) in María Zambrano's thought. Only by accepting the mystery of eternal return may we unravel the movement of becoming.

---

32 Simmons, *The Entangled Trinity*, 151.
33 Christopher Ben Simpson, "Divine Life: Difference, Becoming and the Trinity," in Shults and Powell-Jones, eds. *Deleuze and the Schizoanalysis of Religion*, 62.
34 Shults and Powell-Jones, eds., *Deleuze and the Schizoanalysis of Religion*, 64.

4. Aurora's Trinity: Wisdom, Love, Might

Emotional dimension, being invisible, finds materialization in the poetic word and in the rhythm of life beyond one single generation.[35] The authentic being is uncovered in my text through the elaboration of short poems based on the anecdotes the informant (my mother) highlighted through the story.[36] Aurora, my given name, is the heirloom passed down from my grandmother to my mother. It is the poetic word that has given me, just by poetic luck, the opportunity to illuminate my self-introspection and my historical writing.

Aurora's Wisdom

Wisdom, Love, Might;
endless as an ocean's tide

Memory Alfacar, 1942

My mother was born on July 5, 1933, in the village of Alfacar, just outside of Granada, known to outsiders as the place where Federico García Lorca was executed. She inherited her name from her mother, as was custom. I am called Aurora too. That is the precious heirloom I received at birth. The story of many Spanish women in the twentieth century can be told through the lives of these three generations of Auroras. My grandmother, Aurora Sánchez Jiménez, was illiterate. My mother, Aurora Gómez Sánchez, went to school until she was nine years old, when she was diagnosed with a pleural mass. The antidote, milk, was something my grandparents could not provide in the midst of the postwar hunger years. The solution was to send her to work at a milkman's house to take care of an infant in exchange for the life-giving white elixir.

More than the war itself, I remember the postwar. Because I am the youngest, I can only remember the misery that came after the fighting was over. It was a very difficult childhood, one with many needs but few satisfactions...of having to go to work before I was grown up.

She was tiny when she went to work, a small child with stick-thin legs doing women's work. They dressed her in a smock that hung about her knees and gave her an unsteady stool to stand on so that she could reach the laundry sink. The milkman and his wife weren't cruel, just indifferent. She wasn't their child, after all. Maybe it was the times, or maybe it was the tradition, but nobody said anything about a young girl forced to labor for her food. In Spain, this was no time for sentimentality. This was no time to be a child, either.

---

35 María Zambrano's line of thinking follows Spinoza, Saint Augustine, Pascal, or Nietzsche's "the heart reasoning;" see Ana Bundgaard, *Más allá de la filosofía* (Madrid: Trotta, 2000).

36 On the use of poetry in constructing oral history narratives see: Valerie J. Janesick, "Using Poetry in Oral History to Represent Someone's Story," in *Oral History for the Qualitative Researcher: Choreographing the Story* (New York: The Guildford Press, 2010), 129-33.

My mother proudly describes Alfacar as "a village rich with water...and very good bread" but in the same breath, as a village that could only provide for half its people.[37] *When I ask her to explain this, she says: "I mean that those who had a piece of land or had a shop could feed their families. But people like my father, a man with no land, no skills, and no shop, had to send his children away. My father was a peasant...who collected and brought dried sticks from the mountains to feed the bread ovens. Sometimes the Civil Guard, those who were supposed to protect people, would take the wood from him, leaving him with nothing for his day's work.... You can imagine how we grew up...my mother with six needy children and almost nothing for them to eat."*[38]

Her family lived at the edge of the village in a neglected collection of dwellings called "Las Canteras," where the poorest were segregated from the merely poor. My mother remembers a school for boys and girls which she briefly attended. "I did not have a book to read. At the one-room school there were some books, and the teacher would put us in a row of five or six to read aloud a line each, as he instructed. I had a small slate that broke if dropped and a little chalk, which would break if dropped as well. When I came home crying with the broken slate or chalk, my mother would scold me: 'now you have nothing, because I cannot buy you another one'...it is amazing that I can even speak properly."[39]

The daily routine in the classroom is vivid in her memory: "I studied in those books, did additions and subtractions on my slate and then erased them...then would do other exercises the teacher would tell us to do. ...He used to hit us a lot. On one occasion I remember he was teaching me with a stick on a map and a girl tapped me on my back. As I turned around to her, he came towards me and slapped me on the face...only for that. He wore two rings that left a mark on my face for days. My parents did not even bother to go find out what I had done and why he had slapped me. I don't know why...maybe it was fear...."[40]

Hunger, hunger
Hidden bread
Mother's offering
Blessing said

Aurora's Love

Wisdom, Love, Might;
rolling in fullest pride,

Memory, Granada 1972

---

37   Aurora Gómez, interview by author, 1994.
38   Aurora Gómez, interview by author, 1994.
39   Aurora Gómez, interview by author, 1994.
40   Aurora Gómez, interview by author, 1994.

I don´t know how to conjugate the subjunctive. Today, I also have my typing test. Don Vicente will blind me with his white handkerchief to see if I can type without looking at the keys. ASDFG lefties, ÑLKJH righties.

Father Miguel is standing at his usual spot at the top of the stairs overlooking the concrete soccer field. He knows the secret to decipher the subjunctive, even the pluscuamperfecto. I need to talk to him so he can help me. Presente de subjuntivo del verbo ser. Only ask yourself, ¿Que yo sea? And that is the secret question...the key that will unlock the conjugation.

Yo sea, tu seas, él sea, nosotros seamos, vosotros seáis, ellos sean.

¿Qué será? ¿Será? With don Vicente? With me...after all these years, my typing is good but I always look at the keys.

A girl's school uniform is not complete without the proper shoes. White shirt, dark blue jumper down to the knees where the edge of the skirt meets the edges of high socks, and then, the bulky black leather shoes. They have to be sturdy; they are your foundation to sustain and carry you through the day's ups and downs. Papa shined those shoes every night for the three of us. My younger brother and sister are my responsibility on our walk to school. I am the big sister, already nine years old. This morning we are running late. My shiny shoes are nowhere to be found. Mama remembers she forgot to pick them up from the shoe repair shop yesterday evening. Instead, I have to wear my white canvas tennis shoes, which belong with the gymnastics uniform, not this classroom one. Bad foundation to start the day. I know this is not a good beginning. I will have to be extra careful not to step in any mud or puddles on our walk to school.

Ay no! Mother Pilar is at the school entrance checking everyone's uniform.

I try to rush through the door unnoticed. Then, I hear her screechy voice pronouncing my name. With her right hand in the air, she motions for me to come closer.

When she looks at my feet, her face puckers in disgust.

¿Qué será, será? Forty years later, I find myself with a blue American passport and a closet full of shoes and a keyboard with no ñ.

Hunger, hunger
Hidden bread
Mother's offering
Blessing said

Aurora's Might

Wisdom, Love, Might;
through the earth far and wide
let there be light.

Memory, Alfacar, Granada 1937

Anda, Aurorilla, sube arriba que te he puesto un pedazo de pan debajo de mi colchón!

　The four-year-old runs up the stairs, mouth watering, to hunt for the piece of bread her mother has hidden carefully under the mattress. Hunger's invisible thumbs open her mouth wide, as wide as her beautiful dark eyes. Excitement, anticipation, and a cramping belly propel her feet up the stairs. High steps, one, two, three, she uses her hands too in the ascension to communion, into her parents' bedroom to collect a meager piece of black bread, waiting hidden under the matrimonial mattress, like a treasure, for her. Her mother knows how hard it is for her to eat at the family table. Six children to feed. Aurorilla is the baby. Everyone sits around a common pot and digs in during the last supper of the day. But the baby is too small to reach, and she always scalds her mouth. Her mother knows she is hungry all the time. The little piece of hidden bread is their secret. That bitter black bread is the token of love between them, a memory my mother has not forgotten to this day.

The Trinitarian metaphor is not static but rather perpetual motion in tune with Deleuze's eternal return, fueled by the agapeic historical representation proposed by María Zambrano. The motion in the triune metaphor nurtures a giving and receiving, the gift of life self-generating. Being transforms into water. Always water, whether solid, liquid, or evaporated.

　Lovingly, the grandmother tries to hold her granddaughter's tiny arm. The invisible **wisdom** of the photographer's eye behind the lens captures the **might** in the old woman's gesture supporting me. The recipient of their **love**.

Hunger, hunger
Hidden bread
Mother's offering
Blessing said
Transubstantiation
In the flesh

PART 2

Intro Part II
Time and Invisible Things: Working Class Narratives

A Klee painting named "Angelus Novus" shows an angel looking as though he is about to move away from something, he is fixedly contemplating. His eyes are staring, his mouth open, his wings are spread. This is how one pictures the Angel of History.
Walter Benjamin, "Theses on the Philosophy of History. IX"[1]

Figure 14: *Angelus Novus (Klee Painting)*

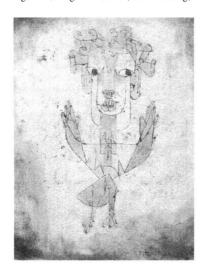

---

1   Benjamin, "Theses on the Philosophy of History: IX," 257.

Metaphors are conduits aiding us in capturing what proves elusive to analytical reasoning. Klee's "Angelus Novus" inspired Walter Benjamin's metaphor of the Angel of history, an image useful to reflect on the concept of "Angel of the Home"[2] enshrined in the Francoist rhetoric of domesticity. Working class women, however, redefined conventional notions of domesticity, of "Angel of the home," and turned into agents of their own destinies—"Angels of History a la Benjamin." A few of them raised me and, years later, sat with me intently in conversation as they contemplated and shared their lives' paths with renewed insights. Their stories told of constant adjustments to their shifting circumstances, of reinventing themselves in their invisible quotidian routines. In the process, these women turned into historical agents, "Angeli Novii," in my eyes.

Well aware of their condition as outsiders, they felt their life stories had little to contribute to the master historical narrative. We know near to nothing about them as they inhabit the dark side of history, what Unamuno called intra-history. Alessandro Portelli reminds us: "In the literary imagination of the industrial age, the shape of the working class is unknown, its place is darkness, its language silence—thus making the working class a sort of general signifier for all that is repressed, marginal, and unspoken in society. Identified with the passive inertia of tired bodies and minds, the working class can be only represented by negation, only be named where the text breaks down."[3]

Invisible in plain sight; hidden behind their daily routines and rituals, these ordinary individuals and their personal experiences lack historical density, shape, form, and yet constitute the indispensable substratum of the public official history, the visible side of our lives. Our collective being in time hangs heavy on the indispensable lightness of their non-being. "Every day includes much more non-being than being...," noted Virginia Woolf, "...a great part of everyday is not lived consciously. One walks, eats, sees things, deals with what has to be done; the broken vacuum cleaner; ordering dinner; ...washing; cooking dinner...."[4]

For those existing outside of history, the quotidian is suspended in a state of "non-being." Ostracized, their lives are invisible, suppressed, like quiet currents under still waters. Yet, such nondescript, unthinking *modus vivendi* is crucial to propel and sustain the grand public "being moments" of those others who lead in our master historical narratives. Certainly, here we are. Nourished, delivered, and

---

[2] María del Pilar Sinués y Marco, *El ángel del hogar: estudios morales acerca de la mujer* (Madrid: Imprenta Española Torija, 1862); Carmen Morán, "El ángel del hogar era una esclava," *El País* (June 13, 2012). https://www.catarata.org/media/catarata55/files/book-attachment-1586.pdf.

[3] Alessandro Portelli, *The Text and the Voice: Writing, Speaking, Democracy and American Literature* (New York: Columbia University Press, 1994), 243.

[4] Virginia Woolf, "A Sketch of the Past," in *Virginia Woolf Moments of Being: Unpublished Autobiographical Writings*, ed. Jeanne Schulkind (New York: Harcourt Brace & Company, 1985), 70.

saved in a chain of invisible non-being moments. Rhythmic heartbeats, breaths, words, and silences.

An arrhythmia makes dangerously evident the importance of the trivial forgettable healthy heartbeat. An asthmatic attack chokes us, gasping for air, for life, for refuge, for protection. Only with the protection of the invisible metronomes of life may we enjoy the privilege of being in time. Raoul Vaniegem pointed out in 1963 that "the vast majority of people have always devoted all their energy to survival, thereby denying themselves any chance to live. But in their daily attempts to cope with an alienating environment, ordinary individuals engage in countless acts of defiance."[5]

Oral history offers the best tool to unveil their multiple acts of defiant agency for at least two reasons. First, the interview exchange articulates a space in which the visible and the invisible meet in the remembrance of things passed. Second, the conversation opens a well of emotions not so readily accessible through conventional archival, scholarly research.

When applied to the practice of oral history, the theoretical apparatus provided by María Zambrano's "poetic reason" promises to be fruitful in unveiling the invisible and also to re-examine the time element in the binary space/time that reverberates throughout this book.[6] In order to accomplish this task, I examine the narratives that follow utilizing two important aspects of María Zambrano's poetic reason: first, the acoustic/musical thought intrinsic to the notion of poetic reason which Zambrano puts forward in her exploration of rhythm as inherent to her understanding of time. The Zambranian lyrical explanation of rhythm as essential to life is ontological. Second, Ortega y Gasset articulated "I am I and my circumstance" through his notions of ratio-vitalism. As his student, Zambrano's exploration of the Orteguian dictum, however, helps us understand how oral history and memory inevitably intertwine and allows us to explore the historiographical mandate of truth and objectivity in a new light and a new sensibility. María Zambrano carries further the dictum "I am I and my circumstance" by contemplating the emotional nerve in human thinking process. As she puts it, "In the deepest realm of the howling, the weeping, and the groaning resides the core, the insoluble seed of our being, of the word itself."[7] That emotional element only emerges through poetry revealing an authentic universal being rather than simply a factual objective representation.

---

5   Gerd-Rainer Horn, *The Spirit of '68: Rebellion in Western Europe and North America, 1956-1976* (Oxford: Oxford University Press, 2007), loc. 207 of 4087; see note 25 loc. 764 of 4087, Kindle.

6   Between 1924 and 1927, María Zambrano (1901-1991) studied under José Ortega y Gasset (1883-1955) and followed his teachings on the quest to rethink Western thought from vital experience.

7   "En el interior más hondo del reino del sollozo y del llanto y del gemido habita tal vez el núcleo, semilla indisoluble ha de ser, de la palabra misma [...]" [my translation]. Zambrano, *De la Aurora*, 124.

Finally, the emotional language of poetry in the stories that follow is strengthened with photographs the informants provided me. In order to analyze their hidden significance, I apply John Berger's understanding of the concept *photo-Roman* or visual bildungsroman. As Berger notes, a photograph preserves a moment of time: "Between the moment recorded and the present moment of looking at the photograph there is an abyss."[8] Such abyss is the space/time reconstructed in the interview, the story harvested in the process of recalling the past outside of the photograph frame and History.

The Invisible Sound Time

> Una conciencia que sólo dispusiese de un oído afinado [...] podría medir los cambios habidos y los cambios que se preparan en la historia, podría escuchar cómo se gesta el futuro." María Zambrano, *Delirio y destino*[9]

> "En el principio era el canto y antes del canto el silbido que anuncia la aparición del 'logos'" María Zambrano, *De la Aurora*[10]

To embark on an exploration of the invisible we must close our eyes. To unveil those "countless acts of defiance" we need to reassess the many acts of renunciation, of self-effacement as the means to open opportunities for the next generation, to better their offspring's odds. The journey promises to be illuminating but, paradoxically, it requires that we dwell in the dark and rely on intuition rather than vision.

> You have to fall asleep above the light.
> We must wake up in the intra-terrestrial, intra-corporal darkness of the different bodies which terrestrial man inhabits: that of the earth, that of the universe, his own.
> There in "in the depths," in the infernos of heedful heart, it reveals itself, reignites itself.
> Up in the light, the heart succumbs itself, cedes itself, surmises itself. It sleeps at last without sorrow. In the embracing light where no violence is suffered. Because

---

8   John Berger and Jean Mohr, *Another Way of Telling* (New York: Vintage International, 1995), 87.

9   "A conscience that only had a fine-tuned ear [...] could measure the changes passed and the changes to come in history, it could listen to how the future is gestated" [my translation]. María Zambrano, *Delirio y destino* (Madrid: Mondadori, 1989), 158.

10 "In the beginning it was the chant and before the chant it was the shrill which announce the birth of the 'logos'" [my translation]. Zambrano, *De la Aurora*, 104.

it has reached that point in that light, without forcing and even without opening any door, without having crossed lintels of light and shadow, without effort and without protection.[11]

It is in the shadows where those outside of history dwell. From a young age, Zambrano had shown an interest in the poetics of culture and sought to illuminate the dark interstices of life, go beyond the Orteguian rational vitalism, gain understanding of human affect as manifested in cultural symbolism and the arts. Her thought sought a cognizance of authentic/emotions rather than the conventional scientific objective/dispassionate truth the Enlightenment championed. Zambrano unmasked the prevalent "divorce between life and philosophical truth." To connect the two, she advocated a history of compassion, of love, of mercy, as the only guide to life devoted to truth. In her argumentation the philosopher distinguishes between *eidetic* and *acousmatic reason*. The former focuses on a Cartesian truth, which relies on the visual rational inquiry. Zambrano characterizes this as a rigid reasoning based on the classical discursive rendering, which may be understood as male centered. The *acousmatic reason*, by contrast, she regards as more fluid because *acousmatic reason* relies on listening, on the acuity of our ear. As Francisco Martínez González points out: "reasoning means to stop and listen. It resides in the ability to grasp that which vibrates, which flows and is in constant angst. Such reasoning is in pursuit of heterogeneous, polyphonic, polyrhythmic beings/entities/circumstances in the world. Such acoustic reasoning is focused on unveiling beings/entities/circumstances' harmony"[12] or in some cases their dissonance. This second reasoning is what Zambrano calls "poetic reason," which needs to be understood as female driven and emotionally centered.[13] Felt in the attentive listening, as Zambrano puts it:

> While I, without noticing, attended immobile to the distant murmur of an invisible source. Gathered into myself, my whole being became a marine snail; an ear, just hearing. [...] I became hearing and when I turned to look, nobody listened to me.[14]

---

11   María Zambrano, *Claros del Bosque* (Madrid: Cátedra, 2011), 149, quoted in Lola Nieto, "Metáfora, repetición y musicalidad: María Zambrano y Chantal Maillard," *Dicenda: Cuadernos de Filología Hispánica*, 33 (2015): 179-93.

12   Francisco Martínez González, "Introducción al pensamiento musical de María Zambrano," *Revista de Musicología* 28, no. 2, Actas del VI Congreso de la Sociedad Española de Musicología (2005): 1019.

13   Important here was the influence she received from another great Spanish thinker, Xavier Zubiri (1898-1983), in particular the notion of "inteligencia sintiente" (the intelligence of feeling, or emotional intelligence).

14   "[M]ientras yo, sin apercibirme, atendía inmóvil a un rumor lejano de la fuente invisible. Recogida en mi misma, todo mi ser se hizo un caracol marino; un oído, tan solo oía. [...] Me

Zambrano shows an increasing interest for the acoustic after her reading of Marius Schneider's *El origen musical de los animales-símbolos de mitología y escultura antiguas* (*The musical origin of the animals-symbols of ancient mythology and sculpture*). This ethnographic study proposed that in the beginning was sound, rhythm, and sonorous substance, which constituted the world:

> Greek culture began with ancient mysticism and, when it ended in an aesthetic game, it snatched acoustic thinking from the human being. Sight increased its radius, as the ear weakened and the sculptures, created according to the canon of aesthetic forms, replaced those other fabulous beings. In classic culture there is no lack of ancient mystical elements. Even the theory of the music of the spheres is known; however, all these elements are already in full decline, and are only relics of a high mystical old.[15]

For Schneider, the ear is the "mystical organ" par excellence. In turn, Zambrano considers the ability to listen to be "ear" akin to having a perceptive, sensitive attitude towards life; a sound existence in tune with our emotional self. The Spanish Civil War and her long exile altered Zambrano's philosophical pursuits. The distance between philosophical truth/reason and life/emotion had deepened so profoundly that she only found refuge in mysticism. The religious piety that reverberates in Zambrano's writing is linked to Unamuno's tragic sentiment of life and the pre-Heideggerian poetry of Antonio Machado. Poetry was considered as the instrument to restore the connection between reason and emotion, to endow with number, weight, and size all the things that have none.

For Zambrano, "the word"—language's minimal expression—symbolizes all the arts, including music and poetry. According to Humberto Ortiz Buitrago:

> The word is not only an expression of a suffering subjectivity [...] but rather it is the concrete objectification, which under precise measured rhythm, like that of music and poetry, has always marked and invited us to participate in temporality's dance.[16]

---

fui volviendo oído y al volverme para mirar, nadie me escuchaba." María Zambrano, "Diótima de Mantinea," in *Hacia un saber sobre el alma* (Madrid: Alianza Editorial, 2008), 222.

15   "La cultura griega se inició con el misticismo antiguo y, al concluir en juego estético, arrebató del pensar acústico al ser humano. La vista aumento su radio, a medida que el oído se debilitaba y las esculturas, creadas según in canon de formas estéticas, sustituyeron a los seres fabulosos. En la cultura clásica no faltan los elementos místicos antiguos. incluso se conoce la teoría de la música de las esferas; sin embargo, todos estos elementos ya se hallan en plena decadencia, y solo son reliquias de una alta mística antigua." Marius Schneider, *El origen musical de los animales-símbolos en la mitología y la escultura antiguas* (Madrid: Siruela, 2010), 154, quoted in Martínez González, "El pensamiento musical de María Zambrano," 196.

16   "La palabra no sería solo la expresión de una subjetividad padeciente [...] sino una objetivización concreta que bajo la medida precisa de un ritmo, como el de la música y la poesía han

The rhythm of poetry is the materialization in words of the acoustic/musical nature that permeates Zambrano's thought. Rhythm and tempo are inherent to each other and constitute the heart's thinking in Zambranian terms. She says: "Language has a sound (intonation), which in its most primary form supersedes words."[17] In her view, there is in music something transgressive that escapes logic as it reaches us emotionally. Poetry is the closest we can come to articulating our thoughts in a musical form. The intonations, the silences, the laughter, and cries in the oral history practice embody the musicality of the message. In deploying the poetic reason method with our eyes closed, we may listen intently and reach the revelation of the invisible quotidian acts of empowerment and their emotional contours. Their rhythms unveil an original non-human language, and so through poetry and music it is recaptured:

> Music and poetry rescue the continuity of the screech, and of all non-human language, sacrificed to the discontinuous word. That song of all creatures rising incessantly forms the ground of the word which would be required, if minimally sentient word, to become the sky that gathers that hymn without end. The music of the universe.[18]

There is a correlation between the non-human sound and the non-being with the rhythm of speech and the erasure of historical narrative of those inhabiting the intra-history of Unamuno. Therefore, paying attention to the way they deliver their stories is revealing. The whispers, and the high pitch utterances, the silences and the facial expressions disclose enigmatic significations. The informants in the narratives that follow resort to repetition, almost as if they were singing the chorus of a song-refrain. As if they were the chorus of a Greek tragedy.

I propose to embrace poetry as a means to capture the invisible acts of self- empowerment revealed in my conversations with the informants.[19] It is the architecture of a poem that allows us to seize the contours, density, and volume of that, and

---

sabido 'desde siempre' marcar, invitase a la participación, al baile a la temporalidad." Humberto Ortiz Buitrago, *Palabra y sujeto de la razón poética: Una lectura del pensamiento de María Zambrano* (Caracas: Universidad Central de Venezuela, 2013), 247.

17   Zambrano, *De la Aurora*, 130.
18   "La continuidad del silbo, y de todo lenguaje no humano, sacrificados a la discontinua palabra; la música y el poema los rescatan. Y ese cántico de todas las criaturas que se eleva sin cesar forma el suelo de la palabra que estaría obligada, si lo siente mínimamente, a convertirse en el cielo que recoge ese himno sin fin, si es que obedece plenamente a lo que la sostiene, a la música, a esa música del universo" [my translation]. Zambrano, *De la Aurora*, 140-41.
19   See Janesick, *Oral History for the Qualitative Researcher*, 129-36. There is a rich historiography on gender and feminist analysis in oral history. To mention just a few, see: Joan Sangster, "Telling Our Stories: Feminist Debates and the Use of Oral History," *Women's History Review* 3, no. 1 (1994): 5-28.

those outside of history, and explore feminist dilemmas scholars have discussed over the last four decades: periodization, agency, becoming visible. Questioning the traditional periodization in historiographical analysis illuminates the dark side of history (the intra-history in Unamuno's terminology) shining on minute acts of agency. These women's invisible acts of resilience many times were rooted in the desire to better the odds of their offspring. The informants emotionally tell us about something we might think is insignificant, but if we amplify its resonance in the conversation, it will allow us to gain understanding of the actions and choices made by these ordinary women (or any other subaltern) and therefore bestow them with number, weight, and size.[20] In the words of René Lourau, "When we dwell in the small fleeting moment a conscious course of action reveals itself and turns something regarded as insignificant into something visibly powerful. The 'moment' is, under the sign of immanence of the everyday life, like the caress of an angel's wing, a passing fling with transcendence."[21]

The narratives that follow are poeticized and may be characterized as creative non-fiction essays, which emulate a ficto-critical technique. Ficto-criticism is a postmodern feminist approach to the text composition by which the boundaries between theoretical analysis and creative writing collapse. This approach is particularly fruitful in the realm of autobiography within cultural studies. In my rendition, the hybrid nature of the text intends to invoke poetic reason. As Anna Gibbs explains:

> Ficto-criticism does not illustrate an already existing argument, does not simply formulate philosophy (or anything else) in fictional terms. It is not translation or transposition: it says something which can't be said in any other way: because it is not reducible to propositional content. It is, in essence, per-formative, a meta-discourse in which the strategies of the telling are part of the point of the tale.[22]

---

20 To explore time, Henri Lefebvre's *Rhythmanalysis* describes the body as the "metronome of living experience." A haiku will encapsulate each story. I chose haikus because they impacted western avant-garde writers such as the Imagists in the English-speaking world and the Generation of '27 in Spanish. The essence of haiku speaks to the thinker as poet described in Dilthey's and Heidegger's philosophies and unveils the invisible of the "I am I and my circumstance." Haikus inspired my analysis in several ways. First, like haikus each story reveals in simple words profound signification. The simplicity and impressionistic nature of the haiku encapsulates what I as a historian am in search of: revealing what feminist/gender historians are invested in, what we called "becoming visible." On visibility, see Bridenthal et al., *Becoming Visible: Women in European History.*

21 René Lourau, "Lefebvre 'parrain' de la Maffia 'Analise institutionnelle," xiii, quoted in Elden, *Understanding Henri Lefebvre*, 171.

22 Gibbs, "Bodies of Words." See also Barone and Eisner, *Arts Based Research*; Kerr and Nettelbeck, *The Space Between*; Pattinson, "Discovering the Self."

Ficto-critical narratives may be rendered in multiple ways. I write short paragraphs followed by poems. Likewise, I utilize font size to represent **whispers** in opposition to louder **INCANTATIONS**; I wrap explanations of the speaker's delivery, whether laughter, tears, or facial expression in between brackets []. In some cases, the narrative turns into a poem or, on some occasions, I resort to Haibun style,[23] combining a lyrical paragraph followed by a few verses that expand the meaning of said paragraph. In this way, the stories possess an internal rhythm, a heartbeat of sorts, and may be enacted almost like mini plays, theatrical, a dance, movement at the heart of listening. A short poem, whether a haiku or a free verse, allows us to make a complete stop of time in a detail. This means to pay attention to silence as well.[24] As María Zambrano explains, "The word can recover its lost innocence only by simultaneously being thought, image, rhythm, and silence, and hence become pure action, creational word."[25] Therefore, it is imperative to pay attention more

---

23   Haibun combines prose and haiku first utilized by seventeenth-century Japanese poet Matsuo Bashō See Matsuo Bashō, *Bashō's Haiku: Selected* Poems, trans. David Landis Barnhill (Albany, NY: SUNY Press, 2004) Originally the content of the prose refers to travel, landscape, or quotidian vignettes followed by a haiku, which elaborates or expands the sentiment of the preceding prose. The Haibun genre is now universal and has experienced a revival in recent years in English.

24   Haiku is no stranger to Spanish poetry. It reached Spain at the turn of the nineteenth century, having an impact on the literary Generations of 1898 and 1927. Our own *seguidilla* has the same verse structure 7-5-5-7. Some of the poets of the generations of '98 like Miguel Unamuno or Antonio Machado wrote haiku. Likewise, the importance of imagist poetry at the beginning of the twentieth century will make European poets gravitate towards the Japanese form. The poets of the Generation of '27 in Spain who cultivated haiku include Federico García Lorca and Juan Ramón Jiménez. After the Spanish Civil War the genre experienced a decline but came back in the early 1970s with the publication of the classic by seventeenth-century Japanese poet Matsuo Bashō's *Narrow Road to the Northern Provinces*, Matsuo Bashō, *Sendas de Oku*, trans. and ed. Eikichi Hayashiya and Octavio Paz, 2nd. Ed. (Girona, Spain: Ediciones Atalanta. Some of the Spanish poets that cultivated the genre in the 1970s include: Verónica Aranda, Frutos Soriano, Elías Rovira, Toñi Sánchez, Félix Arce, María Victoria Porras, José Luis Parra, and Isabel Pose. See also Pedro Aullón de Haro, *El jaiku en España* (Madrid: Hiperión, 2002); Fernando Rodríguez Izquierdo Gavala, *El haiku japonés* (Madrid: Hiperión, 1972) https://www.thehaikufoundation.org/omeka/files/original/e76226e68e309a763bdbbaca a8ed51b1.pdf https://haikunversaciones.wordpress.com/400-2/haiku-de-japon-a-espana/.

25   "Porque solamente siendo a la vez pensamiento, imagen, ritmo y silencio parece que puede recuperar la palabra su inocencia perdida, y ser entonces pura acción, palabra creadora." Zambrano, *Hacia un saber sobre el alma*, 49, quoted in María Carmen López Saenz, "Merleau-Ponty y Zambrano: el 'logos' sensible y sentiente," *Aurora* 14 (2013): 116. López Saenz cites Merleau-Ponty as well: "Hemos de considerar la palabra antes de que sea pronunciada, sobre el fondo de silencio que la precede, que no cesa nunca de acompañarla, y sin el cual no diría nada; hemos de ser sensibles a esos hilos de silencio de los que el tejido de la palabra se halla entreverado." Translation: "We must consider the word before it is spoken on the background of its preceding silence, which never ceases in accompanying it, and without silence

to the cadence of the speech rather than just focus on the logic of the argument of the chain of words.[26] Indeed, the threads of silence are woven into the fabric of speech. This ficto-critical technique promises to be useful in interpreting women's lives. Their vulnerability and self-effacement turn, hence, into courage and resistance for the sake of the next generation—a generation shaped in the somber side of history, not the luminous one.

In Pursuit of Authentic History: Zambrano's Philosophy and Poetry

Zambrano's thought is the sum of Unamuno, Machado, and Ortega's.[27] She also carries further German romanticism as in the Nietzschean new notion of philosophical language through metaphor, and the Heideggerian notion of language understood as "the house of being." Indeed, Zambrano inherited the European and Spanish intellectual traditions: on the one hand, philosophical critique and, on the other, poetic production. She expounded on the central role played by the individual's interaction with an "Other," for the subject to achieve a sense of self, a sense of authenticity, a sense of purpose. Zambrano proposes to transcend the binary male/reason versus female/emotion and, as argued above, proposes to combine both reason and emotion through her *Poetic Reason*.

She accomplishes this union by incorporating and further expanding the Orteguian concept of "radical reality" of life as encapsulated in her professor's dictum "I am I and my circumstance" as mentioned above.[28] Her focus on emotions, and the invisible connections they articulate among us, guides the analysis of my oral histories as purveyors of a higher truth—authentic, ontological, revealing the invisible in the human condition.

---

      the word would not say anything; we must be sensitive to those threads of silence weaved in the word's fabric."

26   López Sáenz, "Merleau-Ponty y Zambrano," 116. López Saenz points out how "It is striking that in all the work of Zambrano, especially in *Hacia un saber sobre el alma* and in *Filosofía y poesía*, there are so many coincidences, not only with Merleau-Ponty's *Phenomenology of Perception* (1945), but even with the *Visible and the Invisible* written in 1959 and left unfinished as a result of his sudden death." *Visible and Invisible* was published posthumously in 1968.

27   Antolín Sánchez Cuervo points out how María Zambrano's poetic reason always drew from a literary tradition: Senecaism, mysticism, Cervantes' realism, Galdós' narrative, the cultural world of the Institución Libre de Enseñanza, and García Lorca's romances. Antolín Sánchez Cuervo, "The Anti-Fascist Origins of Poetic Reason: Genealogy of a Reflection on Totalitarianism," in *The Cultural Legacy of María Zambrano*, ed. Xon de Ros and Daniela Omlor (Oxford: Legenda, 2017), 61.

28   Concha Fernández Martorell, *María Zambrano: Entre la razón, la poesía y el exilio* (Madrid: Montesinos, 2004), loc 581 of 1171, Kindle.

"Authentic" historical writing happens in the practice of oral history because it forces us to rethink the relationship between past and present as the informant and the researcher engage in conversation. The formula, "I am I and my circumstance," that Ortega gave us to decipher our "authentic being" is radically concrete and profoundly empowering, but it is also male centered, blind to female nature, and dismissive of a woman's value. However, the dictum is radically concrete in the sense that it is grounded in the historical moment in which each generation is immersed. It is also infused with empowering potential because it situates human ratio-vitalism as unfolding, enduring time. Therefore, it may apply usefully to the examination of any subaltern experience, allowing in the process of examination, and argumentation to reveal oppression as located in a grey zone where individual action carries the potential for self-affirmation and historical agency. However, we need to go against Ortega's premise that women are not an intrinsic part of historical action and apply his historical reason (what he called the *Aurora of Historical Reason*) in tandem with the poetics of Zambranian analysis. How do we unveil *authentic gendered beings*? While men are bound to act toward their destiny, in the case of women, Ortega resorted to essentialism and hollow eternal feminine immanence. He speaks of historical rhythms to elucidate his historical reason:

> One of the most curious meta-historical investigations would consist in the discovery of the great historical rhythms; ...for example, the *sexual rhythm*. There is an insinuation of a pendulum character in historical eras influenced by the predominant male power and others with the dominant feminine influence. Many institutions, habits, ideas, myths until now unexplained, are clarified in surprising ways when we realize that certain epochs have been ruled, modeled by the supremacy of the feminine.[29]

The historical world is constituted by human actions and, Zambrano reminds us, it is necessary to bring understanding to life, human life in its totality. Following in the steps of her teacher Ortega y Gasset, she understands life as the primordial reality, and all reason is born of that radical reality that is life. To accomplish an authentic historical self, we must radically humanize our understanding of history.

As Alberto Santamaría points out, Zambrano's objective is "to open the way to a new historical sensibility within which writing will emerge to reveal the cen-

---

29   "Una de las más curiosas investigaciones metahistóricas consistiría en el descubrimiento de los grandes ritmos históricos. Porque hay otros no menos evidentes y fundamentales que el antedicho; por ejemplo, el ritmo sexual. Se insinúa, en efecto, una pendulación en la historia de épocas sometidas al influjo predominante del varón a épocas subyugadas por la influencia femenina. Muchas instituciones, usos, ideas, mitos, hasta ahora inexplicados, se aclaran de manera sorprendente cuando se cae en la cuenta de que ciertas épocas han sido regidas, modeladas por la supremacía de la mujer." José Ortega y Gasset, "La idea de las generaciones," (1923) https://www.ensayistas.org/antologia/XXE/ortega/ortega3.htm.

ter, the being, the place from where everything comes."[30] Poetry would serve as the language for new historical understanding, born of a ratio-poetic process. The mystery of life to unveil in Zambrano's outlook is a mystical endeavor. In order to reach the core, the center which links us to our past within, I propose to explore the Bergsonian method of intuition discussed below. Intuition will prove instrumental in articulating an inclusive historical narrative, which weaves the personal and the collective, the self and the other.

How then can we articulate an inclusive, whole, authentic being? This question leads us back to the way Ortega approaches the question of being as intrinsically bound up with the radical reality of human life. Human life for him is nothing else but history: "Man has no nature, man has history."

Ortega, and more so Zambrano, draw on their Catholic sense of life and individual purpose. For the latter, authenticity will be accomplished through a compassionate, love-centered pursuit of the self in constant unfolding through social interactions with others. As Hannah Arendt remarked, "For love, although it is one of the rarest occurrences in human lives, indeed possesses an unequaled power of self-revelation and an unequaled clarity of vision for the disclosure of *who*, precisely because it is unconcerned to the point of total unworldliness with *what* the loved person may be, with his qualities and shortcomings no less than with his achievements, failings, and transgressions. Love, by reason of its passion, destroys the in-between which relate us and separate us from others."[31]

Like Arendt, Zambrano proposes a sacrificial history. The poetic reason proposed by Zambrano is rooted in compassion and love and turns into a bold re-elaboration of the Orteguian "historical reason." In her essay, "Para una historia de la piedad," she remarks:

> Reality, and philosophers discover this fact again, occurs somewhere previous to knowledge, to the idea. The Spanish philosopher Ortega y Gasset developed the concept of "vital reason" based on his discovery that the reality is prior to the idea, contrary to what Idealism formulated. The rationalist believes that reality is given through an idea or thought and that only by reducing reality to thought he can understand it. Mercy is the feeling of the heterogeneity of being, of quality of being, and therefore it is the yearning to find the ways of understanding and deal with each one of those multiple ways of reality.[32]

She reinterpreted "I am I and my circumstance" and the radical reality of historicity by appealing to the centrality of emotions in the human condition. The authen-

---

30   93.
31   Arendt, *The Human Condition*, 242.
32   Zambrano, "Para una historia de la piedad." See Appendix I for translation by María Asunción Gómez.

tic being of Zambrano is even more radical than that of Husserl because, as Ana Bundgaard points out, she is looking for essential, radical, and many times unconscious "facts" not accessible to rational intelligibility.[33] Through poetic reason the historian turned poet uncovers the suffering and overcomes violence by actively exposing the power of forgiveness. This line of thought claims the emotional as characteristically feminine and conventionally regarded as passive and outside of history.

While Ortega's philosophical stance makes women the "second sex," it is through the poetic reason proposed by Zambrano that authentic historicity, authentic being, may be conquered. Zambrano proposes a return to what she called the "Auroral origin" in her work, *De la Aurora*.[34] The origin, the birth, is where word/language/poetics and the thought/reason/philosophy come together. Only through the act of poetic creation will we be able to grasp the core of our individual and collective "authentic being."

For Zambrano, art (poetry) creates the most absolute truth and shapes the *authentic being*.[35] As Clare Nimmo explains, Zambrano's Poetic Reason is "a form of knowledge through union: that is, a knowledge not attained through the intellect alone, but the fruit of the intellect and of the poetic, guided and directed by the latter."[36] In other words, "I" only becomes "I" in interaction with an "Other." The practice of oral history turns into the most useful tool to achieve, if not absolute objective historical truth, at least historical authenticity—variations of Being in the world through time.

In *Poetry, Language, and Thought*, Heidegger points out how the genuine language of thought is no other than poetry, because poetry is the saying of truth.[37] "Poetry has an indispensable function for human life: it is the creative source of humanness

---

33   Bundgaard, *Más allá de la Filosofía*, quoted in Ortiz Buitrago, *Palabra y sujeto de la razón poética*, note 3, 13. See also: Bundgaard, "Ser, palabra y arte,"7-12.
34   Zambrano, *De la Aurora*.
35   María Zambrano, *Filosofía y poesía* (Mexico City: Fondo de Cultura Económica, 2012), loc 962 of 1589, Kindle.
36   Clare E. Nimmo, "The Poet and the Thinker: María Zambrano and Feminist Criticism," *The Modern Language Review*, 92, no. 4 (1997): 893-902. Nimmo argues that Zambrano adopts a critical position against rationalist male-centered philosophy "through her explicitly poetic reinterpretation of the dominant element of philosophical discourse: reason, or the *logos*" (894). This, in turn, reveals a "Gynocritical" approach like that of her contemporary Helene Cixous' work. The influence of German Romanticism, from Hölderlin or Novalis to Nietzsche, Dilthey or Heidegger, is evident in María Zambrano's poetic reason. The Spanish philosopher draws from this tradition and from her fellow country thinkers (Ortega, Unamuno, Zubiri) to elaborate on the central role played by social interactions with one another to achieve a sense of self.
37   Heidegger, *Poetry, Language, and Thought*, x.

of the dwelling life of man."[38] History's main purpose, to unveil the truth through impartial objective analysis (reason), may be enriched by the idea of poetry as the most genuine means to attain human/historical understanding rather than simply historical representation. In *Hacia un saber sobre el alma*, Zambrano points out how philosophy and poetry have always sought the word to create the "self," but the former has as its only objective to "discover a new use of reason."[39] By contrast, Zambrano's poetic reason masterfully engages metaphoric language to deliver the authentic origin of the human condition, what the Greeks called *poesis*. For Zambrano, the literary genre, and more specifically poetic language in the image of the Greek tragedy, unified rational and mythical thought and represented a historical attitude of consciousness—the human attention to feeling, which will lead to the revelation of the most authentic truth of the human condition. Therefore, literary genres are forms of consciousness, and poetry is, in this sense, an act of creation, an act of humanness, an act of empathy, mercy, and reconciliation.

The artistic creation of a poem that captures the sentiment of a moment is understood in Zambranian terms as action, as the process of recognition of our "selves." In that instant when an informant dwells and retells us, the invisible may become apparent, if only briefly, and rather than just retrieving a fact, the interviewer experiences the emotion of introspection and revelation with her interviewee.[40]

Out of this communicative experience arises the "thinker/ historian as Poet." Because the historian-turned-thinker does as the poet: *poetiza, compone, articula* (poeticizes, composes, articulates).[41] Poetic reasoning maintains rigor and critical insight while making the symbolic nature of language work in its favor, opening the door to the emotions and malleable nature of the human condition. Zambrano suggests that the purpose of thinking is "to open up and take true measure of the dimension of our existence."[42] Such introspection is what will make possible the unveiling of the "authentic gendered being" I am pursuing in the analysis of these interviews. Such thinking is a recalling, remembering, memorization, but also implies a responding and an autobiographical immersion into the analysis. Past and present meet in the moment informant and historian talk to each other. As in the first part, the stories that follow trigger my memories. These are the women who shape my sense of self, and the rhythmic telling of our shared paths illuminates the tempo of our lives across time and ocean.

---

38 Heidegger, *Poetry, Language, and Thought*, xv.
39 María Zambrano, *Hacia un saber sobre el alma* (Buenos Aires: Losada, 1950), 135, quoted in Fernández Martorell, *María Zambrano*, loc. 592 of 1171, Kindle.
40 Heidegger, *Poetry, Language, and Thought*, xii.
41 Heidegger, *Poetry, Language, and Thought*, xi.
42 Bundgaard, "Ser, palabra y arte."

Poetry and art contribute to fill life with meaning. As Concha Fernández Martorell explains: "It is not about trying to explain history, not even about telling the life histories of individuals, because history as an objective temporal process is only an abstraction, a fiction; it is only possible to show life through human experiences, the actions, creations, and works true pieces of the past, the traces that something must had happened."[43] It is through art that the past lives in the present; our history is embodied in our creations. These creations are the repositories of our knowledge and passions and incarnations of ourselves. Therefore, Zambrano teaches us that the only way to make visible what we cannot see is through artistic creation, "to expose the entrails of life, to shed a soft light on the hidden feelings of people, only through the collective language the poet expresses herself, does her work to resuscitate the history contained in the words open a new path, a new understanding."[44] Love of other is love of self. According to Humberto Ortiz Buitrago, for María Zambrano love is the original force that must be revealed through a compassionate reasoning with a loving conscience.[45]

"The word" symbolizes in Zambrano all the arts and their power to make us reach an affective maturity and introspection into the human condition. She makes a distinction between philosophical and poetic word. The images and symbols formed by poetic language show historical and individual affective directionality. A word is not just a word, looking back to the Platonic concept of compassion as the virtue of the ethical man and therefore the rational self. Zambrano proposes a compassionate attitude to return to the human condition origins, the Greek original (Auroral) rationalism, nothing more than poetic knowledge as testament of the human suffering and the compassion that it has endured.[46]

There is also a transient nature to Zambrano's thought, what Ortiz Buitrago calls "emotional mobility." For those outside of history, for women, the authenticity and verity of the self is only possible to measure through the impact on the other, on the next generation. Its vital weight is realized in the fulfillment of the empowerment intimated (not expected but only hoped for) by the first generation. The invisible renunciations have meaning only in the fulfilled success of the yet to come. If our works, our artistic traces, are our only physical manifestations of the past, the gift of empowerment is the lived history bequeathed to us by the sacrifices of our mothers and grandmothers.

---

43 Fernández Martorell, *María Zambrano*, loc. 606-1171, Kindle.
44 Fernández Martorell, *María Zambrano*, loc. 621-1171, Kindle.
45 Ortiz Buitrago, *Palabra y sujeto de la razón poética*, 253.
46 Ortiz Buitrago, *Palabra y sujeto de la razón poética*, 248. For example, the symbolic dichotomy virgin/whore has been registered in collective memory and is the manifestation of a past sentiment part of Western Christian tradition.

Memory and Oral History

Maria Zambrano points out Henri Bergson's consideration of time as the conduit intertwining memory with what she calls a compassionate history:

> The philosopher Bergson has provided a masterful criticism of this linear conception of the passage of time, which has been represented as a series of dots that follow one another and that they are consumed as they pass by. Time, according to Bergson, is growth with multiple forms, in which every instant penetrates and is penetrated by other instants; instead of destroying, time creates. This fundamental thesis of contemporary metaphysics casts a bright light on our topic, since feelings, in their history, do not destroy each other. Therefore, Mercy can be the mother to all positive or amorous feelings, without being swept by them, as they come.[47]

Memory is essential to articulate, to convey a compassionate account of our human condition— past, present, and future. How do we understand memory? As Deleuze points out, Bergsonian "duration is essentially memory, consciousness, and freedom. It is consciousness and freedom because it is primarily memory."[48]

There are two inseparable aspects of memory: recollection memory and contraction memory. We need to ask by what mechanism does duration turn into memory in fact, not only in principle. According to Bergson, memory is coextensive with duration and consciousness coextensive with life. Our subjectivity is born out of this threefold operation. Deleuze explains in *Matter and Memory* how Bergson identifies five aspects of subjectivity: 1) *need-subjectivity*, this is the moment of negation based in the circumstances at hand which makes us question the false statement of the problems to solve in our present reality; 2) *brain-subjectivity*, this is the moment of indetermination, dislocation which creates an interval/gap in which our brain offers us the opportunity to choose our course of action; 3) *affection-subjectivity*, the moment of pain or pleasure in our evaluation; 4) *recollection-subjectivity*, this is the moment of recalling, what fills the interval created in between the negation and the execution. It is here where the first aspect of memory resides. Finally, 5) *contraction-subjectivity*, the actualization of the memory as the fusion of the previous moves.[49]

These five aspects are arranged in two directions: matter and memory, perception and recollection, or objective and subjective. The first two aspects of subjectivity belong to the matter/perception/objective line of inquiry and the last two to the memory/recollection/subjective one. Crucial in linking both lines is the third

---

47   Zambrano, "Para una historia de la piedad."
48   Gilles Deleuze, *Bergsonism*, 51.
49   Deleuze, *Bergsonism*, 52-53.

aspect, affection-subjectivity, which is essential in the deployment of the method of intuition. The difference between the two lines of inquiry is a difference in kind between present and past, between perception/matter and recollection/memory. There is, however, a false problem when historians approach memory as a repository of recollections. The question "where are recollections preserved?" is a fallacy based on our understanding of the past as that which no longer is, which according to Deleuze is based on our "confusing Being with being-present," but "the present *is not*, rather it acts," as it is pure becoming, always outside of itself. Its proper element is not being but the active or the useful. The past, on the other hand, has ceased to act or to be useful. But it has not ceased to be. Useless and inactive, impassive, *it is* in the full sense of the word. It is identical with being in itself. It should not be said that it "was" since it is in-itself of being. Of the present, we must say at every instant that it "was" and of the past that it "is," that it is eternally for all time. This is the difference in kind between the past and the present.[50] The past, therefore, is pure ontology. When we engage in recollection, we leap into being, we seek ontological significance. Pure recollection requires an adjustment, like the "focusing of a camera." The next step is the actualization of the memory, what Bergson calls contraction of all our past in every single instant of our life. All our past coexists with each present moment that we try to make sense of, and duration is revealed in all its intensity. The past and the present do not succeed each other but, rather, they are two different kinds of entities or elements which coexist.

Oral history provides a useful tool to unlock Memory's ontological dimension. Through the interview we enact the affection-subjectivity aspect as we facilitate the intersection of Matter/space and Memory/time in the conversation with our informants. In the process we move from the virtual to the actualized recollection, which gives meaning to our present moment. There, two simultaneous movements applied here that Bergson explains as follows: One move is that of translation, the other that of rotation upon itself that contemplates the most useful action. The narrative out of the interview is a translation of the ontological significance behind the memory or recollection our informant is providing in the conversation. To follow Berger, this translation, which is our narrative, may be like the silence in a speech. Simultaneously, and with the aid of intuition, the narrative manifests a rotation as well, a turn towards the present to reveal the "useful facet" in the union of the two. "Recollection," Deleuze points out, "enters into a kind of circuit with the present and rotation prepares the ground for this launch into the circuit." The motor behind the actualization of a memory is the interview, which relies on the method of intuition and the affect emerging in the conversation.

---

50   Deleuze, *Bergsonism*, 55.

The Method of Intuition

Henri Bergson's (1859-1941) understanding of intensity, duration, and free will help us understand better Berger's explanation of the semantics of image residing in the duration/intensity of the moment; Zambrano's poetic reason may better discern her understanding of radical vitalism through musicality, rhythm, tempo. Indeed, the three thinkers are elaborating on the concept of duration as key to understanding the inner self and the realization of true free will. According to Bergson, intensity, duration, and agency/freedom are as inseparable as they are intangible. In *Time and Free Will* (1910), Bergson[51] states:

> Psychic states seem to be more or less *intense*. [sic] Next, looked at in their multiplicity, they unfold in time and constitute *duration*. [sic]
> [...]
> Intensity, duration, voluntary determination, these are the three ideas which have to be clarified by ridding them of all that they owe to the intrusion of the sensible world and, in a word, to the obsession of the idea of space.[52]

For Bergson there are two different selves: one, the external projection of the other, "its spatial, so to speak, social representation."[53] The inner self is only reachable through introspection, which "leads us to grasp our inner states as living things, constantly *becoming* [sic], as states not amenable to measure, which permeate one another and of which the succession in duration has nothing in common with juxtaposition in homogeneous space. But the moments at which we thus grasp ourselves are rare, and that is just why we are rarely free. The greater part of our time we live outside ourselves, hardly perceiving anything of ourselves but our own ghost, a colorless shadow, which pure duration projects into homogeneous space. Hence our life unfolds in space rather than in time; we live for the external world rather than for ourselves; we speak rather than think; we 'are acted upon' rather than act ourselves. To act freely is to recover possession of oneself, and to get back into pure duration."[54] Just like in the photographs that Berger studied.[55]

Intrinsic to the duration is movement and multiplicity, heterogeneity yet oneness unmeasurable:

---

51   On Henri Bergson see the entry in Stanford Encyclopedia of Philosophy. https://plato.stanford.edu/entries/bergson/.
52   Henri Bergson, *Time and Free Will: An Essay on the Immediate Data of Consciousness* (1910) (New York: Dover Publications, Inc., 2001).
53   Bergson, *Time and Free Will*, 231.
54   Bergson, *Time and Free Will*, 231.
55   Bergson, *Time and Free Will*, 234.

If time [...] were, like space, a homogeneous medium, science would be able to deal with it, as it can with space. [...] [D]uration, as duration and motion, as motion, eludes the grasp of mathematics: of time everything slips through its fingers but simultaneity, and of movement everything but immobility. This is what the Kantians and even their opponents do not seem to have perceived: in this so-called phenomenal world, which, we are told, is a world cut out for scientific knowledge, all the relations that cannot be translated into simultaneity, i.e., into space, are scientifically unknowable. [...] [I]n a duration assumed to be homogeneous, the same states could occur over again, causality would imply necessary determination, and all freedom would become incomprehensible.[56]

This statement calls for a reconceptualization of historical writing to reflect the human condition/experience as unfolding, located in the depths of time and our inner selves. This turns into an emotional, empathic exercise, which Bergson and Zambrano will cipher in love and compassion utilizing a method of intuition.[57] As Deleuze reminds us, "intuition is the method of Bergsonism," a fully developed philosophical method which articulates Bergson's three fundamental concepts: duration, memory, and *Élan Vital*.[58] The methodological deployment of intuition as proposed by Bergson aids us in ascertaining meaningful knowledge. Intuition as method involves three interventions, according to Bergson. First, it is concerned with the statement of true or false problems; second, it seeks to unveil differences in kind rather than degree; and finally, it aspires to discover real time.[59] Signification is the method's fundamental pursuit and life/experience itself its conduit.

How we formulate our questions, state the problem, will lead to the conditions and steps towards a solution. "The history of man," remarks Deluze, "from the theoretical as much as from the practical point of view is that of the construction of problems. [...] In Bergson the very notion of the problem has its roots beyond history, in life itself or in the *Élan Vital*. Life is essentially determined in the act of avoiding obstacles, stating and solving a problem."[60] Our agency resides in stating the problem to better solve the obstacles at hand. That is the first step each and every one of the women whose narratives follow unconsciously engaged in. They resorted to imaginative ways of solving predicaments which seemed impossible to overcome. The outcome they sought informed the way they stated the problem, many times meaning their own self-effacement for the betterment of their families and loved ones.

---

56 Bergson, *Time and Free Will*, 234-35.
57 Zambrano, "Para una historia de la piedad"; Henri Bergson, *The Creative Mind*, trans. Mabelle L. Andison.
58 Deleuze, *Bergsonism*, 13.
59 Deleuze, *Bergsonism*, 14.
60 Deleuze, *Bergsonism*, 16.

The second intervention in the Bergsonian method of intuition values difference in kind rather than degree, or quantity of the problem at hand. This second task is particularly important to decipher those false problems Bergson characterized as "non-existent problems" and defined as problems "whose very terms contain a confusion between 'more' and 'less.'" These are problems of "non-being," in which Bergson explains how non-being includes "more" than problems of being, how there is more in disorder than in order, more in the possible than the real.[61] In our confusion we tend to focus only on the differences in degree rather than in kind. Bergson says it is critical to apply intuition. This means to go against the visible and seek the signification in the negation, and the absences in the silences. Intuition as a method is one of division, of breaking the problem at hand into pieces in order to uncover the difference in kind and avoid the illusion of difference in degree. In order to reach the difference in kind, we need to go beyond our state of experience toward experience at its source and beyond.

The final intervention deployed by the method of intuition involves thinking in terms of duration. This is a purely temporal thinking in which Bergson identifies the true differences in kind devoid of spatial connotations, which he asserts only presents difference in degree, measured, divisible.

To summarize, in Gilles Deleuze's words: "intuition forms a method with its three rules: This is essentially a 'problematizing method' (a critique of false problems and the invention of genuine ones); a 'differentiating method' (carving outs and intersections) and a 'temporalizing method' (thinking in terms of duration)."[62]

---

61 Deleuze, *Bergsonism*, 17.
62 Deleuze, *Bergsonism*, 35.

Figure 15: Feria del Corpus, Granada c. 1958

(In)Visible Images

Radiant faces, full of joy, mothers and daughters are crammed into the carnival ride. Every spring Granada celebrates Corpus Christi. Flamenco music floods the night for ten days of continuous celebration. A parade announces the small circus. Sugar spins into cotton candy. These are days for forgetting. My mother sits in the front row in between two of her cousins, holding the pretend driving wheel with the help of the youngest. In their summer dresses, they all smile on cue as if they knew I would be looking at them across time. Do not fret, they seem to be telling me, as they happily await the bumpy ride ahead.

The following narratives are populated by photographs of the informants, which they offered to illustrate their stories. They are enigmatic when isolated. As I contemplate them, my own story comes alive. An in-visible narrative is born from the interplay between theirs and my memories of the events displayed in the photographs.

John Berger reminds us of the two different uses of photography:[63] one ideological for public consumption present in state propaganda or advertising; the other private, which evokes an emotional chord in the viewer. The images I include in the following stories belong to the private, emotional realm. Yet they convey an important relationship to the public as they are manifestations of how the private lives of these women, while invisible to the larger historical events, had an impact on the next generation and therefore, represent an example of how the subjective interacts with the social and political, unnoticed in the public grand narratives.

Photographs reveal a story all their own. They provide another way of telling about experience and therefore they have commonalities with language. Images in a photograph are coded like a message, and we decipher the message by association and context. Berger points out how "appearances reveal resemblances, analogies, sympathies, antipathies, and each of these convey a message."[64] However, modern science has deprived images (the visible) of any ontological function. They are opaque and in need of explanation, of words to explain what they represent—purely aesthetic objects.[65] The aesthetic becomes our emotional refuge where our personal feelings may be expressed. However, what we see is only a manifestation, a code to be deciphered. The viewer partakes in the revealed meaning the visible image contains. The viewer becomes a storyteller who explains and makes sense of what lies hidden in the image. Berger remarks, "appearances are so complex that only the search which is inherent in the act of looking can draw a reading out of their understanding. It is the search with its choices which differentiates...and the seen, the revealed, is the child of both the appearances and the search."[66] The revelation insinuates further; it goes beyond the image displayed, and the viewer fills in the gap in an autobiographical search for introspection and meaning. The revelation is difficult to verbalize, and the aesthetic emotional component provides the means to capture the unknown invisible meaning.

Insisting on the linguistic nature of images, Berger distinguishes between the qualitative difference between a photograph and a painting, likening them to speech forms. While the photograph, he explains, resembles a quotation, the painting is akin to a translation of appearances. This appreciation has a profound significance in the deciphering of meaning behind the images we contemplate. While the painter's rendition of an image is the result of a deliberate conscious process and some "pentimentos"[67] (or regrets), the photograph arrests a moment

---

63   Berger and Mohr, *Another Way of Telling*, 111.
64   Berger, *Another Way of Telling*, 115.
65   Berger, *Another Way of Telling*, 115.
66   Berger, *Another Way of Telling*, 118.
67   The definition of pentimento: Pentimento, (from Italian pentirsi: "to repent"), in art, the reappearance in an oil painting of original elements of drawing or painting that the artist tried to obliterate by overpainting. If the covering pigment becomes transparent, as may happen

in time, isolates an instant, a memory flash in our mind. The photograph produces an interruption to the historical continuity of one's life. A frozen moment in time, the photograph only gains meaning if we lend it a story. As quotations, photographs show the instantaneous void of significance until time passes and we gain perspective. But as Berger points out, the legibility of the photograph depends on the photograph's quotation quality, more specifically, its length—understood not as the time exposure set by the photographer but the temporal length, its duration not in time but in signification.[68] Like a short poem, a haiku, a photograph shortens for the viewer a meaningful event in our lives brought back to life in the swell of the emotions it triggers. Those emotions emanate from the consciousness of things passed, as photographs show the image of that which no longer is. Photographs preserve a moment in time in similar ways to how we store images in our memory.[69] Berger remarks:

> Memory is the field where different times coexists.... Among the ancient Greeks Memory was the mother of all the Muses and most closely associated with the practice of poetry. Poetry, at the time, was a form of storytelling as well as an inventory of the visible world...metaphor after metaphor was given to poetry by way of visual correspondences. The muse of photography is not one of Memory's daughters, but Memory itself. Both the photograph and the remembered depend upon and equally oppose the passing of time. Both preserve moments and propose their own form of simultaneity in which all their images can coexist. Both seek instants of revelation for it is only such instants which give full reason to their own capacity to withstand the flow of time.[70]

As I engage in the contemplation of the image of the six women above, the photograph's moment brings theirs and my life together. In that sense, my looking at the photograph functions like the mind recalling a memory.

Certainly, the void between that which is apparent in the photograph and that which is absent, invisible, is filled in by my own auto-biographical sense of self. The narrative is the sum of both the visible and the invisible story that encapsulates.

> Perhaps at the beginning
> time and *the visible*,

---

over the years, the ghostly remains of earlier marks may show through. *Pentimenti* most occurs owing to slight repositioning by the artist of the outlines of figures or of their clothing. Many signs of such "repentances," or pentimenti, are found among the thinly painted Dutch panels of the seventeenth century. One of the most famous examples is a double hat brim in Rembrandt's "Flora" (c. 1665; Metropolitan Museum of Art).

68 Berger, *Another Way of Telling*, 120.
69 Berger, *Another Way of Telling*, 89.
70 Berger, *Another Way of Telling*, 280.

> twin makers of distance,
> arrived together,
> drunk
> battering on the door
> just before dawn.
> The first light sobered them,
> and examining the day,
> they spoke
> of the far, the past, *the invisible*.
> They spoke of the horizons
> surrounding everything
> which had not yet disappeared.[71]

The language of poetry can express the simultaneity of multiple temporalities because it is the linguistic form that procures feelings with a home and neglects sometimes mere functional communication. Poetry is about rhythm, about tempo, the metronome of life. We sense time through our lives passing at different speeds depending on the intensity[72] of experience of the moment we are going through. The more intense, the longer it feels.

Diótima's Daughters

> Be clever, Ariadne!
> You have small ears, you have my
> ears: Put a clever word into them!
> [...]
> I am your labyrinth.[73]

Home constitutes the center of the worlds inhabited by these women in the following narratives.[74] Home is also where I return, over and over again, to harvest the original words they sang, threads connecting me to my origins. Their words are meant to be listened to, not just read, with the ear as the privileged organ of the human soul. In Zambrano's words, "the acoustic plane of a word matters more

---

71 John Berger, *And Our Faces, My Heart, Brief as Photos* (London: Bloomsbury, 2005). [Italics mine].
72 Bergson, *Time and Free Will*.
73 Friedrich Nietzsche, *Thus Spoke Zarathustra: A Book for None and All*, trans. with a preface by Walter Kaufmann (New York: Viking Penguin, 1966); Gilles Deleuze, "Ariadne's Mystery," *ANY: Architecture New York*, 5, (1994), 8-9. https://www.jstor.org/stable/41845627.
74 Berger, *And Our Faces*, 64.

than its semantic meaning whose precision responds to a parallel piano, but lower than purely musical."[75]

Diótima se va convirtiendo así en criatura
del sonido y, por ello, no puede escribir;
lo que le es natural es hablar y [...] Diótima, criatura casi del mundo
natural, posee esta capacidad de captar realidades
que están a punto de ser, posee una
extraña sensibilidad hacia lo fragmentario y
lo evanescente, y esto se debe, según ella
misma, a que nunca ha pensado, es decir,
nunca intentó formar palabra, nunca se
sometió a ninguna lógica. Sus movimientos
han sido siempre <<atraídos invisiblemente
como las mareas>>, y la reguladora de las
mareas es, como se sabe, la luna (p. 95)

La luna es, simbólicamente,
la señora de las mujeres, afecta tal como a las
mareas su ciclo fisiológico. La luna y su luz ida
es tomada como guía del lado oculto de la naturaleza,
Es una duplicación de la luz solar, un
reflejo, es decir, una luz que no es luz por si
misma, pero que la recibe de una forma pasiva;
por eso representa la pasividad, lo femenino, con
toda su carga de saber intuitivo. (p. 96)

Nos dice Diótima:
<<En ese medio de visibilidad
(las cosas) ni se mueven ni
están quietas, no sufren estado
alguno, son. Respiran en la luz,
en una luz que no vibra ni por
ello está muerta>>(nota 23 Diótima p. 193) (p. 96)

Diótima es también la madre de las almas
que en ella se hunden cuando se quedan sin cuerpo.
Pero no de todas las airnas, apenas de las de
<<aquellos que no hablan tenido nombre>> (nota 24 p192 Diótima) (p. 96)

---

75   Zambrano, "Para la Historia de la piedad."

Qué quiere significar este otro medio de
visibilidad? Parece que Diótima hubiera alcanzado
la mirada inteligible, una contemplación
directa de las ideas como pretendía Platón: ver
en el medio de la verdad. Ver en un medio donde
no hay diferencia entre el ver y lo visto; haber alcanzado un estado donde la constante dicotomía
obstaculizante del conocimiento, la separación
sujeto-objeto, no produjera distorsiones.
Un acceder, pues, a las cosas mismas, no mediatizadas
por un modo de percepción. [...] Después Diótima vió al modo de ver del
poeta; y este modo de ver era como si estuviera
bajo el agua. Por otro lado, se vuelve a
destacar la presencia del ritmo: las imágenes bajo
el agua variaban de luz y de intensidad, pero partían
de una imagen modelo que luego < (p 98)

El ritmo aparece una vez más como elemento
fundamental, primigenio, participante de
todas las cosas. El ritmo es música y la música es
un arte que se realiza en el tiempo. Necesita del
tiempo como elemento donde vivir, así como el
pez necesita del agua. Diótima, criatura del sonido,
empieza entonces a <<respirar en el tiempo
(...) hasta entrarme en su corazón. (Nota 33), y, al penetrar
en el corazón del tiempo, penetró en todas
las cosas, pues <<no hay cuerpo, no hay materia
alguna enteramente desprendida del tiempo>> (nota 34).
El tiempo es, pues, condición de la vida. Llegar
a ser coincide con empezar a latir desde un ritmo
propio, empezar a caminar por su tiempo. [...] Esta es, pues, su posición: Madre, origen anterior
a la separación entre luz y sombras, y anterior a
la diferenciación de los ritmos y sonidos; ella es
potencia, toda Eros, toda tensión a punto de realizarse. (p. 99)

Chapter 7
Patrocinio 101

> It remains – to remain? –
> The flesh wounded. There is a scar.
> And the mind – the mind? – wounded
> wounded? No, there is no wound.
> If there were one there would be blood.
> There is a scar. No, Neither.
> If there were a scar, it would be evident.
> They do not always show, they say.
> Certain words are used instead of others,
> they say. When there are not enough
> words. Better when there's nothing.[1]
> Chantal Maillard, *Hilos* (2007)

I stand in the middle of the room, my hand pressing down on top of the round dining table. My five fingers are not enough anymore to count my age. Six years old, three feet tall, two eyes closed, and one mouth shut, I stand stiff, straight, my free right hand tightly squeezing my mother's. The hot sterilized sewing needle pierces my pearly earlobe. Inside my mouth I scream, as a flood of salty tears washes over

---

1   Permanece—permanecer?—la carne
    herida. Hay cicatriz.
    Y la mente—la mente?—herida.
    Herida? No, no hay herida. Si
    la hubiese habría sangre. Hay
    cicatriz. Tampoco.
    Si hubiese cicatriz, sería
    Evidente. No siempre se ven, dicen.
    Ciertas palabras se utilizan
    en vez de otras, dicen. Cuando
    no hay palabras suficientes.
    Mejor cuando no hay
    cosa. Chantal Maillard, *Hilos* (Barcelona: Tusquets, 2007), 15.

my eyes. My aunt pulls the alcohol-laced thread through the tiny opening as if stitching a label to my skin.

On the Point of a Needle

> Night of four moons
> and a single tree
> On the point of a needle
> There's my love,
> Spinning![2]

My aunt Patro is my godmother and my mother's cousin. A seamstress by night, and a butcher by day, she is very skilled with knives of various sizes, scissors, pins, and needles. The perfect piercing artist. She pierces with her voice too.

> *Ya está, Ya está, Ya está...*/ There, there, there...
> *eso no es na!*/ That is nothing!
> *Qué valiente es mi niña*/ My Little girl is so brave
> *y*/and
> *qué guapa va a estar*/She will be so beautiful
> *con sus zarcillos nuevos*/with her new earrings
> *p'a su primera comunión!*/ for her First Communion

When the ordeal is over, a storm of kisses drenches my face. They are Andalusian kisses, accompanied by a chorus of chirping birds.

Patro was born on September 12, 1917, in Granada, one of five siblings. When she was four years old, she was gifted to the childless Escribano family, the owners of the butcher shop where her father worked. In those days, it was not uncommon for spare children to be given to relatives or others in an informal kind of adoption. This was done sometimes out of economic necessity and other times as a token of *compadrazgo*, or kinship.

Patro refers to her adoptive parents as her "Aunt" and "Uncle," even though they were not blood relatives. She is not clear on the details of the transaction, but this was not some hidden family secret. Patro still saw her biological parents and siblings—they all lived in the same neighborhood and her father continued to work in the butcher shop—and thought nothing unusual about this arrangement. As she

---

2   Federico García Lorca, *Selected Poems*, trans. Martin Sorrell (Oxford: Oxford University Press, 2007), 91-93.

tells it, her "aunt" had taken a liking to her when both families lived in the same building. When her aunt and uncle moved to a new house, Patro, along with the furniture, went with them:

> When they bought the house in the Escudo del Carmen...that was when I left with them, I was only four years old. Because my aunt had no children and I was a very sweet little girl, she loved me very much. When we lived in the same building I would say... 'Oh my auntie is coming'...and filled the jar with fresh water....

Moving to the Escribano house took Patro out of the crime-ridden Manigua neighborhood and also provided her with a more comfortable life.[3] "I used to go in the afternoons to see my aunt's sister at the 'Thirty-two' [restaurant] where we had our afternoon snack. Then, some days in the summer we would visit that sister in the village of Zubia where she owned a *cortijo* (farmhouse). Well, we would go to the *cortijo* in the summer afternoons to visit for a little while. We always went in the afternoon and we had to ride the trolley car...of course!"[4]

Patro loved her aunt, accompanying her everywhere, even the butcher shop where her father still worked. An outgoing, social girl, she preferred the vibrancy of the market to the drudgery of school. When she turned twelve, she asked her aunt if she could quit school to help out in the store. "All I wanted was to sell. I told my aunt to let me sell lemons and parsley." She extends her tiny hand towards me, turns it up, making a little bowl shape with her fingers where she holds an imaginary lemon, while with the other hand, she pretends to braid a strand of parsley. "... It would cost a 'perrilla' or a 'gorda'[5].... And so that's it, I liked to sell. I began selling in the market next to the butcher shop."[6]

When she turned fifteen, a handsome young man from the neighborhood, Juan, started noticing her. Her aunt was not so keen on the advances of a *rodaballo*, a *turbot*, she called him, nine years older than Patro, but there was little she could do to prevent the two lovebirds from liking each other. As were the rules of courtship, Juan and Patro could not talk to each other without a third party present at all times. That responsibility fell to Patro's younger brother, Paco.

I talked to him [Juan] through an iron gate at the Escudo del Carmen house, and sometimes someone came in and I ran up the stairs to the first floor...and he would push and try to slip his foot in to hold the door ajar.... That would scare me, so he would quickly retreat.... One

---

3   The local newspaper IDEAL published the story of the Manigua neighborhood: "Comienza el derribo de la Manigua," June 16, 2015. https://granadablogs.com/terecuerdo/2015/06/16/comienza-el-derribo-de-la-manigua/#more-1342
4   Patrocinio Martínez Sánchez, audio recording by author, Granada, December 2012.
5   Currency units that do not amount to even a penny.
6   Patrocinio, recording, 2012.

*day my uncle showed up...I don't know why or what might have happened for him to all of a sudden show up but I darted up the staircase while my husband [to be] stayed downstairs. And then when carnival time came, and everyone in masks, that's when my Juan finally asked my uncle's **permission** to climb the stairs to talk to me.*[7]

Figure 16: Patro and Juan

Patro and Juan got married after four years of courtship. She was nineteen. Their wedding took place in the spring of 1936, just prior to the beginning of the Spanish Civil War. They got married in the San Ildefonso Church in the Triunfo district where Patro's parents lived, though the bride departed to the church from her aunt and uncle's home in the Escudo del Carmen. She recalled her nuptials fondly.

"My husband gave me 20 *duros*[8] for both my wedding dress and the dress for the day after. I also had enough to buy fabric to make some curtains," she recalled with pride. "The wedding dress cost one *duro* per meter...because it was sateen...so shiny and beautiful...the sleeve required a least one meter of fabric as it was all gathered at my wrist so." She wraps her fingers around her tiny wrist to demonstrate, as if she were touching the sateen once more. "And my veil...and my bouquet...." She remembers how Juan also paid thirteen *duros* for a six-car procession to transport the wedding party from the Escudo del Carmen Street to the church. In a melodic tone she loudly sings, *"SIX CARS."*

---

7   Patrocinio, recording, 2012.
8   A *duro* was a five pesetas coin, equivalent to approximately five cents.

Figure 17: Patro and Juan's wedding photo

They moved into a one-bedroom pied-a-terre in the Boqueron district, which she recalled warmly: "The house…well I furnished a very suitable home. Look, …there was my bed, which I still have! That one will remain my bed until I DIE!!… My armoire and two stone-topped bedside tables…. And one of those old washbasins with a water jar…have you seen those? I also had sewn myself a beautiful peignoir, which by the way…there is a history behind that too…a lady who lived on the Aranda's street made me this peignoir along with some embroidered linens and so on…. Later, I made a blouse out of it, a vivid pink sateen piece with brown embroidered embellishments…." She paused for an instant. "You see, I also had a bridal bedcover…a dining room table with its tablecloth…two pedestals with their doilies, two grid chairs, and my sister-in-law Indalecia made me some round cushions with some Chinese designs…. My sister-in-law was so talented…. And then in the kitchen we had an *espetera*, the *cantarera*, the table…that's thanks to Tito Emilio who crafted all those household things for me…. And also, one of those little pantry cupboards. And a trunk for my clothes."[9]

---

9   Patrocinio, recording, 2012.

The accumulation of household furnishings and fittings at the time of marriage was mostly the responsibility of the bride and was supposed to portend a successful union. While modest, their home was more than adequate for a skilled worker and his wife. Juan was a cook who expected his young bride to stay at home and forget about butcher shops or selling in the market.

Juan had five siblings: three sisters, Indalecia, Virtudes, and Dolores, and two brothers, Nicolás and Miguel. Indalecia was dear to Patro. They were almost the same age. Originally, Indalecia was to marry her boyfriend, a mailman, before Patro and Juan, but they decided to wait. She sadly remembers how Indalecia lost her boyfriend in the early days of the civil war. The war was not easy on Patro either. She got pregnant right away, and Juan was sent to Sevilla to serve as cook in the home of General Queipo de Llano, the brutal commander of the Nationalists' southern forces.

Patro, a woman who was never particularly interested in politics, doesn't seem to grasp the implications of her husband working for the general responsible for the massacre of so many Spaniards during the civil war. She spoke about Juan's position as if it were just another deployment: "They picked him and another guy up and took them to Sevilla to cook for Queipo. He told me they [The Queipos] were very good people...especially his wife, *buenísima*. But my husband found himself with the other guy who was not trustworthy and...my husband got scared, sick. He obsessed about what the other guy might do.... If something happened to Queipo they might blame it on the cook for poisoning him or something. My husband got a bladder infection from worrying. The General's wife, who was very sweet, had a conversation with her husband and...she went ahead and gave Juan FIVE DUROS!! and sent him back to me in Granada. I remember how cousin Miguel was coming down the street yelling, 'he is coming, he is coming, Juan is coming!!' And suddenly, my husband appeared at the front door.... He, poor man, looked so sick...THAT WOMAN gave him five *duros*!!...for the trip back because she was so kindhearted.... He [Juan] had had a talk with her...and the other scoundrel stayed behind...."[10]

I am listening in silence, trying to process in my head how to render the story, her story, that now is mine to tell and which suddenly makes the enemy a close personal subject. The alien nature of evil suddenly enters the room, and its ghost sits in on our conversation. Ronald Fraser tells us how "all those denounced by 'law-abiding citizens' as assassins, left-wingers, trouble-makers, non-churchgoers were certain to be court-martialed."[11] There is no question Juan was terrified to be working for someone like Queipo. However, the way he managed to return to

---

10   Patrocinio, recording, 2012.
11   Ronald Fraser, *Blood of Spain: An Oral History of the Spanish Civil War* (New York: Pantheon, 1979),158.

his pregnant wife in late December 1937 with money in his pocket is suspicious. Patro continued, "My husband did not belong to any political party, unlike his sister Indalecia.... My sister-in-law was into politics. She was with the workers, but my husband was not. One night, as he approached his house, Juan saw some of the workers meeting on the terrace, and he told them, 'Oh you're going to bring us ruin.' But my husband did not turn them in…. He went into his house…I mean he was so righteous. And then they caught them…that was terrible. Aunt Indalecia participated in the Casa del Pueblo persecution, as it was known…. But as she did not know how to sign her name, nothing happened…otherwise, God knows what would have happened to her. And yet she had a boyfriend who was a postman, who ran with people who were you know [she implied they were leftists]…in Casa del Pueblo or in the bar…they would meet, and they would talk. My dear…and they took thirteen postmen and in twenty-four hours they shot them. My sister-in-law went every day to the cemetery…and we were going with her…with my children, and I went to the cemetery myself. The awful thing that happened…that she was going to get married."

Like all families who lived through the Spanish Civil War, there are secrets that do not easily give themselves up. I had never heard about Juan's involvement with Queipo de Llano during the war, or the Casa del Pueblo persecution in which my aunt's sister-in-law, one of the collaborators, was somehow spared on a technicality. Patro takes all these events at face value, never questioning the role her husband played.

As with many Spanish families in the south, loyalties were often split. Patro had been adopted into the right-wing Escribano family. Her memories of workers out to harm her adoptive relatives, owners of various enterprises, show a distinct right-wing bias. To her, the ones who just happened to disappear in the early years of the regime, some from her own family, were being indiscreet or worse, disloyal.

"I lived with the Escribanos, and you would hear them," Patro recalled. "I do not say that Franco was behind it, but there were many abuses…hatred and people being killed and blaming Franco. The tito of Aunt Consuelo's husband, you know your mother's sister…he was a man who talked a lot…and they took him out of the way…left him on the highway. And yet he had a brother who was pro-Franco. But because he spoke…one of those men who talks and talks and doesn't know what he is saying…with his eight children…they took him out of the way."

As Patro and Juan reunited and welcomed their first child in the winter of 1938, they still had to endure another year of war. Their marriage would last only seven more years. Seven more years, three more children, and twenty-four hours of agony.

He Died at Dawn

> My husband. Gone,
> gone, gone, GONE.
> white little darling face.
> Green, purple, red
> All of his body
> gone, gone.[12]

"Within twenty-four hours he was dead," she shared. "That photo, niña, HE DID NOT SEE, qué lástima de mi marído! Oh, my poor husband!" Juan had filed some paperwork to get an apartment in the new Figares district. The government had built some affordable housing for large families. Having a minimum of four children qualified them for the petition. As part of the paperwork, the family had their picture taken.

Figure 18: Patro and Juan with three of their four children

"He got septicemia. It seems that he cut himself working, you know. He must have cut himself with a can, and people started to say he got tetanus...no, no, no...HE DIED of septicemia.... They treated the wound...in his hand...but that thing was bad. They prescribed some pills and all day long he took those pills and retched at night...so very sick. I did not know what had taken over him, I was so young.... And then something started to show in his arm. My husband knew he was dying. I cannot forget those patches all over.... [she touched her arm up from her hand

---

12   Patrocinio's words as she retells her husband's death. Interview by author recording, 2012.

to her shoulder] He kept looking at those patches crying... 'do not look at them anymore.' The doctor was going to return in the morning to amputate the arm. My husband told me, 'You will have to return to sell [in the market].' I remember those last words. At nine in the morning the doctor came to take him to the hospital but by then he was already dead. My two little boys stood shivering in their undershirts, next to the bed. The neighbors came to see...as is customary...they laid him on the ground.... What a tragedy! In the evening...they took him to the cemetery. Only a little bit of his face remained white. The rest was black.... He was 38 years old and I...not 29 yet. [long silence] With four children."[13]

Patro was alone now. Her parents were taking care of one of her siblings, Pepe, the youngest brother, sick with tuberculosis, making it impossible for her to move back home. "Yes, my husband told me, 'You will sell;' it was my destiny," she remembered. "Within a year of his passing I was in the market. But first I started sewing. In our neighborhood, down the street there was this factory where they made overalls.... I started sewing overalls for them at home on my sewing machine because the pension I received did not cover all our needs.[14] I received 468 *pesetas*,[15] three *duros*[16] which gave us enough to eat but not much more. People would ask me, 'What are you going to do with four kids? How will you survive? You surely will place the older ones [in an orphanage]....' And I said, all right, while I have things to sell in the house, we'll see about that."

"I couldn't survive on only three *duros*. NO WAY!! So I worked. I used to pick up the materials in the factory and sometimes Amelia, my neighbor, also a widow, would help, and the two of us made a little extra money. I remember how one day she came home all agitated because unintentionally she had cut one of the pieces wrong and so was panicked we would not get paid. I told her not to say a thing. Then, I folded all the pieces very nicely and put the defective one in between the good ones."

"I also remember how one day, another neighbor, Maria's husband, the coal worker, sold me fifteen *duros* of coal, and I took it to my living room and threw it on the floor and re-sold it to the neighbors! ME!! In my own house. I was not going

---

13 Patrocinio, recording, 2012.
14 Juan died in 1946.
15 After 1939, the Bank of Spain's objectives were set by the Francoist Ministry of Finance. Spain was excluded from the Marshall Plan and implemented autarchy or self-sufficient economy. After the Pact of Madrid in 1953 with the US, Spain wasn't able to escape the misery of the postwar years, the 1940s, known as the Hunger years. In 1959 the exchange for $1 was 60 pts. This was thirteen years after Patro became a widow. On the financial history of the National Spanish Bank see Pablo Martin Aceña, *The Banco de España, 1782-2017: The History of a Central Bank*, in *Estudios de Historia Económica*, 73 (2017). https://www.bde.es/f/webbde/SES/Secciones/Publicaciones/PublicacionesSeriadas/EstudiosHistoriaEconomica/Files/roja73e.pdf.
16 One *duro* was a coin of five pesetas, the equivalent of a nickel.

to stay just with three *duros*. NO WAY!! You not only had to feed the children but to dress them and pay rent and electricity...I had four children.... The next year I got a stand in the public market to sell the meat offal from the butcher shop. I sold, tongue, heart, tripe...."

Figure 19: Patro in the market stall

I remember my aunt at her stand in the public market, dressed in blood-specked white, holding a butcher knife in one hand and a gigantic cow's heart, our dinner that night, in the other. Hers was in one of two rows of stands occupied by other women also dressed in white, hawking their wares to the passersby. At various times on my aunt's marble counter you would find squishy brains resting next to rubbery pigs' feet or a gigantic, mute, fleshy tongue. Entrails draped from meat hooks behind Patro's smiling face. Amid the animal carnage, Patro was in her element, selling to the women, like my mother, who needed the cheap meat to flavor the soups, to feed their growing families from their husbands' meager wages.

Figure 20: Empty market stalls

The offal sellers were all women. The butchers were all men. This unquestioned hierarchy was indicative of the way working class women under Franco were relegated to the helping class. Having recently emerged from the worst of post-war deprivation, these women were in no position to question this hierarchy. They were just happy to have their own little white tile stalls and the castoff pieces of meat to sell. What looked like a scene from a horror movie was their sanctuary. Here they enjoyed a lively fellowship amongst themselves and the housewives who came daily to haggle.

Figure 21 (left): Patro and two others at the market stall
Figure 22 (right): Patro cutting meat

Butchery Business

The butcher shop that belonged to Patro's adoptive family, the Escribanos, ended up in the hands of her older brother, Felix. "When my uncle died…my aunt left the butcher shop to her sister," Patro shared. "Of course, she was not going to leave it to me!! You understand? And then, she hired my brother Felix, paying him thirteen *pesetas* a day…. One day she showed up at the butcher shop and said… 'Felix, I want nothing with this butchery, you can have it!' That simple! And then Uncle Paco [her younger brother] arranged the paperwork and the butchery went entirely to FELIX [she declares with an intense look into my eyes]…. And me, the one who grew up with them…[pause] what do you think of that?"

This is particularly painful for her because when she asked Felix to supply her with offal to sell in the market, he at first refused. No, that was not a job for his sister. But Patro begged and begged him until he finally relented. She needed him to provide the offal meat for her to sell in her little stall to be able to support her family.

Without a source of steady income, women had to rely on the charity of men. For Patro, this was not an attractive option. Once her brother finally agreed to supply her with his discarded scraps, she was on her way: "I was a good seller. Everyone got to know me. Some days my sister Dolores would come down and other days she would help with the children. In the end, I do not know who said…I do not know if it was your grandmother or Aunt Nieves, 'Go ahead and bring cousin Aurora to take care of the kids'…and that's how your mother came to live with me."

My mother was thirteen years old when she moved in with her first cousin Patro, a widow with four young children. Theirs turned into a happy relationship as my mother would be living among family rather than being a domestic servant in the houses of strangers, while my aunt, a young widow, would have someone she trusted looking after her children and the household while she worked in the market. They lived on San Isidro Street in a centrally located neighborhood behind the city's patroness, Virgin of the Sorrows Basilica. Patro and her four children would have qualified for public housing as a large family, but the paperwork got lost after her husband died and she never applied again. The San Isidro home was always open to family, neighbors, and friends from near and far. It was in that living/dining-room that I stood in tears while my aunt pierced my earlobe on a spring afternoon in 1969.

The apartment was small, located on the top floor and arranged around a central patio where the windows faced inward. "So much hard work," she reflected, "...and your mother with the children there. Then I came, we sewed, we made dinner, we did so many things together. Look...the house was like this, you went in and there it was, the dining room with a balcony. And our uncle from Noalejo made me a bar from side to side to hang some drapes that the kids said was the theater curtain...but it served us better as a divider. When the kids got dressed and undressed, we would draw the curtain and split the room. And then from the same room [to the right] there was another small room and there is where I put Grandpa [her father]. Grandma [her mother] had occupied it the same before him...until she died there, while your mother lived in my house too. You know that I did not grow up with them [her biological parents, the grandparents of her children] and yet both died here with me.... You realize what...what life is all about. When Grandma died, Grandpa was living with Aunt Dolores [Patro's younger sister]. Aunt Dolores went to the butcher shop on San Juan de Dios Street...and asked me, 'Can you take care of Papa?' 'Oh, well, then send him to me,' I said, and Grandpa came to live with me, and I put him in that small room."

After twenty years of working in the market, raising four children, and caring for her ailing parents, Patro was beginning to get sick. "I was exhausted. Papa was always getting up in the night. 'Niña, turn on the light.' 'Papa, what do you want?' 'Turn on the light. I have to pee.' After that I would return to bed...in a little while again, 'NIÑA...!' I do not know how much time in between...in a little while...again I got up. 'NIÑA...!' Then, I would come back from work and Patrico [her oldest daughter] would tell me, 'Grandpa is waiting for you with soiled hands from wiping himself....' I would wash his hands...He did not want to eat until I came back from work.... Well, this happened day after day.... Then, well, then Uncle Antonio and Aunt Dolores came to help take care of Papa...'so you can sleep.' But Papa would say, 'no, no, no, my PATROCINIO only!' And I was right next door where I have the bedroom. Well, I would not sleep either. Then I fell. They told me it was a bad heart. I needed to stop working and rest."

Patro was forced to retire. She eventually regained her health but didn't return to the market. She still cooked and cleaned and even helped her seamstress daughter Patrico with some sewing. Keeping track of her four children and many grandchildren became almost a second job.

In today's world, a four-year-old girl who was freely given away by her parents to a wealthier, childless family might be expected to have issues. Another girl, only thirteen, lent to a new widow to help her raise four children, might also be expected to harbor some resentment. But this was not the world in which my Aunt Patro and later my mother, Aurora, grew up. Their world was one of civil wars, dictators, and years of hunger, where the suffering of working-class women was part of the collateral damage.

Far from feeling sorry for themselves, these women learned how to survive in a world in which their men were conscripted, co-opted, and often damaged. They cooked and sewed and cleaned house. They raised families and took care of the elderly. And they worked in the markets, stalls, and shops to make the little bit of money that kept their families housed, fed, and clothed. These working-class women were more practical than political, but their underlying fortitude made a statement all its own. The lie that women were the weaker, more fragile sex was hard to accept when growing up with working-class women like Patro. The strength they showed was not lost on my generation, nor was the blatant injustice they suffered at the hands of men and a patriarchal regime. The implicit lesson that these women taught us was that only we knew how to provide for ourselves.

Patro died on October 22, 2018, of a stroke. One hundred and one years old, sharp as the knives she used to cut the fibrous cow's heart in the market stall so many years earlier. My mother, who she liberated from a life of penury in the village, still lives. I sit here writing these stories because of them.

Chapter 8
Pura's Rashomon Effect (1926-2013)

> To be free is not a gift, it is a reconquest, and it is necessary to remain silent to build that story that is saved like a long secret that nobody witnessed.
> To be free is to nurture a mystery upon which our life is built.
> Chantal Maillard, "Spell to tell lies and build truths" (1999)[1]

As I listen now to the tape recording of that hot June 2002 afternoon, from my air-conditioned house in Miami, the street noise from the recording triggers a host of memories. I am transported to that hot, sticky afternoon, frustratingly trying to unlock the truth, any truth, from my aunt's tightly guarded memory vault. She does not want to tell me what I want to know. I am hearing her talk, but I am not really listening because I know she is not confiding in me. She knows I know her story, or at least the outlines. I am her family.

She is good at this game, though, presenting her fiction while I pretend to not be aggravated. Because I am family, I don't have the same authority as an outsider. The truth, after all, can be uncomfortable when you have to keep living with someone. I tell myself that this is just one wasted afternoon, me pretending to listen, she pretending to tell the truth, as her yellow canary intermittently chirps on the slowly unfolding tape recording of that afternoon on June 30, 2002.

---

1 *Ser libre no es un don, es una reconquista,*
y es preciso callar para construir
aquella historia que se guarda
como un largo secreto del que nadie es testigo.
Ser libre es tener cuidado de un misterio
sobre el cual se construye nuestra vida.
Chantal Maillard, "Conjuro para decir mentiras y construir verdades," *Nómadas: Revista Crítica de Ciencias Sociales y Jurídicas* (1999): 135-36. https://webs.ucm.es/info/nomadas/0/chantalmaillard_1.pdf.

Pura's Narrative

Figure 23: Pura as a child, 1927

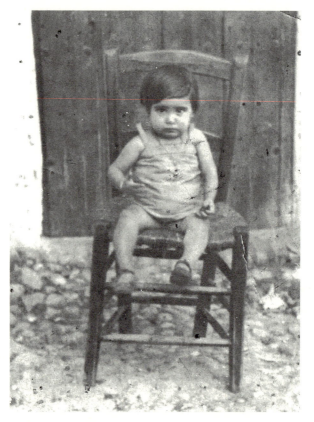

Pura was born on the 5th of September 1926 in Alfacar, a small village only seven kilometers from Granada, and raised in a nearby village called Huetor. When she turned twelve, the family moved to Granada. She remembered going to school in Huetor Santillán: "…Well, it seems to me that I entered school at four or five years of age. I decided to go on my own, not because anybody encouraged or sent me there." With an ironic laugh she remarked, "I was on the wrong path!…had high expectations!… I went to school with a medicine book under my arm." She stares me in the eyes with pride, "…and then, the teacher asked me, 'Did you bring your textbook?' And I replied, 'Yes, here it is.'"

I can see her satisfaction in retelling that memory as she repeated the teacher's remark as if we were in her presence: "Oh my, we are starting the house in the wrong place.... You see, my Uncle Gaspar, my mother's cousin, lived with us and he was in medical school, so I took one of his medicine books to MY school.... I indeed was starting the house from the wrong place!"

Pura is my aunt on my maternal side. Her father, Miguel, and my grandfather, Jose, were brothers. Both had many children and endured tremendous hardships to raise their families as a result of the Spanish Civil War and the immediate misery that followed.[2] Pura was the oldest of eight: three males and five females. Only ten years old when the war started, she remembered with bitterness having to leave school to go to work and support the family: "I stopped going to school when the war started. We moved to Granada and I, being the oldest, had to help my mother and also work for money. Sewing. In the sewing industry, always sewing. And that way I helped my mother and the household.... She was alone and the two of us had to care for the children...my siblings. My father worked for the telephone company. First, he had worked for the electric company, Conpañía Sevillana, and then he moved to the Telefónica.... I am not sure exactly what he did, only I know he went to work for the telephone company, and he did whatever they asked him to do. Sometimes he would be inside the plant, sometimes on some other site outdoors, but I am not sure because he never talked about his work."

When I ask her to tell me more about her childhood memories of the war, my aunt gets aggravated with my question: "Look, about the war, no...I do not remember anything, and I do not want to remember it. Because I had enough of wars as I have experienced too many. I do not even want to think about it. And as far as my childhood, well, I was very happy. Because I had everything I wanted...although, with the war I had to start helping at home...helping my parents...but my childhood was very happy."

It is clear that her childhood was far from ideal, but it is also clear that Pura is in no mood to talk about it. I try to steer away from this touchy subject and follow with a more personal question pertaining to her coming of age. I ask her about her first period. When I interviewed her in 2002, I was immersed in research for my second book on sexuality and body politics under Francoism. My question was met with similar exasperation. *That happened so many years ago I DON'T REMEMBER. I*

---

2   The bibliography on the Spanish Civil War (1936-1939) is too copious to list here. A very short list of works include Hugh Thomas, *The Spanish Civil War* (New York: Harper Row, 1961); Ronald Fraser, *Blood of Spain: An Oral History of the Spanish Civil War* (New York: Pantheon, 1986); Stanley Payne, *The Spanish Civil War* (Cambridge: Cambridge University Press, 2012); Paul Preston, *The Spanish Holocaust: Inquisition and Extermination in Twentieth-Century Spain* (New York: W. W. Norton & Company, 2013). On gender see Mary Nash, *Defying Male Civilization: Women in the Spanish Civil War* (Denver: Arden Press, 1995). For Granada see Rafael Gil Bracero y María Isabel Brenes, *Jaque a la República (Granada 1936-1939)* (Granada: Osuna Editores, 2009), along with the extensive work on García Lorca by author Ian Gibson.

DON'T REMEMBER. Determined, undaunted, I ignore her attitude and ask if she was shocked or if knew about it when she had her first menstruation:

"Well, girls always know. In the same way they know about it now. When we were young, we also knew. We knew where babies came from and how things happened. That is common knowledge [irritated tone] always. That was then, now, and a long, long time ago. Since the beginning of times.... Mothers might have seen it as taboo, but girls?... We know much more than our mothers gave us credit. Exactly the same as now."

When I suggest that maybe there was less information available at the time due to Catholic morals, she dismissively replied: "The same, LIFE CONTINUES...those things...I really do not see any difference. Seriously, I do not see it. No, girls always know about our things, and they have always known. Because if you don't know about something, I would tell you and then that passes from mouth to mouth. It was always common knowledge."

"Is that how you found out?" I pressed.

"THE SAME WAY YOU FOUND OUT! And that other one, and that other one. The way everybody finds out about anything. Or about how babies come...when you get married, etc.... We all know those things the minute we are old enough. Because if you do not know something, I will tell you and the next one, and those things pass from mouth to mouth. There are some people I have encountered who pretend to be stupid...and those who pretend to be naïve, but they are not! In the end, they have behaved worse than those others who supposedly were very worldly.... ALWAYS THE SAME THE SAME...YESTERDAY, TOMORROW AND FOREVER...."

I have upset her now.

"That's how some pretend...pretending they are naïve until it is obvious that instead they are too smart for their own good. Those things...Aurora...I do not appreciate it."

I move to what I think are safer waters, asking her about her leisure activities as a young woman. Did she go to the movies or read novels? She replied, "ME?!... No, reading novels has not been my choice. I only liked to read serious educational books. Novels and comics were not to my taste. I used to read books that sometimes fell into my hands, sometimes not. Instead of reading a novel I would rather sew or embroider or do something else. But not for me...most certainly not novels...I did not even like to listen to them."

Pura was most likely referring to the "radio novelas" popular at the time among homemakers. She continued, "Nowadays, perhaps I find some entertainment in listening to them because I cannot sew very much as I have bad eyesight. But really for me, whenever I find a good history book or something like it.... A good book always rather than a novel...not interested.... You see, for me, let me tell you...since I was a little girl I wanted to learn and could not.... Well, I did not want to waste any time reading something I would not like.... I would have studied medicine if

I could. That was my dream and even now...look, I have collected medical books, about medicinal plants, and I have devoured them but not a novel. If I have an ailment, I know how to take care of myself, better perhaps than other people who are not familiar with home remedies...this herb or that other is good for that or the other.... When I visited a doctor, rather than using the medication he prescribed I would use herbal treatments of my choice. [...] Because I have studied all those things.... It is what I am trying to tell you.... When a person likes something.... Let's see, why do you know about history? Because you like it, right? And seek information, right? Now you are researching, seeking information, learning from me.... Well, in my case, I like medical stuff...everything on the subject I have been able to learn, I have read, studied...I brought some medical books from France ...but some boxes with my books were lost in the move...."

Her mentioning France gives me a chance to ask her about her experience abroad. I know she got married to Juan, a Spanish man who came all the way from Algeria to marry her. I would like for her to tell me about how they met that day in August 1958 when he came from Oran across the Mediterranean. Pura's response, unsurprisingly, is not very revealing: "It is of no consequence, how I met him...because it was my destiny. He had to come to meet me. You know, that man did not live here, he lived in Algeria...and he came to visit Uncle Jeanot who was his friend[3].... He came, we got to know each other, and he fell in love with me...and I liked him. So, we arranged everything and got married here [in Granada] in the Iglesia del Salvador, of course, where else? Perhaps I could have gotten married in another church but since we had to do it quickly before his return and had very few days in between.... Because as soon as he met me in person...we met on August 2, got married on the 28, and he returned to Algeria on August 30."

"You did not know that, right?" She looked intently into my eyes with a half-amused smile. "We got to know each other before through correspondence and photographs...I saw him first in that picture over there." She pointed to a picture of her husband displayed prominently on the other side of the room. "He sent me a portrait so I could see him. When he came in person, I liked him, his presence, his manners...and so we got married...I was almost thirty-one.... Then, I had my Mari and my Carmen [their two daughters]."

---

3   Jeanot had married Mercedes, one of Pura's younger sisters, and was in Granada. Jeanot, also Spanish, and Juan had been neighbors and friends in Oran for years.

Figure 24: Pura (on the right) on a stroll with her sister Mercedes and her husband, a close friend of Juan's who showed him this picture, which led him to pursue Pura

I asked Pura about her first impression of Algeria, when she arrived in Oran. That was her first time outside of Granada. "When I arrived there, I thought it was paradise. Because I was used to...you know, Granada in those days, Granada was a very beautiful city. It shined with its cleanliness and so on.... Granada may have been a small town but it shined like a silver cup. It was clean as fresh spring water. When we came early in the morning to work, down the Calderería hill from the Albayzin to downtown...the street sweepers were finishing scrubbing, street by street. Now our streets are dirty...now Granada is grimy, but then, it was like a precious little silver cup, everything gleaming clean. No one could shake out even a tablecloth out their window because you got a fine. Today we only see filth. So, I was used to Granada and when I arrived in Oran, well...upon arrival I was not very impressed. It was in the evening that your uncle took me out for a stroll...because we lived, let me think how best to explain it to you.... Like our Gran Via, there was the main avenue in the city center and we lived in what we call here in Granada Elvira Street, parallel to our Gran Via, just like it. So, when we went out at night for a walk down the main avenue...I was enchanted, really enchanted. For me it was...a Little America...that is what Oran was for me...an America in miniature. Because...how can I describe it to you?... I saw everything with impressionable eyes.... If you go to a place you never saw before and you see it in all its grandeur.... Well, let's see.... What did you feel when you arrived in America? After your departure from a beautiful town like Granada...."

Figure 25: *Their wedding in Granada, August 28, 1958*

Obviously, my aunt had never visited America. What I believe she is trying to tell me is how foreign her new home felt. She tries to connect her experience with my own when she compares it to my move to the United States in 1989 to pursue a Ph.D. at the University of New Mexico in Albuquerque. I tell her my experience was amazing as well, not wanting to explore with her my own difficult truth. As an interviewer you are not supposed to interject your own story, but in a way you do. When I listen to my words on the tape, I reflect on the true experience of displacement in a foreign land in order to imagine what my aunt might have experienced being alone in a foreign country, away from her hometown of Granada, for the first time in her life.

My mind drifts uncontrollably to August 9, 1989, when, after twenty-four hours of flying (Málaga to Madrid, Madrid to Dallas, and Dallas to Albuquerque), I finally arrive, exhausted, in Albuquerque, New Mexico. The airport feels small, more like a bus station. No one is there to greet me, so I take a taxi to the motel that had been recommended by the parents of an exchange student from the University of New Mexico that I had briefly met in Granada a couple of months earlier. The driver drops me off at the front office of a motel on the main street to the university, Central Avenue. A disproportionately large flickering neon sign of a smiling cowboy beckons weary travelers to the "Highway House." It hits me that I am truly in America and not the America of glamorous Hollywood movies. This feels more real, real in the sense that the working-class neighborhoods of my childhood feel more real than the fairytale palace of the Alhambra. The rooms all face inward, giving the guests unobstructed views of the dusty sedans and trucks slotted into the rectangular courtyard. A large woman at the motel's registration desk asks me to pay in advance and in cash for my three days' reservation. Who am I to question the customs of my new country? As I pull out my wallet to pay, I notice a couple of older men lounging on the red vinyl couch in the tiny lobby. One of them, smelling of beer and cigarettes (something strangely familiar to a Spaniard of my generation) and dressed in jeans and a stained t-shirt, wordlessly slouches over to take my blue hard-case Delsey. I am momentarily confused. In Spain, hotel employees are readily identifiable by their uniforms and high standard of grooming. Shoes are shined like mirrors and shirts starched and pressed. I make a mental note of this cultural difference. I stifle a laugh as I watch the overweight man strain to lift the manuscript-laden suitcase before leading me down a concrete path to my temporary home.

It occurs to me that I have not thought this adventure through well enough. When I call my parents, I assure them that everything is fine. The local news telecast offers an update on all the murders in town. After double-checking the lock on my door, I call the local family who I had met briefly in Granada months earlier and ask for the number of the police department. In fifteen minutes, they are at my doorstep, whisking me away to their house and leaving behind the prostitutes, drug dealers, and drunks that inhabit this stretch of neon-lit motels along Central Avenue.

My point is, what my aunt was telling me was a fairytale. What I knew to be true was that Pura was fed up with her life before she turned fifteen but could not get out of Granada until she was thirty-one. Her ticket out was her marriage to a stranger with a French accent, owner of a prosperous pâtisserie, La Colombe, in Oran. She flew across the narrow Mediterranean waters and became Madame Casquero in the summer of 1958. Seven years later, war and violence forced them to start all over again in Toulon, France, as one of many relocated pied-noir families.

Pura tells me her husband was a Spaniard who had migrated to Algeria when he was sixteen years old. He held on to his Spanish but also learned to speak French and Arabic. According to Pura, learning French was not an issue for her as she picked up the language by watching TV and through her daily interactions with others. She tells me Juan was the love of her life, and even after his death, that she has not been able to find anyone to replace the void his departure left in her heart: "He...He was the love of my life. Very special to me because he gave me everything in exchange for nothing."

Figure 26: Pura and Juan, Souvenirs D'Oran

When I ask her if her parents had any objections to her marrying and moving away, she replied with a defiant tone: "WHAT OBJECTION COULD THEY POSSIBLY HAVE? I WAS ALREADY THIRTY YEARS OLD. Of course, my mother suffered because of my decision because I was truly everything for her, as if she were losing her feet and her hands. But that was my decision, and nobody was going to deter me. I met him in person at night and I did not...really feel a spark.... And thought, 'he will go back and that's that. In the very same plane that has brought him here, he will leave tomorrow.' But the following day, when I saw him again, I changed my mind. I liked him better. I liked his presence, his kind manners, his demeanor. He was very elegant, and I liked him very much. And I thought to myself, 'Oh no, you are not getting away from me.'...It was fate; he was meant for me."

"We had to wait three months to be reunited after the wedding.... I took the train from Granada to Alicante and from there, I flew to Algeria. That was my first time flying. My Mercedes and Jeanot went on vacation to Algeria with their little son Juanmi, so they accompanied me to be with my new husband. You see, I could not go with him after the wedding but rather had to wait for him to claim me as his new wife. I got my passport to cross the sea and leave Spain...to go to a strange country where they spoke French.... France had to give me a visa and someone had to claim me as his wife, you understand...and that is how I was able to leave because in those days you could not leave Spain just because you wanted to. Once I arrived, I applied for my national card and went to the Spanish consulate to register as a legal. It took three months between our wedding in August and my arrival in Oran when we reunited."

I interject casually, "Uncle Juan was a widower, right?" "*NO!*" she replied emphatically, "he was not a widower or was never married ever before. I was his first and only wife."

Figure 27: Pura's arrival in Oran with Mercedes, Jeanot, and their son in 1958

Her answer surprises me. All the family knows Juan Casquero was a widower. I don't press her, knowing that that would be a dead end.

I switch to the topic of work. Pura explained, "I never worked abroad, I only worked when I lived in Granada. Clearly, I was very aware of what I could do. All my life...I have been...I have considered myself not just a girl but a woman. Young but very mature. First of all, because as the oldest of eight siblings, I had a lot of responsibility and knew how to handle it. I was only fourteen years old when I first went to work in a factory, and I remember I was not welcomed by any of the women who were there. I MADE FUN OF THEM!! OF THEM!! [with emphasis] being just a kid, fourteen years old. My mother had no need for us to work as domestics, and Aunt Paca, my father's sister, told me, 'Oh [Pura changes her voice to a contemptuous tone] my child, you should do what Prima Josefa has done.' '…What has Prima Josefa done?' 'Well, she serves in a house.' [Pura changes to a contemptuous voice again] 'And they dress her and feed her…and the salary she earns is for her to buy her trousseau.' And you know what I told Aunt Paca, may she rest in peace [changes to a resentful and grave tone], 'Why don't you put your own daughter to serve?' I asked her. 'Why don't you put your daughter to serve, Aunty?' [again, Pura changes to a contemptuous tone in her intonation as if Auntie Paca were in the room with us]. 'Because my daughter is not like you!'"

Then Pura uttered an angry, triumphant reply, looking intently into my eyes. "'NO?! OH, MY COUSIN IS NOT LIKE ME? Well, it so happens that you are my father's sister, and I'll SERVE NOBODY !!' Because I have two hands to work…. Today I'm in the factory working, in a factory…maybe tomorrow I'm at home working in another way. But to serve…I would rather work in the factory and start sewing, embroidering, and just working in my own house, without needing to go anywhere. Because I WAS A LADY and I did not have to go to another girl like me and call her 'Miss'…NO, NO, NO."

"Because in our house we were poor; in our poverty, we have lived it behind closed doors…but not in public! What has happened in my house has never been known out on the street. So, we did not give the impression of being poor. Do you understand me?… Because nobody knew about me…if at home we missed eating one day…we did not go around saying we did not have anything to eat. In my house that never happened…EVER! We worked. Everything I earned I gave it to my mother so we could get ahead. But nobody ever knew what was missing in my house…. Because we showed ourselves well to the world…well dressed, well groomed…because we made our own clothes, because my mother sewed for us and made her own clothes and when we were older, we did it ourselves. We have never given the impression that we were poor."

"Living abroad I have done nothing outside the home. Although I wanted to, Juan never let me go out and work because he felt he made a good living with the bakery. And so, I had my children in a private clinic with a private midwife. I never had to step in a hospital. Everything was private and paid for."

They lived in Oran for seven years until the Algerian war forced them to leave their prosperous business and happy life behind. Pura recalled, "We had to leave because we could not live among the Moors. We are not Moors...we are Europeans.[4] I returned to Europe and left Africa. We moved to France. Toulon, because it was similar in climate to Oran, close to the seaside. And we stayed in Toulon another seven years and after that we came to Granada. We were from Granada and once we got our retirement, where else would we go? If it had been up to me, we would have stayed in France. I liked it there much more than here. But Juan wanted to return to his Spain, and I could not say no. I liked everything about the foreign countries we lived in. Everything, everything, everything...I liked everything. I lived very well, very comfortable, very respected by everyone. Everybody appreciated me...even strangers treated me with kindness. At the beginning it is hard but once you acclimate yourself...it is the best. Surely, there is good and bad everywhere, but you have more freedom. The world and its people are all the same everywhere."

When I ask her about the escape from Oran, she said bitterly, "We closed down our business and left everything behind. They stole everything from us. I did not say I was leaving for good but rather that I had bought a flat abroad and was sending some of my furniture to that new apartment and on our return I would buy new furniture for our place in Oran.... We could not sell the business...the bakery. We had to turn the key, close the door, and flee. Leaving everything there. House, business, a lot of land we had bought to build a little summer house...EVERYTHING. We left to start from scratch. Zero. Juan wanted to open a new business [in Toulon] but I did not want him to. I told him we would only open another business when we were living in our own country.... But while we were living in a foreign land, he better work as an employee and earn a salary. No more businesses...as any day another crisis could explode and they all tell you again that you don't belong in this land...whatever we were to invest in it must be in our homeland so nobody could claim ownership. Only when we returned to Granada did we open a little bakery. So, in Toulon he started working at a bakery as an employee and did not want me to work but I did want to. There was an opportunity to work in a sewing workshop for me, but he did not let me."

---

4   Clearly, Pura is using the term "Moors" pejoratively. The significance of the term is best explained by Eric Calderwood: "In modern usage, the term can refer to many distinct categories, including Muslims (a religious category), Arabs or Berbers (ethnic categories), inhabitants of al-Andalus (a historical designation), and the people of North Africa or Morocco (regional or national categories). Like the term "Oriental," the word "Moor" tells us more about the person who uses it than it does about the thing it supposedly describes. It is thus best understood as a category of the Spanish imagination rather than a descriptor of peoples or cultures." Eric Calderwood, *Colonial al-Andalus: Spain and the Making of the Modern Moroccan Culture* (Cambridge: Harvard University Press, 2018), loc 613 of 9328, Kindle.

Rashomon Effect

When trying to understand my aunt's story so many years later and after she had passed away, I realized that there were lots of missing pages, pages that she deliberately tore out and threw away. I decided to find others who might be able to ghost write her past with me. I reached out to her two daughters and also to her younger sister, Pili, who lived with the family for almost two years in Oran. Over the course of various conversations held on the telephone and in person over the course of a year, the four of us reconstructed some of the highlights of my aunt's life. My pursuit is best described by what is called the "Rashomon Effect," based on Japanese director Akira Kurosawa's film *Rashomon* (1950).[5] Kurosawa utilized an unconventional non-linear narrative in his adaptation of the story "In a Grove," by writer Ryunosuke Akutagawa (1892-1927). Set in eleventh-century Japan, "In a Grove" tells of a heinous crime: the rape of a noblewoman and murder of her Samurai husband, supposedly by a bandit in their journey through a forest. Kurosawa utilized flashbacks to re-tell the incidents through four witnesses' testimonies (the woman, the woodcutter, the bandit, and the Samurai's ghost). The film provides a valuable artistic reflection on the relativity of truth and the unreliability of memory. These two accusations have been the main criticism at the core of oral testimonies as accurate primary sources in History's noble pursuit of "objectivity." I use this technique not to uncover some objective truth of the events of Pura's life, but rather to understand the process of constructed memory in historical retelling.

The most important moment in Pura's life was no doubt her marriage to Juan Casquero in 1958. Her move to Algeria and then France in the next long decade had a profound effect on her family's life. Twice she had to start a new life from scratch in a foreign land. Yet, she whitewashed much of the hardship from her life's narrative. Her power resided in her conscious forgetting, rewriting, and refashioning of herself as an adventurer rather than a victim. In her telling she is almost heroic. Listening to the testimonies of her two daughters and her younger sister who lived with them in Oran the last year of the revolution gives us another perspective.

Pura's life according to her daughters Carmen and Marian

According to my cousins, Juan Casquero was born in Almería in 1906 and lost his mother at the age of twelve. When his father remarried, he and his two brothers were sent away to Oran, Algeria, to live with his aunt, who worked as a doorkeeper

---

5 On the "Rashomon Effect," see *Rashomon*, directed by Akira Kurosawa (1950; Tokyo: Daiei) htpps://www.criterion.com/films/307-rashomon.

for the city's historic newspaper, *L'Écho d'Oran*.[6] He did not attend school in Oran but rather started working as an apprentice in a pastry shop where he learned the trade that would eventually make him a successful businessman. When he arrived in western Algeria, he was not in strange territory. The Andalouses beach and Oran region had been under Spanish control on and off since 1509. After the earthquake of 1792, the Spanish crown turned Oran into the Algiers Regency, and in 1830 the French became the colonial power in the region.[7] Nonetheless, the Spanish presence in the Oran region grew during the nineteenth century. The agrarian crises caused by droughts and floods in the Spanish southeast during the second third of the nineteenth century were the primary causes of the Spanish emigration to the Oraine district. The geographical proximity of Oran with the Spanish ports of Alicante and Cartagena and the climatic similarities between the Algerian territory and the Spanish Levante drew many day laborers from Alicante and Almería to embark on an uncertain and risky move. Initially this emigration was temporary, but by dint of repeating the cycle, many ended up staying to work in the cotton or tobacco plantations as well as in the vineyards. Others came to build the railroad between Algiers and Oran. In 1840, Spaniards represented almost half of the Europeans in the cities in the Algerian territory and were almost the only ones in the rural areas. The French Constitution of 1848 divided Algeria into three regions: Algiers, Oran, and Constantine. Of the 257,000 European inhabitants in the 1850 Oran census, 65% were of Spanish origin.[8]

In 1882 more than twenty thousand Spaniards arrived at the port of Oran, half of them from Almería. Three years later the Spanish colony in Oran had 80,000 individuals permanently established in the region, 30,000 of them residing in the capital. In the districts of Oran and Sidi-Bel-Abbés, the Spanish population was double in number to that of the French.

To address this problem the French issued a series of laws headed by the decree of June 28, 1889, and later by another of July 23, 1893, which imposed, without exception, French citizenship on all foreigners born in Algeria. The law of automatic naturalization was like a magic trick that turned Spaniards into French

---

6   *L'Écho d'Oran : journal d'annonces légales, judiciaires, administratives et commerciales de la province d'Oran* (184?-1963) ; see Bibliothèque Nationale de France, Département Droit, économie, politique, JO-13582 http ://catalogue.bnf.fr/ark :/12148/cb32759772v.

7   On the Spanish presence in North Africa see: Sasha Pack, *The Deepest Border: The Strait of Gibraltar and the Making of the Modern Hispano-African Borderland* (Redwood City, CA: Stanford University Press, 2019); Calderwood, *Colonial al-Andalus*; Juan Ramón Roca, *Españoles en Argelia: Memoria de una emigración* (Alicante: IES Luis García Berlanga, 2016); Susan Martin-Marquez, *Disorientations: Spanish Colonialism in Africa and the Performance of Identity* (New Haven, CT: Yale University Press, 2008). For a history of Algeria see James McDougall, *A History of Algeria* (Cambridge: Cambridge University Press, 2017).

8   Roca, *Españoles en Argelia*, 29-33.

overnight. This bureaucratic solution to the Spanish overpopulation did not immediately change the reality of the immigrants but, combined with French-only schooling for their children, subsequent generations became more French than Spanish.[9] The Oraine district's Spanish population decreased from 102,433 in 1891 to 78,000 in 1930. The French population grew in the same period from 98,724 to 273,000.[10] However, the presence of Spaniards in the region continued to grow. When Juan arrived in 1919, new trades started to grow alongside the agricultural jobs. After the First World War, the ice cream and pastry confectioners, canvas shoe and leather apparel artisans, anise distillers, and potters from different provinces in Alicante established their businesses in Oran. Many set up their factories in Algeria to avoid tariffs.[11] Women were employed as workers in factories and shops, as domestics, shopkeepers, and concierges. Juan lived with his aunt, who worked as a concierge. By 1931, according to historian Juan Ramón Roca, 65% of the foreign population came from Spain. The Spanish Civil War added the Republican exiles to the labor migration with around 15,000 newcomers who fled repression from Franco's regime.

The best-known incident of Republicans fleeing Spain concerns a coal ship, *The Stanbrook*,[12] which sailed on March 29, 1939, with more than 2,600 passengers. Upon arrival in Oran they had to wait six days before women, children, and the sick were allowed to disembark. After twenty days on board, a typhus epidemic broke out, and the ship was quarantined. The French decided that they could no longer accept the growing number of refugees flooding their North African shores. Thirteen thousand were imprisoned in seven concentration camps south of Algiers, some located in the middle of the desert. Many had to wait until the American liberation during the Second World War to be freed.

In 1954, after France's refusal to develop a decolonization plan for Algeria, a liberation war broke out that culminated in the country's independence in 1962. It was at the beginning of this revolutionary war that Pura's marriage began.

Pura got pregnant soon after she arrived in Oran. This event might not have been such a happy occasion for a number of reasons, as I learned in my conversa-

---

9   Roca, *Españoles en Argelia*, 60.
10 Roca, *Españoles en Argelia*, 71.
11 Roca, *Españoles en Argelia*, 77-78.
12 For a detailed account of the *Stanbrook* event see Juan Bautista Vilar, "Guerra civil, éxodo y exilio: La aventura del *Stanbrook*, Alicante-Oran, marzo 1939," *Estudios Románicos* 2 (Universidad de Murcia, 2007-2008): 213-27. Available at: http://revistas.um.es/estudiosromanicos/article/view/94691/91111. Juan Bautista Vilar is the authority on Spanish emigration to Algeria; see: Juan Bautista Vilar, *La emigración española a Argelia* (Madrid: C.S.I.C., 1975); *Los españoles en la Argelia francesa* (Madrid: Centro de Estudios Históricos, C.S.I.C., 1989, 1989); *La emigración española al Norte de África, 1830-1999* (Madrid: Arco-Libros, 1999); *El exilio en la España contemporánea: Las emigraciones políticas españolas en los siglos XIX y XX* (Madrid: Ed. Síntesis).

tions with Carmen, who was born in 1959, and Marian, her younger sister. Their recollections may explain why Pura told me she was Juan's only love and wife. Maybe she happened to be his only true love but, certainly, she was not his only wife. Marian explains why:[13]

Figure 28: Family portrait, 1963. Pura holding Marian, with Juan standing behind Carmen

"Of course, that was a secret. It was a thing that…look, we found out because we were very curious girls, my sister and me. And we liked to enter into my parents' bedroom to go through their drawers, to see what we could discover. And we found the Family-Book,[14] and so, one day reading it, we must have found it on a table or something because they were using it for something…we noticed it said HE was a widower! And my sister and I secretly read it. '…Oh look there it says that Papá was a widower!' But nothing happened, we let it be a secret. Later, Auntie Pepi, I remember, she did tell us something more about it…how they met and so on…. Although it was nothing bad to hide…. Well, no, no! Well, I do not know. She [Pura] did NOT like to talk about it. Also, my mother was badly regarded by his first wife's family. When she arrived in Oran, the first wife's family still lived there. That woman had not been able to have children, and they blamed it on my father. He had a number of nephews and nieces, all aware of and expecting my

---

13 Marian CasqueroGómez, phone interview recording, June 2, 2018.
14 Married couples registered each new birth in the Family Book, the official Spanish government registry. The Francoist regime rewarded prolific families, starting at four children.

father's inheritance. When they saw my father show up with a younger woman and that she became pregnant...then their inheritance...went poof!! and disappeared. Ah see? ...when my mother got pregnant the gossip ensued: 'Who knows who the father might be?' etc.... You know? Surely, that's why she did not talk at all about that, and that family disappeared from my father's life the hard way...because they distanced themselves from my father, but that's why. Because the family wanted the inheritance. 'If he does not have any heirs then everything is ours,' they thought...."

Pura was not interested in motherhood, according to Marian. If it had been left up to her, she would have been happy with only one child. "So I believe that my mother," Marian speculated, "after having raised 8 or 10, or 12 or whatever number of siblings, she might have thought, 'Me again taking care of children?'...and knowing my mother's character...as she was a woman with a strong personality...with a lot of determination...a woman who always fought and overcame everything, and endured many troubles and hardships...because they had not gone hungry since my grandfather worked for the telephone company and food was never lacking, but clothes, shoes, and other things were scarce for so many children. And then my mother grew restless, she wanted to learn and could not, wanted to go to school and could not. She worked very hard, driven by her eagerness to learn, learn, and learn.... But she was my grandmother's hands and feet and...the family stifled her thirst for freedom...they clipped her wings. And of course, when she saw an easy way out, she must have said, 'Well, I'll get married and get out of here and start again...or I can live differently, be happy, have time for me.' ...And so, then my sister came; they did not expect that pregnancy but the gossip...well, it so happens that my sister was the spitting image of my dad.... My dad was older, and she didn't like the idea of having more children very much.... But my father insisted, and I came to exist because of him, otherwise...[she laughs]. He was more paternal and he said that a girl alone was not right...since he had had that yearning...that is why I was my daddy's girl and my sister was my mom's...I simply adored my father. ...I remember that my father had a red leather armchair and the two of us fit in it [giggle]. It was my perfect place...for me. And if we went for a walk, I was always with...my father. And my sister, as she was also born with health problems, and maybe my mother was more concerned about her. I do not know; but they always have been very fond of each other...very close."

Marian and Carmen's first years of schooling were in French, which meant a hard adjustment for them when the family relocated to Spain from Toulon in 1971 after their father retired. It was the French school that played a decisive role in the social cohesion of the European collective in the colony. The only public school run by the Spanish state was in Algiers, and it had closed its doors in 1870 due to lack of resources. The Spaniards sent their children to French schools that had better resources and offered advantages. Carmen went briefly to a school run by nuns. Many Spaniards became bilingual or even trilingual (Spanish, French, and Arabic), as was the case with Juan. From all this mixture of languages was born the so-called "patuet" dialect, a mixture of the three that in the Oran region received the name of "chapourlao," from the Spanish "chapurrear"(jabber, to speak a broken language).

On October 1, 1954, the war of independence in Algeria began with a series of terrorist attacks claimed by the FLN (Front of National Liberation). The conflict lasted seven years, eight months, and three days, finally forcing the pied-noirs, the Europeans in Algeria, to choose between fleeing the country or resisting within the clandestine OAS (Organisation de l'Armée Secrète or Secret Army Organization).[15] In France the pied-noirs were often seen as primitive and uneducated people.[16] Of the entire foreign colony (Spaniards, Italians, Maltese, Swiss, and Germans), the Spaniards represented the group with the lowest cultural capital because they came from the most impoverished ranks of society. At that time in Spain, only 31% of men and 9% of women knew how to read and write. In addition, the emigrants came mostly from the southeast of Spain, one of the poorest regions in the country with the highest illiteracy rates. In Algeria, relations between the French and Spaniards were not always cordial. The Algerian administration and the French press in general were suspicious of them. The Spaniards lived grouped and isolated from the French community. Throughout the twentieth century, a strong feeling of belonging to the country was formed by the pied-noirs, regardless of their origin; they felt they were Algerians. Some came to dream of a "Free Algeria" of France. OAS, the pied-noirs' clandestine resistance group, came to confront the French army and the French colonial establishment. When the conflict broke out, many Spaniards living in Algeria actively participated in the OAS.

When Juan Casquero originally married a French woman, he renounced his Spanish citizenship. He built a successful business in Oran and felt at home in that city. But with the revolution he lost everything and had to leave with his family to save their lives. According to his daughter Marian, "He lost everything. He lost it

---

15   Roca, *Españoles en Argelia*, 104-06. The OAS was founded in Francoist Spain shortly after General de Gaulle started negotiations with the FLN for independence. Some French military officers met in Madrid after the 8 January 1961 referendum on self-determination and established the OAS, a right-wing dissident paramilitary organization that carried out a violent counter-terrorist campaign in the next year until Algeria's independence was proclaimed on 5 July 1962.

16   Pied-noir was a term first used by Algerian indigenous peoples to refer to the military and first French colonists, referring to their black shoes and boots they wore. A term originally applied pejoratively, during the war of Algeria, it was embraced with pride. On a contemporary assessment about the pied-noir community in Algeria in 1962, see Alfred Sherman, "Climax in Algeria: The O.A.S. and the Pieds Noirs," *The World Today*, 18, no. 4 (Apr., 1962): 134-42. Available at: https://www.jstor.org/stable/40394178. The Algerian War remains an emotional issue in contemporary French Politics. In 2014, the ultra-right leader of the Front National (FN) Marine Le Pen addressed a letter to "the Harkis and pied-noirs" in which she declared De Gaulle had abandoned them.

because he was not intelligent in that regard. But my father, with his caring quiet character, everyone loved him. Because he had an affable personality, he was calm, he was a man who didn't care if they were Moors or not...he made no distinction and was a man who got along well with people. So, they told him, 'Mr. Casquero, leave. Take your girls and your wife and leave or you will lose everything. They won't give you anything.' But my father was stubborn. Because, of course, with so many years living there, he asked how they were going to take away what was his and what he had worked so hard for. It did not enter his mind that he was going to lose everything. And he did not understand that things were getting worse.... Well, I remember...Aunt Pepi who came from Granada when I was born, was there with us...bombs were falling.... And the revolutionaries attacked.... They put a bomb over here, a bomb over there. And Aunt Pepi would take us into a closet every time she would hear a plane or anything...or every time sirens sounded.... And she hid us in the closet.... Once, later on, my sister and I...we were traumatized by that.... Because growing up every time I heard a plane I became paralyzed and I had to wait for the plane to pass...one day I told my sister. I said, 'Carmen, is this happening to you?' And she tells me, 'Yes,' and we asked Tita Pepi, as she liked to tell us things about the time she was in Oran...and one day...she had repeated it many times, but we had never realized.... And that time she told us again, 'And we were in the closet and you were crying a lot.' And these are lingering images I have of when there was so much trouble...." The fear my cousins expressed was never revealed in my conversation with my aunt. She never mentioned the hardships they all endured in the seven years of the war.

Fear is still vivid in my Aunt Pepi's recollection of the two years she spent in Oran with her older sister. Pepi was almost twenty years younger than Pura. When Marian was born, she went with her father to meet her nieces. Pura asked their father to let Pepi stay at least for a year so she could learn French and help with the babies. That was the summer of 1961. Pepi was thirteen years old and remembers how well established and comfortable she found her sister. Pura from Granada had become the prosperous Madame Casquero. "So, the truth is," Pepi remarked, "that I did not suffer any scarcities.... We had plenty of food...I only remember the FEAR!" According to Pepi, her sister Pura made a great choice marrying Juan and escaping the gossip in the little neighborhood in the Albaycin. Pura borrowed the wedding dress of a neighbor and got married within a month of Juan setting foot in Granada and three months later left for Oran. "I remember," she told me, "we read her letters aloud, 'Mama, I'm very well, this is a paradise for me'.... Well, indeed, it was a paradise, because Juan was doing very well economically. The bakery they had was called 'La Colombe'... 'The Dove.'"[17]

---

17   Pepi Gómez Sánchez, interview recording, Granada, June 17, 2019.

Figure 29: Wedding cake by Juan La Colombe pastry shop

Pepi also liked Oran. Pura and Juan decided enrolling her in a school to learn French might not be a good idea since the tensions started to heat up shortly after her arrival. Instead, Pepi started taking classes with a neighborhood French girl a few years older than her. To practice speaking French, Pepi would spend time in the pastry shop talking to the attendants Juan employed. There were also two men who worked with Juan, one of them a young Arab who fell for Pepi: "Then at that time things started to become violent.... And she [Pura] realized then, 'I cannot send you back, neither can we leave.' Juan, [Pepi gets agitated and starts crying] for me, he was like a father [choking with silent tears]. He would say, 'You don't have to be here.' And to my sister, 'Pura, send her back.' [Crying] And my Pura would say, 'I can't. How do I send her? How do I send her?' Then, at the pastry shop there was...a young Moor. And the Moor, well look...he fell in love with me. And Juan told me, 'Don't come downstairs.' 'But, Juan I only....' 'DON'T COME DOWNSTAIRS! Don't go down, I'm going to get into trouble!' Of course, they could not send me back. Well, I was there and of course I couldn't leave. Then there were the two baby girls. Pura had to go out to shop...and then.... They started putting bombs in different places and businesses. Juan was never a target, never bombed because he was loved by both the Christians and Moors as well as the Algerians and whoever else owed him favors. The young Moors who worked for him would repeatedly tell him to leave: 'Señor Casquero, leave! Otherwise you're going to leave with nothing! Then they will kill you.' 'No, no ...,' he would say, 'How could they kill me? I have grown up here, since I was twelve, and I am one of them? I haven't messed with anyone...I don't matter...why would they kill me?' But he did not understand that every day the situation would worsen. We did not leave until the very last minute."[18]

During the almost two years Pepi stayed with her sister, the teenager had a front row seat to the Algerian revolution: "Every day...maybe...first thing in the morning I remember I went to open the window and [she makes a gesture of terror] and heard FERME LA PORTE!! And I did so...OH MY GOD!! OH MY GOD!! Then, the entire street was...you know, because it was not very wide, the street was not very wide, the Rue Fondu(?)...it was not very wide...and when I went to open the window I discovered that the street was full of military or the gendarmerie...then everyone shouting, 'CLOSE THE WINDOW !!' and 'PURA!!' and she told me, 'CLOSE IT AND COME AWAY FROM THERE!' And it turns out that they were occupying the premises. They were searching all the floors...and searching people as well."

According to Spanish historian Roca, in a letter addressed to the High Commissioner of France, the Consul of Spain in Oran protested strongly against the police searches carried out in the homes of several Spaniards, presumably suspected of being members or sympathizers of the OAS. Almost sixty years later, Pepi[19] recalled these searches with acute anxiety:

"Then my sister, so they would not take anything away from us, she had already made...because we already knew that this happened from time to time in other places and we had been warned...she sewed something like a purse...a pouch, she told me...one for her and one for me. But mostly for me because she could be searched more easily than me, since I was a young girl. Then, in that [the pouch] she put money, because we could not have it in a bank or anything...all the money that she had and the jewels. In one side and in another side. But of course, I put it underneath [my clothes] because they did not search you if you were a child. For me, the baby girls were my only refuge, I always protected them...always had them with me...and of course my sister Pura...yes. But no, they came in and asked us where we were from...they started telling us this and that...asking who we were

---

18   Casquero Gómez, interview, 2018.
19   Gómez Sánchez, interview, 2019.

and...but Juan was downstairs [at the bakery] because he could not get out either. ...He downstairs and...and us upstairs. Then they entered and searched the house and saw that there was nothing...they were looking for.... Yes...looking for weapons...weapons because below lived...the girl who was my French tutor and she had a boyfriend, a French pied-noir.... Then this young man was in that [referring to OAS]. And in our VERY FRONT DOOR [lengthens the syllables] I saw it...they killed him. I saw it. They killed him. So handsome he was. They killed him. And I saw it. And I saw everything, maybe I would look out on the balcony, because, you see, there was a family who lived across the street, a family that was...I do not remember right now...Madame Martínez...and many times she called out, 'INSIDE!!' They said, 'Pequeña, inside!' And I...and I said, 'Why?' 'Inside! Because I have three children and all three are in the revolution.' Of course, when something was about to happen, she would warn us, 'Inside' and if she said, 'Tell Madame Casquero to look out the window,' I would say, 'Pura, they are calling you' and Pura would tell me, 'Go inside with the girls' and... 'Inside, Madame Casquero.' 'All right,' and we would close down and go inside. Then, they [the gendarmes] would search the houses, and eventually they found a basement with weapons."

"And, of course, you can imagine the scare... one day I was on the street casually walking when a Moor came running from behind and killed a man right there. So, the first thing I would do was close the windows and run inside. While on the street the gendarmes, the local police, the military...with machine guns...the French pointing to all the balconies."

"I remember one day Carmen, my poor little angel...because, you see, my sister had two clothes lines on the balcony to hang out the laundry and there was a chair that Carmen would climb up on and she got tangled in between the two ropes. I noticed something out in the balcony, as I always paid close attention and saw her...and I said, 'CARMEN, CARMEN GET OFF!!' The girl was entangled and could not come down...and I yelled, 'CARMEN FOR GOD'S SAKE'...and I picked her up swiftly and took her inside."

"The house was like this [she drew the rectangular shaped floor plan with her fingers on the table] the entrance of the street here and as you entered there was a long corridor, here was the bedroom, here was the dining room, and here was the kitchen. There were balconies in each room which overlooked the street...."

"To the left as you came into the house there was a closet. I slept in the dining room on a folding sofa bed. Of course, if the machine guns started to fire, the bullets crossed the windows...and entered here into the corridor. Then, the safest place to hide was here in the large closet, sitting on a chair with the two girls and that's where we hid.... Of course, I sat in the chair, took baby Marian in my arms and Carmen sitting on my other leg. I was so young, and they were so attached to me. I tightly embraced both of them... [she cried again] and thought, 'my god,

Chapter 8. Pura's Rashomon Effect (1926-2013)   201

what do I do if something happens to me? What if my sister does not come back?' [she paused to wipe her tears]."

Figure 30: Pepita and the girls, 1962

Algeria's independence was proclaimed on 5 July 1962. While the members in the OAS in France were mostly fascists, in Algeria they were politically diverse among the pied-noirs (French, Spanish, as well as Sephardic Jews). However, the FLN violent propaganda issued the slogan "The suitcase or the coffin" among the European colonists, provoking a mass exodus of people with their two allowable suitcases starting in April 1962. Between the 5th and 7th of July, the notorious "Oran massacre" took place. This massacre was an internal mass killing of Europeans living in the city. The death toll report varies from low estimates of 95 up to 453 casualties and missing. According to William Kidd, there were "3,000 European victims of FLN kidnappings and murders in the final months of the conflict whose remains have never been found."[20] As the conflict escalated, the Casquero family started to make plans to leave. First, they had to evacuate Pepi. To do so, the consulate told

---

20 William Kidd, "(Un)packing the Suitcases: Postcolonial Memory and Iconography," in *France's Colonial Legacies: Memory, Identity and Narrative* ed. Fiona Barclay (Cardiff: University of Wales Press, 2013), 129-49 and 131-32.

Juan they needed a letter from Pepi's father in Spain reclaiming her. Once the letter arrived, they had to go to the consulate in person to sign the paperwork. It was already late May 1962, close to the end of the war and very risky for Europeans to be walking on the streets. Pepi recounted the terrifying experience of going to the Spanish consulate located in the middle of the Arab quarter:

"Back then the consulate was in the Moors' neighborhood. We had to go from Oran [she was referring to the urban downtown] to the Moors' neighborhood. I had to go with Juan. He told me, 'Pepi, take my hand...and hold on to my jacket. DO NOT LET GO!!! But...if they catch me...GO AWAY!! RUN!! HIDE'... and I was only fourteen years old...the Moors...were all around us...like in the movies that you see.... That's why I don't like to watch those because people say, 'you are traumatized.' No, I'm not traumatized...but, ...yes, I still remember the fear. [she choked back tears] there are things that I can't stand even today...when you find yourself surrounded by a crowd and you are caught in the middle...."

"Well, we got through all that successfully. We arrived at the consulate. When they opened the door they were alarmed. 'Monsieur Casquero, por Dios!' and Juan said, 'I had no choice but to bring her because she has to sign.'.... They took us inside, gave us some water. I do not remember exactly. They sat me on a bench...they gave me water [and told me to] 'calm down' and I said 'yes, yes, I'm calm.' Meanwhile, my brother-in-law was in an office with the paperwork...whatever happened inside...all I know is that he cried, he cried...inside I don't know what happened but when he came out, he came out with red eyes from having cried.... He said, 'come on, we can go.' They took us back home in a car."

"When we arrived at the house Pura was beside herself with worry and began to cry. 'I thought you weren't coming back, not coming back, not coming back,' and the babies started to cry, especially Carmen in her toddler language, saying 'Don't go, don't leave me, DON'T LEAVE DON'T LEAVE ME.' Naturally, I spent all day taking care of them...they were so little.... The next step was complicated as well...because they told us that Franco was going to send a boat to repatriate the Spaniards, but only children and women, because...because...all the Spaniards, or almost all of them...or many of the Spaniards there were refugees from the war in Spain [the civil war.] So they COULDN'T return! Those poor people...but there were also people who didn't escape from the war...like Juan who had been a child, who had not run away from war but poverty. He could have returned, come back...everything. Pura could have evacuated with the girls...but she refused. She felt staying with her husband was her obligation. And I suggested, 'Pura, I'll take the girls.' And she said, 'Pepi, how could I let you take the girls by yourself?' 'Pura, I'LL TAKE THE GIRLS!' [Supplicant intonation] [crying silently]."

For Pepi, the return to Spain was as traumatic as the preparations. She traveled by boat from Oran to Alicante by herself with the two allotted suitcases on a ship packed with desperate people. A family temporarily adopted her so she would not be harassed by the sailors. After a terrifying night and half a day more, the ship arrived in Alicante, where a family friend was waiting for her. She spent one night and then the next day boarded a train to Granada. She remembers how a man sat next to her on the train and kept asking questions, offering her something to eat. The man proved to be useful as he scolded some young soldiers who later boarded the train and started harassing her. The man turned out to be a police officer who made sure upon arrival in Granada that the people waiting on the platform were indeed Pepi's family.

My Aunt Pura did not mention any of this ordeal when I interviewed her in 2002. What she didn't relate to me then, now takes on a larger significance. In historical narratives what is not included is often just as important as what is. Imagining different perspectives or, as in this account, looking for them, is essential to filling in that space.

My cousins tell me their family sent some of the furniture, and their father salvaged many documents, contracts, bills of purchase, and the blueprints for a bungalow they planned to build by the seaside on a plot of land they had bought—everything that could fit in his two suitcases. But they lost everything. No recourse. They were foreigners in a foreign land, with no rights, and despised by the French in Toulon, where they stayed until their father retired: "I remember my mother saying that they had to close the store door and flee...everything lost. They had bought a piece of land on the beach that they also lost. And they had to leave by boat to Alicante. And with very little…. I do remember how my mother told us she hid money in the head of one of the dolls my sister and I carried in our arms."

"My father…went first to Paris because my Uncle Jeanot was there. But he didn't like it…a very big city…he liked more coastal and warmer places. Of course, Oran is on the coast too…it's on the same Mediterranean coast. And then also, all the French who lived in Algeria, the vast majority arrived in the area of the French Riviera. The pied-noirs settled in Marseille, Toulon, Nice, Cannes…that whole area is where they went, most of them because of the weather, the sea, because of the environment they went there. And there we stayed in Toulon."

An important contingent of French pied-noirs connected or sympathetic to the OAS established themselves in Alicante, Spain. According to Juan David Sempere, during the first three years following independence, a few dozen OAS activists resided in Alicante and even "commands were prepared with the mission of attacking De Gaulle." All this was possible in the midst of the Francoist dictatorship.[21] The

---

21 "It is difficult to know how many people passed or settled in the city and in the province due to the absence of specific counts and the internal diversity of the collective: Spaniards who simply returned to their villages and neighborhoods of origin; French who did not want or did not think about going through the French consulate reopened at that time, people who no longer had contacts in the place of origin of their ancestors. There are figures that usually

city of Alicante, which had been a small provincial capital, became a cosmopolitan enclave with the arrival of the newcomers. The pied-noirs even established a French school and a newspaper called *Le courrier du soleil* and brought important economic and social changes to the region. However, Juan decided to relocate in France rather than stay in Francoist Spain.

In evaluating their mother's decisions, my cousins are clearly impressed by her fortitude. Carmen admires how Pura overcame adversity and was able to start anew again and again:

"To begin with, my mother was brave to go to an unknown country and without knowing the language…that was her first life…a first stage…then she had to change again to a different country, even if it was still the French language, and started over again…. Because my father had to start over. He stopped being an entrepreneur and became a simple worker in a bakery…. And then when my father retired, they came here to Granada and it was again having to start from zero here too. And she was always a rock…. If it hadn't been for her and her sheer determination… [her voice trailed off] Because my father was more…do you remember? Quieter…very quiet."

"My mother was the one in charge and the one who made decisions and the one who moved forward…braver in that respect, no? …To remake our lives three times. Also, when they returned to Spain, they only had a small retirement pension, as they were not able to be compensated for the many years they had contributed in France and especially Algeria…. The latter was lost. We had to look… my father had to work again after retirement for a while in the bakery Olimpia, on the Gran Vía [in Granada]…until they were able to open a little place on Avenida de Pulianas."

---

range between twenty and forty thousand people, and especially of the 30,000 pieds-noirs mentioned in the magazine they created, *Le courrier du soleil*, and with which Antoni Seva Llinares titled his book in 1968. But in the absence of sources of information and knowing if they refer to the city or the province, it is not possible to confirm this figure. Reliable counts are well below the indicated figures. In 1970 the French consul in Alicante had six thousand French registered, most of them from Algeria, although he estimated between ten and fifteen thousand the number of French people living in the province. On the other hand, in the 1965 census of the municipality of Alicante only 2,778 people originating in Algeria had been counted, but it allows us to confirm that they had a balanced structure by age and sex, that they were mostly merchants, employees, and workers, and that initially they were distributed throughout the city but especially in the neighborhoods of the Center, Carolinas, and El Pla." See Juan David Sempere Souvannavong, "Cincuenta años con los pies negros," *Información* July 26, 2012. https://www.diarioinformacion.com/arte-letras/2012/07/26/cincuenta-anos-pies-negros/1278748.html. Antoni Seva Llinares, *Alacant, trenta mil pieds-noirs* (Alicante: Eliseo Clement, 1968) was one of the original studies of the diáspora. See also: Juan David Sempere Souvannavong, *Los 'Pieds Noirs' en Alicante: Las migraciones inducidas por la descolonización* (Alicante: Publicaciones Universidad de Alicante, 1998).

Figure 31: Juan Casquero with his daughters, after he retired to Granada in 1971

Marian also applauds her mother's choices, in particular marrying her father: "Well, that's why I say that when my mother met my father...and he told her, 'Look, I can't have children. Does that matter?' And my mother replied [Marian laughing], 'Me? Matter to me? I have raised eight already!!' [laughs heartily] She must have thought, 'You are the perfect husband! The perfect husband...look, you get me out of here. [she speaks with emotion] A new life! A new life in which I will not have to work even one day, a life without children? [she says with emphasis] Right now I'll sign whatever, whenever, where do I sign?' ...A month it took her to decide...A month!! You know what I mean, now?"

"And so the first baby arrives unexpectedly...because it was not in her plans and the second one...another?...yes, yes, yes, yes...Another...And I know that she got pregnant with another child who was a boy...because they...expected me to be a boy and so they would have the pair, boy and girl...but the stork brought a girl...me, the mistake [she laughs] And with the mess in the war and all that...."

Although Marian and her mother did not always get along, she has tender memories of the final years caring for her mother after Pura suffered the ultimate act of forgetting— Alzheimer's: "Although it was difficult...because I was not close with my mother...neither in my adolescence, nor when I married or anything.... Then I saw my mother as far away [short pause] would be for that...because we looked like each other...because we didn't get along.... Then comes the disease...she stopped eating...." Pura forgot how to swallow, and the doctors decided it was not worth it to try to retrain her, as swallowing is not an involuntary action. But Marian was adamant and took her in her arms like a baby, massaging the food down her throat, every day, until her last breath.

Chapter 9
In Antigone's Shadow: Valentina

"But my story is bloody. All, all history is made with blood, all history is blood, and tears are not seen. Crying is like water; it washes and leaves no trace. Time, what does it matter? Am I not here without time now, and almost without blood, but by virtue of a story, entangled in a story? Time may pass, and the blood does not run anymore, but if there was blood and ran, the story continues to stop time, entangle it, condemn it. Condemning it. That is why I do not die, I cannot die until I am given the reason for this blood, until history goes away, letting life live. Only living can you die."[1]
María Zambrano, *La tumba de Antígona*

One has to be brave to live without living. Valiant indeed is she, Valentina, like Antigone, both from the same lineage. The myth of Antigone has captivated our imagination in multiple plays and operas.[2] María Zambrano wrote *La tumba de Antígona* as a play during her residence in La Pièce, France, and published it in 1967 in Mexico. As Anna Formentí points out:

> While in the work of Sophocles, Antigone is moved by her anger for being misunderstood and abandoned by these gods to whom she had devoted herself and she ends her life once she enters the grave; in Zambrano's adaptation of the myth Antigone will be reborn in her grave with a single purpose: to give herself the form and content never enjoyed in life. Actually, Zambrano's version is the only one that allows a true existence of Antigone as a person, and that is why Zambrano differs from Sophocles when he says that she committed suicide in

---

1   María Zambrano, *La tumba de Antígona* (Madrid: Alianza Editorial, 2019), loc. 570.
2   Euripides' play written in (480-406 BCE) is now lost. While Sophocles' adaptation (497-406 BCE) is the most famous, numerous more have been adapted over the centuries, such as by Bertolt Brecht, Jean Cocteau, and Jean Anouilh, Carl Orff, among others. The most recent adaptation is a 2019 film by Canadian filmmaker Sophie Deraspe. In Spain, Catalan writer and poet Salvador Espriu also adapted "Antigone" in 1939 as a commentary on the Spanish Civil War in the same vein as Zambrano's.

her grave: "But could Antigone kill herself, she who had never disposed of his life?" [Zambrano's words] That way Zambrano turns the tomb of Antigone into the cradle of her nascent being. Zambrano tries to illuminate what in the tragedy of Sophocles is dark; the interior of her main character, the reason and unreason that Antigone keeps in her entrails not able to come to light, her fears and her grudges, everything she does not know about herself and will discover as she approaches her end. Zambrano intends to rescue Antigone's life not lived, since, as the philosopher points out in the prologue, Antigone's essence in life was that of sacrifice: "This essence was substance, the raw material of sacrifice that sacrifice can only consume."[3]

It is precisely that non-living or non-being that Valentina incarnates, just like Antigone. Valentina buried her needs and feelings early in her life in support of those around her. Yet, she represents the tenacious resilience of women, mostly outside the view of history, whose sacrifices were significant for the survival of Spain after the civil war and its ultimate emergence as a modern European democracy.

Born in 1943, Valentina, the oldest of five siblings, quickly learned to accept she had to put herself last when it came to family matters. The 1940s were the "hunger years," years of autarchy and misery for a devastated population after the cruel civil war. Hunger and violence were quotidian comings and goings in her life.

---

3   "Si en la obra de Sófocles, Antígona, movida por la furia de la incomprensión y el abandono que siente por parte de estos dioses a quienes se ha consagrado enteramente, pone fin a su vida una vez entra en la tumba, en la obra de Zambrano ésta renacerá en su tumba con un único propósito: darse el ser, la forma y el contenido que en vida nunca se dio. En realidad, la opción de Zambrano es la única que permite una verdadera existencia de Antígona, de la persona Antígona, y por esto Zambrano difiere de Sófocles cuando dice que ella se suicidó en su tumba: 'Mas ¿podía Antígona darse la muerte, ella que no había dispuesto nunca de su vida?' De esa forma convierte Zambrano la tumba de Antígona en cuna de su ser naciente. Zambrano intenta alumbrar lo que en la tragedia de Sófocles queda a oscuras; el interior de su principal personaje, las razones y sinrazones que Antígona guarda en sus entrañas y que no han podido salir a la luz, sus miedos y sus rencores, todo aquello que desconoce de ella misma y que va descubriendo a medida que se acerca a su fin. Esa vida no vivida de Antígona es lo que Zambrano pretende rescatar, puesto que, como dice en el prólogo, su esencia en vida fue la del sacrificio: 'Esta esencia era sustancia, materia prima de sacrificio que el sacrificio solo puede consumir.'" Anna Formentí, "La tumba de Antígona" (México: Siglo XXI, 1967). http://www.ub.edu/smzambrano/resenyas/LA_TUMBA_DE_ANTIGONA.pdf [my translation].

ACT I: Early Life

La historia, niña Antígona, te esperaba a ti, a ti.
Por eso estás aquí, tan sola. Por la historia[4]

I was born in Córdoba on July 18, 1943. My siblings were born there too. Three. One more was born in Granada. And my parents were in Córdoba for about 4 years or so […] After about 4 years or so, it's when I came back from there, from Córdoba. We moved into my grandparents' house, a very large house they owned.

They were a well-to-do family. And in the war, they had to move to the other side, as they say. To communism, because his brothers [referring to her father's siblings] fled while two women stayed behind here. And because of terror, of fear, because they [referring to the fascists] hunted them, took them out, and mistreated or raped them, they fled too. And when they came back, [after the war] they found the house was plundered…because anyway…they had paintings…good paintings and some relics, and they had land. They had everything and then from having had everything they found themselves with no more than night and day.

Well, my mother and my father also left. They lived in the Guadix's area and decided to get married because everyone was telling them to get married. But then when they came back to our village, they were told those marriage papers were invalid, so they had to remarry in Atarfe, in the church, and in court and everything. So, they are married for good. They got married by the church, yes. And then as life was so hard in those years, oh so bad…well, they migrated to Córdoba. Because let's say like an emigration, you know? In Córdoba there were better off people who rented land to work. And then, at the end of the year's harvest the foreman received a percentage. So, my parents left for Córdoba. While my mother sewed in the owner's house, my father got the job of foreman.

What happened? Well, after four years, seeing that they did not pay him or give him any explanations, my father went and asked the owner what was happening. He said he wanted to clarify before he continued or stop working the land. And then, you know what that man did? He called them one by one into his office with a gun in his hand…and told him [Valentina's father] to sign as if he had given him his money. [she paused] My father told me that story and did not want me to ever repeat it. But now I'm telling you. Because they [referring to her parents] were afraid. And then, they had to go in and sign one by one and after signing and not giving them anything, they had to come back to our town without a penny, without a house, with nothing. Luckily, my uncles had not sold the family house and we all moved in with my uncles and lived there for a number of years. After a few years, they sold the house and distributed the money…so then we left. My parents built a house, where we were raised. Until I was 18…because I remember RATION CARDS [she emphasized] since I was the oldest girl in my house and my mother was going to serve the family…because my father,

---

4 "History, my child Antigone, was waiting for you, you. That is why you are here. Because of history." Zambrano, *La tumba de Antígona*, loc. 737 of 1423, Kindle [my translation].

being from a well-to-do family, he didn't want us to be servants of anybody, or to work in the fields...nothing. Better to starve because once we had been a well-to-do family. However, my mother was doing housework for his family. She was, let's say, cleaning up their shit [pause]. To clean, to wash clothes, to help with the matanza,[5] everything. And then she would come back with sticks of tobacco we would burn for cooking. With the tobacco sticks we cooked and all that. What happened then? That is when I was about to turn eight years old, and my parents had their last baby. That meant I couldn't go back to school or anything anymore. I had to stay home to help raise my sister. I was only eight years old...not quite, because my sister was born in February and I turned eight in July. Well, of course, my mother she couldn't do it...because his [referring to her father] family didn't give her, let's say only...old leftover bread and used oil after having fried the fish. LEFTOVERS. IN A WORD, LEFTOVERS! But you had to shut up. For my parent's sake I had to shut up. Because they came from rich people and we could not complain. Well, ALWAYS REPRESSED. You could not talk. However, we never did go to bed starving. Truth be told. But we had to eat whatever someone else did not want and left for us.

I fed my sister, this little baby girl. I gave her bottles of goat's milk because my mother did not have breast milk. And then, I used to buy a quarter of a liter of goat's milk and when I was older, I used to dunk bread in it, you know? And some other times, I made toasted flour gruel...I roasted the flour [Valentina recalled with pride] and sometimes I added a little extra water [laughing] for me to try a little spoonful of the gruel...only eight years old. My sister slept with me. Of course, there were no diapers available like nowadays, so I was soaked in pee every morning. I had to wash my clothes, close the door, in my underwear, and hang the clothes to dry. Then, I put them back on and with my sister I did almost the same thing with her, with the little baby girl, as in those times they were thick fabric wraps and all that...and I had to remove them when she peed and it smelled and the stink really bothered me.

We had a portal entrance...a zaguan (hallway). There were the houserooms and there were these portals about three meters wide. Then, in what is the middle, there were cobble-stones like a river basin and my father, I remember him throwing water over the cobblestones and I on my knees with a... [thinking] a ...a heavy rug mop...you had to tame that rug and I dried the stones until they shined. And my father was such a brute that he kept throwing the water...pouring it with a pail, he threw the water like that...buckets, imagine going out on the patio...while I kept kneeling down...drying that...The house was always clean. I was eight or nine years old, but I was a tiny girl. My father always closed the door so nobody would see him doing housework. Because they would think he was no longer a real man.

Later on, when I was ten, I started to embroider veils. My mother taught me how to sew; she taught me how to make patches; she taught me how to make underpants. I did all that without going to school after I turned eight years old. I still kept my school bag. [she giggled] So, I grew up without knowing how to read or write.

---

5   Traditional community or family-centered pig killing to preserve meat for sale or consumption within the family.

We raised pigs, chickens. I did all that. I remember the smell of brown bread and potatoes, which we fed to the pigs...The bran, that was it...and I wanted to eat that. And I ate it every once in a while...I ate the bran. I liked it. And almost every year my father worked in the drive of the sugar production at a factory in la Vega. But they always fired him by Christmas and we sacrificed a pig...we had to kill a pig and a few chickens, ten, twelve chickens for Christmas. He used to return and simply go to bed.

Well, we had to sell the chickens. We had to sell the pig.... And in addition to all that, I had to cook, and I remember my mother used to give me two or three duros[6] *and she sent me to the market and said, "Daughter, try to bring enough for lunch and dinner." I brought the best I could, to make a noodle casserole, or beans, or chickpeas, or whatever. Because I've always been a little devil* [mischievous smile] *I went to the butcher shop and demanded, "Give me two or three pieces of that meat" and then I would say, "I have only this much* [referring to money] *and the butcher would say, "but this is all you pay me?" And I replied, "that's all I have. And you also have to give me that little piece over there because it's the one I like." And* [laughing] *because the butchers loved me, they gave it to me. Then, I was able to cook and my mother...that was in the winter season and the tobacco season, she went to harvest tobacco and in the summer season, it was the corn. My mother, because my father continued with the same ideas that we were well-to-do people and we couldn't* [do manual] *work. My mother could, but we could not. That went on until I turned eighteen. When I turned eighteen, there were four months of storms and my twelve-year-old brother was already working in a bakery. And they paid him with a bread loaf and a half and a duro and with that we maintained our household.*

Sometimes my mother would get some old dresses from our relatives, and the poor woman made new garments out of such rags. She cut them up and made all new clothes. But in the first wash, they would come apart on the washing board. All of this until I turned eighteen years old. By that time, my brother was already fed up with his job at the bakery because he was only given twenty duros a month and one and half loaves of bread. But he would start at five in the afternoon and work till dawn. He wouldn't arrive at the house until seven in the morning. So, the poor thing was very fed up and he had already turned twenty years old. So, it happened that an uncle of mine from Córdoba had migrated to Barcelona. We found out he was in Barcelona, and my brother wrote to our cousins and then my uncle, and they said we shouldn't think twice about coming, and even if we all slept on the floor, we were welcome to move in with them. My brother left two months before me. And my father and I followed him in September. I remember we arrived on the festivity of the Virgin of La Merced...in '61. There we were, three families in three bedrooms, a kitchen, and a dining room flat. [Valentina paused] *There we went. On the Day of our Lady of the Merced, a Saturday or Friday, and by the following Tuesday we were looking in* La Vanguardia *newspaper for jobs. We realized they preferred to hire Catalans for these jobs; we were not welcome. They did not want us...not at all...They did not speak Spanish to you because they wanted you to learn it* [Catalan].

---

6   A *duro* equaled five pesetas.

Nowadays they are more willing to speak Spanish than in the 60s. So, I arrived...I arrived on a Saturday, as I've already told you, and the following days we grabbed La Vanguardia *on Monday, on Tuesday....*

On a Monday I arrived at my first job and the manager saw me. He was Catalan and he told me...in his house they did not even like Andalusians...so I said, "Very well..." as in those days there was plenty of work in Barcelona and I would go elsewhere. But then, he said "I don't know why I like you," ...because, you see, there [referring to Barcelona in those times] *they were very respectful towards you.... He said, "Come back tomorrow, Tuesday, and I will test your skills." And he tested me and hired me. The test consisted of making a bra within an hour and a half, and I finished it in three quarters of an hour. So, he hired me.... Then he said, "Come on Friday. We start the week on Friday, from Friday to Friday." I had left a small village and suddenly found myself as if in New York...because Barcelona was just like our New York at that time.*

That was my first job, 23 Condal Street, a corsetry workshop which produced bras, swimsuits, underwear, what else was it? [Valentina paused to remember] *girdles...I mean underwear of all kinds. And I specialized in bra cups, built with some padding. There was another girl who also made the bra cups, but she made them two sizes smaller and I made sure to stitch a little further out. So the boss told her to try to make them a size larger because hers were returned. You see a size 95 must be 95 and hers felt more like size 90. And I made them exactly 95.*

So, if it were supposed to be 95 it was indeed size 95. The boss really liked my work and made me a specialist in making the bra cups and for making the salesmen's samples.... Yes, samples were my job too. Even lace samples, and the boss paid me a bonus for those. Because I would work on the lace for twelve hours.

They paid me one cent for some, and two cents for others. The most laborious were worth two and a half. And I earned in those times per week over 3,000 pesetas, almost 4,000 pesetas in the sixties...that was about 12,000 or 13,000 pesetas. Well paid, of course it was...but I worked twelve long hours.

Figure 32: Corsetry factory employees pose in their uniforms, Barcelona c. 1962

And then, I would return home to make lunch for my father and for me. That went on for three months...cooking for my father, for my brother, and for me. It was during those three months when suddenly my father decided that he did not like Barcelona and told us he wanted to return to Andalusia. We told him we were not going back there to so many debts and no work. So my father suggested we go out for a ride on the bus to the city center and when we saw him acting so kindly...something we had never seen from him as he was never affectionate, but of course, that kindness had a motive.... He was a typical brute as men were in those days.

Figure 33: At work in the corsetry factory

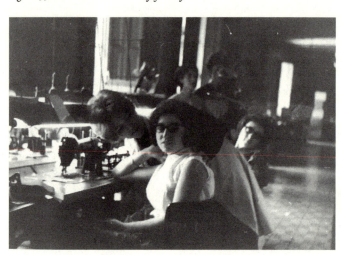

And then I said, "All right, Papa, where are we going?" And then he said, "To buy the tickets to return home." THEN, I pulled the emergency stop cord on the bus and it stopped and we three got off. My brother got off and I got off…well, he [Valentina's dad] had to get off. When we got off, we took a walk to a nearby park. He kicked my brother… [nervous laugh] and he gave me a big pinch and slapped me across my face…that…I will not forget in life. And I told him that if he wanted to take the train back to go ahead and my brother took my side. "Papa, do you realize what problems we left there in Granada, even suffering what we are going through here…. And my dad said, "I cannot stand the Catalans," [severe tone] and we replied, "We come to take away what is theirs; it is like the one who goes abroad." Well, we are not the same because we are all Spanish but…still, we came to take, as we say now, from those around here. We came to take their work…and that's how it happened. Neither his hitting us nor his raging anger would move us…. We stayed there, and so did he.

The worst was not over. He started to drink heavily, like my uncle. My father used to drink a little but then being so unhappy made him and my uncle drink and drink. You see, he used to give me half of his week's pay and my brother gave me the entire week's pay except for some pocket money. And I saved my entire week's wage. We had to save money for a deposit in order to move out of my relatives' flat. I HAD TO COLLECT 40,000 PTS THEN IN THE 60S… [Valentina emphasized] and then, buy furniture. It was not worth bringing furniture from the south because it cost you more than buying it there second hand.

So, my father every night asked me when no one saw us, "Give me money." And I would say "Money? I don't have it anymore; I am truly sorry." …From an angel girl I turned into an evil girl. Already, my rebellion within overpowered me more than anything else, because it was always beatings, slapping me around, and punishing me nonstop…just the way it *was in those times. THAT ABUSE IS WITH YOU FOREVER, NOTHING IN THE WORLD MAKES IT POSSIBLE TO FORGET....*

Well, he kept asking me for money and I kept saying NO...he would go into a rage, checking my suitcase, he then would search me, search my uncle...everyone...and I would tell him that I had the money in a sacred place. And he screamed, "If you have opened a savings account, I assure you that I'll kill you. ...He would not...he was not going to kill me because he was my father. The money was in a missal that I...see...in my youth, I was so pious...as they forced me to be...and in a missal inside a sheath cover I had been hiding the money in between the pages. Every page would guard a twenty duros bill note, another sheet of the book, another twenty duros bill. Little by little until I saved...I don't know...about sixty or seventy thousand pesetas. I PUT IT IN THERE! That missal had its cover, with the engraved word "Missal," which kept my father at bay.

Valentina looked at me with great pride, triumphant, as she revealed the beatings she endured to save the little fortune. In her tone she cogently conveyed how every blow was worth it. How resisting the blows was more powerful now that she unveiled the secret, sacred bank. Every blow made her feel freer. She continued her story:

If I hadn't done so I would not have been able to save a cent. Because he started drinking and I needed my mother to join us in Barcelona because I could not throw away my life. I could not endure it any longer. I remember in the house where we lived there was a young man who had studied. He was a nephew of an aunt of mine. Someone with enough schooling to be able to attend college if he had wished to. We had a long bus and subway ride to work every day...and one day I told him I could not read and write. He said, "Tina, really, you cannot write?" And I said, "Well, I don't know how to write, Pepe; I don't know how to read or write."[7] So, he gave me a book and said, "If I give you some homework, would you learn?" And I said I would do as he said.... "You could study on the subway," ...he said...and I would say, "Do you know how to teach me, Pepe?" And he said, "YES." So, I said then, "Make it so that I will study and bring the homework to you to review it and correct it every night." YES! AFTER TWELVE HOURS OF WORK, I went back to housework, making dinner, and the next day's meal...and I studied on the public transit. And SO, I LEARNED TO READ AND WRITE. I read my books. I don't read now as much as I read then. I do not read now because of my poor eyesight...I LEARNED TO READ AND WRITE. Those books about famous people. Leftists rather than rightists' books, you know? ...But I can't tell you the titles. They were small books and then he gave me an encyclopedia that was quite from the left rather than the right....

---

7   Not unusual, given Spain's high illiteracy rates.

Valentina—Tina—learned to read and write, saved enough money to bring the rest of the family to Barcelona where they stayed and were able to move to their own flat. She reached her full potential, a strong independent woman.

ACT II: Love and Marriage

Y ahora necesito saber el porqué
de tanta monstruosa historia.[8]

The virgins are here to prove a point.

The virgins are here to tell you to fuck off.
The virgins are certain there's a circle
of hell.
dedicated to that fear you'll never find
anyone else.[9]

Figure 34: Young women posing in the courtyard

My father...when I had any suitors...there was this woman, a neighbor in our village...and when a young man...a suitor was waiting for me to go out...we would say a sort of

---

8 "And now, I need to know why so much of a monstrous history." Zambrano, *La tumba de Antígona*, loc. 748 of 1423, Kindle [my translation].

9 Fragment from Analicia Sotelo, "Do You Speak Virgin?" in *Virgin: Poems* (Minneapolis: Milkweed Editions, 2018), loc 70,76,85 of 786, Kindle.

boyfriend...that neighbor sneaked up on us and would tell my parents...and then my father and mother would order me to take off my dress. I would cry and complain, "I have done nothing wrong." "TAKE OFF THAT DRESS YOU ARE NOT GOING ANYWHERE." ...Then I finally found out that the neighbor was telling them. You see, having many suitors was not right because then you were considered a whore...I was a very happy, very friendly young girl... ...Well, I didn't know anything about sex [Valentina emphasized]. *Nothing at all. When I got my first period, I knew nothing. I found out more about it from a girlfriend who told me.* [pause] *And I put on some rags that I took away from my mother. I used to wrap them in newspapers or some sort of papers and hide them under the mattress. Can you imagine? Of course, my mother didn't know that I had gotten my first period and that I was now a woman. At thirteen, I got it...just in July, I got it...I waited for her to leave the house for me to wash my rags. I hid them...because I was embarrassed and because I believed...I don't know...that whatever was happening to me was something bad.*

Sex? More of the same. Sex, I had never in my life heard talk about sex at all in my house. I just remember how I heard my mother moan many nights. Two and three times. My father must have been rather potent or...a brute or whatever. And then I saw them...because there were no doors separating the rooms, only curtains. But after two or three times she would get into bed with me. She would whisper, **"make some room for me."** *And I used to say,* **"Mama, did Papa hit you?"** *Of course, because I could hear her moan. So, I feared that my father might have hit her or something and that is why my mother got into bed with me. My father might have been demanding...and she was running away...because she didn't want any more children. We were already all big kids and enduring so much misery she didn't want any more children. And that's the only thing I knew about sex.* [Valentina reflected, looking at me intently] ***I know now****, what all that was...all that.*

And like that, over time I found a boyfriend. My boyfriend was, well, as I tell you, a ladies' man. A man who knew women...a man seven years older than me...handsome...with great presence...but he also liked going out, he liked women, he liked a glass of wine. He grew up with his grandmother...well...his parents...he didn't love them...he really didn't love them. He grew up with his grandmother; his grandmother gave him everything...heaven if need be. But still he had to give his parents his wages and they didn't give him any money. Even during his military service, he would work when visiting the family because his father had little handyman jobs.

I remember, I went to Camas in the Sevilla area to the festivities and stayed with relatives fifteen days and so I came back a little chubbier and wearing pretty summer dresses an aunt of mine, who was well-to-do, made for me. I came back that year that I turned fourteen and Antonio noticed and liked me. But he was older...and my father worked with him in construction. Whenever Antonio had a construction job, he would hire my father as his helper. So, what happened with Antonio? Well, he lived in a house on the same street and his balcony overlooked mine. But he just looked at me...observed whenever I went out and when I came in after lunch. He used to read many Wild West novels. He would tell his mom, "I am going upstairs, if I fall asleep, wake me up." But it was a lie. He would start reading on the terrace but the terrace was covered like this...walled up...made of perforated bricks like a thick lattice and all he wanted was to look out to see me leave and to see me enter. But he never got to speak to me until I turned eighteen. He liked me in silence all that time and never said a word to me.

Only a week before I was to go to Barcelona, he stopped me. Because, you see, I had at that time three suitors and my parents wanted to kill me...they followed me to death...my mother...whenever there was a dance they forbid me, "don't go to dance." "Mama, I'm not going." ...The minute I arrived at the dance...because, you know, maybe my girlfriends would convince me, "How is your mother possibly going to find out? ...How is she going to find out?" I don't know what it was...if she had telepathy or what...but the instant I reached the door of the dance my mother was already there. And she pulled me back home, beating me all the way to our house [Valentina recounted all this while laughing] for having lied to her. Because one could neither lie nor could one blaspheme [continues laughing] nor could anyone do anything fun...you had to be a saint. If I were to say "darn," she would slap me in the mouth. [Laughs] Anyway, I then resigned myself to not going to the dance. On Wednesdays there was something called "femina" which meant that the girls could enter for free if accompanied by a guy. She, my mother, knew it somehow. If we planned a stroll downtown, she was already at the cinema's entrance waiting for me to take me back home. My friends were free, and I had to go home. [Pensive pause] So about sex NOTHING. Sex...I didn't even know how to kiss, or touch...I didn't know where they would touch me. You washed yourself and there were times when I went to where we had the chickens and pigs for privacy. I washed up there...I would put water in a pot on the stove and then and there [referring to the corral] I washed. But you had to go out dressed and you had to get out of it... Many times I had put water on the stove and was not quick enough, so my brothers took it and I had to wash up with cold water. We had to go get the water at the well because we didn't have a water tank. **A lot of hardships, Auri** [she called me by my childhood nickname, lovingly] ...*in every sense of the word.* Because then you had no intimacy or trust to confide in your own mother. "Mama, look, this is happening to me...Mama, that other thing happens to me." ...Once, I remember during Holy Week the Via Crucis took place. Well, I already told you I was very pious then...I was with my girlfriends out during the...the Via Crucis and they let out all the young soldiers from Grana(da) [she laughs] and we had two or three soldiers following us. I became so agitated that I got an awful nosebleed. And then I remained in bed for a month, and they gave me some transfusion and all kinds of things to recover. It was as a result of the terror...that it gave me...just to think that I was followed by three soldiers and that my mother and that my father would kill me if they saw me.

Well then, I went to the dances and I don't know what the hell happened to me that one guy really liked dancing with me. By the time I went back home my mother knew who I had been dancing with, whatever I had done, whatever I had not done...even more than what I had really done. DANCE! "Mama, please I have not done anything but dance"..."YOU HAVE BEEN DANCING FLAMENCO?... DID YOU TURN AROUND?".... I would say, "Well, of course in a dance you turn around and around,".... "AND WITH THE CANCAN DRESS

YOU WORE YOU HAVE SHOWN YOUR LEGS?".... "Mama please, I haven't...been looking down"...to all that yelling I tried to respond very calmly...you know?...I have never in life ever been able to dance with a person who I did not know. He always had to be known by the people in the village and have an upright life. Let's say they would say, "That guy drinks, or he is a womanizer." ...It had to be exclusively like that, otherwise I would have to sit in a chair and not dance at all...all night long. That was my life!!

My parents did not like Antonio as a boyfriend for me. A week before I left for Barcelona, Antonio told me, "Look, I've liked you for so long. I didn't want to say anything because your parents are going to object. Because they know that I love women, like any man, and that if I get drunk...I do drink a glass of wine occasionally. Your father knows me very well and I know he does not want me to pursue you." Because you see...there was a class rank between our families...meaning that, although we did not have a cent, I belonged to a well-to-do family, something important at the time, and Antonio came from a lower-class family.... Well, we started to write letters to each other and one day my father found one of his letters and said, "What is this?" Antonio's family was known by the nickname "Pollero" and he was called Antonio Pollero...."Are you corresponding with the Pollero's son?" ...I said, "Well, yes." ...And he said, "Well, look I'm going to tell you something, I do not like it." ...I said, "Well"...by then we were in Barcelona...and I said, "Look, I'm truly sorry, but I like him."...[Valentina paused] He replied, "Well, I'm going to tell you something in one word." ...He did not tell me "Antonio is a womanizer,"...he called him "a whoring man and a drunk" and added, "but you will never lack something to eat in your house nor some money to put away." I mean he said something good and something bad. Then they talked...of course because they [referring to her parents] knew I was seeing him, so, they talked and Antonio proposed.

Well, it turns out that Antonio came at the end of the year. He used to come visit once a year to Barcelona because he migrated to France...when he became my boyfriend...I moved [to Barcelona] in September and he had moved in January to Strasbourg in France and visited us for Christmas. Every Christmas. He stayed fifteen days in my house.... Where would he stay otherwise? Not at a pensión because we all had known him from our village, so he stayed at my house. He stayed in the same room with my brother. Well, after two or three days he asked permission from my mother.... "Look, I'm leaving soon...since here in Barcelona there are cinemas with matinees showings, Tina could leave work a little earlier...a couple of hours earlier and that way we would come back with her sisters after they finished work all together." SO, we went to the movies! [Tina and Antonio, alone without chaperons] And I kept pulling him to the front rows...and he said, "no, no here in the back," ...and I thought it odd...to go so far back to see the movie, well,...but we did go to the back. And when we sat down I said, "Oh, Antonio there is nothing but couples here [Valentina giggled happily] all kissing, kiss comes and kiss goes. I told myself, "Here I perish." Of course, he gave me a kiss, a small quick one. Well, I liked it so much, to be frank, and after that first one there were seven or eight or I don't know how many more. [We both laughed and relished the moment of happiness she was describing] I became so skilled in such a short time.

Then the time came for him to depart again and for two years...in those two years [she paused] *there was a crisis between the leftists and the rightists...Antonio was always for the workers and immigration found out and made sure that he could not come back, because what he defended was left-wing; then he left and he could not come back for two years. Exiled, because if he came back, they would lock him up...as a political prisoner. In those two years he proposed marriage by proxy and my parents didn't want to...and I...it took me three or four months to write. And in those three or four months, as I had already kissed him, I believed that the kiss brought pregnancy. Well, I sobbed constantly* [laughing], *"He has impregnated me and now he's gone, and does not write to me...and now what do I do? How do I tell my parents?" ...And although my period came regularly, I was convinced I was pregnant. Until his sister wrote to the consulate asking about him since he didn't write. And then he sent her a letter, writing, "Sister, please leave me alone. I don't write to my girlfriend and you certainly must not write to me.* [silence] *Tell my girlfriend that I love her and I will love her till death. If she wants to wait for me so be it; if she doesn't, she is free to do as she wants. I can't say any more." I had other suitors, but I...I liked...my husband-to-be, no one else.*

Well, that was in [19]64 and he could not come until [19]66, and he asked me to take care of the paperwork as he planned to return in '66 for us to get married...when he came back here from France. But I told him that I would not arrange any papers because with the experience I had had not knowing the reason why he did not write, I would not do it.... Then he asked for a month leave to go to Barcelona and on November 15, 1966—a Tuesday it was—we got married. Civil and church ceremonies, because he was not a church supporter, but I was and my family also and because then it was very frowned upon to marry only in court.... We got married. I spent a very happy day, very happy [emphasis]. *I sincerely tell you from my heart.*

That was my first time. He noticed I was so very nervous and took me for a stroll down the Ramblas to a hotel. In that hotel...he saw that I was still very nervous. I did not bring any luggage. I did not want anyone to know that I was just married. Imagine how little experience. [Valentina ran out of words, frustrated by her memories of that moment] *My innocence was so great. He was a man with a lot of experience. Well, he called the hotel but they said that there was simply a room with two beds and so we said yes...he said yes...well, a room with two beds. I only carried an overnight bag because we planned to stay in that hotel four days, and I only carried a bag just to change and he had told me to bring a bed sheet...or rather, a bath towel... just that.* [She stopped. Silence] *"Antonio, what do I want a bath towel for?" And he said, "Bring one with you, I will explain...nothing might happen, but something may happen." Well, I was trembling like...but also full of desire* [with emphasis] *to be able to hug him...I'm telling you, Auri* [Valentina called me by my childhood nickname again].... *At the wedding banquet he whispered in my ear all the things in life we were going to do.... It was unforgettable, but he kept noticing my anxiety. Anyhow, he asked for the hotel room and we went in. We acted like a normal couple. They asked us at the hotel, "Do you have any more luggage?" And he replied, "No, because I come from France...we come from France," and he said, "We didn't bring anything more than this luggage because* we are leaving soon." ...So each one of us sat on a bed and started talking normally.... "How did you enjoy the day," etc.... to put me at ease...I was very tense and he continued the conversation always very casually to distract me. Until he said, "Do you want to take a shower?" And I quickly said I would really like a shower. Then he said, "All right, go into the bathroom...in the bathroom, take your shower and if you brought a nightgown or you brought something special to wear, put it on if you want or not, if you do not feel like it. Do as you want." Well, I put on my nightgown, my underwear, my bra, my nightgown.... [She enumerated, amused, the multiple garments she wore in the bathroom] *I put on ALL those clothes. AND JUST STAYED THERE. And fretted, "Now, how do I go out dressed like this?...* [She laughed looking at me] *and "Now, how can I possibly come out? My God, how embarrassing to show myself in my nightgown!! Oh no, how distressing!"* And then suddenly I hear him on the other side of the door, "Tina, are you all right?" and I replied, "No, no, no." He said, "Don't worry, take all the time you need." Trying to make me feel better...to reassure me because I was so scared and anxious that I had not even eaten all day.... Eventually, I walked out and then he exclaimed, "My God, YOU ARE BEAUTIFUL!" Those were his first words...and he gave me the first kiss and then...then he got in the bathroom and put on his pajamas...and we started talking again. He was sitting on his bed and I sitting on the other. This went on and on until at least five in the morning. At five in the morning, we couldn't take it anymore. We constrained ourselves a lot. At five in the morning he started...and he told me not to worry that...he would behave as the true gentleman that he was. Because he started this and the other...I did not know what that thing was. BUT IT WAS NOT TRAUMATIC AT ALL. FOR ME NONE. [Valentina remarked emphatically] *It wasn't traumatic. Just that I was so extremely nervous because we tried intercourse for the first time...and I again went into a panic as I expected that would be worse of an experience and at the same time felt so much desire...so much that it did not happen, anything painful...* **just... just a small blood stain... a little** [soft voice] *and that's it.* But suddenly I began to cry, and cry, and cry, and cry, and cry. And he soothingly asked me, "Why are you crying?" and I told him I didn't know why. Then he tried to comfort me.... "There must be a reason;...do you regret it?"..."NO, Antonio, I AM NOT SORRY." "Have I hurt you? Do you feel bad?"..."NO, Antonio I do not feel bad." ...And then he started crying too. And it was my turn to comfort him. "Antonio, and now what happened to you? And now what happened to you?" "Well, it moved me to see you cry."

The next day...I told him, "I do not want to exit the hotel at ten or eleven in the morning. Please let's go out early. I don't want people to notice anything; I've been told it shows [she referred to having had sex] when walking...this and that...." So that was what we did. At 8:30 in the morning we left and went to the airport, to see the airport, just to go somewhere.... Well, then came the second night, and we started the...the same talk, and talk and with a lot of patience...much too much patience and again I began to cry because my nerves got in my stomach. I wanted to eat and could not and poor Antonio said that it could not be like that, that it could not be...that I had to eat. [emphasis] *And so he started crying again.* [Valentina laughed nervously, recounting the moment] Then I told him...I said, "Antonio, what is wrong with you?" And he then asked, "No, what is happening to you? Is it hard for you to have lost your virginity and marry me?" And in that instant I reassured him, "NO." [She started crying softly] *I told him that the only good thing that had happened to me in my life at my age was to have married him.* [I held her hand and we stayed silent for a little while. Tears rolled down her beautiful sad face.] *I said it then and I keep saying it; even after I had our children...WELL, THE GREATEST HAPPINESS OF MY LIFE WAS MY HUSBAND ANTONIO* [she continued crying. I cried too].

Antonio died of liver cancer in 1985. He was forty-nine years old. He fathered three children: two girls and one boy. Tina was forty-two when he died. *And I don't miss going out. I long for solitude. I like being alone. With his memory. With his image here.* [she pointed to his picture on the other side of the room] *I talk to him. He grants me everything. Maybe it's a coincidence but whatever...he grants it to me up to this day. And with regard to my parents...I was taking care of them until the last moment...they died too. Antonio died in my arms. I helped the nurses get his body prepared to be buried and now I live...with the loving memory of my husband. Now I live the joys my grandchildren grant me, but I miss him dearly.*

ACT III: Without Antonio

Me dejas sola con mi memoria, como la araña. A ella le sirve para hacer su tela. Esta tumba es mi telar. No saldré de ella, no se me abrirá hasta que yo acabe, Hasta que yo haya acabado mi tela.[10]

Figure 35: Construction workers posing on top of a scaffold

---

10   Zambrano, *La tumba de Antígona*, loc. 761 of 1423, Kindle.

> We openly raise the word
> from hard ground and roots.
> From every dark blow received
> we openly give you testimony.
>
> This is our voice and our struggle,
> our blood shed, inevitable
> like the bitter sweat of the hours
> endlessly worked without a beginning.
>
> Our skin stings, this second
> skin of night men, which does not arise
> from the light, but from death,
> in the rain, the sun and from the lash.
>
> There were not just three. We remained
> all on the shocked ground,
> discovering suddenly, once again,
> the hidden meanings of things.
>
> We have not cried, it is true. This pain
> it doesn't fit within naked tears.
> it only emerges if it is shared
> with every man and transformed into acts.[11]

Antonio was seven years older than Tina. He had worked in construction since he was a teenager and had migrated to France around the same time Tina moved to Barcelona with her father and older brother. Through the labor movements in France and Spain he had been involved in leftist politics.

According to an October 1969 study on the evolution of prices and the cost of living carried out by the Vice Secretary of Trade Union Organization in Granada, the wage of a construction worker in Granada was not only insufficient to meet

---

11   Luis González Palencia, "Granada, July 1970," in *Andalucía: tierra cercada* (Bilbao: Zero, 1977): *Abiertamente alzamos la palabra desde la tierra dura y las raíces. De cada golpe oscuro recibido os damos testimonio abiertamente. Es esta nuestra voz y nuestra lucha, nuestra sangre vertida, inevitable como el sudor amargo de las horas trabajadas sin fin y sin principio. Nos escuece la piel, esta segunda piel de hombre nocturno, que no surge desde la luz, sino desde la muerte, bajo la lluvia, el sol y el latigazo. No fueron tres tan solo. Nos quedamos todos sobre la tierra sorprendida, descubriendo de pronto, una vez más, las ocultas razones de las cosas. No hemos llorado, es cierto. Este dolor no nos cabe en las lágrimas desnudas. solo tiene lugar si es compartido por cada hombre, y transformado en actos.*

the minimum needs of clothing, furniture, appliances, health, transportation and leisure, but did not even cover basic food costs. At that time 34% of the population were connected to the building trades. According to the Bank of Bilbao, in 1955, Granada occupied the last place on the national list, with an average income per inhabitant of 5,613 pts (about $500 in today's money) compared to 24,777 in Guipuzcoa, which was the first.[12]

During the era of "desarrollismo" (economic development plans), Granada was able to access the aid provided by the International Monetary Fund and the World Bank. Thus, in 1969 these grants arrived in Granada as part of the Second Development Plan of 1968-71. With them, Franco invested in infrastructure such as the construction of the airport. However, job creation expectations were not fulfilled for more than 48% of the population, which resulted in an increase in emigration from the province. Tina and Antonio represent the changing face of labor in the early 1960s. According to Carme Molinero and Pere Ysàs, 1962 marked the beginning of a stage of mobilizations driven by economic transformation and the new labor activism marked by the birth of the so-called CCOO. CCOO benefited from the regime's attempt to liberalize labor relations. General Secretary José Solís[13] and the National Delegate of Trade Unions bet on the new formula of collective contracts and elections of union representatives. This is how the Communist Party and other trade union organizations such as HOAC were able to participate in union elections and to negotiate better working conditions.

Established in 1943, HOAC operated with the directives of the Vatican in the spirit of re-Christianizing the labor movement. In the regime's sponsored union elections of 1963, the HOAC and the JOC gained support. The encyclical *Pacem in Terris*, published that same year by Pope John XXIII, was instrumental in opening the dialogue between Catholics and Marxists in both the workers and student movements. Likewise, the participatory assembly became a new legal venue to claim labor rights within the new opening formula the Labor Ministry articulated.[14]

CCOO was legalized in 1967 and shortly after, Antonio joined and became a union liaison in the organization for the construction guild. Valentina remembered the time when he went to training: "Antonio was in the union, yes. In CCOO. ...They chose him at work.... He was a representative...sure, ...yes! And he had to do a training or something over there at...what is that?... They gave him a framed

---

12 Enrique Tudela Vazquez, *Nuestro Pan: La Huelga del 70* (Granada: Comares, 2010), 42-43.
13 Molinero and Ysàs Solanes, *De la hegemonía a la autodestrucción*, loc. 742 of 10995, Kindle.
14 Carme Molinero and Pere Ysas, *De la hegemonía a la autodestrucción*, loc. 650 of 10995, Kindle. See also Espai en Blanc, ed., *Luchas autónomas en los años setenta: Del antagonismo obrero al malestar social* (Madrid: Traficantes de sueños, 2008). On CCOO see: Alfonso Martínez Foronda, *La conquista de la libertad historia de las comisiones obreras de Andalucía (1962-2000)* (Sevilla: Fundación de Estudios Sindicales, 2005) Archivo Histórico de CC.OO.-A Segunda Edición.

diploma that I still have.... It has on it the hammer and the wheat spikes and what else is it? You know, Comisiones? Well, that was there. He had to do a workshop, but I did not know much about it. Whatever they did...there on the avenue, that building where there is now a fancy hotel...what was there? The unions headquarters...the unions...well, there is where he did a workshop and they gave him a certificate, yes. I didn't go, because he didn't tell me," she paused. "Antonio did not tell me...what he was going to...the workshop or anything...I recently threw away all those papers, but I do keep the diploma...."

Figure 36: There were not just three. We remained all shocked on the ground, discovering suddenly, once again, the hidden meanings of things.

Labor conflict increased significantly in the 1960s. According to the Ministry of Labor's official report for 1970,[15] workers' conflicts in the Basque Country and Asturias played a leading role in the first half of the 1960s, particularly in mining and heavy industry. In Andalusia, the construction workers in Sevilla and Granada were the ones who led the more violent protests, most tragically in Granada during the summer of 1970 with the death of three workers in the confrontation with the regime's armed police. The report responded to the guidelines of the Organizació Internacional del Trabajo (International Labor Organization) and noted 1,595 workers' conflicts for 1970, 317 of those taking place in Granada in July, and 54 in October.[16] The conflicts increased 30% in the construction industry as a result of the urbanization and tourism infrastructure boom of the so-called "development years."[17] Granada benefited, as mentioned above, from government investments in 1969 as part of the second five-year development plan. Nevertheless, Granada's working class endured extreme poverty. Emigration to the more prosperous north or to other European countries was often the best means of survival. Between 1950 and 1970, Granada lost almost 300,000 people, half of its population. Every year about 15,000 people left, bound for Catalonia and other developed regions in Spain, and to the richest European countries.[18] There were also many people, like Antonio and Valentina, who, after they married, moved to Granada from villages such as Aterfe and Maracena.

Remigio Mesa Encinas describes the terrible working conditions of the construction workers. Apprentices received the lowest wages, about 1,200 *pesetas* per week, including payments, permits, and family bonuses. They worked ten hours per day, six days a week. The practice of piecework and unreported overtime was widespread, causing a high level of unemployment and underemployment. Contracts were generally four to six months. It was common for workers to go from one company to another on a recurring basis, in addition to having frequent periods of inactivity. Often, workers were fired or had to move from job to job, making it nearly impossible to gain any seniority. Most of the workers' wives worked as domestic servants. The tragic floods of 1963 precipitated the mass relocation of workers' families to the newly established district of La Virgencica where the HOAC and CCOO found their base. Young college students like Socorro [see chap. 2] visited the temporary government housing to help alleviate the suffering and encourage

---

15 Ministerio del Trabajo, *Informe sobre conflictos colectivos de trabajo 1970* (Madrid: Colección Testimonio, Serie: Informes, Ministerio del Trabajo, 1971), Publications Collection, International Institute of Social History, Amsterdam.
16 Ministerio del Trabajo, *Informe sobre conflictos colectivos*, 19.
17 "In this period 1961-1973, there will be a 7% cumulative annual average growth, multiplication by three of industrial production, 5 and finally, the great boom of the 'Spanish miracle.'" Blanc, *Luchas autónomas en los años setenta*, 35.
18 Remigio Mesa Encinas, "La huelga de 1970 en Granada" in *Luchas autónomas en los años setenta*

women to support their husbands' political and trade union activism. In La Virgencica the parish priest Antonio Quitián, a construction worker himself, lived among the poorest of the poor, and organized the first neighborhood association to demand from the town hall basic services like garbage collection, paved streets and electricity.[19] Quitián was instrumental in facilitating the collaboration between the workers and college students. The repression against the construction workers of Granada in the summer of 1970 spurred the students' protests at the beginning of the academic year that ended with the regime's proclamation of the State of Emergency in December and the persecution and incarceration of students.

The summer of 1970 was a bloody one in the history of Granada's labor movement. Since the civil war, there has not been a workers' mobilization of such caliber and violence. Three workers were killed by the police,[20] and army forces were deployed in the city streets by order of the civil governor of Granada. The conflict raged until, after a long and difficult negotiation between the workers' representatives and the employers to settle the demands for a fair contract, a "convenio colectivo" was agreed upon. The negotiations had started in June and after four unsuccessful meetings, living wages remained the point of heated disagreement. The workers had lowered their initial request of 300 *pesetas* a day to 240 for beginning mason laborers. Employers were offering 170 *pesetas*. On July 21, around 6,000 workers descended into the city and stood around the Official Union Headquarters on Calvo Sotelo Avenue (now called Constitution Avenue). An anonymous testimony reports: "From the different distant points of Granada, groups of bricklayers arrived at eight o'clock in the morning, picking up on the way their fellow workers who went to work in the different sites, because they had not heard about the strike, not having attended the gathering the day before." An estimated 12,000 workers participated in the strike.[21]

---

19 The neighborhood was demolished in 1984. See the chapter on Socorro and Jesus story in this book. On La Virgencica see: Andreo Sánchez, "La Virgencica"; Tudela Vázquez, *Nuestro Pan*; Quitián González et al., *Curas obreros en Granada*.
20 The three workers were: Antonio Huertas Remigio, 22 years old from Maracena; Cristóbal Ibáñez Encinas, 43 years old from Granada; and Manuel Sánchez Mesa, 24 years old from Armilla.
21 Quoted in Mesa Encinas, "La huelga de 1970 en Granada," 123.

Figure 37: Aerial view of La Virgencica bee-hive shape design housing for the poor, 1969

Valentina was still afraid to talk about the strike and the tragic episodes that unfolded on July 21, 1970. To this day, she is convinced Antonio prematurely died as a result of the beating he received in prison that summer. I asked her where she was when the conflict between the construction workers and the police started on that day. It is then that she opened up to me, on the other side of the phone line across the ocean. Me in Miami, pacing around my house while she speaks into my ear from a seaside town by the Mediterranean. She is spending the summer with her youngest daughter and grandchildren. Her voice remains as strong now in 2019 as it did seventeen years after our first recording.

He was working as foreman for Juan[22]...that day at the Sacromonte hotel.... That day a workers' protest took place, and everything fell apart. As he had to pass by the very site of the protest on his way home...he saw some young men from our village and decided to stop and greet them. And that's when everything exploded. The troops from Sevilla and Málaga had already come and I don't know from where else...the police. And that's when everything went crazy. They [referring to the police] started...shooting and they caught him because they arrested many.

He was hit. He had marks all over...from the beatings, bruises on his legs...and I don't know any details as Antonio spoke so little about it. But I did see clearly that he had been badly beaten...I saw those bruises...it all started on July 18 and lasted until July 25 or more.... It lasted at least ten or twelve days...locked up,...yes. They kept them more days at the police

---

22 This is not his boss' real name. I have changed all names and places to respect Tina's wish for their privacy.

station than was legally permitted. And then they took him to jail. I did not go to visit him in jail, because my father-in-law didn't want me to. And Miguel [referring to a neighbor in their building who was very religious and sympathetic to the regime] was the one who pleaded for help...I told him, "Miguel," I said, "Miguel, can you see about Antonio?" And he said, "I was going to ask you, but those things are very delicate...and I didn't know if you wanted my help or not." And then he added, "But do not worry, this afternoon I'll bring you an answer about when they might let him go." He assured me, "Do not worry, he [Antonio] will come back to you very soon." And sure enough, the next day they let him out.

She paused for a second and retraced the events to make sense in her mind of the circumstances leading to the debacle.

I found out...because, you know...I went down to the drugstore to buy a can of paint, and the shop attendant told me, "Do you have a construction worker in your family? Do you know what is going on?" And I had left my baby boy in the cradle and my little girl in the carriage. And then she, the store clerk, told me, and I replied, "Yes, my husband," and she said, "and do you know where he is?" and I said, "the Sacromonte Hotel," and she goes, "Let's phone right now to see where he might be." The owner answered and told me that a workers' patrol had stopped by the work site where there were other construction workers like Antonio. The masonry workers patrol threatened them if they did not stop working; they stoned them. ...So then Antonio and the rest of his crew stopped working...they got off and my Antonio called the owner, Juan, to let him know, and Juan said they could all go home. Then Antonio took his motorcycle to come back home, but as he passed by the Union Headquarters on his way, he stopped, took a look around and stopped. And then, it was then the police arrived from Málaga and Sevilla. At that moment a truck loaded with bricks drove by. Some say that they were called [truck drivers]. Of course, since they [the police] started with gun shots, they ran to the truck and began to throw bricks at the police. And then they took him. [pause] **And they hit him?** *Of course, they hit him. And now three [referring to the three killed workers]...and some others...they died later after the confrontations from the beatings they endured. I don't know if Antonio...because nobody told me anything, Antonio never said a single thing to me...and whenever I mentioned it, he would reply, "Don't ask me, don't ask me, Tina; I have lost sleep over this...don't ask me, please." And I, so he would not suffer...would resign myself, "Let's shut up..." and that's it. He got sick as a consequence, of course. He was already sick with liver problems. But then, they tortured him and all that...and he suffered so much too. Because there were young people who were also Communists who had been caught, and he used to tell me they were beaten to death. [pause] That's all I know. Nothing more.*

My darling...I loved him so much that I slept all those days...wearing the same dress I was wearing the day they arrested him...day and night. AND I COULD DO NOTHING MORE THAN SEEING HIM AT ALL HOURS...AND SEEING AND SEEING HIM...and there staying with me were my in-laws and my parents. My father-in-law kept telling me, "Don't talk, don't talk...say nothing," [urgency in the voice] just in case something happened to my Antonio...and I Shut Up, Shut Up, did not go out...to the street. Buried alive so I would not risk talking. Because you couldn't speak up in those times. So...I remained in my house with my children and with them [referring to her in-laws and her parents] **there**. *My father-in-law brought something to eat to Antonio while he was in jail. I prepared the food for him...but he would not give me his consent to accompany him to the jail.*

He was in jail at least ten or twelve days...I think I even...started to stink because I slept in my dress; I would not take it off. In case they came looking for me...in case I had to run.... [urgency in her voice] *And I lay awake in that light blue dress I had.* [pause] *That happened...that way. And then when he came out...for not making him suffer...well, I asked him but as he did not answer, and his tears flooded his eyes...for all the young people from our village who were beaten just because they were Communists. These were young men from the village.... They had been throwing leaflets...and he knew them, of course...they were from the village and he knew them. Yes.* [pause] *So that happened. I don't know if the disease got worse because of all this or he would have had it anyway. He had had...hepatitis, then cirrhosis, but of course as they hit him so bad and that...well...because on his leg, as I told you, he had a black bruise from his groin to the knee...black like a demon...and everywhere else as well. ...You would think he would be compliant, right? No, he was stubborn like a mule!! Like me...a mule. Maybe a while...but eventually the one who looked for him, because he found out...it was his own boss...who found out...because I had called the Sacromonte Hotel. I spoke with Juan...he looked for Antonio in the hospital, not knowing where he would be. ...Looking for him, he went everywhere looking for him...and the motorcycle, Antonio had left it parked in the gardens* [near the Unions Headquarters building], *and we had to go...Juan and I went to fetch the motorcycle and he kept it in his garage. His own boss was the one who warned me about what was going on. He came to my house and left me 20,000 pesetas[23] on top of the fridge. He said, "Take it! You might need it." Yes, it was his own boss who went to the hospital.... "Don't worry...we won't give up on him...we do not know where he is, though," Juan would tell me. Because you went to the police station and they would tell you that he wasn't there. But there they were indeed, because they were only supposed to be held for forty-eight hours, right? And I think they kept them for at least four or five days. In the Plaza de los Lobos precinct. Yes. They made them stand all the time, all in the same cell. And they slept standing up! leaning on each other's shoulders...Yes. So, don't write our names...don't write our names. Let's NOT tempt luck and after all those years, now they put me in jail.*

---

23 About $200, a significant amount of money in 1970.

Valentina's fear still lives with her. Now seventy-six years old, she pauses and worries about being punished for remembering and telling about what she was told to bury and relegate to oblivion. But time has given her the ability to inhabit her solitude and dwell in her Antigone lineage. Valentina is in a tomb of her own making like Antigone, where she deploys her self-effacing modus operandi for the sake of love and self-respect. In Zambrano's words:

> Concealment occurs in this class of beings--(characters and exceptionally human creatures) in a different fashion: when given a grave, and a time of forgetting, of absence as if in a dreamlike state. With this obliviousness they are given time. The time they are owed, which coincides with the time humans require to attain some revelation arising from within themselves. Those are clearings emerging in the forest of History.[24]

I am humbled in her presence, full of might.

---

24 "La ocultación se produce de otra manera en esta clase de seres—personajes y excepcionalmente humanas criaturas—: una tumba cuando se les da, y un tiempo de olvido, de ausencia como en el sueño. Con este olvido se les da tiempo. El tiempo que se les debe, que coincide con el tiempo que los humanos necesitan para recibir la revelación, que de ellos surge. Claros que se abren en el bosque de la historia." Zambrano, *La tumba de Antígona*, loc. 369 of 1423, Kindle.

Chapter 10
Esperanza's and Adoración's Cartographies of Mercy

Irse.
Decidir irse. O mejor, quedarse.
porque es demasiado largo,
decidir. No hay paciencia.
Hay infinitos puntos, como
en el trayecto de Aquiles, o el de la flecha
que nunca alcanzará la diana.
El irse
se divide en fragmentos,
la decisión en otras decisiones,
y estas a su vez
se subdividen.

Irse:
Salir de la ciudad, pero antes,
de una casa y antes aun,
de una habitación y para ello,
levantarse, poner
orden entre los huesos
y cerrar el cuaderno y previamente,
dejar de escribir para qué?
Si: irse. Irse quedó atrás. Se escribió más arriba,
o en la página anterior.[1]
Chantal Maillard, *Hilos* (2007)

---

[1] *Leaving. Deciding to leave. Or better, staying. Because it's too long, deciding. There is no patience. There are infinite points, like in the path of Achilles, or that of the arrow that will never reach the target. Leaving is divided into fragments, the decision into other decisions, and these in turn subdivide into more decisions. Leaving: Leaving the city, but first, leaving a house and even before, a room and for that, getting up, that is the problem, getting up, putting the bones in order and closing the notebook and previously, stop writing for what? Yes: leaving. Leaving fell behind. It was written above, or on the previous page.* [my translation] Maillard, *Hilos*, 83-84.

*Mystery is not found outside;
it is within each of us,
surrounding and enfolding us.
We live and we move within mystery.
The guide to avoid getting lost in it resides in Mercy.*[2]
María Zambrano, "Para una historia de la piedad" (1989)

*Irse.
Decidir irse. O mejor, quedarse.
porque es demasiado largo,
decidir. No hay paciencia.
Hay infinitos puntos, como
en el trayecto de Aquiles, o el de la flecha
que nunca alcanzará la diana.*

Figure 38: Esperanza with her son on his First Communion day, Bilbao, c. 1957

---

[2] "El misterio no se halla fuera; está dentro y en cada uno de nosotros, al par que nos rodea y envuelve. En él vivimos y nos movemos. La guía para no perdernos en él es la piedad." Zambrano, "Para una historia de la piedad."

Espe's life and times as "bonne à tout faire"

Espe was born on February 24, 1923, in Ermua, a town in the province of Vizcaya in the Basque Country. Her father never laid eyes on her, having died only a month before. Her mother was left a widow with two little girls and a newborn. Perhaps these circumstances led the young mother to optimistically name the girl Esperanza. Hope was literally all she had left.

Espe's mom worked as a cook, and her late husband had been the chauffeur for the noble Chávarri Salazar family in Bilbao. The couple met in 1918 while working as part of a staff of eighteen domestic servants in the renowned Chávarri palace.[3] After the death of her husband, the young widow had no choice but to send her two oldest daughters away. She placed her middle child with relatives and the oldest in a nunnery boarding school in Larrauri (Munguia), keeping baby Espe with her in Bilbao. Mother and baby would share the attic quarters in the Chávarri palace with two other servants.

From birth Espe was sickly. "As soon as I got wet, I caught colds," she explained. One of the other servants suggested the possibility of sending Espe to Carranza, a pastoral rural town. There the little girl's health would improve under the care of this woman's mother, who would take Espe in for a small payment. But the arrangement did not go well with that lady in Carranza, "because **she threw me out the window**," Espe declared.

Thinking that I misunderstood her I ask her to explain. With a small nervous laughter, she added: "Well, I did not like milk…. And then, she said that I put soap in the milk…maybe I did, I do not know." Espe was seven years old when this happened. She fell from the window into nettles, where she sat crying. A neighbor passed by and heard her. "He saw me in such a state and took me to a family who brought me into their home," she explained. This family offered her shelter, not knowing where she came from or who were her relatives. They fed her and sent her to school. Seven years later, Espe reunited with her mother, who still believed she was living where she had placed her in Carranza.

I used to attend the Sacred Heart school located near the train station and one day, while I was in class, I turned my eyes to the window and saw my mother passing by on the street. "MY MOTHER! MY MOTHER!" I screamed. And the teacher, startled, said, "but what's wrong with you?" and I kept yelling "MY MOTHER!" So, they fetched her and indeed…there she was…my mother walking, WALKING BY MY SCHOOL…AFTER SO MANY YEARS. So, I then took her to the house where I was truly living and I introduced her to that kind family. "This is my mother," I told them. And they said, "Oh well then, child, you must go with her as

---

3   Now the Chávarri palace is the site of Bilbao's Civil Governor's office.

she is your mother." ...*And then I told my mom, "I have lived all these years with this family who I call my grandparents, and Aunt Anita, Aunt Enriqueta," and my mother was shocked.*

After their reunion Espe's mother took her back with her to Bilbao where she joined her two older sisters. It was 1936, the beginning of the Spanish Civil War. They lived in Bilbao during the three years of civil war and Espe, now a teenager, started to work as a kitchen aide in the cooking school of a restaurant called "El Cano." There she met Victorino in 1937, in the Playa Moyua.

I met him there. He came along with a group of friends. Then, when he turned eighteen he went to the front.... He fought for the Republic in the Ebro battle...very famous. He said to me "I want you to be my war sweetheart," and I said, "all right."[4] *We wrote to each other and I made him a sweater; I remember sending it to him. He wrote love verses and drew for me.... He had a little notebook, with some flowers on one side...and then written all over with poems for me.* [Espe smiled].

Espe remembers the advance of General Mola and how he died in a plane crash, and then she mentions Queipo de Llano who in her opinion was much worse than Mola, and how the alarm sirens are still vivid in her mind, and the bombing of Guernica enters into our conversation.

Well, the ones who bombed Guernica were the Germans! My uncle who lived in Guernica knows this very well. My sister had lived with them for a while. Luckily, by then she had returned to Bilbao to live with my mother. But my uncle and his family still lived there. He had a workshop that made engines...to export abroad...huge machinery.... And he always said..."I dare anyone to ask me, who did it..." because Franco was saying, "the reds have burned Guernica." And he [referring to her uncle] *used to say, "REALLY? ASK ME! I WAS THERE." People took refuge in the church....* [she repeated her uncle's words to me]: *"I saw the planes, how they bombed the city...they bombed Guernica," because the Basque government was there in Guernica. Because the Fueros of the Basque Country were in Guernica. But they*

---

4   The "madrinas de guerra" were women who volunteered as pen pals, writing to soldiers. The women wrote letters to more than one soldier, many times unknown to them. The purpose was to raise the morale among the troops. The practice was institutionalized on the rebels' side while the Republican side introduced it later and for a shorter period. Many of the letters from the republican godmothers are lost, since they might have been destroyed after the Francoist victory. Not only did these women send letters and postcards but also clothing and food. See: https://journals.openedition.org/bulletinhispanique/4284#tocto1n3; Mary Nash, Rojas, *Las mujeres republicanas en la Guerra Civil* (Madrid: Editorial Taurus, 1999); J. Martínez y N. Rodríguez, "Cartes d'un soldat republicà" en www.aasit.com/informatiu/hemeroteca/ [...]; Carmen Ortiz and Manuel de Ramón, *Madrina de guerra: cartas desde el frente* (Madrid: La Esfera de los Libros, 2003).

didn't bomb the official buildings or the church. ONLY THE PEOPLE, YES! The people...they knew what they were doing.

During the war, Espe kept corresponding with Victorino and working at the El Cano restaurant. This training helped her to get a job with the Chávarri's children (her parents' employers) when they moved to Madrid in 1939. The Olábarri Chávarri family owned an entire building on elegant Genova Street. The couple had eight children and a staff of eleven domestic servants. Then sixteen, Espe was hired in 1939 as a kitchen aide with a monthly wage of thirty-five *pesetas*.

Between 1940 and 1950, more than half of the female labor force in Spain worked in domestic service, which was more than simply a job for poor young women. As historian Eider de Dios points out, domestic work for poor women represented an essential piece in the National-Catholic political agenda emerging after the Francoist victory in 1939. In the new Spain taking shape after the civil war, being a servant meant a kind of indentured servitude for many poor women who belonged to the vanquished side.[5]

The whole building belonged to them on Genova street...they were big capitalists. ...They had two floors. Below were the service rooms and a bathroom. Upstairs they had the laundry and a line to hang their clothes. When my mother was in their service, they employed twelve or fourteen servants. When I was there, we were eleven. They had a cook and a kitchen aide, a waiter to serve meals, and his scullery maid. She and I were the helpers and mops [she laughed softly]. And then they had one woman to iron clothes all day. Another one to handwash clothes, because at that time you washed clothes by hand. ....They had a chauffeur, a chambermaid for the husband, a chambermaid for the wife, a nanny for the boys and a nanny for the girls, and a head housekeeper. Can you imagine?

In the year [19]39...when the war ended...in the [19]40s these people had all that...I worked for them three years from 1939 to 1942. They had a villa in Bilbao, in Las Arenas, and every summer we all went there to their chalet to serve them...I used to make breakfast for twenty-two people every morning. I baked bread every day...white bread YES! Because the Master

---

5   Eider de Dios Fernández, *Sirvienta, empleada, trabajadora de hogar: Género, clase e identidad en el Franquismo y la transición a través del servicio doméstico (1939-1995)* (Málaga: Universidad de Málaga, 2019). See also: Sescún Marías Cadenas, "Las empleadas de hogar durante el franquismo y la transición democrática: entre el paternalismo y la marginación (1939-1981)" in Ana Antón-Pacheco Bravo et al., eds., *IX Jornadas Internacionales de Estudios de la Mujer* (Madrid: Editorial Fundamentos, 2011), 297-307; Cristina Borderias Mondéjar, "Las mujeres autoras de sus trayectorias personales y familiares: a través del servicio doméstico," *Historia y Fuente Oral* 6, (1991): 105-21; María Jesús Espuny Tomás and Guillermo García González, *Relaciones laborales y empleados de hogar reflexiones jurídicas* (Madrid: Dyckinson, 2014); Rocío García Abad and Arantza Pareja Alonso, "Servir al patrón o al marido: Mujeres con destino a la Ría de Bilbao," *Arenal* 9, no. 2 (2002): 301-26.

went to Cuatro Caminos to buy flour and all that. They had to...because there was rationing at the time. We [referring to the poor] got just a piece of hard bread that you could bounce off the floor! BUT they [referring to the rich] were given...white bread. As I say, WHAT DISCRIMINATION, really!? I think about it and say...lucky I served the rich.

The 1940s were known as "The Hunger Years." Ration books were in circulation until 1952. A year earlier, Cardinal Vicente Enrique Tarancón had published "Our Daily Bread," a pastoral letter denouncing the utter destitution of the larger population while the Francoist establishment controlled much of the black market. Gerald Brenan recorded in his travel log a visit to Spain in 1949 when "the ration consisted of a small roll of bread a day, a quarter of a liter of olive oil, and three ounces of sugar a week, with minute quantities of chickpeas and rice, very irregularly distributed. Even these rations are not always honored. And on the black market the bread are twelve *pesetas* the kilo—just the average daily wage."[6]

Espe felt fortunate that she was able to secure a good job with the rich during the early postwar hunger years. Thirty-five *pesetas* a month allowed her to save a little money and buy her trousseau. "In Madrid I bought the fabrics," she recalled, "every month I would buy some sheets.[7] In 1939 Victorino was stationed in Valladolid to fulfill his mandatory military service. He paid her a visit to Madrid, and they got engaged. In 1942, once he completed his military service, they both moved to Bilbao and got married in the San Vicente parish in 1947.

What happiness Espe experienced was short-lived, as her husband soon became sick with active tuberculosis.

We got married and went on our honeymoon to Haro, in La Rioja, and stayed at his uncle's place. He [Victorino] kept coughing, and coughing, and coughing at night...for eight days.... He kept on coughing and coughing when we returned to Bilbao and I said, "We have to go to the doctor" but he would say, "Why go to the doctor. They will just have me rest and I'm not going to stop working." I would insist, "Well, I'll work! Do not worry, I will work," I'd say to him. We were living with my sister and my mother in my mother's attic...the house being as big as it was. And one day, we would have been married no more than two months, I said, "Today it's happening, I'm taking you to a private doctor." I took him to a lung and heart specialist, the best in Bilbao who had a sanatorium for tuberculosis patients. In those days,

---

6   Aurora Morcillo, *The Seduction of Modern Spain: The Female Body and the Francoist Body Politic* (Lewisburg: Bucknell University Press, 2010), 132. See also: Oscar Rodríguez Barreira, *Migas con Miedo: Prácticas de resistencia al primer franquismo Almería 1939-1953* (Almería: UAL, 2008), and also by the same author "Cambalaches: Hambre, moralidad popular y mercados negros de guerra y postguerra," *Historia Social* 77 (2013): 149-74. Hunger was rampant throughout Europe in the 1940s; for Germany see the work of Paul Steege, *Black Market, Cold War: Everyday Life in Berlin, 1946-1949* (Cambridge, Cambridge University Press, 2007).

7   Esperanza, interview recording, 2007.

the clinic in question was crowded because the prisons' inmates were infected. So, I took him to the doctor who said, "Well, he has to rest for at least three months...at least." So, I kept him at home. And one day, a friend of my mother's came to visit; she was coming precisely from another clinic where my husband had gone to be treated before we got married, but now he refused to go back. So, I decided to go there to find out more, and the doctors confirmed, "This young man was here three years ago. At that time, he would have healed in six months, but he didn't want to continue the treatment." [Espe stopped and looked at me sadly] *You see, the problem was there was nothing to eat in those days.... So, that friend who came to visit, she saw how having a sick man like that at home was no good...A young girl, like me, strong, of course, but really...we had been married for just two months. And so, she advised us to contact the hospital's director as there was a pavilion for this illness, a tuberculosis wing. And the director of that pavilion also had a private practice in his home. ...And so, I took him there. He took X-rays and told me, "Come in four or five days to get the results."*

We were still sleeping in the same bed, but I told him from that day on, "Look, you are going to sleep here...but I'm going to sleep in my mother's room," and I went to sleep with my mother. She had two beds in her room. My sister moved out and went to the village as soon as they told us what he had. My mother and I stayed. I went for the X-Ray results and the doctor said to me, "There is nothing impossible for the Almighty. But for science this case is very tough. [She paused] *We have to operate."* [She pauses again looking at her hands] *and then he said..."We can admit him in the hospital." When I got home, he asked, "What did the doctor tell you?" and I said, "Well, nothing; you just have to rest." I never told him what it was. NEVER! And he was admitted to the hospital. I called the pavilion of infectious cases at the hospital and requested someone to come to our home to transport him. They disinfected the mattress, everything, and sealed the room...they did...it was extraordinary...in the year [19]47. THE YEAR 47, that was.*[8]

When we committed him to the hospital, we were relieved. "Luckily I am not pregnant...What a relief!" I thought...because I had my period...in November and December, and I thought..."well, I'm not pregnant." But after four months or more missing it, I went to the doctors and they told me, "You are pregnant." [Espe stared at me in silence] *CAN YOU BELIEVE IT! I told him about it. But of course, he was never with our baby. He saw him from afar in the garden. I was working then as a cook downstairs in the building where we lived, I remember. When he fell ill, they told me they needed a cook and since they lived on the floor below, I went down every day. Also, I took a part-time job cleaning an office. At six in the morning I cleaned the office and then went to work as a cook. So, one morning my mother was walking out of our building when she ran into my mother-in-law and my mother said to*

---

8   On the treatment of tuberculosis in Bilbao see: Antonio Villanueva Edo, "Las instituciones de la lucha antituberculosa en Vizcaya (1882-1957)," *Euskal herriaren historiari buruzko biltzarra* 4 (1988): 201-20 (La crisis del Antiguo Régimen), https://www.ehu.eus/documents/1738121/234 9786/Tuberculosis.pdf.

her, "*Do not go upstairs, because your son is in the hospital,*" and she [the mother-in-law] started shouting, "*MY SON! MY SON IN THE HOSPITAL!*" *She went crazy.*

Victorino's family had concealed his condition to secure the marriage. Espe reflected:

They ought to be thankful that I swallowed that lie...because I never told my son that story because...WHAT FOR? WHAT FOR? My brother-in-law did say to me, half surprised, "Seven years of courtship with him, you hadn't noticed? He had never told you anything?...because you surely must have had some intimacy...." And I said, "NO! NOTHING!" You see, what happened is he [Victorino] *figured, "If I say something about this she will leave me," and his mother told me later, "If I had suggested to my son, 'tell her or leave her'...HE WOULD HAVE JUMPED OUT A WINDOW." That is what my mother-in-law told me...I was lucky he did not infect me...because I had lived with him for a few months of marriage. Earlier in our relationship nothing happened because at that time you did not touch each other...only a stolen kiss and nothing else.* [Espe laughed]

I think he got sick in the war...he went to the front...the front of the Ebro was VERY, VERY HARD! [said emphatically] *and he was sent there...the battle of the Ebro. Then he did three more years of military service in Valladolid, and then the job he had!* [referring to the window cleaning] *always raining in Bilbao....*

Victorino spent two years in the hospital. He never returned home.

In November he fell ill and in January he entered the hospital [1948]. *It was also in January that he died, just two years later. Until I gave birth, I visited him every day. I cleaned the office in the morning and then worked in the kitchen. After I finished at four or five, I went to the hospital every day. Once he entered the hospital, my sister moved back home with her girls to live with us. And she was the one who took me to the hospital to deliver my baby when the time came...My sister and I, I remember we walked all the way to the hospital at two in the morning. ...They would not pay any attention to me until eight in the morning.* [she giggled nervously] *It wasn't very far but still it was a walk.... And they put me to bed and at about six o'clock they came to me, they got me up, and he was born with the help of the midwife. And then I was torn apart and they explained I had a total tear inside and out. Because the child took so many hours of labor to deliver, he was born with such a cucumber shaped head* [she put her hands on her head to show me] *the forceps, you know, to get him out and they said, "Don't worry, his head will go back to normal right away." They told me the doctor had to come.* [She paused for a moment] *And there I was waiting, waiting, waiting. The child had already been taken downstairs with my mother and she knew nothing of what had happened to me. Then, I told the doctor, "Look, my husband has tuberculosis and he is hospitalized," and the doctor said, "Ah, good you have told me. Right now, I am going to call Madrid so they can send us the vaccine...the Bacillus of Koch." And it arrived immediately, the next day. I remember, I would take out my breast milk onto a spoon and mixed it and that's how I gave the vaccine to the baby...that was so he wouldn't catch tuberculosis. Thank God...he has never had anything...never...And I was also lucky that he* [her husband] *didn't infect me.*

Espe was twenty-seven years old when her husband died in 1950. Alone, with a toddler, she sought more work to provide a better future for her son. Even though she had been denied an education, she was determined that her son would not suffer the same fate. A friend told her there was work at the elegant five-star Carlton Hotel in Bilbao. They were looking for a seamstress and ironing maid. She proudly recalled how, while working as a young kitchen aide, she had also attended sewing classes and was ready to take the job at the fancy hotel.

And I worked there for six years. In addition, I continued to clean the office...and whenever anyone needed a cook for a First Communion banquet I would also go to work.

Her work at the Carlton involved both sewing and ironing.

*We had to iron bed sheets, men's suits.... In the laundry room there were about ten women who ironed by hand, four or five who used machine irons, and two more to do the folding. That was so efficient! I became a friend of a girl who worked in the hotel's kitchen and she told me she was moving to Paris. "You know," she said one day, "I'm going to work in Paris. She was also a widow...**So, in [19]56 I went off to Paris**[9]**... just six years after my husband's death.***

---

9   On the migration of Spanish women to work as domestic servants in Paris see: Laura Oso Casas, *Españolas en París: Estrategias de ahorro y consume en las emigraciones internacionales* (Barcelona: Edicions Bellaterra, 2004). There was also a film released in 1971 by the same title *Españolas in París*, screenplay and directed by Roberto Bodegas, with Ana Belén, Máximo Valverde, and Tina Saenz in the leading roles. Some studies on the Spanish migratory movements during the Franco regime include: Alicia Mira Abad et Mónica Moreno Seco, "Españolas exiliadas y emigrantes: encuentros y desencuentros en Francia," *Les Cahiers de Framespa* [En ligne] 5 (2010). http://journals.openedition.org/framespa/383; DOI : 10.4000/framespa.383. Luís M. Calvo Salgado et al., *Historia del Instituto Español de Emigración: La política migratoria exterior de España y el IEE del Franquismo a la Transición* (Madrid: Ministerio de Trabajo e Inmigración Subdirección General de Información Administrativa y Publicaciones, 2009); Pedro José Chacón Delgado, "El Asimilacionismo Nacionalista Vasco: La emigración española al País Vasco en la segunda mitad del siglo XX," *Cuadernos de Pensamiento Político* 45 (January/March 2015): 123-52; José Babiano and Sebastián Farré, "La emigración española a Europa durante los años sesenta: Francia y Suiza como países de acogida," *Historia Social* 42 (2002): 81-98.

According to Laura Oso Casas, the 1960s saw an increase in the number of women migrating to France as domestics.[10] The French government established the National Immigration Office in 1945 to recruit foreign labor to contribute to the postwar reconstruction of the country. In 1956, the Franco regime established the Instituto Español de Emigración (IEE) to regulate the flow of emigrants to the rest of Europe.[11] While these two agencies were officially in charge of implementing the 1961 bilateral agreement between France and Spain, most of the women traveling by themselves like Espe made the move outside of the institutional bureaucracy. Spanish women migrated to Paris during the 1960s and 1970s to work as servants or *bonne à tout faire*[12] for middle-class French families. They followed the connections with acquaintances and other women who had already migrated. Espe's friend worked polishing floors for the French consulate in Madrid. With her connections she helped procure a contract for Espe to work for a family in Paris.

I then realized my options. And remember telling [my friend], "Oh, María, I would go wherever necessary.... Because I ca"t give my son a good education here." My friend understood

---

10   Between 1962 and 1968 the percentage of Spanish women within the emigration influx went from 44% to 47%. The majority of these women who worked as domestic servants for the new bourgeoisie came alone, whether single or widows. They resided in Paris mainly in the 16th district, while other areas also saw a presence of families where the Spanish had settled at the turn of the twentieth century, the so-called *Petite Espagne* in the northern district of Siene-Saint Denis. Oso Casas, *Españolas en París*, 29.

11   Babiano and Farré, "La emigración española a Europa durante los años sesenta," 88.

12   According to Laura Oso Casas, "Some of the women who migrated with their husbands or who were regrouped by them, headed for their arrival in Paris to other less bourgeois neighborhoods of the city, such as the East of the capital (Paris XI, Paris XII, chambres de bonnes Paris XX ...), where they initially rented or roomed in hotels. And they combined this residential strategy with work or multi-employment. However, they often worked as a femme de ménage and had other extra jobs. They were also set up in a stage of occupational mobility for women who started working as bonnes à tout faire. Some of the women who left domestic service as ménage femmes (living in the house environment of their employers) left to work in one or two houses. The advantage of this type of work is an improvement in living and working conditions. The extra work consisted, first, in working as an external servant in several houses. This work could be combined with other occupations such as 'burones' and 'pubelas.' The work of 'burones' is, in the jargon of the Spanish diaspora in France, office cleaning, which is done in the morning early or at night. The 'pubelas' consisted of cleaning the stairs and taking out garbage in buildings that had an electronic intercom rather than a concierge/doorkeeper. One other occupation of Spanish women in Paris was sewing. The XI district of Paris was characterized by sewing workshops, where some Spanish were employed, who could take their work home to sew a few hours before bedtime." Laura Oso Casas, "'Chambras,' 'porterias,' 'pubelas' y 'burones:'" estrategias de movilidad social de las españolas en París," in *Un siglo de inmigración española en Francia* (Vigo: Grupo de Comunicación Galicia en el Mundo, 2009), 88-90.

and told her boss, a French diplomat, ..."Sir, she is desperate because she really wants to give her son an education." I was indeed an unhappy sight to see as I was not able to provide him with a good education. I would have liked to study myself. Because I liked it but couldn't do it because of the war. The war prevented me.... When my friend told me about a job...I asked to see the conditions of employment...I needed a passport, travel money...and they agreed to cover everything. So, I got my passport, bought a train ticket, and left. I made 700 pesetas working in the hotel while in this job I was offered 2,000 plus room and board. SO, I said "I'M GONE!" I said, "I'm going alone to try and see if it works for me or not. It is better to expose myself alone without my child." My mother said, "Oh dear, you are crazy, crazy...You think 'streets are lined in gold.'" "No, Mom," I replied, "I only see that here my son is growing up and I am not able to give him a good education."

I left. I went with that French family; he was a doctor and diplomat. I learned a little French with the little ones. The older boy would say "regarde le papillon." ...He was two and a half years old or three years old. "Regarde le papillon."

Espe laughed as she remembered and said the words in French, and I am able to see the butterfly flying between us. She continued: *He was a diplomat. Then, just nine months after I arrived to work in their home in Paris, he tells me, "Look, we are going to Madagascar and there you have nothing to do but take care of the children. Because there, black servants will do everything...cleaning...everything. You will just take care of the children." But when I found out this move was for three years...the thought of going without my son...no, I could not do it. I accompanied them to Marseille to take a ship to Madagascar. I spent the day after they left sightseeing in Marseille and then returned to Paris.*

I stayed with a couple from Bilbao...Communists, of course. They were exiles from the war there and they worked as janitors/doorkeepers of the building.[13] *It was a good place they had, I remember, rooms for those seeking employment in the city. I stayed there with other girls, and they assured me, "Don't worry, you'll find work right away...."*

Espe's predicament was similar to that of many Spanish women who arrived by themselves to the big city. Many of them found refuge in the Residence Saint Didier located on Rue Saint Didier (Paris 16th district) and run by the Sisters of Mary Immaculate nun order, the Adoratrices Order, or the Spanish mission on Rue de la Pompe, also in the 16th district. In this center the newcomers could find a temporary place to stay and the nuns would help them find a job. A network of volunteers waited at the train station for their fellow Spanish women, and they would bring them to the shelter.[14]

---

13   Many families lived as doorkeepers in bourgeois buildings. The ground floor quarters were small and lacked services but allowed many to combine a paid job with family living arrangements.

14   Oso Casas, *Españolas en París*, 37-38.

Espe did not use these shelters but rather stayed with her exiled Communist friends who helped her find another job right away.

Indeed, I found a family right away, but they told me I was too fancy of a cook for them. I had already learned to prepare some French dishes...I made her dessert.... It was in this house that the owners got me the legal paperwork for a permanent work permit. The lady wanted me to pay her for my travel expenses as part of all the paperwork, and I said, "Non merci, c'est moi qui ai payé le voyage." I said, [Espe looked at me with pride] *I said no, my former employer had paid for my travel expenses and then deducted monthly from my wages what I owed him little by little. I also asked them to let me bring my son, and they wanted him to be put in a boarding school. I did not like it. I was not about to do with my son what they wanted but rather what I decided as his mother.*

This family let her go, and Espe returned to Bilbao, where she found employment as a cook with a German family until she was able to arrange for another home in Paris. This time, bringing her son was a condition she was not willing to negotiate. Her son was already ten years old when she was able to bring him to live with her in the house where she worked. He arrived at the Gare Austerlitz accompanied by another friend who also worked in Paris like Espe. She remembers fondly how this woman and her husband admired her dedication to her son.

I would take him to visit them, this Spanish couple...we called them pop and mom...who were Communists...The kindest people, very good people...they helped me so much with my son.

Espe sent her son to school as she had always dreamed of, and he was a dedicated student who quickly learned French. The home employer where she moved in with her son was supportive. She advised her to become a French citizen so her son could have access to the financial aid benefits. As Espe put it, "I became French and immediately my son along with me." Her son learned French in a summer while she took extra work with a friend of her employers who had young children and asked her to be their cook during the summer vacation.

We were there three months and he learned French perfectly as he was spending his day with the other children playing and so on. Then he completed his four years of High School and sat for the graduation exam. When I went to speak with his professor and told him, "Now that he has completed his diploma, Monsieur Professor, I would like him to go into technical education." And he said, "Vous-êtes malade? Vous n'avez pas de travail?" and I replied, "No Monsieur, Oui, je travaille," and he told me, "You ask me an impossible thing; how many French would I wish were like him!" And then, I understood. "No Monseiur, on ne parle plus," I said with conviction. "Let's not talk anymore; my son must continue his education." So, he finished his studies. He did the bachelor's first and then studied industrial engineering.

Espe paused for a moment and looked me in the eye with pride. Like in Bilbao, she worked for two generations of the same family during the next twelve years. These families she worked for helped her achieve her goal of seeing her son succeed.

And there in that house I stayed six years. And then I worked for the daughter who married an American from Wisconsin, another six. Twelve years with the same family, I was. The daughter had an apartment in Cannes where we spent the summers...all summer.... They had a pool! And a large yacht where they entertained guests...well, Americans and so on....

This couple helped my son while he was studying engineering because he was required to do an internship on site and write a report. The first year he worked in Paris at Citroën. I remember in the year [19]68, the student revolution in France; he did not strike. I remember that his friends were saying, "You are a strikebreaker," and he would tell them, "But if I go on strike I risk them taking away my scholarship, NO. I have a scholarship! The state pays for my studies."

Espe is quick to point out how not everyone she worked for was so kind and generous. Referring to the parents of the wife in this family, she recalled:

Just the opposite of her parents, who were so tight and mean.... I had to tell that lady once, "Madame, with this food my son does not have enough. If you buy three steaks and my son eats one, that means I haven't eaten."

Espe stopped to make the point clear to me. *I did tell them one day, you know?* She switched to French to repeat the moment she told her employer,

"Non madame, c'est moi qui ne mange pas." Because, you see, she entered the kitchen and we [she and her son] were eating and she remarked, "Of course we have to support your son here," and I immediately replied "NON, MADAME! non madame, c'est moi qui ne mange pas. S'il mange, je ne mange pas." But the daughter and her American husband were kinder.

Espe's son was able to do some internship work in the American factory owned by her employer and eventually found a career as an industrial engineer in the United States. He got married and moved to America. After twenty-two years living in France, Espe found herself alone and decided to return to Spain. Looking back, she considers her move to France the best decision she ever made in her life.

When I arrived in France, the difference was...well, like water and wine. It was like that...totally opposite. Absolutely...not only people's life, eating, the everyday and all that...it was the way they related to each other.... I mean, they would walk out of the subway and would kiss each other, and I did not see that in Spain. I remember how one day my husband put his arm like that over my shoulder in the park and a police guard came to scold us.... There were so many things I experienced...it was that freedom! That was the "thing" in France. They indeed were twenty or thirty years ahead of us. It's true, in everything. Because in those days Spain was VERY, VERY poor. Even the Basque Country, because the Basque Country was not the worst in Spain, but it was behind....

It was very, very bad.... So people emigrated, many, many people. Those from the south went to Germany. Large numbers of young men from the countryside went to Germany to work, while in France, we were mostly domestic servants. And in Germany it was more country men like Luis Mariano the Spanish actor and singer; he was first working in the French grape harvest...he sang so beautifully.... Those rural country men came to work every summer.... Yes, because the conditions of work were very good; they had their little barracks, their showers, very good. At least in France, in other places I do not know, but in France they were fine.

Espe's eyes lit up when she spoke of Luis Mariano.

I went out with my friends to the movies and that.... Yes. I remember that we went to see Luis Mariano...if we used to go out.... We had a center. In the French parish there was a Spanish priest, Asturian. They let us use a chapel where they gave Mass for the Spaniards, the Spanish priest. And we prepared the mass for us. It was a huge center. We used it to teach children the catechism...to have parties on Sundays. And each one made a meal and brought it to share at dinner. ...Well, there we were, our center. The priest gave us a key...and...we made meals...each one carried what he wanted. First there were my son's in-laws. He was the president and he told me, "You are going to be my secretary," and I said, "Good," but when he stopped being president, they ELECTED ME! And I was the president until I came back to Spain.

We gave informative talks too. Because many Spaniards were not paid by insurance, I had to go with some to make a claim. I would say, "Look, you, madam, you don't pay this." I knew because we were going to the UGT union, one of my friends and me. We were going to see what rights we had. Sure, homework too. But, let's see what rights we had. You have the right to this, this, and this. ...Then we used to give talks. "We have the right to this, this, this. And if the employer does not pay you, you have to protest. But you also have the responsibility to do the work properly and punctually."

I remember someone who hadn't been paid, and I went with her because she didn't speak French. "Madame, I'm sorry, but you haven't paid Edurne," I said. And I went to another session with someone else too, and the employer said, [thoughtful pause] How did she tell me? [Speaking to herself] "Let her speak too...because she also knows French," she told me, because I was going with those who didn't know French, to help them.

Espe's story shows the often fraught relationship the Spanish émigrés had with their French employers, and the larger problem with the way foreign workers are in general treated by the country that needs and benefits from their work. The cognitive dissonance on the part of the French was partly reconciled by creating simplistic caricatures of the foreign workers, and in this case, the female Spanish domestic employee. The maid's job is the one that fed the most prevalent stereotype of most Spanish immigration in France, personified in the character of "Conchita." As Bruno Tur points out, "the stereotypes of the sixties in France are not born ex nihilo: they are inspired, prolonged, perpetuated or modified preconceived ideas existing since the beginning of the XX century, some of them inherited from the XIX, while the most ancient date back to the modern era, sometimes before to the French Revolution (1789)."[15] Tur explains how in 1968, when the novelist Solange Fasquelle published in the Albin Michel editorial a humorous work on the maids of Paris, *Conchita and you: Practical manual for people who employ Spanish maids*, Conchita was already a stereotype well known to the French. Before "Conchita the maid" there was "Conchita the Spanish woman," who lived in Spain and was not an immigrant. The stereotyped character appears in the light comedies of the Parisian capital (théâtre de boulevard), in literature, and in songs like the one by Luis Mariano:

> *This is the wonder*
> *That you repeat daily,*
> *Because the young seamstress*
> *Becomes a fairy-godmother in Paris.*
> *Miracle of Paris, Paris, Paris,*
> *In silk and lace,*
> *Girls who live, live, live*
> *Making others' dreams come alive*[16]

The Spanish woman of the French imagination is a brunette, beautiful, seductive, with the potential to do great harm. She knows how to dance, how to move her body. Like Mérimée's *Carmen*, Conchita is often portrayed as a gypsy, Andalusian. Her character embodies something inaccessible and, ultimately, wanton. This character follows that of Bécassine, a French comic strip character inspired by the earthy maids from Brittany who left the farm to work in Paris.[17]

Espe returned to Spain in 1977 after her son married and moved to the United States. She was fifty-four years old. With the money she had saved she bought a small delicatessen in Bilbao, in the Basque country, her native country. There she

---

15   Bruno Tur, "Estereotipos y representaciones sobre la inmigración española en Francia," in Grupo de Comunicación Galicia en el Mundo, *Un siglo de inmigración española en Francia*
16   Esta es la maravilla/Que a diario repetís/Porque la modistilla/Es hada en París. /Milagro de París, París, París,/En seda y encaje/Muchachas que vivís, vivís, vivís/Haciendo soñar. [My translation] "Milagro de París," song lyrics sung by Luis Mariano, a famous tenor in France, Spain, and Latin America in the 1940s through 1960s. Luis Mariano was born in Irun, Basque Country, but grew up in France where his family migrated after the war. Esperanza was one of his most devoted admirers.
17   Tur, "Estereotipos y representaciones sobre la inmigración española en Francia," 130-31.

worked until her retirement. Espe's move to France was, in the end, the key to making her return to Spain more comfortable. She followed the pattern of migration with the objective to save and return home.

Historian Eider de Dios utilizes oral history to reconstruct the experiences of the domestic servants during the Franco regime. She divides her study into three parts, according to three categories she designs to characterize the worker in each period: first, the servant (1939-1959); second, the housekeeper or "empleada de hogar" (1959-1975); and finally, the domestic worker or "trabajadora del hogar" (1975-1995). Espe belonged to the first category, although she would take charge of her own destiny by moving to Paris where labor conditions and pay for domestic servants were better. Three years after she migrated to Paris, the decree of March 17, 1959, established a Montepío Nacional del Servicio Doméstico as an official policy for Spanish domestics working abroad. The Women's Section of Falange partly directed it between 1960 and 1970, the years that Espe was working in France.[18]

In retirement, returning Spanish domestics who had worked abroad typically had to rely on different sources of income. For Espe that meant a partial pension from the French government for the years she paid into its system and also a partial retirement from the Spanish government. The wage disparity for female domestics in Spain and France is what made the biggest difference for Espe and thousands of others like her who could barely subsist in Franco's Spain but could live a relatively comfortable life outside of it. The higher wages and the advantages of living in the booming, modern, postwar Europe paid even more dividends for her son. In France he had access to a better education and to job opportunities that did not exist for the son of a domestic in Spain. In order to achieve her objectives, Espe, like so many of the other Spanish domestics, had to be bold. She had to leave everything she had known—people, culture, language—and adopt another country's language and culture as well as its way of life. What she discovered when she moved to Paris is that life under Franco for poor Spaniards was mostly a dead end. They were locked into a life of servitude with little hope of advancement. Their work was indeed needed to take care of the Spanish elite, as illustrated by the large number of domestics employed by the families for which her mother and father, her husband, and even she had worked. The indignities of being a "Conchita" in France and having to organize to demand justice from unscrupulous employers or businesses, however insulting, were a small price to pay for the opportunities afforded by working abroad. The truth, as Espe came to realize, was that the domestic servant was not going to be treated well by the upper classes, whether in Spain or in France, so she might as well take the money. That made all the difference.

---

18   Fernández, *Sirvienta, empleada, trabajadora de hogar*, 131.

Dori's Many Returns

> El irse
> se divide en fragmentos,
> la decisión en otras decisiones,
> y estas a su vez
> se subdividen.
> Irse:
> salir de la ciudad, pero antes,
> de una casa y antes aun,
> de una habitación y para ello,
> levantarse, poner
> orden entre los huesos
> y cerrar el cuaderno y previamente,
> dejar de escribir para
> que? Si: irse. Irse quedó atrás. se escribió mas arriba, o en la página
> anterior.

Dori was born in December 1940 in Alhama, a village in the southern coastal town of Almería.

My parents had never left the town.... I mean my mother had never traveled.... The farthest she ventured was perhaps Barcelona.... She, once, had visited Granada...and talked a lot about the times when she was young and used to go to Linares because they had some relatives there and so, I think, in her youth she had visited Linares.... My parents had seven children, six daughters and the last one a boy. My father was a wine barrel maker. Here the grape industry began to provide a lot work, and he spent almost all year making barrels. There are several barrel making workshops in Alhama. And then when the time of the grape harvest came, they called it the "labor" season...he had a lot of work.

My mother stayed home taking care of the children. There was nowhere for women to work either...that's what happened to me and other people my age. My father did not want us serving the rich...cleaning and so on. My father never could stand that we were cleaning anyone's home, so he would prefer working as many hours as he had to. We only worked during "labor" harvest...cleaning grapes...then everyone worked, including married women and all the young, worked as we did not go to school. Nowadays everyone goes to school, right?

So, I had already left school...very small...I did not graduate...I attended school for a very short time.... I was eleven years old. My mother would go to work at the harvest, and I stayed home taking care of my siblings. The little bit I know I have learned on my own. I did not even finish learning my multiplication tables.

During the civil war, Dori's father fought on the Republican side along with one of his brothers. "He was a Communist, my dad," she remarked, "but after the war we had to make sure to keep our mouth shut." Dori's family was not religious either. Her parents never got married, even after being pressured and harassed by the village to "sanctify" their union in church.

They didn't get married...no one could convince them to get married...and then the gossip.... "Oh, you all are going to be bastard children, bastard children," and then of course the fear seeps in because the village people put you in a box with a label. At home we didn't talk about anything; my father was a very quiet man. I was forced to go to mass every Sunday while I went to school and made my First Communion without even putting much thought into it. No special dress, no party, nothing to celebrate.

Alhama's provincial values kept young men and women strictly separate.

Chapter 10. Esperanza's and Adoración's Cartographies of Mercy   251

Figure 39: Newlyweds, Munster, Germany, 1963-64

I had had a boyfriend or two before I left for Germany. My father worked packing grapes in another village. He used to stay with a family there and became very friendly with them. So, a son of this family was the one I started seeing as a suitor. In Alhama we went out only with other groups of girls. We went for walks just on Sundays...Sundays or holidays, but not every day. Women did not often go out in public. You would embroider or learn to do some handcrafts or clean the house. Occasionally, there were parties, mainly in the summer, and we were allowed to go dancing a bit or go to the movies on Sundays. I went to the cinema a

lot with my sister and her boyfriend as a chaperone. In Alhama there was a summer terrace cinema and a winter cinema. I remember the first movie I ever saw, because they opened the cinema when I was a young girl. I remember Jorge Negrete and María Félix. They distributed the film advertisement in the cinema when you entered. It was a flyer with the title of the film, the cast names, and a beautiful picture of the movie. I remember that my sister collected them.

There was another very nice winter cinema; it was like a theater. Later on, they demolished it to make flats, but it was very beautiful; it had an orchestra and mezzanine with the peanut gallery upstairs. That was where the troublemakers sat. [She laughed] *The couples courting sat farther back for all the petting. Of course, it was dark and one could do certain things. When the characters were about to kiss on the screen, they always cut it. A cut kiss caused an uproar in the cinema.* [She laughed]

Dori was twenty-one when she got engaged. Her husband-to-be was a distant relative whose family were bakers. He had migrated already to Germany with a friend, and one of the summers he returned to Spain for the holidays. That's when they became boyfriend and girlfriend.

I became his girlfriend before he returned to Germany, and we had a short time of courtship, she remarked with a smile, *maybe a year and a bit. He was very handsome, and I fancied him.*

During that year they exchanged love letters:

It was hard for me to write, but I wrote,

she reminisced with a happy laugh.

I would get up early to post my letters in time for it to go out the same day.

They got married on June 2, 1964 and spent their honeymoon in Granada.

In those days honeymoons were modest,

she was quick to note. As soon as their honeymoon was over, they traveled together to Germany.

Germany had signed a bilateral agreement with the Franco regime in 1960. The German government policy of active labor recruitment took place between 1960 and 1973.[19] The Bundesanstalt für Arbeit (BAA, or Federal Employment Office) was

---

19 According to historian Carlos Sanz Díaz, between 1955 and 1982, approximately 800,000 Spaniards migrated to the Federal Republic of Germany, of which 86.1% returned to Spain

the official German body in charge of implementing and monitoring immigration matters under the Spanish-German agreement. On the Spanish side, the agency was the IEE. To execute the agreement, the BAA established a technical delegation office assigned by the IEE in Madrid, the so-called German Commission. It opened in April 1960 with fifty employees in the Spanish capital in addition to various mobile teams of contractors and doctors from the BAA. These teams traveled to different Spanish provinces to recruit applicants for the job vacancies in Germany.

There were three types of Spanish emigration to Germany. The first, named *first path*, was regulated emigration in which the IEE and the BAA controlled the entire process. This first path could be through open recruitment or by nominal request (Namentliche Anforderung). The second variety of emigration, called *second path*, was accomplished through an entry visa, issued by the German consular representatives in Spain. Dori's husband went in 1962 under this second path.

They sent him a contract...there was another friend of his working in Germany already...because no one could go except with a contract from Germany. There, in Germany they admitted workers, but with a work contract. A friend who was already working there arranged for the employers to send two contracts, one for my husband and another for a friend. That's how they went to work in the paint factory called Glasurit. A big factory with three thousand workers in the district of Hiltrup in Münster, the city where we lived. When I arrived, we rented a room with a little kitchen. I was fortunate to have a stove. There was the bedroom, a hallway, the kitchen...but there was no toilet, only outside in the stairs shared by all the neighbors. I had to wash up in our room with a washbowl.

---

in the same period. The years of greatest emigration were: 1964 (81,818 emigrants); 1965 (82,324); and 1970 (61,318). Carlos Sanz Díaz, "Las relaciones del IEE con Alemania," in Luís M. Calvo Salgado et al., *Historia del Instituto Español De Emigración: La política migratoria exterior de España y el IEE del Franquismo a la Transición* (Madrid: Ministerio de Trabajo e Inmigración, Subdirección General de Información Administrativa y Publicaciones, 2009), 168-188. See also: Antonio Muñoz Sánchez, "Una introducción a la historia de la emigración española en la República Federal de Alemania (1960-1980)," *Iberoamericana* 46 (June 2012): 23-42; José Babiano y Ana Fernández Asperilla, *La patria en la maleta: Historia social de la emigración española a Europa* (Madrid, Ministerio de Trabajo y Emigración, 2009); Antonio Muñoz Sánchez, *Entre dos sindicalismos: La emigración española en la RFA, los sindicatos alemanes y la UGT, 1960-1964* Documento de Trabajo 1/2008 (Madrid, Fundación 1º de Mayo, 2008); José Manuel Azcona, "Tratamiento político de la emigración exterior española en el tardofranquismo (1974-1977)" *Estudios Internacionales* 182 (September-December 2015): 9-35.

Figure 40: Newlyweds cooking in their apartment in Münster, 1964

Dori's experience is that of many thousands of southern European and Northern African workers who migrated to Germany as part of the so-called *Gastarbeiter* or "guest worker" program developed after World War II.[20] There was also a *third path* of entry. This was when the emigrant arrived in Germany as a tourist and later obtained the legal working permits (work and residence) to stay. The Spanish IEE did not play any role in the second and third paths, leading to tensions with German authorities whose practices hampered the Spanish authorities' ability to control Spanish migratory flows.[21]

The regulated migration followed a series of official controls and protocols. Workers who wanted to accept the jobs offered by German employers had to register at the regime's local Syndical Union offices. They had to go through a double selection process. First, technicians from the IEE or the Falangist Trade Union Organization checked their professional qualifications and administered a first medical examination. Those who passed this screening phase underwent a second medi-

---

20 During the 1950s and 1960s, West Germany signed bilateral recruitment agreements with a number of countries: Italy (22 November 1955); Spain (29 March 1960); Greece (30 March 1960); Turkey (30 October 1961); Morocco (21 June 1963); Portugal (17 March 1964); Tunisia (18 October 1965); and Yugoslavia (12 October 1968).
21 Sanz Díaz, "Las relaciones del IEE con Alemania," 174.

cal clearance and review of their trade skills, this time administered by the mobile German Commission teams sent to different provincial capitals.[22]

Those selected received a bilingual contract, usually effective for one year. In addition, the German government issued a visa and work permit and detailed information about the working terms and conditions they should expect in Germany. The IEE and the German Commission coordinated the travel arrangements of emigrants by rail in "joint transport" every week. They crossed the Spanish-French border through Irun, in the Basque Country, and reached their destination at the Cologne-Deutz railway station in Germany. An average of 800 Spanish workers arrived in Germany each week during the 1960s. Representatives of German employers and labor authorities received them at the station with great pomp and publicity.[23] Most Spaniards continued their journey in smaller groups until they reached their final destinations, which, in the case of Dori and her husband, was Münster.[24] The 1960 bilateral agreement between Spain and West Germany provided for family reunification (article 17) under the requirement that the emigrant had "appropriate housing" for the worker and his family, while the German State did not have any obligation to accept the requests for family regrouping.

Dori did not speak a word of German when she arrived, and yet she told me she found herself in "wonderland."

Newlywed, in love with my husband and...I don't know, everything was so very different. It was truly a wonderland! Just going to the supermarket, something we did not have in Spain yet; well at least in Almería, but a superstore where you could buy everything from a tub of butter to a car?! So, all that for me made a great impression. In Spain we would buy a small can of foie gras, and we would have to spread it so very thin so everyone could have a taste, but in Germany you could buy whatever because you knew you could afford it with your wages. Also clothing in Spain, you had it made, homemade, while over there [Germany] you could

---

22   Sanz Díaz, "Las relaciones del IEE con Alemania," 175.
23   On September 7, 1964, only a couple of months after Dori and her husband arrived in Germany, Armando Rodrigues de Sa, a 38-year-old Portuguese carpenter, was welcomed as the one millionth guest worker by a German delegation and journalist who recorded how he was given an award and a motorcycle.
24   Those who decided to emigrate on their own opted for requesting a work visa at the German consulates in Spain before traveling to Germany or entering as tourists. Approximately 30% of Spaniards who emigrated to Germany did so without the assistance of the Institute of Emigration. This irregular emigration was especially high between 1960-1967. For the same years, illegal practices of intermediaries were also detected. These intermediaries provided Spanish emigrants with the transfer to Germany and entry into the country through poorly monitored border crossings with a payment of a fee. Sanz Díaz, "Las relaciones del IEE con Alemania," 175-76; and Carlos Sanz Diaz, *Clandestinos, ilegales, espontáneos emigración irregular de españoles a Alemania en el contexto de las relaciones hispano-alemanas, 1960-1973* (Madrid, CEHRI, 2004).

buy an already made dress with great ease. Everything for me was amazing. I liked it very much at the beginning. Then, little by little, I started to miss my family and my hometown.

Dori soon started to work too. Having two salaries made it more affordable to access the consumer economy in her new home country. First, she worked in a clothing factory where she met other young women, many from southern Spain, and a few from Italy. She recalled how hard working German people were and how she took pride in showing her dedication to them by doing a good job. After a few months she went to work at the same paint factory where her husband was employed.

*They paid us well. In Germany we lived better because we earned two salaries. Women there worked too. All of us who migrated, even those who had never worked in Spain, went to work when they moved there [Germany]. And that was that, two salaries, husband and wife worked. Because in my village there was no work for women at all. You see, we **were going to save money to return home**...what men and women worked for then was to save some money. We lived off one salary and sent the other wages home to save up to build a house or start a business and be able to make a better life.*

Dori became pregnant two months after they arrived in Münster. Instead of losing her job, as she probably would have in Spain, she was paid for two months leave by the German social security system.

Social security was very good [in Germany]; better than in Spain. You could not even fix your teeth and all that in Spain, and there [Germany] you could go to whatever doctor you chose, everything covered by social security. I had my first baby girl, and they gave us four weeks before and four weeks after the delivery. When I returned to work, I used to leave my baby with a German neighbor. She was married and also took care of her sister's baby; the sister was a single mother. Germans did not look down on single moms. There were many German girls who had children and weren't married. Young people used to leave their parents' home when they were of a certain age; even the parents encouraged them to be independent, very different from what we did here [Spain]. We sheltered our children too much.

When the baby turned six months, Dori and her husband decided it was better for her to return to the village. She had been in Germany a little over a year.

Because I got pregnant again and already had my baby girl, we decided it was best. I already wanted to come back, to tell you the truth. So during our vacation visit my husband said, "Look, you're going to stay. I can send you the money, and here you don't have to work and you have some help from the family." So I stayed in Spain, and he went back to Germany.

Cristi was born and then when Santos was born...in [19]67 my husband came back to set up a greengrocer shop here in Alhama, and in the greengrocer shop the customers began to order rosquillas,[25] and so, we started making rosquillas to sell in Almeria too. Our customers began to ask for more rosquillas, more rosquillas, more rosquillas, and we closed the greengrocer business to become bakers. BUT again, he had a longing for Germany and decided to go back alone for a while. He would visit us twice a year, get me pregnant, and leave again. I had four babies in a row. I missed having him by my side. So many departures and so many returns.

*Raising children is a big responsibility, you see? Having two, three children, they would get sick and in the middle of the night I found myself looking for help...a lot of responsibility for a mother to have a child and not have the father there...**to be alone!*** [she uttered in a whisper] *My family helped me. I was living in my parents' house when I first came back pregnant with my second baby boy, Cristi. But then, after he was born, we rented a house, and I went to live on my own with the children. My sister sometimes would stay the night so I would not find myself all alone with the children. Ana was born in Germany, Cristi in Alhama fourteen months later. Then Santos and then baby Dori were born a year and thirteen days apart in Alhama. So, I had four babies in four years. Dori was born in the house I moved to by myself with them, and then and there I learned the business of baking "rosquillas." In that house we built a big storage shed and a bakery workshop. We opened the bakery, and my husband did not return to Germany anymore. Eventually, we bought a plot of land in the village to build this house* [where we were holding the interview] *and the business in the same place. The truth is that after we had been working abroad and endured separation after separation, we did save a little, but not enough to build the house...We weren't away that long either...not so many years...a short time really. And also, I had to sustain myself and the children here while he also had to live there and send money to us. I saved a little but not so much. Then with our savings, we had to buy an oven and build the storage to be able to work in the first house we rented. So, when it came to building this house, we had to do it...little by little. We bought a plot first, and since at that time things were not as expensive as they are today, we were able eventually to do it but the materials we picked were the basics, so the house ended up costing around 500,000 pesetas. We brought the equipment from the other workshop in the house we had been renting and established ourselves here.*

Dori spent most of her young adult life taking care of her family. A few years after her husband returned for good from Germany in 1971, he fell ill and after nine years of a chronic illness, he died in 1987. By then, they had had another child, a baby girl they named Sofia, only ten when her dad passed.

Dori expressed some regret that the two boys ended up staying closer to her to help with the business rather than going to college.

---

25 Round-shaped bread with a hole in the center.

They had to get to work. They were still very young. Santos was still going to middle school. Both boys were still in school. But my Santos, I had to wake him up a little earlier in the morning. He was small. We started working early before they would leave for school. They would help me make the bread dough. I would maybe wake them up at seven o'clock or around then so they would help me a little before leaving for school.

I sit listening in admiration of this tiny woman who was able to accomplish so much in her life, not only for herself, but also for her entire family. She tells me she was always thin, never weighed more than 130 pounds maximum. Yet, she is the incarnation of strength and grit. Her workday starts at five thirty in the morning and doesn't end until sunset. When I ask her if she is still able to lift the heavy flour sacks, she very calmly explains she does not have to as she utilizes a baker's pourer and works the dough into pieces. The only tiring aspect of her routine, she confides, is the fast pace.

I work very fast because these are doughs containing yeast and you have to watch them closely, you have to guard the oven, and you have always to work in a hurry. And to tell you how many hours? I have no set schedule or fixed hours. I get up at five thirty, have breakfast on the go without stopping. At noon on the mark, I prepare lunch and many times dinner too. My sister comes for lunch to make sure I eat, and she eats with me. Sofía sometimes used to come for lunch when she was at school, sometimes not.

Dori gave her youngest child a name that she wears well, Sofía. Sofía means wisdom, and she is indeed wise. Sofía is a respected historian of contemporary Spain, now a professor and a prolific author whose works focus on the experiences of those outside of history in the violent Spanish twentieth century.[26] Dori has a clear sense of her historical non-being as she reflects on her life.

Well, I don't know.... I have not done anything.... I believe that I have not been an exceptional woman in anything. I've accepted my position as it was dealt to me. I learned with my husband side by side in the bakery and always worked here with him at the oven. Then, my children, as they grew older, also helped and took on more responsibilities. Now, even to run the business paperwork and so on, it is Santos who is the one in charge. Old age is not important for me. I am not afraid of getting old. I am not scared of dying. No, no. I neither

---

26   Some of Sofía's publications include: Sofía Rodríguez López, *Memorias de los nadie: Una historia oral del campo andaluz (1914-1959)* (Sevilla: Centro de Estudios Andaluces, 2015); *El patio de la cárcel. La Sección Femenina de FET-JONS en Almería (1937-1977)* (Sevilla: Centro de Estudios Andaluces, 2010); *Quintacolumnistas: Las mujeres del 36 en la clandestinidad almeriense* (Almería: Instituto de Estudios Almerienses, 2008); *Mujeres en Guerra: Almería (1936-1939)*

fear death nor old age. Having the bakery makes me get up in the morning. When I hear people talking about that so and so has more money or...I say, "I BELIEVE WE HAVE MORE THAN PLENTY." We must always look back and down, not look upward to someone else having more than you. Instead, I look back on those who have so little, not even food to survive. We have enough to eat, we have enough to dress ourselves, we have enough to buy ourselves a treat now and then. **Accumulating money is not necessary;** *only just having what you need and a little more in case you want to buy yourself a treat or you want to take a trip. So, for me there is more than enough.*

*What have I lived? Well, I have lived the life that happened to me, and I regret it was not a life such as it is lived now that we enjoy other choices, another way of living. THAT I would have liked to live. I would have preferred that life had not been so...well as I told you...***so difficult.*** *We have endured and persevered through everything because we were young and did not realize how hard we had it. Now, we look back and see things differently, but that was what life was like. We thought nothing of it, just that that was the way to live. But of course, as one grows older, one sees that life need not to be so hard. I would have liked that life would have been, as it is now...***a life of freedom.*** *In sum I have lived an ordinary life...nothing special.*

Dori does not say this with false modesty. She really believes that her life was nothing special. She had been conditioned to think that women's sacrifices, women's work, was of little worth. Spain under Franco was also conditioned to take women like Dori for granted. Spanish women were given a role in National Catholic propaganda, but that role was as support for heroic men forged by the regime. The reality was that Dori, like so many Spanish women of her era, was the driver of both the domestic and the economic spheres of her family. She was a business partner, a babysitter, a cook, a listener, and moral support for an extended family. She cared for the past and future generations. Instead of being the tail wagging behind, these women were the head of their families, leading the way.

* * * * *

Espe and Dori's delivery of their stories is diametrically different. Espe's is a knotty narrative, untangled urgently, populated with parenthetical clarifications, backtracks, and fast-forwards. Hers is constructed of those details, sparks of her own logic. The narrative switches from Spanish to French in a re-enactment rich in dialogue. Constant through her rhizomatic storyline is the sheer determination and fixed aspiration to provide a better life for her son.

By contrast, Dori's diction is slow and deliberate. She speaks almost with detachment about her own life, embracing, dwelling in her non-being. She rides waves of the storm as they come. But she too is determined to provide a better life for those who come after, her children.

I am a migrant, an expat like Espe and Dori, the subjects in these two stories. Their given names predict their lives' paths. Esperanza (Espe) means hope in Spanish. Adoración (Dori) means adoration. My name, Aurora, dawn, has illuminated my journey into the unknown. Theirs and mine are "nomadic histories"[27] impelled by survival, grit, and the acceptance of life's unkind terrain. The sole purpose of falling is to lift ourselves up again and again. Guided by the plural "us," we venture across physical and metaphorical borders.

As Deleuze and Guattari write, "[i]t is true that the nomads have no history; they only have a geography."[28] We *nomad(ologists)* realize that "History has always dismissed the nomads."[29] Deleuze and Guattari also point out that "the nomad is not at all the same as the migrant; for the migrant goes principally from one point to another, even if the second point is uncertain, unforeseen, or not well localized. But the nomad goes from point to point only as a consequence and as a factual necessity."[30] Espe's and Dori's motions mark those of migrants, but they are also nomads. Their moves respond to life's necessities. Their names, Hope and Adoration, poetically propel them in their quests. Espe's and Dori's testimonies illustrate the concept of "nomadic subjects" afforded by feminist scholar Rosi Braidotti as well as María Zambrano's notion of "Sacrificial/Merciful history." According to Braidotti, a nomadic subject is a:

> [T]heoretical figuration for contemporary subjectivity. A figuration is a politically informed image of thought that evokes or expresses an alternative vision of subjectivity. [...] The black feminist writer and poet bell hooks in her work on postmodern blackness, describes this consciousness in terms of "yearning." She argues that "yearning" is a common affective and political sensibility that cuts across boundaries of race, class, gender, and sexual practice and *"could be a fertile ground for the construction of empathy—ties that would promote recognition of shared commitments and serve as a base for solidarity and coalition."* [my emphasis][31]

The affective yearning described by Braidotti is clearly articulated in María Zambrano's poetic reason. Recognizing each other's neglect borne out of our evanescent

---

27 The inspiration for this chapter comes from a Deleuzian nomadic model as presented in Gilles Deleuze and Félix Guattari, "1227: Treatise on Nomadology—The War Machine," in *A Thousand Plateaus* (Oxford: Bloomsbury, 2016), 409-92. Also see Rosi Braidotti, *Nomadic Subjects: Embodiment and Sexual Difference in Contemporary Feminist Theory* (New York: Columbia University Press, 2011); Craig Lundy, "Nomadic History," in *History and Becoming* (Edinburgh: Edinburgh University Press, 2012), 64-103.
28 Deleuze and Guattari, "1227: Treatise on Nomadology," 459.
29 Deleuze and Guattari, "1227: Treatise on Nomadology," 459.
30 Deleuze and Guattari, "1227: Treatise on Nomadology," 443.
31 Braidotti, *Nomadic Subjects*, 22.

experiences of isolation and displacement (inner and worldly) may only be overcome by our yearning to be free. Such yearning is the force guiding the invisible nomad subjects in their paths. Zambrano's sacrificial history is a quest for revealing the mystery that connects us as one. Zambrano calls mercy such a yearning in her 1989 essay "Para una historia de la piedad" (For a History of Mercy). She defines mercy as "the feeling of the heterogeneous quality of being," and therefore it is "the *yearning to find the ways of understanding* [my emphasis] and dealing with each one of those multiple ways of reality. ...Mercy is knowing how to deal with what is different, with that which is radically other than us."[32] For Zambrano, poetry is the language of mercy. The emphasis on the rational leads us to "only know how to deal with those which are almost a reproduction of ourselves. ...And that is how," she explains, "we ended up alone; alone and unable to deal with 'the other.' But if we put together the various kinds of 'otherness,' we realize that it is nothing but reality, the reality that surrounds us and where we are anchored."[33]

Espe's and Dori's testimonies of migration are infused with yearning, mercy, and self-empowerment. They epitomize Braidotti's nomadic subject notion, a notion only possible to historicize in tracing their lives' paths. Theirs are two emotional cartographies of hope and adoration. Espe's and Dori's moves crossed national borders, but they were informed by their trespassing inner boundaries and limitations of class and gendered specific expectations. Esperanza and Dori made themselves anew, the former as a maid in Paris during the late 1950s, the latter, as a factory worker in Germany in the early 1960s.

Spanish emigration at the end of the 1950s is part of a broader migration system that included nine countries: Portugal, Italy, Greece, Yugoslavia, Turkey, Morocco, Algeria, and Tunisia. These countries provided cheap labor to northern European countries: France, Great Britain, Germany, Sweden, Belgium, Holland, and Luxembourg. By the mid-1970s, around eight million migrants resided in a European country other than their own. The movement of this labor force was sanctioned by a series of bilateral agreements between the receiving and sending governments. Franco's regime signed the first agreement with Belgium in 1956; West Germany in 1960; and France, Switzerland, and Holland in 1961.[34] Leaving Franco's Spain as an emigrant allowed many to escape the regime's economic repression. The regime signed with more developed European countries a number of "guest worker" programs, which led many of the poor to find employment abroad to provide for their families. In most cases, the emigrants planned to return to their home countries

---

32 María Zambrano, "Para una historia de la piedad," in Aurora G. Morcillo et al. eds., *The Modern Spain Sourcebook: A Cultural History from 1600 to the Present* (London: Bloomsbury Press, 2018), 35-41. Translation by Asunción Gómez.
33 Zambrano, "Para una historia de la piedad," 38-40.
34 Babiano and Farré, "La emigración española a Europa durante los años sesenta," 82.

after a few years. However, there were some who did not feel the need to return to a country in which they felt like second-class citizens or as outsiders in their own land.

Realizing from afar that a strange land provides more for you and your family than your own birthplace became in many cases (and today as well) a blunt riposte to hollow patriotic and nationalistic slogans. The truth for many Spaniards in the 1950s and 1960s was that the Franco regime could not provide the sustenance of the more democratic neighbors to the north. While Spain languished as a quaint culturally and morally stifling backwater autocracy, the free democracies of Europe and the United States raced ahead of it. Instead of exporting its products and ideas like other countries, Spain could only offer its workers to clean the houses and make the goods for others. Ironically, these workers and their perambulations created cracks in the regime's wall, where subversive ideas seeped through. The act of working abroad also loosened the loyalties of many people who saw that the outside world was doing more for common Spaniards than even their own government.

Espe and Dori did not see themselves as part of the resistance to the regime, but in actuality they were. Their form of resistance was to dare to go abroad to seek a better life. What they brought back from their travels were tales of a better world and the yearning to remake Spain so that their children and their children's children would not be forced to make the same perilous choice.

Chapter 11
Luz Invisible

Si en el firmamento poder yo tuviera,
esta noche negra lo mismo que un pozo,
con un cuchillito de luna lunera,
cortaría los hierros de tu calabozo.
Si yo fuera reina de la luz del día,
del viento y del mar,
cordeles de esclava yo me ceñiría
por tu libertad.

¡Ay, pena, penita, pena -pena-,
pena de mi corazón,
que me corre por las venas -pena-
con la fuerza de un ciclón!
Es lo mismo que un nublado
de tiniebla y pedernal.
Es un potro desbocado
que no sabe dónde va.
Es un desierto de arena -pena-,
es mi gloria en un penal.
¡Ay, penal! ¡Ay, penal!
¡Ay, pena, penita, pena!

Yo no quiero flores, dinero, ni palmas,
quiero que me dejen llorar tus pesares
y estar a tu vera, cariño del alma,
bebiéndome el llanto de tus soleares.
Me duelen los ojos de mirar sin verte,
reniego de mí,
que tienen la culpa de tu mala suerte
mis rosas de abril.

¡Ay, pena, penita, pena -pena-,
pena de mi corazón....[1]

"Luz Invisible" is a *copla*, or Spanish song, popularized in the 1940s and appropriated by the Franco regime to symbolize the essence of Spanish character. Like the relationship of jazz and blues, *coplas* are a cousin to flamenco, *cante jondo*, the guttural, deeply emotional, and emblematic Andalusian music. In the *café cantantes* of the mid-nineteenth century, singers, musicians, and dancers popularized *coplas*, elaborating on the rawer, less flowery Flamenco. *Coplas*, an amalgam of "poetry, narrative, music and theater,"[2] appealed to urban middle and upper classes. Their roots go back to the oral tradition of popular poetry during the Middle Ages, composed of four stanzas of four lines each with no more than eight syllables per verse and with assonant rhyme in the even-numbered lines. Poets of the Generation '27, such as Federico García Lorca and Rafael Alberti, cultivated this poetic form. It was García Lorca who designed the original *copla* format when in 1931, he recorded a series of popular songs called "Las calles de Cádiz" with singer and performer Encarnación López Júlvez.

---

1   If I had any power in the firmament this night dark like a well, with a little moon knife I would cut the grilles of your jail. If I were the queen of daylight, of wind and sea, I would tie myself in slave ropes for your freedom
    Ay sorrow, little sorrow, sorrow... sorrow of my heart that flows inside my veins with the strength of a cyclone It's like a cloudy spell, of darkness and flint it's a runaway colt that doesn't know where it's going It's a sandy desert -sorrow- it's my glory in a penance Ay penance, ay penance ay sorrow, little sorrow, sorrow!
    I don't want flowers, money or cheers, I want them to let me cry your sorrow, and to be by your side, my dear drinking the tears of your loneliness My eyes hurt as I look but cannot see you, I hate myself Guilty for your bad luck, my April roses
    Antonio Quintero (dramatist), Rafael de León (lyricist), Manuel Quiroga (composer). https://lyricstranslate.com.
2   Stephanie Sieburth, *Survival Songs: Conchita Piquer's 'Coplas' and Franco's Regime of Terror* (Toronto: University of Toronto Press, 2014), 46. This is the first scholarly book on the *copla*, a popular genre of music during the 1940s and 1950s. The performers were mostly women: Concha Piquer, Juanita Reina, Imperio Argentina, Estrellita Castro, Lola Flores, and Marife de Triana, to only mention a few, became the equivalent of Hollywood stars for the Spanish audiences during the 1950s and 1960s. Likewise, gay men identified with the *copla* genre, including Rafael de Leon. Miguel de Molina, the most iconic gay male *copla* singer, was brutally persecuted and lived in exile during the dictatorship. The cross-dressing community has been portrayed in Pedro Almodóvar's films. Some other works on the significance of the popular flamenco music and cultural politics include José Colmeiro, *Memoria histórica e identidad cultural: De la postguerra a la postmodernidad* (Barcelona: Anthropos, 2005); Jo Labanyi, "Musical Battles: Populism and Hegemony in the Early Francoist Folkloric Film Musical," in *Constructing Identity in Contemporary Spain*, ed. Jo Labanyi (New York: Oxford University Press, 2002). In 2009 the Biblioteca Nacional de Madrid offered an exhibit recorded in the catalogue entitled *La copla en la Biblioteca Nacional de España*.

Stephanie Sieburth's *Survival Songs: Conchita Piquer's 'Coplas' and Franco's Regime of Terror* draws from Freudian concepts such as repression, projection, and "working through"[3] to explain the psychological power of these songs. The *coplas* offered the vanquished the opportunity to express the pain they were forced to repress in the context of the regime's new "normalcy." They also offered a space of recognition not only for the vanquished, who listened to the lyricists' anguished stories of prostitutes, sailors, and the down and out, but also for the victors who saw the genre as the ultimate cultural marker of Spanish national identity.[4] The pathos, tragedy, and artistry of the *coplas*, though, are not completely fiction. They are rooted in the authentic experience of the Spanish people.

The story of Luz, my father's younger sister, unfolds like a copla. It is full of pain and suffering that morphs into something heroic at its conclusion. It is a story that informs as well as entertains, giving quiet dignity to the suffering and perseverance of a generation of working-class women growing up in the shadow of Franco's Spain.

I remember the sounds of flamenco blasting from my Aunt Luz's home.

> *Ay sorrow, little sorrow, sorrow...*
> *sorrow of my heart*
> *that flows inside my veins*
> *with the strength of a cyclone*
> *It's like a cloudy spell,*
> *of darkness and flint*
> *it's a runaway colt*
> *that doesn't know where it's going*
> *It's a sandy desert -sorrow-*
> *it's my glory in a penance.*

Luz's husband Miguel was crazy about flamenco and an avid aficionado of *coplas*. His favorites were the usual suspects: Lola Flores, Mari Fe de Triana, and Juanita Reina. "He liked flamenco a lot," Luz explained. "Mari Fe especially; he liked her voice a lot. When Mari Fe came to the theater, he took me to see her."[5]

---

3 Sieburth, *Survival Songs*, 7.
4 Sandie Holguin, *Flamenco Nation: The Construction of Spanish National Identity* (Madison: University of Wisconsin Press, 2019); Alfredo Grimaldos Feito, *Historia social del Flamenco* (Barcelona: Ediciones Península, 2010/2015); Alberto del Campo and Rafael Cáceres, *Historia cultural del Flamenco* (Almuzara: Edición Almuzara, 2013). On the history of bullfighting, see Adrian Shubert, *Death in the Afternoon: A History of the Spanish Bullfight* (New York: Oxford University Press, 2001).
5 Luz Morcillo, interview by author, audio recording Granada, June 18, 2006.

Lux/Lucem/Leuk[6]

Luz is petite, with enormous brown eyes and a piercing laugh. Her hands, all day immersed in water, are pink and puffy. Not a natural blond, she started bleaching her hair when she was young. It was part of practicing her trade of coiffeur or coiffeuse, a hairdresser. She was born on the tenth day of November in 1945, right in the middle of the hunger years, following the unexpected death of another baby girl, María Luz. Her family economized even in the choice of names, recycling the name of Luz and only dropping María from the dead sister. María Paz, the second oldest sister, was the self-designated guardian angel of the new baby and would be Luz's *angelus novum*.

Luz was never particularly affectionate to me or my siblings when we were children. She was, at best, indifferent. This puzzled me at the time. What would have made her so distant from her brother's family? Over the years, though, I have developed a more meaningful relationship, and even more importantly, an appreciation for her. Whenever I go back to Spain, I always make a point to visit her, and we enjoy long conversations about the family, her life, and my work. Now in her seventies, she is a kindred soul, offering up alternating spoonfuls of unadulterated wisdom and affection. To say that she has mellowed would not be exactly the truth. There is nothing mellow about her. Life's tragedies have smoothed some of the rough edges, but I also have come to see her in a different light.

I was born on Calle Real de Cartuja. And I was a very calm girl, but very vivacious. I liked to play a lot with scraps of fabric, making rag dolls. I went to a school called Divino Maestro; my mother signed me up for the school canteen to receive daily lunch. One day, I'm going to tell you, one day the nun...they served beans ... and that nun made me eat three servings. I got so sick with bad indigestion...vomiting.... And I didn't want to go to school anymore.... Well, I was about 8 years old...and I already left school, played truant from school. I would leave with my girlfriends, we would go down the San Antonio road to the hill known as El Tambor. We ran, and sat around, and picked wild flowers and when we came back home my mother would ask me; "Why are you coming home so dirty?" and I would say, "I was playing in the school patio during recess."

I ended up leaving school because I didn't like the food they served. I told my mother, "Look, Mom, I'll go to school, but I won't go to the dining room, because of that nun Sister Manoli." ...She was a horse, that nasty woman...made me eat that awful food twice!! She would not leave me alone. Every opportunity she had she would punish me by pulling my ears. So, whenever I saw her, I would see the devil!! I didn't want her near me at all. And so,

---

6   Meaning "light," brightness, from Latin Lux/lucem and proto-Indo-European root Leuk. The latter is the root of Leukemia.

my mother said, "All right, if you do not want to go to the dining room, you come home for lunch." That was that for a couple of more years.

When I turned ten, I made my First Communion in the church Cristo de la Yedra. I wore a beautiful white, short dress made by a dressmaker named Mercedes who lived on Cazorla Street. A lovely dress! My mother also took me to get a perm at the Navarretes' beauty parlor, in our neighborhood....but they burned my scalp! And to top everything off my ears got infected too, when my mother got me some new earrings. [She laughed] *The whole ordeal was terrible. It does not show in my portrait, you know. They took me to have my picture taken at Reyes Católicos Avenue Photography studio.... And, oh yes! they made a special merienda of chocolate and churros to celebrate* [she said with a singing voice] *and nothing more...that's it.*

As soon as I turned 13, I left school for good and started to work. First, my mother wanted me to learn to sew in order to become a dressmaker, but I hated it. When I turned 14, I started to work as an apprentice at a beauty parlor. But I developed eczema on my hands, so I had to stop working at the salon, though I really enjoyed it. And then I found work in a noodle factory where I stayed for two years. In the noodle factory the machines resembled looms, where they produced the pasta, and we would cut it and package it. That was my job. After two years that factory closed, and I got a job at a bleach factory on Calle Real. I washed glass bottles, removed the seals from the bottles, and filled them with bleach. I left the bleach factory not long after I started. Then, I started working in a chocolate factory but also stayed only a very short while. I guess I just didn't fit in anywhere. They paid so very little... 6 pesetas...SIX PESETAS!...and in the noodle factory I was paid TWO PESETAS...a week!! TWO PESETAS!! It was around the year 1959 or so.

Figure 41: Luz as a young girl

In the end, I decided to go back to the hairdresser business. I looked for a job in a salon in Calle Recogidas called Isidro Hair Salon. The owner made a pass at me; it was very unpleasant. He told me, "Well, we need to test you to see your skills and decide if we are interested or not in having you stay." Well, well, I didn't know what his intentions were, of course,...so I did the task just fine...but that so-called fine man only wanted to take advantage of me! And I told him...NOT AT ALL! [She paused with indignation, remembering his advances] *The same thing happens now with bosses. They always want the same thing: to harass you* [She meant sexually] *but I said...NO! Well then, since I didn't succumb...and I had done*

the test just fine...well, that so-called respectable fellow threw me out. I filed a complaint with the police, but he didn't show up, of course. I turned around and left to look for work in another salon where I ended up staying ten years. By then my hands had gotten used to the water or chemicals or whatever, so no more eczema.

Luz was fifteen years old when she met her future husband, Miguel. She fell head over heels for him. He lit her fire, not like Jim Morrison but rather like Manuel de Falla's bewitched love.

> *Lo mismo que el fuego fatuo*
> *Lo mismito es el querer*
> *Le huyes y te persigue*
> *Le llamas y echa a correr*[7]

Their love story unfolds like a copla with its intense emotions leading to its ultimate, inevitable tragedy.

I used to go out with my friend Mari Trini who also lived on Calle Real.... One day she said, "Let's go to that dance where the boys hang out on Hornillo Street," and I said, "Well, sure, let's go." I added, "But, girl, how are we going to go like this? We are dressed like little girls...they won't let us in!" But she insisted.... "Well, let's see what happens." So we were able to enter the party, and I saw Miguel and right away I liked him! And you know what happens. Boys ignore you and you...as a young girl, because we were so innocent and young...kept coming back on other Sundays. My friend started dating one of the other boys, and we all started to go out together every Sunday. The photos of those times are hilarious. When carnival came around, we used to throw parties and get dressed up. [She laughed while showing me the photos] Miguel was a king and I was a princess. All dressed up, we went down Gran Via Avenue to eat some cake. I remember the "gypsy's arm"[8]*...it was delicious...in the Alcazar confectionery. Your parents had already gotten married and they moved to the same street where Miguel's family lived in Calle San Isidro. My family was not happy about my seeing Miguel.*

---

7 Like phosphorescent fire is love When you run from it, it follows you If you seek it, it runs away [my translation], excerpt from, "Canción del fuego fatuo" or Song of wildfire (Will-o'-the-wisp) in the ballet composition *El amor brujo* (1916) by Manuel de Falla (1876-1946) and libretto by Gregorio Martínez Sierra (1881-1947).

8 A sponge cake roll dessert from Spain. https://www.spanish-food.org/desserts-spanish-swiss-roll.html.

Figure 42: Luz and Miguel in costume

> Every day a fight...an argument...they beat you... would say, "I don't want you to go down there...don't go...don't go looking for him...that's not your place...to go looking for him...HE should be the one who comes to you..." You know how it is. But the more they told me not to do something the more I wanted to. It came to blows and a slap, but I said, "I don't care how much you punish me! I will do as I please!" [She paused] I was only 15 or maybe 16 years old, so very naive [In a reflective tone she goes on] You know...If I had known better, like I do today, I would have not disobeyed. To tell you the honest truth, I should have had more self-esteem; I should have made others see my worth.
> And I spent every day...EVERY DAY, morning, afternoon, and night, at all hours, in his pursuit. I was so in love with him [She paused a moment] I could not see anything else. I could not see he had no future...because he really had no future...but I was so very young.

Her pleading eyes, as she recounts her love affair, resonate with the Lorquian cadence of *Zorongo*:

> *I have blue eyes, I have blue eyes*
> *and my little heart is just like the tip of the flame.*
> *By night I go out in the courtyard and I cry until I´m spent*
> *seeing that I love you so much and you don´t love me at all.*[9]

One day, I wanted to go to the wedding of a friend in the neighborhood. My mother told me, "You are not going to the wedding! I told you, you are not going to the wedding! Much less with that boy." **I escaped through the window.**[10] *I jumped out the window to the patio and went to the wedding. We came back at three in the afternoon. Auri, WHEN I SAW MY MOTHER AT THE DOOR I said, 'Miguel, go now!" and he replied, "Why do I have to go? I haven't done anything wrong." My mother slapped me so hard that blood ran out of my nose. Luz silently looked at me and then in a whisper she said, "That was the way." And I told myself, "Well, you hit me.... I don't care."*

Miguel wanted to come to the house to ask permission from my mother and father to be my formal boyfriend, but then my father died. Then he (Miguel) came to the wake, asked for a chair, and sat there among everyone else...and after that moment...after that day of the wake he started coming to our house regularly. That was how our official engagement began! He just asked for the chair to sit and pay his respects when my father was already dead and we were watching him.

We saw each other very little because he had to work with his sister in her churro shop. Many times he came to pick me up too late. My mother always told us, "Do not come back later than nine!" I took little Pepe, my nephew, as our chaperone. I had to take the child even though I did not like to have to bring him. ...I thought, "What can my boyfriend possibly do to me?...My boyfriend...a kiss and a hug?" I told my mother, and she would not budge. "I do not know what, I do not know how much...patatín, que patatán."

---

9   *Tengo los ojos azules, tengo los ojos azules Y el corazoncillo igual que la cresta de la lumbre. De noche me salgo al patio y me harto de llorar De ver que te quiero tanto y tu no me quieres ná.*
     Federico García Lorca, *Zorongo*, https://lyricstranslate.com/en/zorongo-zorongo.html.
10   They lived in a ground floor apartment.

Figure 43: Luz and Miguel at the fair

> The moon is a shallow well,
> the flowers aren't worth anything,
> what is truly worthy are your arms
> when they hug me in the night,
> what is truly worthy are your arms
> when they hug me in the night.[11]

One day we wanted to go to the cinema. Miguel came to pick me up with the tickets. I can see him now as I am talking to you. I said, "I don't have any stockings! And I don't have high heels!" But Concha [her oldest sister and Pepe's mother] had bought some spectator perforated pumps in black...beautiful! And she also had silk stockings. So, I said to myself, "These things, I'm going to wear them!" I remember that day. I wore a nice pretty flowery dress with a bolero jacket. Then, I put on the pumps. Before I put on the shoes, Concha had warned me, "Do not even think about wearing my new shoes. I haven't worn them yet," and I replied, "No, no...I don't wear heels and don't know how to walk in them; why would I do that?" And my mother also told me, "Don't wear your sister's shoes. She will start fighting and raging." And I said to myself..."Right, why not? I am wearing those shoes AND THE SILK STOCKINGS...TODAY!" Well, once outside, I put them on. I went out the window into the patio [She looked at me with mischievous smile] so my mother wouldn't see me. I took

---

11   *La luna es un pozo chico, las flores no valen nada. Lo que valen son tus brazos Cuando de noche me abrazan. Lo que valen son tus brazos Cuando de noche me abrazan.* García Lorca, *Zorongo.*

the shoes in their box. Then took off my shoes and put the new ones on. I placed mine inside the box and threw the box into the bedroom through the window.

As Miguel and I were walking down Dr. Oloriz street around the area where the Granada garage was at the time, one of the heels broke [She laughed loudly] and with great alarm I told Miguel, "Oh if we don't fix this heel they're going to kill me, THESE SHOES ARE NOT MINE!!!" So, we decided to go into the Granada garage and asked the man who was there on guard, "Would you have a hammer and a nail? My girlfriend broke her heel, and she is limping." Well, the man went in the back and found the tools to hammer the heel...badly...and I said to Miguel, "Let's go." I was barefoot then; "Let's go, I don't want to wear these shoes anymore." When I came back home, I cleaned the shoes very well, took off the stockings and realized I made a big run in them, and I thought, "Oh, no!" This happened on a Saturday, and on Sunday my sister went to put on her new shoes, and she screamed at the top of her lungs, "MY SHOES ARE BROKEN. YOU WORE MY NEW SHOES." Oh my! She started a big fight.... What a disaster.... My mother hit me, pulled my hair.... And I said, "But, aren't you ashamed to hit me now that I am already so big? I am fifteen years old; aren't you ashamed of hitting me?" "Noooo, because I warned you...I didn't want you to put on her shoes, I didn't want you to wear her stockings."

The rebellious temperament of a young woman in those times was risky business. Luz was mischievous, but not malicious. Obdurate, impertinent, indomitable. There was no punishment harsh enough to change her. She wanted Miguel and she would have him. Their courtship lasted nine tempestuous years.

You know how things are and what happens when people are dating. Some days, you are all right, get along and other days you are in a bad mood, regretting the day you laid eyes on each other. I was working at the hairdressing salon and, on the side, also started working at home. And I remember telling the girls at the salon where I was working, "When I get married, I will not work anymore," and one of them said,… I can almost see her now as I remember this...her name was Conchi, "Don't believe that, honey; you will work until you die." And I said, "Oh please don't tell me that, Conchi, I don't think so. My boyfriend works at his sister's churro stand." Then shortly after, out of the blue, my boyfriend said, "I would like to learn your trade." I could not believe my ears, "Oh, my God!" I said. So he started coming every Sunday, after he finished working at the churro stand. He learned to put curlers on, wash hair, prepare and apply the coloring dyes.

This stopped when he got drafted into the military. They sent him to Viator, Almeria. My boyfriend was already coming down with some bad stomach illness!! When he returned from his service, I decided to quit my job in the salon where I was working and go into business with him. I remember how difficult it was to tell my mother. I said, "Look, Mamá, I am quitting the salon because I am opening one with Miguel." She was so upset. "What are you talking about?" she said, "You cannot stop providing your wage here at home." "Mamá, please, wait, let me explain myself...I am planning to bring my same wages to you every week," and she replied, "Sure, you say so now...I do not want you to quit your job.... You have no idea what you are getting into, leaving your job and starting a business with your boyfriend, you alone with him? My God...what will people think? What about your reputation?" I told her, "I am twenty years old and I know how to take care of myself." In the end she accepted my decision, as she saw I was not going to change my mind.

Miguel and I rented a flat for 2,500 pesetas per month. My mother was terrified. "How are you two going to be able to pay that rent? You only charge 25 pesetas per head!!" I reassured her; it is true, we had to work very hard to make the rent every month plus pay for utilities too: water, electricity, and the business license. To be honest, Miguel gave me the seven pesetas I used to make in my old job, but you know I once complained to him, "So you give me the seven pesetas I used to make in my job, those same seven pesetas I give to my mother, and I am so overworked here from eight in the morning to ten at night. For just seven pesetas!" And he would tell me, "Well, whatever we can save will go to our wedding fund," and so on. So, I thought, since I only get seven pesetas and I have to give them to my mother, I will start working on my own at home on Sundays to make some extra money for my expenses. And I did get lots of customers on Sundays, but of course those people stopped coming to our beauty parlor. Anyway, the business prospered a little, one way or another, and we hired some young girls, apprentices, you know. One of them, a girl named Clara, started flirting with Miguel, and he was flattered. Ha! So, I told him, "Look here, this can't continue. We are either going to get married or break up. I will split the business with you too. That means the three standing hairdryers I bought will come with me, and you keep the single one you purchased."

I had taught him the trade, and he thought he was going to be my boss?[12] What nerve. I was the one working fourteen hours a day and making seven pesetas a week. When I questioned him about that girl, he would say I was hallucinating. "No, no, no, no; I am not imagining things," I told him. "The customers are the ones telling me what you two are up to. Do you think I am stupid?"

Despite their problems, they eventually did get married.

---

12   The regime first re-enacted the 1889 Civil code in 1938, and there were no reforms until 1958. Even under this legislation, women were legal minors and needed permission from their husbands to even open a bank account. See Morcillo, *True Catholic Womanhood*.

Figure 44: Luz and Miguel outside work

After the wedding celebration, we went down to our apartment. Although it was late, we went for a walk. And I remember my mother had told me, "Girl, cover the sheets with some towels when you go to bed." And I wondered, "Why towels on the bed? What will happen to me on the wedding night? What is my mother trying to tell me? What is the wedding night about?" I was so uninformed. I went ahead and laid my towels on the bed. Miguel looked surprised. "Why do you put that on the bed?" I said, "Because my mother told me to, just in case the bed gets dirty." [She laughed] And he said "Oh, come on!!!" He was more worldly than I. Well, the wedding night passed. And I thought, "That was a big disappointment." Those were my thoughts. "THAT WAS IT?" I might be a very cold person; sometimes I would tell him, "Stop!!! you are hurting me!! I can't stand this; I can't stand this!" Really, instead of enjoying myself the whole thing was an ordeal. [She spoke in an indignant tone] The *morning after the wedding night, someone knocked on the door very early, and IT WAS MY MOTHER-IN-LAW. I felt so embarrassed and ran into the closet. I didn't want to come out. I felt so mortified to have to see her!!!* [She said emphatically] *I don't know why she came.* [She spoke outraged with shame] *AH! BREAKFAST!!! BREAKFAST?!! The sweet woman did it with good intentions. Miguel opened the door and let her in, and she asked, "But where is Luz?" And he, amused with the whole scene, replied, "Well, she's in the closet. She doesn't want to come out." And I was so ashamed...SO ASHAMED!!* [She almost blushed again] *That was my wedding night. NADA!!*

Figure 45: Luz and Miguel's wedding photos

I could not get pregnant, so I had to go to the doctor. I remember my mother-in-law accompanied me to a very invasive test. I got so sick after it that when she saw me coming out, she told me, "As soon as I see my son, I will tell him there is no way you can have any more of these tests. It does not matter if you don't have any children."

Eventually, Luz and Miguel got pregnant; not once but twice. Two sons came five years apart. Miguel started to get sick right after the first baby was born. That was the beginning of a very painful time.

Miguel started to get sicker when the first baby was born. He managed to last almost fourteen more years before he died, but each year he became sicker. He was only forty-two when he died. The youngest boy was eight and the oldest fourteen. My mother died in July and Miguel had stomach surgery in August the same year. Exact years and dates don't stick in my head. Yes, he was 42. He had stomach cancer; he was so very sick, truly sick, sick. The doctor did not want to alarm me by telling me about the cancer at first, so I wondered all the time, "Why is my husband so very ill?" His skin turned yellow. He was vomiting all the time. I decided one day I had to talk to the doctor, and he questioned me, "Luz, you really don't know the kind of ordeal your husband went through?" and I said, "I just thought he had stomach surgery." Then he revealed to me what the reality was. "We removed the stomach completely because your husband has cancer." She slowed down her speech and looked at me with sad eyes.

> *Ay sorrow, little sorrow, sorrow...*
> *sorrow of my heart*
> *that flows inside my veins*
> *with the strength of a cyclone*
> *It's like a cloudy spell,*
> *of darkness and flint*
> *it's a runaway colt*
> *that doesn't know where it's going*
> *It's a sandy desert -sorrow-*
> *it's my glory in a penance*
> *Ay penance, ay penance*
> *ay sorrow, little sorrow, sorrow!*

I walked out of the hospital weeping, barely breathing, as if I had lost my mind. Everything we had suffered started to make sense at that moment. He had been sick many nights, and we had had to rush to the emergency room [she told me this in a whisper] *at two, at three, at four in the morning. That time when he had awful itching...horrific itching.... That must be the worst possible thing to suffer. One day I remember, I arrived home from the salon and found him all burnt, his skin raw, because he got so close to the stove to alleviate the itch. Apparently the heat helped. I arrived and found him, poor creature, all burnt, with blisters all over, and I asked him, "My darling, what have you done?" and he tearfully replied, "Oh Luz, Oh honey, I am so sick, I am so very sick; I am dying. I will jump out that window," and I yelled, "What are you talking about? WHAT ARE YOU TALKING ABOUT? JUMPING OUT A WINDOW?" Nothing more...one day, and another day, and another day...*[she hit the table with her fist].

> *The hands of my love*
> *are weaving a cape for you*
> *with a trim made of wallflowers*
> *and a hood made of water.*
> *When you were my boyfriend,*
> *back then in the white spring,*

> *the hooves of your horse*
> *were four sobs made of silver.*[13]

Nine years.... Well, really almost from the very moment I met him, Aurorita!!
     After I had my first baby, they did the surgery and the doctor told me, "We have fixed him for another five years or so." He improved so much and that's when I got pregnant with the second baby...in those five years. And I thought, "The doctor lied to me; he doesn't have cancer." And I went to see the doctor and said, "You know, doctor, I think you might have made a mistake." And he replied softly, "No, Luz, dear, I did not make a mistake about your husband's prognosis." Sure enough, Miguel started to get sicker again, yellow again, pain on the side, pain in the stomach area. Now I found myself with two little boys and a sick husband to look after.
     He could barely work. I was working at our salon, taking care of the housework, [she changed the cadence of the speech to reflect the monotonous routine], *the kids...taking them to kindergarten.... One night, I had to leave the house at three in the morning, alone. Go down those dark streets looking for a taxi. He vomited, and I had to gather some of it from the bucket where he puked to take it to be analyzed to the hospital so they could determine what was wrong* [she stopped talking and looked into my eyes intently.] *Auri. That?! That was the worst.*
     As he was really sick, he was always in a bad mood...always fighting, irritable around the children...yelling at them, spanking them. Many times, I pleaded, "Don't you pity them? They are so little; that's not something one does." [she spoke with an imploring tone, as if Miguel were in our presence] *He would spank them on the butt or slap them on the face, and I would tell him, "Miguel, for God's sake, that is not something to do to little children. You make me suffer." But then I would reflect and tell myself, "He is not well." He developed a horrible temper. I had never seen that before, not when I met him. That was the disease acting out.*

---

13   Las manos de mi cariño te están bordando una capa con agremán de alhelíes y con esclavina de agua. Cuando fuiste novio mío por la primavera blanca, los cascos de tu caballo cuatro sollozos de plata. García Lorca, *Zorongo*.

Figure 46: Nieces in flamenco dresses

Well, I liked him. I liked him the minute I saw him. I felt my heart stop!!! Auri, when I saw him, I knew, "That one is mine, my destiny." That's what I think, Auri!! To tell you the honest truth, I feel I was more in love with him than he was with me. [She spoke softly with revealing emphasis] **I was blind...crazy about him**. I had met another guy, but only for a short time. MIGUEL was the only one. After he died, no one else, never...nothing. I suffered enough, you know? One day, and another day, and another day, and another day, and another day [her voice rose in crescendo] AND ONE MONTH, AND ANOTHER MONTH,...AND ONE YEAR, AND ANOTHER YEAR...THAT WAS NINE YEARS. [She stopped. Then continued] With a disease. I got married in [19]70. And he died in [19]86!! [She looked at me with indignation] How about that? Sixteen years married and nine more dating.

> García Lorca considered songs, like people, living entities.
> The songs are creatures, delicate creatures, which must be taken care of, so that their rhythm is not altered at all. Each song is a wonder of balance, which can be easily broken.
> [...]
> The songs are like people. They live, they improve, and some degenerate, they fall apart until we only have those palimpseptos full of gaps and contradictions.[14]

My aunt's life was like the *copla* lyrics Miguel used to listen to, blasting from their record player at every family gathering. Like the *copla*, her life was full of passion, defiance, and ultimately tragedy. A cancer devoured her only love, right in front of her eyes. She was so close to happiness but was robbed of it by her husband's illness. Miguel was never able to be the man she thought he was. The sickness turned the handsome flamenco-loving young man into a bitter and unloving husband and father. So much hope, yet so much disappointment. No one's fault but fate.[15]

She continued talking in her wounded tone:

> *That's why I tell you.... If I had known better...I swear to you.... I told my mother one day, I said, "Mamá, if I had known how very little enjoyment I was in for in my marriage I would have slept with him BEFORE."* [Her indignation now turned into defeated exasperation] *...WHEN I WAS YOUNGER, BECAUSE I NEVER ENJOYED MY MARRIAGE. I DID NOT ENJOY ABSOLUTELY ANYTHING.* [She was upset and fell silent] *I ONLY DEALT WITH ILLNESSES. ONE DAY, AND ANOTHER DAY, AND ANOTHER DAY, AND ANOTHER DAY.*

Pimpan
Pimpan
Pimpan

---

14 "...las canciones son criaturas, delicadas criaturas, a las que hay que cuidar para que no se altere en nada su ritmo. Cada canción es una maravilla de equilibrio, que puede romperse con facilidad: es como una onza que se mantiene sobre la punta de la aguja. [...] Las canciones -prosigue- son como las personas. Viven, se perfeccionan, y algunas degeneran, se deshacen hasta que sólo nos quedan esos palimpseptos llenos de lagunas y de contrasentidos." Federico García Lorca, *Obras completas* (2006), 459, quoted in Marco Antonio de la Ossa Martínez, "Federico García Lorca, la investigación musical y las *Canciones Populares Españolas*," *Quadrivium Revista Digital de Musicología* 9 (2018): 3 https://dialnet.unirioja.es/servlet/articulo?codigo=6836540.

15 Manuel Vázquez Montalbán, *Cancionero XX*, quoted in Sieburth, *Survival Songs*, 54.

Maruja's Brilliance

Figure 47: Maruja

Maruja was in the hospital when her father broke the news. The new baby was a girl and they decided to call her Luz. "Luz?" she asked, puzzled, "what kind of name is that? Where did you find it?" "Oh well," he replied, ignoring the question, "We liked it."

Maruja, Luz's older sister, had been in the hospital for a few months after a life-threatening accident. The accident was horrific. She whispered into the cassette microphone the memory of it all:

I had gone to a friend's house after school, but my mother had to go shopping. She had been pregnant before with a baby girl who died [You know,...the one who died?] and was pregnant again. It was then that my mother told me, "Maruja, come over, I am going to Hornillo Street to shop. I want you to blow the brazier." I used to go fetch the wood from the factory where my father worked, and he would give me a sack, a basket of firewood. So, as usual, all the kids were around me to get warm, and then I was blowing at the brazier. There were two boys in a car from El Fargue[16] *where the military powder magazine was located, you know?*

16　In his study of the powder factory of El Fargue, Francisco González Arroyo tells the important history of this site. In his thesis, he argues that the factory's history goes back to the year 1230, "almost certainly" to the existence of two powder mills before the Nasrid period. There

They made bombs there. The driver was going to fetch children at the school and take them home. But in the house next door to where we were standing there was a pile of sand, a lot of sand. Of course, as the guy was driving so fast, he did not see the pile of sand, drove into the sidewalk, and hit the lamppost and it fell on me. It took me rolling all down the street. The lamppost…of course…it was made of iron. I went rolling, rolling, rolling. Well, I almost reached Hornillo Street where the lamp stopped. They called my poor mother. "Emilia, there has been an accident!" Well, they took me to the hospital. My poor mother, I could no longer see her. I think she had the baby girl in the summer in July. She gave birth and I was still in the hospital when they told me the name of the new baby. They did not plaster my entire body, but they plastered me from here [She pointed to her hip] *to the very tip of my foot. All this is a fake bone.* [She touched her thigh to show me the length of the prosthetic bone they implanted].[17]

Maruja spent a year in the hospital. The cost was covered by the army as it was one of their vehicles that almost killed her. She was thirteen when she left the hospital and started to work. First, she learned to sew in a tailor's shop. A quick learner, she became skilled at sewing all the suit pattern pieces. Proudly she told me she was able to complete a full suit, trousers, vest, and jacket. One of the employers she worked for gave her extra work to take home.

I sat on a chair that I placed on top of the table in the main room in our home in order to be able to see the sewing. There was a weak illumination from a lightbulb of 10 watts or so. Then later, when readymade clothing started appearing, and my eyesight became worse and worse, I sought work braiding the cane seats of chairs. I used to work outside our front door in the

---

is evidence of the production of gunpowder in the Muslim era and during the subsequent reign of the Catholic Monarchs, who delegated management to the governor of the Alhambra. The mills came under the control of the Royal Treasury during the Napoleonic occupation (1810-1812). In 1819, two private companies ran the factory until 1850, when the Artillery Corps assumed technical management in collaboration with the Royal Treasury. In 1865 the army took control of the mills. In El Fargue projectiles, torpedoes, and breaker grenades were used successfully, according to the press of the period, in the war with Morocco well into the 1920s. According to González Arroyo, the high point of production took place during the Civil War: "The factory was from day one the main reason why Granada was a crucial target for the Francoist troops, because it could guarantee them the ammunition supply they needed." During the conflict, more than 980,000 kilos of gunpowder and more than 1,250,000 kilos of explosives were produced. There was hardly any dependence on the outside. Almost everything in El Fargue's high tech factory was locally made. Francisco González Arroyo, "De la Real Hacienda al Instituto Nacional de Industria pasando por Artillería 1850-1961" (thesis, Universidad de Granada, 2013) https://granadaimedia.com/la-fabrica-que-decanto-la-guerra/.

17 María Morcillo Miranda, interview by author, Granada, October 23, 2006, tape audio recording.

building courtyard. Whenever there was nothing else to work on, I would just go for the day and work in the fields, gathering wood, picking onions, potatoes, whatever, to survive.[18]

In 1961, as the tourist industry took off in Spain, Maruja emigrated to Mallorca, seeking more stable employment as a maid in the hotels on the Mediterranean island. She tried unsuccessfully to convince Luz to come with her rather than get married. She realized after rejecting a marriage proposal herself, that she did not have the temperament to put up with any man. Her freedom was too important to her. After working in Mallorca for a few years, she returned to Granada where she quickly found a job as a maid in the Colegios Mayores.[19]

---

18   Morcillo Miranda, interview.
19   In Spanish universities, from the late Middle Ages until the end of the 18th century, Colegios Mayores or Major Colleges were associated with instruction and conferral of undergraduate and graduate degrees (bachelor's and doctorates). In addition, the colleges provided accommodations for students. Sometimes they were an extension of a university and other times gave birth to universities. They functioned with great autonomy; the professors taught in the colleges while students would take their exams at the university. The resident students governed the administrative and economic aspects of their college and elected and appointed a rector among themselves. In sixteenth-century Spain there were six Major Colleges; four in Salamanca, one in Valladolid, and another in Alcalá de Henares. Maruja was part of the housekeeping staff in The Royal College of San Bartolomé and Santiago in Granada, founded in 1649. Other European universities also had their University Major Colleges, but the heirs of this tradition were Oxford and Cambridge, where the colleges became the main feature of university life, both as teaching and social life epicenters, leaving the examining functions and collation of degrees to the university.
A decree of September 19, 1789 ordered the extinction of the Major Colleges in Spain due to a crisis of corruption and elitism. There were attempts to re-open them in 1815 and 1831 that did not succeed. In 1910 the Free Institution of Learning established the Residence of Students in Madrid, which sought to emulate the tradition of the English Major Colleges model. Their aim was to encourage broad education and training as an extension and crucial complement of the university life. In 1915 the Women's Residence was created, under the direction of María de Maeztu. The Residence had a formative mission, not only as a residential site for merely 15 students, but with the objective of educating the elite in an exclusive cultured and creative environment. The rationale behind the elitism was to bring Spain closer to the scientific, technical levels of Western Europe. To this end, the most outstanding professors of the Spanish university, distinguished writers, thinkers and foreign scientists (Lorca, Alberti, Buñuel, Dalí, and also dozens of future scientists) stayed at one point or another in the Residence. A decree of August 25, 1926 provided that each university district capital establish a Board with the mission to rebuild and reorganize the Major Colleges. The Spanish Civil War destroyed this venture, although many of the residents and their professors collaborated in exile in the development of Latin American political and intellectual institutions. Olegario Negrín Fajardo, "Los Colegios Mayores durante el franquismo," in *L'Université en Espagne et en Amérique Latine du Moyen Âge à nos jours. II : Enjeux, contenus, images* (Tours : Presses Universitaires François-Rabelais, 1998) http ://books.openedition.org/pufr/5977.

Known colloquially as a "scout" in the English parlance, her housekeeping duties were performed during morning hours for the students' and professors' rooms. The rest of her workday included cleaning and maintenance of communal living areas: kitchens, bathrooms, as well as serving meals (breakfast, lunch, and dinner), laundry and ironing.

The Franco regime re-established by decree of September 21, 1942 the Major Colleges with two fundamental goals: the control of the students and the training of the intellectual and political elites of the regime. In the restoration of the Major Colleges, the regime used the national Catholic principles: imperial university, revival of the Golden Age Spanish past, traditional Christian education under the Catholic Church's purview, and finally, rejection of everything foreign. These colleges were segregated by gender. Each college had a chaplain, and all the residents received political instruction in the Falange principles. Other educational purposes stated in the legal regulations included cultural, social, artistic, and physical and sports education. The Education Act of 1970 reformed the Major Colleges. They would no longer be considered elite training places, as in the ideological presuppositions of national Catholicism, nor were they to be the educational centers par excellence any longer. Their new function was ambiguously stated as "formation and educational coexistence."[20]

Maruja witnessed the college life of the privileged male, exclusively law students at the Colegio San Bartolome y Santiago, located in the adjacent area of the Plaza de los Lobos where the students arrested in the State of Emergency of 1970 were taken. Her life, though, was not affected much by the unrest taking place right under her nose. For her, the job provided the stability to be able to live a quiet life and to help her younger sister raise her two nephews.

Luz was profoundly grateful for the support given to her by her sister.

She helped me so much! Since I got married...every day she would come by from College...every day she brought a basket E.V.E.R.Y D.A.Y. Meat, eggs, bread, fruit...EVERYTHING. Apart from that, every month she gave me money. [Luz looked at me with complicity and paused, then continued listing what her sister provided in terms of financial security for her] *She paid my social security. One day I was combing Concha's hair* [their

---

20   The legal text laid the groundwork for the forging of the ideal Spanish gentleman, following the criteria rooted in conservative Hispanic tradition. The decree of November 11, 1943 established the mandatory residence of university students in the colleges unless they were native residents living with their parents. The same decree established the political control of the appointment and dismissal of the rectors, who would be nominated by the Rector (President) of each university, following a report from the General Secretariat of Falange. The decree-law of October 26, 1956 and the law of protection of Major Colleges of May 11, 1959, solidified the Francoist policy in matters of University Major Colleges. Negrín Fajardo, "Los Colegios Mayores durante el franquismo."

oldest sister] *here in the beauty parlor and Maruja came, like she did every afternoon. At around half past four in the afternoon she would always be here,* [Luz laughed with satisfaction while remembering] staying *until 9 at night. And my Concha suddenly said to Maruja, "Obviously, you have time to visit with this one, but you don't come to my house to see me. You only love Luz." And Maruja, she might have been in a bad mood, replied, "Well YES! Of course, for sure I love her...MORE than I love YOU!"* [Luz paused a little bit to let the story sink in, then gently continued] *Then I told Maruja, "Look, why did you tell her that?" "Because it's the same thing all the time, at all hours, telling me that I come to see you too much, that I give you this and that, blah, blah, blah.... And what does it matter to her? She has her husband who earns good money!"*[21] *I did not have anything but my work at the parlor because my husband did not leave me a pension or anything at all. MY PENSION NOW, I HAVE BECAUSE MY SISTER PAID FOR IT!! That is the simple truth. She used to tell me, "You should have never gotten married to that guy. He was always sick." And I would reply, "So what? If he is sick, so be it. I CHOSE HIM and I LIKED HIM!"*

The lyrics of the copla "A tu vera/by your side" encapsulates the filial love Luz felt for Maruja:

> a tu vera, siempre a la verita tuya,/ by your side/ always by your side
> siempre a la verita tuya,/ always by your side
> hasta que de amor me muera./ Until love takes my life
> Ya pueden clavar puñales,/ They may stab me with daggers
> ya pueden cruzar tijeras,/ they might cross scissors
> ya pueden cubrir con sal,/ they might cover with salt
> los ladrillos de tu puerta./ the bricks of your doorway
> Ayer, hoy, mañana y siempre/ Yesterday, today, tomorrow and forever
> eternamente a tu vera,/ eternally by your side
> eternamente a tu vera./ eternally by your side

Two women alone raising two boys, now men with college degrees. Two women the Regime mostly forgot. One a widow left to fend for herself and her two children, the other unmarried and childless whose role in life was to take care of others. What little joy they had in their life they manufactured in the small cracks of time when they were not working, taking care of others.

---

21   Morcillo, interview.

Coda

Part of the motivation for writing this book was to honor those women who made it possible for me to live the life I have lived. I am a member of the transition generation in Spain. For women this was an especially significant period. It was a time when Spain was forced to consider women as equal actors in a modern society, not just uncompensated and underappreciated supporting roles in an anachronistic pageant put on by Franco's regime. I grew up expecting that I would go to college. And when I got to college, I was not restricted to a few female professions but was told that I could be the first in my family to be a doctor, a lawyer, or in my case a historian. I didn't have to drop out of school to raise younger brothers and sisters, or go to work to help feed, house, and clothe a large, extended family. Getting married young and starting a family, a large family, was not something that was forced on me either. I was raised to be independent and taught not to rely on a man to care for me or to define my happiness. These are all privileges that the women I write about did not have. But it is from their sacrifices and their suffering, I contend, that women like me were able to prosper in a still imperfect, but vastly improved, democratic Spain.

Another motivation for this book was to try to tell these women's stories in a way that better reflected my lived understanding of history, rather than my academically trained understanding of what was an acceptable way to report on the past. This is in many ways my transgression. I do not follow a linear, positivistic arc in which I pretend to know and understand a kind of objective truth. The truth, if that is even the right word for it, is in the emotions felt and poured out by these women and the feelings engendered by their experiences in all of us.

Bibliography

Primary Interviews

Cabrera, Julia. Interview by author. Granada. June 1989.
Camarero Idigoras, Esperanza. Interview by author. February 19, 2007.
Carreño Tenorio, Jesús. Interview by author. September 18, 2017.
Casquero Gómez, Marian. Interview by author. June 2, 2018.
[Ferrer], Amparo. Interview by author. January 8, 2018.
Ferrer, Amparo. Interview by author. Granada. May 15, 1989.
Gómez, Aurora. Interview by author. 1994.
Gómez Sánchez, Pepi. Interview by author. Granada. June 17, 2019.
Marga. Interview by author. Miami. August 4, 2010.
Martínez Sánchez, Patrocinio. Interview by author. Granada. December 2012.
Morcillo, Luz. Interview by author. Audio recording. Granada. June 18, 2006.
Morcillo, María Miranda. Interview by author. Granada. October 23, 2006.
Socorro and Jesús. Interview by author. Granada. May 29, 1989.

Websites

Accidentes mineros mortales del año. http://www.elvalledeturon.net/prensa/1961-1970/1967.
Antonio Quintero (dramatist), Rafael de León (lyricist), Manuel Quiroga (composer). https://lyricstranslate.com.
Archivo de Historia Oral. AHOA, Ahozco Historiaren Artxiboa http://www.ahoaweb.org/.
Carmen de los Mártires. http://www.granada.org/inet/palacios.nsf/xedbynombre/58475794CDC857ECC1257188003A3DA0.
Columbia Center for Oral History (CCOHR) http://www.incite.columbia.edu/ccohr/.
Henri Bergson entry. Stanford Encyclopedia of Philosophy. https://plato.stanford.edu/entries/bergson/.

Historia de CCOO. https://www.uv.es/ccoo/documents/historia_de_ccoo.html.
HOAC militants' report on the 1970 strike. https://drive.google.com/file/d/1yCiiGF EEUIux-MuRqKQCW6iGAkGAs6Qa/view.
International Oral History Association, http://www.ioha.org/useful-readings/.
On Pentimento. https://www.britannica.com/art/pentimento-oil-painting.
Oral History Association http://www.oralhistory.org/resources/.
Seminario de Estudios de la Mujer. http://imujer.ugr.es/.
Seminario de Fuentes Orales http://www.seminariofuentesorales.es/somos/somos.php.
Sponge cake roll dessert, Spain. https://www.spanish-food.org/desserts-spanish-swiss-roll.html.
Unión General de Trabajadores. http://www.fpabloiglesias.es/.

Books, Articles, Music, Films, Interviews

Abrams, Lynn. *Oral History Theory*. London: Routledge, 2010.
Aceña, Pablo Martin. *The Banco de España, 1782-2017: The History of a Central Bank*. *Estudios de Historia Económica*, 73 (2017). https://www.bde.es/f/webbde/SES/Secciones/Publicaciones/PublicacionesSeriadas/EstudiosHistoriaEconomica/Files/roja73e.pdf.
Alberdi Alonso, Javier SJ and Juan Luis Pintos SJ. *Actitud religiosa del universitario español: Encuesta FECUM 1967*. Madrid: Editorial Razón y Fe S.A., 1967.
Andreo Sánchez, Tomás. "La Virgencica, una intervención de urgencia para un urbanismo vivo." PhD diss., Universidad de Granada, Facultad de Bellas Artes Alonso Cano, Departamento de Dibujo, 2015.
Arendt, Hannah. *The Human Condition*. Chicago: The University of Chicago Press, 1998.
Arriero Ranz, Francisco. *El movimiento democrático de mujeres: De la Lucha contra Franco al feminism*. Madrid: Catarata, 2017.
Astey, Gabriel. "La forma de la temporalidad." In *Nacer desde el sueño: Fenomenología del onirismo en el pensamiento de María Zambrano*. Oxford: Peter Lang, 2017.
Auge, Marc. *Oblivion*. Minneapolis: University of Minnesota Press, 2004.
Aullón de Haro, Pedro. *El jaiku en España*. Madrid: Hiperión, 2002.
Azcona, José Manuel. "Tratamiento político de la emigración exterior española en el tardofranquismo (1974-1977)." *Estudios Internacionales* 182 (September-December 2015): 9-35.
Babiano, José, and Sebastián Farré. "La emigración española a Europa durante los años sesenta: Francia y Suiza como países de acogida." *Historia Social* 42 (2002): 81-98.

Babiano, José, and Ana Fernández Asperilla. *La patria en la maleta: Historia social de la emigración española a Europa*. Madrid: Ministerio de Trabajo y Emigración, 2009.

Barone, Thomas, and Eliot Eisner. *Arts Based Research*, 1st ed. Thousand Oaks, CA: SAGE Publications, 2011.

Barthes, Roland. *Elements of Semiology*. New York: Hill and Wang, 1977.

Bashō, Matsuo. *Bashō's Haiku: Selected Poems*. Translated by David Landis Barnhill. Albany, NY: SUNY Press, 2004.

_____. *Sendas de Oku*. Translated and edited by Eikichi Hayashiya and Octavio Paz 2nd. Ed. Girona, Spain: Ediciones Atalanta, 2014.

Basteiro, CM. "Flores por los once de la mina Santo Tomás." *Nueva España*. August 15, 2017. http://www.lne.es/cuencas/2017/08/15/flores-once-mina-santo-tomas/2149847.html

Bautista Vilar, Juan. *La emigración española a Argelia*. Madrid: C.S.I.C., 1975.

_____. *La emigración española al Norte de África, 1830-1999*. Madrid: Arco-Libros, 1999.

_____. *Los españoles en la Argelia francesa*. Madrid: Centro de Estudios Históricos, C.S.I.C., 1989.

_____. *El exilio en la España contemporánea: Las emigraciones políticas españolas en los siglos XIX y XX*. Madrid: Ed. Síntesis, 2006.

_____. "Guerra civil, éxodo y exilio: La aventura del *Stanbrook*, Alicante-Oran, marzo 1939." *Estudios Románicos* 2 (Universidad de Murcia, 2007-2008): 213-27. http://revistas.um.es/estudiosromanicos/article/view/94691/91111.

Benjamin, Walter. "Theses on the Philosophy of History." In *Illuminations*. New York: Schocken Books, 2007.

Berger, John. *And Our Faces, My Heart, Brief as Photos*. London: Bloomsbury, 2005.

Berger, John, and Jean Mohr. *Another Way of Telling*. New York: Vintage International, 1995.

Bergson, Henri. *The Creative Mind*. Translated by Mabelle L. Andison. New York: The Citadel Press, 1992.

_____. *Time and Free Will: An Essay on the Immediate Data of Consciousness*. New York: Dover Publications, INC., 2001.

Blanc, Espai en, ed. *Luchas autónomas en los años setenta: Del antagonismo obrero al malestar social*. Madrid: Traficantes de Sueños, 2008.

Borderías, Cristina. "La historia oral en España a mediados de los noventa." *Historia Antropología y Fuentes Orales*, 13 (1995): 113-29.

Borderías Mondéjar, Cristina. "Las mujeres autoras de sus trayectorias personales y familiares: a través del servicio doméstico." *Historia y Fuente Oral* 6 (1991): 105-21.

Bosque Sendra, Joaquín. Interview June 1989. Transcript provided by Joaquín Bosque Sendra himself. Oral Histories Collection, Archivo Histórico de Comisiones Obreras de Andalucía, AHCCOO-A.

Boym, Svetlana. *The Future of Nostalgia*. New York: Basic Books, 2002.

Bracero, Rafael Gil, and María Isabel Brenes. *Jaque a la República (Granada 1936-1939)*. Granada: Osuna Editores, 2009.

Braidotti, Rosi. *Nomadic Subjects: Embodiment and Sexual Difference in Contemporary Feminist Theory*. New York: Columbia University Press, 2011.

Bundgaard, Ana. *Más allá de la Filosofía*. Madrid: Trotta, 2000.

———. "Ser, palabra y arte: El pensar originario de Martin Heidegger y María Zambrano." *Aurora: Papeles del "Seminario María Zambrano,"* 12 (2011): 7-12.

Bridenthal, Renate, Susan Stuard, and Merry E. Wiesner-Hanks. *Becoming Visible: Women in European History*, 3rd ed. Belmont, CA: Wadsworth Publishing, 1997.

Calderwood, Eric. *Colonial al-Andalus: Spain and the Making of the Modern Moroccan Culture*. Cambridge: Harvard University Press, 2018. Kindle.

Calleja, Álvaro. "La lluvia que silenció el Sacromonte." GranadaiMedia, October 29, 2018 http://granadaimedia.com/50-anos-inundaciones-sacromonte/.

Calvo Salgado, Luís M. et al. *Historia del Instituto Español de Emigración: La política migratoria exterior de España y el IEE del Franquismo a la Transición*. Madrid: Ministerio de Trabajo e Inmigración Subdirección General de Información Administrativa y Publicaciones, 2009.

Campo, Alberto del, and Rafael Cáceres. *Historia cultural del Flamenco*. Almuzara: Edición Almuzara, 2013.

Chacón Delgado, Pedro José. "El Asimilacionismo Nacionalista Vasco: La emigración española al País Vasco en la segunda mitad del siglo XX." *Cuadernos de Pensamiento Político* 45 (January/March 2015): 123-52.

Colmeiro, José. *Memoria histórica e identidad cultural: De la postguerra a la postmodernidad*. Barcelona: Anthropos, 2005.

"Comienza el derribo de la Manigua," June 16, 2015. https://granadablogs.com/terecuerdo/2015/06/16/comienza-el-derribo-de-la-manigua/#more-1342.

Cuevas, Tomasa and Mary E. Gilles. *Prison of Women: Testimonies of War and Resistance in Spain, 1939-1975*. Albany: State University of New York Press, 1998.

Culler, Jonathan. *Roland Barthes: A Very Short Introduction*. Oxford: Oxford University Press, 1983. Kindle.

Deleuze, Gilles. "Ariadne's Mystery." *ANY: Architecture New York*, 5 (1994): 8-9. https://www.jstor.org/stable/41845627.

———. *Bergsonism*. New York: Zone Books, 1991.

———. *Difference and Repetition*. London: Bloomsbury, 2017.

Deleuze, Gilles and Félix Guattari. "1227: Treatise on Nomadology—The War Machine." In *A Thousand Plateaus*. Oxford: Bloomsbury, 2016.

———. *A Thousand Plateaus*. London: Bloomsbury, 2016.

"Devotion to the Sacred Heart of Jesus: Historical Origin," October 2, 2020. http://www.salvemariaregina.info/Reference/Sacred%20Heart.html.

Domínguez, Pilar, Rina Benmayor, and María Eugenia Cardinal de la Nuez, eds. *Memory, Subjectivities, and Representation: Approaches to Oral History in Latin America, Portugal, and Spain*. New York: Palgrave Macmillan, 2016.

Driscoll Derickson, Kate, Lorraine Dowler, and Nicole Laliberte. "Advances in Feminist Geography." In *The International Studies Encyclopedia*, edited by Robert A. Denemark and Renée Marlin-Bennett. Hoboken: NJ, Wiley-Blackwell, 2017.

Elden, Stuart. "Rhythmanalysis: An Introduction." In *Rhythmanalysis: Space, Time and Everyday Life*, by Henri Lefebvre. London, New York: Continuum, 2004. Kindle.

———. *Understanding Henri Lefebvre: Theory and the Possible*. London: Continuum, 2004.

Espuny Tomás, María Jesús and Guillermo García González. *Relaciones laborales y empleados de hogar reflexiones jurídicas*. Madrid: Dyckinson, 2014.

Falcón, Lidia. *En el infierno: Ser mujer en las cárceles de España*. Barcelona: Ediciones de Feminismo, 1977.

Falla, Manuel de. "Canción del fuego fatuo." In *El amor brujo* (1916). Libretto by Gregorio Martínez Sierra.

Fernández, Eider de Dios. *Sirvienta, empleada, trabajadora de hogar: Género, clase e identidad en el Franquismo y la transición a través del servicio doméstico (1939-1995)*. Málaga: Universidad de Málaga, 2019.

Fernández Martorell, Concha. *María Zambrano: Entre la Razón, la poesía y el exilio*. Madrid: Montesinos, 2004. Kindle.

"The Fifteen Promises Granted to Those Who Recite the Rosary," *The Most Holy Rosary*. http://themostholyrosary.com/15promises.htm.

Figuera Aymerich, Angela. "Invierno." In *Obras Completas*. Madrid: Ediciones Hiperión, 1986.

Folguera, Pilar. *Cómo se hace historia oral*. Madrid: Eudema, 1994.

Forest, Eva. *From a Spanish Jail*. New York: Penguin, 1975.

Formentí, Anna. "La tumba de Antígona." México: Siglo XXI, 1967. http://www.ub.edu/smzambrano/resenyas/LA_TUMBA_DE_ANTIGONA.pdf.

Fraser, Ronald. *Blood of Spain: An Oral History of the Spanish Civil War*. New York: Pantheon, 1979.

García Abad, Rocío and Arantza Pareja Alonso. "Servir al patrón o al marido: Mujeres con destino a la Ría de Bilbao." *Arenal* 9, no. 2 (2002): 301-26.

García Lorca, Federico. *Selected Poems*. Translated by Martin Sorrell. Oxford: Oxford University Press, 2007.

———. *Zorongo*. https://lyricstranslate.com/en/zorongo-zorongo.html.

Gibbs, Anna. "Bodies of Words: Feminism and Fictocriticism- Explanation and Demonstration," *Text* 1, no. 2 (1997).

Gómez del Moral, Alejandro. "Buying into Change: Consumer Culture and the Department Store in the Transformation(s) of Spain, 1939–1982." PhD diss., Rutgers University, 2014.

González Arcas, Arturo. Interview transcript, July 2, 2007. Provided by Alfonso Martínez Foronda. Oral Interviews Collection, Archivo Historíco de Comisiones Obreras de Andalucía, AHCCOO-A.

González Arroyo, Francisco. "De la Real Hacienda al Instituto Nacional de Industria pasando por Artillería 1850-1961." Thesis, Universidad de Granada, 2013. https://granadaimedia.com/la-fabrica-que-decanto-la-guerra/.

González Palencia, Luis. "Granada, July 1970." In *Andalucía: tierra cercada*. Bilbao: Zero, 1977.

Goytisolo, José Agustín. *Words for Julia*. Barcelona: Lumen Editorial, 1990.

Gracia, Jordi. *Estado y cultura: El despertar de una conciencia crítica bajo el franquismo, 1940-1962*. Barcelona: Anagrama, 2006.

Grele, Ronald. "Private Memories and Public Presentation: The Art of Oral History." In *Envelopes of Sound: The Art of Oral History*, edited by Ronald Grele. New York, London: Praeger, 1991.

Grimaldos Feito, Alfredo. *Historia social del Flamenco*. Barcelona: Ediciones Península, 2010/2015.

Hamilton, Paula. "The Oral Historian as Memorist." *The Oral History Review* 32, no. 1 (Winter - Spring, 2005): 11-18.

Heidegger, Martin. *Poetry, Language, and Thought*. New York: Harper Perennial Modern Classics, 2013.

Hernández Sandoica, Elena. *Tendencias historiográficas actuales*. Madrid: Akal, 2004.

Holguin, Sandie. *Flamenco Nation: The Construction of Spanish National Identity*. Madison: University of Wisconsin Press, 2019.

Holland, Eugene W. *Deleuze and Guattari's 'A Thaousand Plateaus': A Readers Guide*. London: Bloomsbury, 2013. Kindle.

Horn, Gerd-Rainer. *The Spirit of '68: Rebellion in Western Europe and North America, 1956-1976*. Oxford: Oxford University Press, 2007. Kindle.

_____. *The Spirit of the Vatican II: Western European Progressive Catholicism in the Long Sixties*. Oxford: Oxford University Press, 2015.

_____. *Western European Liberation Theology: The First Wave 1924-1959*. Oxford: Oxford University Press, 2008.

Informe del Departamento de Información del Distrito de Granada. "Situación de los presos políticos en Granada." 14 de abril de 1971. In Archivo Universidad de Granada, Secretaría General del Rectorado, Asociaciones de Estudiantes, 69/71, leg. 23-272.

Iron Chic. "Spooky Action at a Distance." 2013. Track 1, on *Spooky Action*, digital album.

Janés, Clara. *Vivir*. Madrid: Hiperión, 1983.

Janesick, Valerie J. *Oral History for the Qualitative Researcher: Choreographing the Story*. New York: The Guilford Press, 2010.

Jonas, Raymond. *France and the Cult of the Sacred Heart: An Epic Tale for Modern Times*. Berkeley: The University of California Press, 2000.

"José Guerro Campos, obispo emérito de Cuenca," *El Pais*, July 16, 1997 https://elpais.com/diario/1997/07/16/agenda/869004001_850215.html.

Kerr, Heather, and Amanda Nettelbeck. *The Space Between - Australian Women Writing Fictocriticism*. Perth, AU: UWA Publishing, 1998.

Kidd, William. "(Un)packing the Suitcases: Postcolonial Memory and Iconography." In *France's Colonial Legacies: Memory, Identity and Narrative*. Edited by Fiona Barclay. Cardiff: University of Wales Press, 2013.

Labanyi, Jo. "Musical Battles: Populism and Hegemony in the Early Francoist Folkloric Film Musical." In *Constructing Identity in Contemporary Spain*. Edited by Jo Labanyi. New York: Oxford University Press, 2002.

Lakoff, George, and Mark Johnson. *Metaphors We Live By*. Chicago: University of Chicago Press, 2008.

L'Écho d'Oran: journal d'annonces légales, judiciaires, administratives et commerciales de la province d'Oran (184?-1963). In Bibliothèque Nationale de France, Département Droit, économie, politique, JO-13582. http://catalogue.bnf.fr/ark:/12148/cb32759772v.

Lefebvre, Henri. *Critique of Everyday Life: From Modernity to Modernism (Towards a Metaphilosophy of Everyday Life)*, Vol. 3. London, New York: Verso, 2005.

———. *Elements of Rhythmanalysis*. London, Oxford: Continuum, 2004. Kindle.

———. "Henri Lefebvre on the Situationist International." Interview by Kristin Ross, 1983. http://www.notbored.org/lefebvre-interview.html.

———. *The Production of Space*. Oxford, UK: Blackwell Publishing, 1991.

Llona, Miren. "Archivar la memoria, escribir la historia: Reflexiones en torno a la creación de un Archivo de Historia Oral. AHOA, Ahozco Historiaren Artxiboa." In *Historia Oral. Fundamentos metodológicos para reconstruir el pasado desde la diversidad*, edited by Laura Benadiva. Rosario: Suramérica Ediciones, 2010.

———. *Entre señorita y garçonne. Historia oral de las mujeres bilbainas de clase media (1919-1939)*. Málaga: Universidad de Málaga, 2002.

———. "Memoria e identidades: Balance y perspectivas de un nuevo enfoque historiográfico." In *La historia de las mujeres: Perspectivas actuales*. By Cristina Borderías. Barcelona: Icaria, 2008.

Llona, Miren, ed. *Entreverse: Teoría y metodología practica de las fuentes orales*. Bilbao: UPV, 2012.

López Saenz, María Carmen. "Merleau-Ponty y Zambrano: el 'logos' sensible y sentiente." *Aurora* 14 (2013).

Lundy, Craig. "Nomadic History." In *History and Becoming*. Edinburgh: Edinburgh University Press, 2012.

Maillard, Chantal. "Conjuro para decir mentiras y construir verdades." *Nómadas: Revista Crítica de Ciencias Sociales y Jurídicas* (1999): 135-36. https://webs.ucm.es/info/nomadas/0/chantalmaillard_1.pdf.

———. *La creación por la metáfora: Introducción a la razón poética*. Barcelona: Anthropos, 1992.

———. *Hilos*. Barcelona: Tusquets, 2007.

Marfull, Miguel Angel. "La muerte que levantó a los estudiantes contra la dictadura." *Público*, January 18, 2009. http://www.publico.es/espana/muerte-levanto-estudiantes-dictadura.html.

Marías Cadenas, Sescún. "Las empleadas de hogar durante el franquismo y la transición democrática: entre el paternalismo y la marginación (1939-1981)." In *XI Jornadas Internacionales de Estudios de la Mujer*. Edited by Ana Antón-Pacheco Bravo et al. Madrid: Editorial Fundamentos, 2011.

Martin-Marquez, Susan. *Disorientations: Spanish Colonialism in Africa and the Performance of Identity*. New Haven, CT: Yale University Press, 2008.

Martínez, J. and N. Rodríguez. "Cartes d'un soldat republicà." www.aasit.com/informatiu/hemeroteca/ [...].

Martínez Foronda, Alfonso. *La conquista de la libertad historia de las comisiones obreras de Andalucía (1962-2000)*. Sevilla: Fundación de Estudios Sindicales, 2005. Archivo Histórico de CC.OO.-A Segunda Edición.

Martínez Foronda, Alfonso, and Isabel Rueda Castaño, eds. *La cara al viento: Estudiantes por las libertades democráticas en la Universidad de Granada (1965-1981)* vol. II. Sevilla: Fundación de Estudios Sindicales CCOO-A, 2012.

Martínez Foronda, Alfonso, and Pedro Sánchez Rodrigo. *Mujeres en Granada por las libertades democráticas: Resistencia y represión (1960-1981)*. Granada: Fundación de Estudios y Cooperación de CCOO de Andalucía Unión Provincial de CCOO de Granada, 2017.

Martínez González, Francisco. "Introducción al pensamiento musical de María Zambrano." *Revista de Musicología* 28, no. 2, Actas del VI Congreso de la Sociedad Española de Musicología (2005).

Massey, Doreen. *Space, Place and Gender*. Cambridge: Polity Press, 1994.

McDougall, James. *A History of Algeria*. Cambridge: Cambridge University Press, 2017.

McDowell, Linda and Joanne P. Sharp. *A Feminist Glossary of Human Geography*. London: Arnold, 1999.

McLaughlin, Eiland, and Kevin McLaughlin. "Translators' Foreword." In *The Arcades Project*, by Walter Benjamin. Cambridge, MA: Harvard University Press, 1999.

Merleau-Ponty, Maurice. *The Visible and the Invisible*. Evanston: Northwestern University Press, 1968.

Mesa Encinas, Remigio. "La huelga de 1970 en Granada." In *Luchas autónomas en los años setenta: Del antagonismo obrero al malestar social*, edited by Espai en Blanc. Madrid: Traficantes de Sueños, 2008.

Ministerio del Trabajo. *Informe sobre conflictos colectivos de trabajo 1970*. Madrid: Colección Testimonio, Serie: Informes, Ministerio del Trabajo, 1971.

Mira Abad, Alicia, and Mónica Moreno Seco. "Españolas exiliadas y emigrantes: encuentros y desencuentros en Francia." *Les Cahiers de Framespa* 5 (2010). http://journals.openedition.org/framespa/383.

Molinero, Carme, and Margarida Sala. *Una inmensa prisión: Los campos de concentración y las prisiones durante la Guerra Civil y el Franquismo*. Barcelona: Crítica, 2003.

Molinero, Carme, and Pere Ysàs. "La Crisis." In *De la Hegemonía a la autodestrucción: El Partido Comunista de España (1956-1982)*. Barcelona: Editorial Planeta, 2017.

Morán, Carmen. "El ángel del hogar era una esclava." *El País* (June 13, 2012). https://www.catarata.org/media/catarata55/files/book-attachment-1586.pdf.

Morcillo, Aurora G. "Gendered Activism: The Anti Francoist Student Movement in the University of Granada in the 1960s and 1970s." *Gendered Education in History, Theory and Practice-Case-Studies on Women's Education, Gendered Spaces and Performativity of Knowledge, Encounters in Theory and History of Education*, 19 (2018): 90-109.

_____. "In their Own Words: Women in Higher Education." In *True Catholic Womanhood: Gender Ideology in Franco's Spain*. Dekalb: Northern Illinois University Press, 2000.

_____. *The Seduction of Modern Spain: The Female Body and the Francoist Body Politic*. Lewisburg: Bucknell University Press, 2010.

_____. *True Catholic Womanhood: Gender Ideology in Franco's Spain*. Dekalb: Northern Illinois University Press, 2000, 2008.

Muñoz Sánchez, Antonio. "Una introducción a la historia de la emigración española en la República Federal de Alemania (1960-1980)." *Iberoamericana* 46 (June 2012): 23-42.

_____. *Entre dos sindicalismos: La emigración española en la RFA, los sindicatos alemanes y la UGT, 1960-1964*. Madrid: Fundación 1º de Mayo, 2008.

Musser, George. *Spooky Action at a Distance: The Phenomenon that Reimagines Space and Time–and What It Means for Black Holes, The Big Bang, and Theories of Everything*. New York: Scientific American/Farrar, Straus and Giroux, 2015.

Nash, Mary. *Defying Male Civilization: Women in the Spanish Civil War*. Denver: Arden Press, 1995.

_____. *Rojas: Las mujeres republicanas en la Guerra Civil*. Madrid: Editorial Taurus, 1999.

Negrín Fajardo, Olegario. "Los Colegios Mayores durante el franquismo." In *L'Université en Espagne et en Amérique Latine du Moyen Âge à nos jours. II: Enjeux, contenus,*

images. Tours: Presses Universitaires François-Rabelais, 1998. http://books.ope nedition.org/pufr/5977.
Nelson, Lise, and Joni Seager. *A Companion to Feminist Geography*. Oxford: Blackwell, 2005.
Neves, María Joao. "Diótima de Mantinea en la voz de María Zambrano." *Aurora: Papeles del "Seminario María Zambrano,"* (1999): 92-99.
Nieto, Lola. "Metáfora, repetición y musicalidad: María Zambrano y Chantal Maillard." *Dicenda: Cuadernos de Filología Hispánica*, 33 (2015): 179-93.
Nietzsche, Friedrich. *Thus Spoke Zarathustra: A Book for None and All*. Translated with a preface by Walter Kaufmann. New York: Viking Penguin, 1966.
Nimmo, Clare E. "The Poet and the Thinker: María Zambrano and Feminist Criticism." *The Modern Language Review*, 92, no. 4 (1997): 893-902.
Ofer, Inbal. *Claiming the City/Contesting the State: Squatting, Community Formation and Democratization in Spain (1955–1986)*, The Cañada Blanch Series: Studies on Contemporary Spain, LSE. London: Routledge, 2017.
———. "*My Shack, My Home*: Identity Formation and Home-Making on the Outskirts of the City of Madrid." Special issue in *Homes & Homecomings, Gender and History*.
———. *Señoritas in Blue: The Making of a Female Political Elite in Franco's Spain*. Brighton: Sussex Academic Press, 2009.
Ortega López, Teresa. "Obreros y vecinos en el tardofranquismo y la transición política (1966-1977): Una 'lucha' conjunta para un mismo fin." *Espacio, Tiempo y Forma, Serie V. Historia Contemporánea* 16 (2004): 351-69.
Ortega y Gasset, José. "La idea de las generaciones." (1923). https://www.ensayistas.org/antologia/XXE/ortega/ortega3.htm.
Ortiz Buitrago, Humberto. *Palabra y sujeto de la razón poética: Una lectura del pensamiento de María Zambrano*. Caracas: Universidad Central de Venezuela, 2013.
Ortiz, Carmen, and Manuel de Ramón. *Madrina de guerra: cartas desde el frente*. Madrid: La Esfera de los Libros, 2003.
Oso Casas, Laura. "'Chambras,' 'porterias,' 'pubelas' y 'burones:'" estrategias de movilidad social de las españolas en París." In *Un siglo de inmigración española en Francia*. Vigo: Grupo de Comunicación Galicia en el Mundo, 2009.
———. *Españolas en París: Estrategias de ahorro y consume en las emigraciones internacionales*. Barcelona: Edicions Bellaterra, 2004.
Ossa Martínez, Marco Antonio de la. "Federico García Lorca, la investigación musical y las *Canciones Populares Españolas*." *Quadrivium Revista Digital de Musicología* 9 (2018): 3 https://dialnet.unirioja.es/servlet/articulo?codigo=6836540.
Pack, Sasha. *The Deepest Border: The Strait of Gibraltar and the Making of the Modern Hispano-African Borderland*. Redwood City, CA: Stanford University Press, 2019.
Passerini, Luisa. *Autobiography of a Generation: Italy, 1968*. Middletown, CT: Wesleyan, 1996.

_____. *Fascism in Popular Memory: The Cultural Experience of the Turin Working Class (Studies in Modern Capitalism)*. Cambridge, UK: Cambridge University Press, 2009.

Pattinson, Elizabeth. "Discovering the Self: Fictocriticism, Flux and Authorial Identity." http://www.aawp.dreamhosters.com/wp-content/uploads/2015/03/Pattinson2013.pdf.

Payne, Stanley. *Falange: A History of Spanish Fascism*. Redwood City, CA: Stanford University Press, 1961.

_____. *Fascism in Spain 1923-1977*. Madison: University of Wisconsin, 1999.

_____. *A History of Fascism, 1914-1945*. Madison: University of Wisconsin, 1995.

_____. *The Spanish Civil War*. Cambridge: Cambridge University Press, 2012.

Pérez, Janet, and Genaro J. Pérez. "Prison Literature: Introduction." *Monographic Review/ Revista Monográfica* 11 (1995): 9-25.

Polkinghorne, John. *Quantum Theory: A Very Short Introduction*. Oxford: OUP, 2002.

Portela, M. Edurne. "Writing (in) Prison: The Discourse of Confinement in Lidia Falcón's *En el infierno*." *Arizona Journal of Hispanic Cultural Studies* 11 (2007): 121-36.

Portelli, Alessandro. "A Dialogical Relationship: An Approach to Oral History," (1985). http://www.swaraj.org/shikshantar/expressions_portelli.pdf

_____. *The Death of Luigi Trastulli and Other Stories Form and Meaning in Oral History*. Albany, NY: State University of New York Press, 1990.

_____. *The Text and the Voice: Writing, Speaking, Democracy and American Literature*. New York: Columbia University Press, 1994.

Pratt, Geraldine. "Feminist Geographies: Spatialising Feminist Politics." In *Envisioning Human Geographies*, edited by Paul Cloke, Philip Crang, and Mark Goodwin. London: Arnold, 2004.

Preston, Paul. *The Spanish Holocaust: Inquisition and Extermination in Twentieth-Century Spain*. New York: W. W. Norton & Company, 2013.

Quitián González, Antonio et al. *Curas obreros en Granada*. Alcalá la Real: Asociación Cultural Enrique Toral y Pilar Soler, 2005.

Radcliff, Pamela. "Ciudadanas: las mujeres en las asociaciones de vecinos y la identidad de género en los años setenta." In *Memoria ciudadana y movimiento vicinal*, edited by Vicente Pérez Quintana y Pablo Sánchez León. Madrid: La Catarata, 2008.

Ramón Carrión, Manuel de. "Las madrinas de guerra en la Guerra Civil." https://journals.openedition.org/bulletinhispanique/4284#toctoin3.

Rashomon. Directed by Akira Kurosawa (1950; Tokyo: Daiei). https://www.criterion.com/films/307-rashomon.

Ricoeur, Paul. *Memory, History, Forgetting*. Chicago: Chicago University Press, 2006.

Ritchie, Donald. *Doing Oral History (Oxford Oral History Series)*, 3rd ed. Oxford: Oxford University Press, 2014.

Roca, Juan Ramón. *Españoles en Argelia: Memoria de una emigración*. Alicante: IES Luis García Berlanga, 2016.

Rodríguez Barreira, Oscar. "Cambalaches: Hambre, moralidad popular y mercados negros de guerra y postguerra." *Historia Social* 77 (2013): 149-74.

———. *Migas con Miedo: Prácticas de resistencia al primer franquismo, Almería 1939-1953*. Almería: UAL, 2008.

Rodríguez Izquierdo Gavala, Fernando. *El haiku japonés*. Madrid: Hiperión, 1972. https://www.thehaikufoundation.org/omeka/files/original/e76226e68e30 9a763bdbbacaa8ed51b1.pdf.

Rodríguez López, Sofía. *Memorias de los nadie: Una historia oral del campo andaluz (1914-1959)*. Sevilla: Centro de Estudios Andaluces, 2015.

———. *Mujeres en Guerra: Almería (1936-1939)*. Almería: Arraez Editores, 2003.

———. *El patio de la carcel: La Sección Femenina de FET-JONS en Almería (1937-1977)*. Sevilla: Centro de Estudios Andaluces, 2010.

———. *Quintacolumnistas: Las mujeres del 36 en la clandestinidad almeriense*. Almería: Instituto de Estudios Almerienses, 2008.

Rose, Gillian. *Feminism and Geography: The Limits of Geographical Knowledge*. Oxford: Polity Press, 1993.

Ruiz Carnicer, Ángel. *El Sindicato Español Universitario (SEU) 1939-1965: La socialización política de la juventud universitaria en el franquismo*. Madrid: Siglo XXI, 1996.

Ruiz Morcillo, Pedro. "Con la FECUN y contra Franco en los pasillos de Puentezuelas (1968-1973)." [Unpublished mss.; pdf essay provided].

Sainz Martínez, Juan Carlos. "De FECUM a FECUN: Política y Religión entre los Congregantes Marianos (1965—1977)." *Política y Sociedad*, 22 (1996): 103-21.

Sánchez Cuervo, Antolín. "The Anti-Fascist Origins of Poetic Reason: Genealogy of a Reflection on Totalitarianism." In *The Cultural Legacy of María Zambrano*. Edited by Xon de Ros and Daniela Omlor. Oxford: Legenda, 2017.

Sangster, Joan. "Telling Our Stories: Feminist Debates and the Use of Oral History." *Women's History Review* 3, no. 1 (1994): 5-28.

Santamaría, Alberto. "Poetry and Realization: Towards a Knowledge of the Poet's Place." In *The Cultural Legacy of María Zambrano*. Edited by Xon de Ros and Daniela Omlor. Oxford: Legenda, 2017.

Sanz Diaz, Carlos. *Clandestinos, ilegales, espontáneos emigración irregular de españoles a Alemania en el contexto de las relaciones hispano-alemanas, 1960-1973*. Madrid: CEHRI, 2004.

———. "Las relaciones del IEE con Alemania." In *Historia del Instituto Español de Emigración: La política migratoria exterior de España y el IEE del Franquismo a la Transición*. Edited by Luís M. Calvo Salgado et al. Madrid: Ministerio de Trabajo e Inmigración, Subdirección General de Información Administrativa y Publicaciones, 2009.

Schneider, Marius. *El origen musical de los animales-símbolos en la mitología y la escultura* antiguas. Madrid: Siruela, 2010.

"Se inaugura la primera industria del Polo de Desarrollo." 9 January 2012. http://granadablogs.com/terecuerdo?s=gil+bracero.

Sempere Souvannavong, Juan David. "Cincuenta años con los pies negros." *Información* July 26, 2012. https://www.diarioinformacion.com/arte-letras/2012/07/26/cincuenta-anos-pies-negros/1278748.html.

———. *Los 'Pieds Noirs' en Alicante: Las migraciones inducidas por la descolonización.* Alicante: Publicaciones Universidad de Alicante, 1998.

Semprún, Jorge. *Autobiografía de Federico Sánchez.* Barcelona: Editorial Planeta, 1977.

Serrano, Rodolfo. *Toda España era una carcel: Memoria de los presos del Franquismo.* Madrid: Aguilar, 2002.

Seva Llinares, Antoni. *Alacant, trenta mil pieds-noirs.* Alicante: Eliseo Clement, 1968.

Sherman, Alfred. "Climax in Algeria: The O.A.S. and the Pieds Noirs." *The World Today* 18, no. 4 (Apr., 1962): 134-42. https://www.jstor.org/stable/40394178.

Shubert, Adrian. *Death in the Afternoon: A History of the Spanish Bullfight.* New York: Oxford University Press, 2001.

Shults, F. LeRon, and Lindsay Powell-Jones, eds. *Deleuze and the Schizoanalysis of Religion (Schizoanalytic Applications).* London: Bloomsbury, 2016.

Sieburth, Stephanie. *Survival Songs: Conchita Piquer's 'Coplas' and Franco's Regime of Terror.* Toronto: University of Toronto Press, 2014.

Simmons, Ernest L. *The Entangled Trinity: Quantum Physics and Theology.* Minneapolis, MN: Augsburg Fortress, Publishers, 2014.

Simpson, Christopher Ben. "Divine Life: Difference, Becoming and the Trinity." In *Deleuze and the Schizoanalysis of Religion (Schizoanalytic Applications).* Edited by F. LeRon Shults and Lindsay Powell-Jones. London: Bloomsbury, 2016.

Sinués y Marco, María del Pilar. *El ángel del hogar: estudios morales acerca de la mujer.* Madrid: Imprenta Española Torija, 1862.

Sotelo, Analicia. "Do You Speak Virgin?" In *Virgin: Poems.* Minneapolis: Milkweed Editions, 2018. Kindle.

Steege, Paul. *Black Market, Cold War: Everyday Life in Berlin, 1946-1949.* Cambridge: Cambridge University Press, 2007.

Suárez, Ángel. *Libro blanco sobre las cárceles franquistas: 1939-1976.* Paris: Ruedo Iberico, 1976.

Summerfield, Penny. "Discomposing the Subject: Intersubjectivities in Oral History." In *Feminism and Autobiography: Texts Theories, Methods,* edited by Tess Cosslett, Celia Lury, and Penny Summerfield. London, New York: Routledge, 2000).

"The Theory of Moments and the Construction of Situations," *Internationale Situationniste* #4 (1960). http://www.notbored.org/moments.html.

Thomas, Hugh. *The Spanish Civil War.* New York: Harper Row, 1961.

Thompson, Paul. *The Voice of the Past: Oral History*. Oxford: Oxford University Press, 1988.
Thomson, Alistair. *Anzac Memories: Living with the Legend*. Manchester: Manchester University Press, 2011.
Thomson, Alistair, and Anisa Puri. *Australian Lives: An Intimate History*. Victoria, AU: Monash University Publishing, 2017.
Tudela Vázquez, Enrique. *Nuestro Pan: La Huelga del 70*. Granada: Comares, 2010.
Tur, Bruno. "Estereotipos y representaciones sobre la inmigración española en Francia." In *Un siglo de inmigración española en Francia*. Vigo: Grupo de Comunicación Galicia en el Mundo, 2009.
Unamuno, Miguel de. *En torno al casticismo*. Madrid: Alianza Editorial, 2000.
Valis, Noël, and Carol Maier. *Two Confessions: María Zambrano and Rosa Chacel*. Albany: State University of New York Press, 2015. Kindle.
Vaneigem, Raoul. *The Revolution of Everyday Life*. London: Rebel Press, 2006.
———. Interview. http://www.e-flux.com/journal/06/61400/in-conversation-with-raoul-vaneigem/.
Vilanova, Mercedes. "El combate en España por una historia sin adjetivos con fuentes orales." *Historia Antropología y Fuentes Orales*, 14 (1995): 95-116.
Villanueva Edo, Antonio. "Las instituciones de la lucha antituberculosa en Vizcaya (1882-1957)." *Euskal herriaren historiari buruzko biltzarra* 4 (1988): 201-20. https://www.ehu.eus/documents/1738121/2349786/Tuberculosis.pdf.
Vinyes, Ricard. *Irredentas*. Madrid: Temas de Hoy, 2009.
Vosburg, Nancy. "Prisons with/out Walls: Women's Prison Writings in Franco's Spain." *Monographic Review/Revista Monográfica* 11 (1995): 121-36.
Watson, Peggy. *Intra-historia in Miguel de Unamuno's Novel: A Continual Presence*. Potomac, Maryland: Scripta Humanistica, 1993.
Wegter-McNelly, Kirk. *The Entangled God: Divine Relationality and Quantum Physics*. London: Routledge, 2011.
Weinrich, Harald. *Lethe: The Art and Critique of Forgetting*. Ithaca: Cornell University Press, 2004.
Welty, Eudora. *One Writer's Beginnings*. Cambridge, MA: Harvard University Press, 1995.
West-Pavlov, Russell. *Temporalities*. London: Routledge, 2013.
Woolf, Virginia. "A Sketch of the Past." In *Virginia Woolf Moments of Being: Unpublished Autobiographical Writings*. Edited by Jeanne Schulkind. New York: Harcourt Brace & Company, 1985.
Ysàs Solanes, Pere, and Carme Molinero. *De la hegemonía a la autodestrucción: El Partido Comunista de España (1956-1982)*. Barcelona: Editorial Crítica, 2017. Kindle.
Zambrano, María. *De la Aurora*. Madrid: Tabula Rasa, 2004.
———. *Claros del Bosque*. Barcelona: Biblioteca de Bolsillo, 1986.
———. *Claros del Bosque*. Madrid: Cátedra, 2011.

_____. *Delirio y destino*. Madrid: Mondadori, 1989.
_____. *Filosofía y Poesía*. Mexico: Fondo de Cultura Económica, 1996.
_____. *Hacia un saber sobre el alma*. Madrid: Alianza Editorial, 2008.
_____. *Notas de un método*. Madrid: Tecnos, 2011.
_____. "Para una historia de la piedad." *Aurora: Papeles del "Seminario María Zambrano."* (2012): 64-72. https://www.raco.cat/index.php/Aurora/issue/view/19528/showToc.
_____. "Para una historia de la piedad." In *The Modern Spain Sourcebook: A Cultural History from 1600 to the Present*. Edited by Aurora G. Morcillo et al. London: Bloomsbury Press, 2018.
_____. *Persona y democracia: La historia sacrificial*. Madrid: Anthropos, 1988.
_____. *La tumba de Antígona*. Madrid: Alianza Editorial, 2019. Kindle.

List of Figures

Figure 1: Concha with Amalia's family watching TV after lunch for the last time (1990) 42
Figure 2: Socorro and Jesús as college students 55
Figure 3: Socorro as a college student 64
Figure 4: Socorro and Jesús' wedding photo 71
Figure 5: Funeral of the eleven miners killed in the Santo Tomás mine in the Valley
of Turón, Asturias, August 1967 76
Figure 6: College of Theology today houses the Odontology and Library of Sciences
colleges at the University of Granada Campus in the district of Cartuja. From right
to left: Façade, and two views of the main Chapel in 1968 (from the entrance and
from the altar) 81
Figure 7 (left): Rosary
Figure 8 (rght): Prayers of the Rosary 91
Figure 9: Mysteries of the Rosary 92
Figure 10: The College of the Arts. The College of the Arts was located in the
magnificent nineteenth-century palace of the Counts of Luque on Puentezuelas
Street. This was the site of student activism from in the 1960s until the mid-1970s,
when the college was relocated to a new facility built outside the city center in
the northern part district of Cartuja... 96
Figure 11: Amparo, 1968 100
Figure 12: Hymn #466 123
Figure 13: Trifold Mobius Strip 132
Figure 14: Angelus Novus (Klee Painting) 139
Figure 15: Feria del Corpus, Granada c. 1958 159
Figure 16: Patro and Juan 168
Figure 17: Patro and Juan's wedding photo 169
Figure 18: Patro and Juan with three of their four children 172
Figure 19: Patro in the market stall... 174
Figure 20: Empty market stalls 175
Figure 21 (left): Patro and two others at the market stall
Figure 22 (right): Patro cutting meat 176
Figure 23: Pura as a child, 1927 180

Figure 24: Pura (on the right) on a stroll with her sister Mercedes and her husband, a close friend of Juan's who showed him this picture, which led him to pursue Pura 184
Figure 25: Their wedding in Granada, August 28, 1958 185
Figure 26: Pura and Juan, Souvenirs D'Oran 187
Figure 27: Pura's arrival in Oran with Mercedes, Jeanot, and their son in 1958 188
Figure 28: Family portrait, 1963. Pura holding Marian, with Juan standing behind Carmen.. 194
Figure 29: Wedding cake by Juan La Colombe pastry shop............................... 198
Figure 30: Pepita and the girls, 1962 201
Figure 31: Juan Casquero with his daughters, after he retired to Granada in 1971 205
Figure 32: Corsetry factory employees pose in their uniforms, Barcelona c. 1962 213
Figure 33: At work in the corsetry factory 214
Figure 34: Young women posing in the courtyard...216
Figure 35: Construction workers posing on top of a scaffold............................. 222
Figure 36: There were not just three. We remained all shocked on the ground, discovering suddenly, once again, the hidden meanings of things. 225
Figure 37: Aerial view of La Virgencica bee-hive shape design housing for the poor, 1969... 228
Figure 38: Esperanza with her son on his First Communion day, Bilbao, c. 1957............ 234
Figure 39: Newlyweds, Munster, Germany, 1963-64 251
Figure 40: Newlyweds cooking in their apartment in Münster, 1964...................... 254
Figure 41: Luz as a young girl 268
Figure 42: Luz and Miguel in costume 270
Figure 43: Luz and Miguel at the fair 272
Figure 44: Luz and Miguel outside work 275
Figure 45: Luz and Miguel's wedding photos 276
Figure 46: Nieces in flamenco dresses 279
Figure 47: Maruja... 281

Glossary

ACNP: Association of National Catholic Propagandist
APE: Asociaciones Profesionales de Estudiantes (Professional Students Associations)
BAA: Bundesanstalt für Arbeit (Federal Employment Office)
BPS: Brigada Político Social (Socio-Political Brigade)
BR: Brigada Revolucionaria (Revolutionary Brigade)
CCOO: Comisiones Obreras (Workers's Committees)
FAC: Federación de Asambleas Cristianas (Christian Assemblies' Federation)
FECUM: Federación Española de Congregaciones Universitarias Marianas (Spanish Federation of Marian University Congregation)
FECUN: Federación Española de Comunidades Universitarias
FUDE: Federación Universitaria Democrática Española
FLN: Front of National Liberation
FLP: Frente de Liberación Popular (Popular Liberation Front)
FUE: Federación Universitaria Escolar (University Student Federation)
HOAC: Hermandad Obrera de Acción Católica (Catholic Action Workers Fraternity)
IEE: Instituto Español de Emigración
INI: Instituto Nacional de Industria
JEC: Juventud Estudiantil Católica (Catholic Student Youth)
JOC: Juventud Obrera Católica (Catholic Workers Youth)
JUMAC: Juventud Universitaria de Acción Católica (Catholic Action University Youth)
LCR: Liga Comunista Revolucionaria (Revolutionary Communist League)
LOU: *Ley de Ordenación Universitaria* (Regulatory University Law)
MC: Movimiento Comunista (Communist Movement)
OAS: Organisation de l'Armée Secrète (Secret Army Organization)
ORT: Organización Revolucionaria de Trabajadores (Workers' Revolutionary Organization)
OSE: Organización Sindical Española (Spanish Syndicates Organization)
PCE: Partido Communista de España (Communist Party of Spain)
PSA: Socialist Party of Andalusia

PSOE: Partido Socialista Obrero Español (Spanish Socialist Workers Party)
PTE: Partido del Trabajo de España (Spanish Labor Party)
SDEUG: Sindicato Democrático de Estudiantes de la Universidad de Granada (Democratic University Student Union)
SEU: Sindicato Español Universitario (Spanish University Union)
SUT: Servicio Universitario del Trabajo (University Labor Service)
TOP: Tribunal de Orden Público (Public Order Tribunal)
UDE: Unión Democrática de Estudiantes
VV.OO.: Vanguardias Obreras (Labor Vanguards)

Appendix I
For A History of Mercy[1] by María Zambrano (1989)

Before history appeared, there was a prehistory of history: poetry. It is founded by certain poems like *The Iliad* and *The Odyssey*, as well as other poems. They featured the oldest of all civilizations, where the first stories and visions of human events appeared. These stories are poetic; therefore religious, and eminently dramatic. In such poems, only extraordinary individuals appear, and they are agents of large feats. History is the account of great and extraordinary actions; being in history itself means to enter a certain immortality that separates the heroes from the rest of the mortals.

This heroic sense of history has endured remarkably, like all the origins. History as an account of immemorial feats still persists, especially in the *naïve* consciousness of the people. It is the memory of what is wondrous. But history has also been science, and, in this field, it went to pick up facts, mere events, that were decisive and transcendent, but that did not necessarily have to be heroic. To be transcendent means nothing but not ending in itself, that is, to trespass its own limits. Moreover, this scientific way of making history, left aside everyday life; the life that elapses without fanfare and forms the plot, the only scrim where one can draw the extraordinary action or transcendent event.

This anonymous life that did not reach the historical category has been the subject of the novel numerous times. Hence, the best history in some periods of Western culture has been the novel, the best history and the best sociology, since it corresponds to what is now known as the study of "life forms." That is the situation now; more than extraordinary and transcendent individuals and events, it is important to capture the forms of life, the way life is modeled through economic, social, and political relations, among others. But there is something else in the novel and in poetry.

Novel and poetry have reflected better than the historical knowledge, the true life, the truth about the things that happen to people and their inner sense. In order to be complete and truly human, history will have to descend to the most

---

[1] Morcillo et al. eds., *The Modern Spain Sourcebook*, 35-41. Translation by Asunción Gómez.

secret places of the human being, the so-called "insides." The insides are the least visible, not only because they cannot be seen, but because they resist being seen. And the insides are the seat of emotions. But the term "feelings" is so broad that we should stop there because within its field lies mercy, the feeling we are providing a brief history of.

Is it just a feeling? Perhaps, in the realm of the mental life, there is nothing more difficult to define than feelings. When we try to understand them, we realize that they constitute the entire life of the soul, that they are the soul. What would happen to a man if the capacity to feel could be removed from him? He would even cease feeling his own self. Every single thing that can be the object of knowledge, everything that can be thought of or subjected to experience, all that can be desired, or calculated, is previously felt somehow; this applies to the being itself because if it could only be understood or perceived, it would not address its own center, the person. Making an effort to imagine this state, we see it as a kind of abstract dream, a total alienation in which even the things themselves would not be perceived due to a lack of interest, due to the absence of someone who perceives them.

More than any other psychic function, the capacity to feel creates who we are; we could say that while we possess the rest of the psychic functions, feeling is what we are. Thus, feeling has always been the supreme sign of authenticity, of thriving truth; it has been the ultimate source of legitimacy for what human beings say, do or think.

With so brief an observation, we see that if something has the right and the necessity of history is, precisely this vast world of feelings, because its history will be the most accurate history of humankind. However, the difficulty is great, according to a law that seems to preside all human affairs: the greater the need, the greater the difficulty. Feelings are abundant and elusive; since they are the liveliest thing of our lives, they are also the most intangible; the most ready to escape, leaving us with a kind of effervescent vacuum, when we try to capture them.

They are the most rebellious to be defined. That is the reason why poetry and novel have been their best channels. Because what characterizes feelings is the capacity to be expressed, not analyzed. Expression is part of the life of feelings and, when it is achieved, far from fading, they acquire an adamantine kind of entity that makes them transparent and invulnerable to time. Since in our present time, a rationalist notion about the life of the soul has prevailed, knowing about feelings has been decreasing, finding shelter in the most hermetic places. One of the greatest misfortunes and hardships of our time is the inscrutability of deep life, of the true life of feelings, which went into hiding in less and less accessible places. Creating its history, albeit timidly, will be a liberating task.

But what is mercy in the immense and delicate world of feelings? It is perhaps the initial feeling, the widest and most profound; something like the homeland for the rest of the feelings. Although hesitantly expressed, this might seem a very bold assertion, but we hope that along these brief pages, this idea will gain power in the mind of the hypothetical reader. We have to start with an attempt to "present" this feeling, since a definition is, as we have indicated, the most inadequate and clumsy way to approach mercy. But, since feelings –especially mercy—do not have an adequate definition, they must have a history. The objects that have an adequate definition, to the point of coinciding with it, are called "ideal objects": a triangle, a character from a novel, a thousand-faced polygon, and a round square do not have a history. Instead, that which seems impossible to be captured in a definition, is expressed without losing anything in its multiple and successive manifestations; that is, it is expressed in its history.

Mercy cannot be adequately defined, because it constitutes the epitome of a specific type of feelings: the amorous and positive ones. Mercy is not love itself in any of its forms and meanings; it is not charity either, a particular form of mercy discovered by Christianity; it is not even compassion, a more generic and diffuse passion. Mercy is like the prehistory of all positive feelings. And yet, it accompanies them in their history, and mercy itself has a history. And here we have to stop to see the specific form feelings take in their historical path.

The idea we have about the historical path, like any path where time is involved, is one of destruction: "the destructive time" is the image that lingers in the consciousness of almost all human beings; hence, the history of feelings or anything of what constitutes the intimacy of the human condition has not been attempted yet. History seemed to be a sequence of things that destroy the previous ones, a sort of parade of fleeting shining instants that are replaced by other shinning instants. The philosopher Bergson has provided a masterful criticism of this linear conception of the passage of time, which has been represented as a series of dots that follow one another and that they are consumed as they pass by. Time, according to Bergson, it is growth with multiple forms, in which every instant penetrates and is penetrated by other instants; instead of destroying, time creates. This fundamental thesis of contemporary metaphysics casts a bright light on our topic, since feelings, in their history, do not destroy each other. Therefore, Mercy can be the mother to all positive or amorous feelings, without being swept by them, as they come.

Moreover, it is also something that contradicts the common idea that feelings appear in history, instead of appearing all of a sudden. We still have the idea that human beings are formed once, and forever. Maybe so, but it is also true that the capacities or potencies of their being are revealed progressively, while manifesting themselves throughout History. That is why there might be, there is, a history of feelings; because humans have not shown suddenly from the outset of their appearance on Earth, all its fullness and complexity; these are revealed, unraveled. The horrors and sufferings that History is littered with, are "ultimately" justified. Through the vicissitudes of History, the human being unravels, is brought to light; that is, the human being is being born in History, instead of having been born once.

Mercy appears to us as the matrix where the life of feelings originates. Let's see why. Without trying to define it, as has already been said, we must form a certain idea of what we understand by it. To this end, we should dispose of the idea of feeling, since, as it happens with all elaborated and widely used concepts, it carries a load of misconceptions. Moreover, the very term "feeling" corresponds precisely to the stage of thought where Mercy has been more unknown. Thus, if we approach it directly, it seems to escape us. But there is a very old way to get to these entities and it is what theologians have called the negative way. An ancient Hindu mystic referred to God by saying that it is "neither this nor that." This definition has reached throughout the ages the highest theology with Plotinus and the highest mystics. The subtle things that cannot be apprehended by their presence, can be perceived through their absence, through the gap they leave. And we should not be scared by such a procedure, because we surely have experienced it in our own lives: we feel what the loved person or the friend are when we lose them, because of the irreparable void they leave us with; the same goes with homeland landscapes, with health, and with the possessions that are indescribable because of their immensity. They overflow our soul, they flood our consciousness, and they possess us. How do you define them?

To define is to see distinctly the limits of one thing, and seeing it requires to have it at a distance, to distinguish the limits of what is seen, to see it among other things in the same plane, forming a set. Large goods and evils, by contrast, possess us; we feel that they exceed our life and our consciousness. Almost always we need to lose them or to have them concealed in order to recognize them through their absence.

Thus is Mercy. Undoubtedly, it has suffered in recent times an intense eclipse which coincides with the rise of rationalism. Enthusiasm for reason and for its results, the light radiating from rational knowledge seems to have thrown its shadow over Mercy. Since this has been happening for quite some time, we can look with perspective and ask ourselves: what are we missing? That which the wonderful methods of science and technical creations could not give us. Which is our situation as human beings in the Universe? And the answer comes to our conscience immediately, as if it was there, before the question was posed: we are alone, alone as human beings and alone in front and among things: we dominate them, we handle them, but we do not communicate with them. If we were to take mercy as the act of treating people, animals and plants gently, it could seem that such communication exists. But mercy is not philanthropy, or compassion for animals and plants. It is something else: it is what allows us to communicate with them; in short, it is the diffuse and gigantic feeling that places us appropriately among all the planes of being, and among different beings. Mercy is knowing how to deal with what is different, with that which is radically other than us.

The idea that a man is, above all, conscience and reason has led us to consider that only another man can be equal to him. But the process does not stop there, because as differences exist between men and since there are races, nationalities, cultures, social classes, and economic differences, we have come to the quite apparent spectacle of current society. We only know how to deal with those which are almost a reproduction of ourselves. When the modern man looks out to the world, he is searching for a mirror that reflects his own image, and when he cannot find it, he is puzzled and often he wants to break the mirror. We have become terribly incapable to understand that there are people different from us. To fill up this void, the word "tolerance" was invented, a favorite term in the vocabulary of modern society. But "tolerance" is neither understanding nor proper treatment; it is simply, keeping distance, respectfully, with everything we do not know how to deal with.

Other periods of time show us an opposite situation, like the Middle Ages for example, when Mercy was not eclipsed. Naturally, without violence, without speeches or official organizations, medieval people knew how to deal with that which was different in a spontaneous way: in the human world it was the incurable patient, even the monstrous or the criminal. Beyond humanity, there were chimeras and ghosts, angels and Gods. God Himself was not conceived as a great consciousness, it was not reduced to humanity. Instead, the modern man has tried to reduce everything to what he can find immediately within himself; to what he believes is his essence: to conscience, to reason. Everything has been reduced to reason and conscience and that which resisted this transformation, became unknown, forgotten and, sometimes, reviled.

And that is how we ended up alone; alone and unable to deal with "the other." But if we put together the various kinds of "otherness," we realize that it is nothing but reality, the reality that surrounds us and where we are anchored. Thus, we perceive more clearly the vital problem which was hidden under the problem of knowledge in the last stages of Philosophy. It is known that the problem was precisely reality, the apprehension of reality. It seems that consciousness and intelligence by themselves do not provide assurance that we are in contact with reality. And science, with all its splendid results, has also failed to give humans the deep conviction that they are knowing reality, that irreplaceable communion that human beings had in more *naïve* and pious ages.

Reality, and philosophers discover this fact again, occurs somewhere previous to knowledge, to the idea. The Spanish philosopher Ortega y Gasset developed the concept of "vital reason" based on his discovery that the reality is prior to the idea, contrary to what Idealism formulated. And if reality is prior to the idea, it has to be given through feelings. Mercy can be understood as the feelings experienced by a subject, by someone who feels reality not in a diffuse and homogeneous way, but distinguishes instead the "especies" and type of realities that somehow must be favorable to him. That is, a subject who feels reality and at the same time feels himself heterogeneous from it. Awareness of solitude and, at the same time, consciousness of participation, sociability. The rationalist believes that reality is given through an idea or thought and that only by reducing reality to thought he can understand it. Mercy is the feeling of the heterogeneity of being, of quality of being, and therefore it is the yearning to find the ways of understanding and deal with each one of those multiple ways of reality.

This which is evident to us now by contrast, and as we stated above, by absence, was an ingenuous belief before rationalism; ingenuity and the further back in history we look, the stronger this ingenuity was, until we see it constitutes the mentality, the way of life of primitive peoples.

Does human progress inevitably condemn Mercy? Modern ethics has sought to replace it with different virtues or values, such as philanthropy, cooperation, and justice. Today everything is asked on behalf of justice and what it is given is equally awarded on its behalf. Will it be enough? Will values such as justice or cooperation be able to fill that sentimental gap left by Mercy, and feed the flame of creation? Will the heart and the entrails of humans be satisfied with nothing more but what is being granted by justice? Can the anguish that we feel today be dissipated with remedies born in the mind? Reason and justice are sisters, they walk together; one is in practice what the other is in knowledge. But their sole rule will assume that humans only need to know visible and tangible things and to feed from them. But since you do no live from bread alone, justice and reason are not enough.

Won't there be, away from distinct and clear knowledge, the necessity of other knowledge that is less distinct and clear, but equally indispensable? Are not there things and relationships so subtle, hidden and indiscernible that they can only by apprehended by feeling or intuition? Will we be able dispense with inspiration? In sum, let's say the dreaded word that we have been concealing so far. Will it not be a bedrock of mystery supporting everything that is clear and visible, everything that can be enumerated? This would be the ultimate and abysmal bottom of the inexhaustible reality that man feels in himself, filling him up in the happy moments and in suffering; joy and suffering appear endless. And in them it is when we feel that reality not only touches us, but also absorbs us, it inundates us.

Mercy is knowing how to deal with the mystery. That is why its language and its ways have repulsed the modern man who has thrown himself frantically to deal only with what is clear and distinct. Descartes assigned to ideas the qualities of "clarity" and "distinction." Nothing can be challenged but, insensibly, we have come to believe that "clarity" and "distinction" are also the notes of reality. And the truth is that only very few realities can achieve that privilege, those to which we alluded earlier, saying that they are the ones that can be defined. However, there is a vast territory that surrounds us and hugs us, that sometimes reject us, submerging us in anguish and despair, and these feelings are neither clear or distinct. And there they are; we have to deal with them every instant. It is simply our own life. Mystery is not found outside; it is within each of us, surrounding and enfolding us. We live and we move within mystery. The guide to avoid getting lost in it resides in Mercy.

Appendix II
DIOTIMA DE MANTINEA[1] by Maria Zambrano (1987)

And now, who will defoliate the rose over me, who will cry and, most importantly, who will raise his hand saying goodbye and pointing my soul forward, undoing the knot that binds even the souls of the recently dead with the air of life? I did it so first, with those of mine. And then, when they came to seek in my hand the power to carry out such actions that would gradually make me feel and know that love has to become law, and that true laws are moments of love. And now, a foreigner and alone with my God who has become unknown to me, I do not see anyone around me who assures me of being helped at the moment of pulling me from this land of which more than daughter I have been, apparently, a guest. A guest who dwelt too long.

I did not realize that nobody was holding me back, that the host's smiles had long since ended, that the host had disappeared and I myself was not at the table with someone else to share my food with.

They had led me to believe that they needed to hear me, that I would communicate to them knowledge that, like water, escapes imperceptibly from my whole self, as they said; she is not a woman, she is a spring. And me....

And now I remember, my memory is becoming law, I myself was turning more and more towards the original well where my knowledge came from, where I had received it drop by drop. Maybe during times and more times I grew almost dry. And someone piously laid over a white stone of the kind that I had always loved, so that the wound in the earth, which is every spring that no longer flows, would not be visible. And that day, I was dead and buried, while I, without realizing it, attended immobile to the distant murmur of the invisible fountain. Gathered within myself, my whole being became a marine snail; an ear, just hearing. And maybe, I thought I was talking, when words sounded just for me, neither inside nor outside; when they were not already said, nor heard, as I had dreamed, they should be the words of truth.

---

1   Zambrano, *Hacia un saber sobre el alma*, 217-35.

I became hearing and when I turned to look, nobody listened to me. Without a sound space I entered the silence, I am its prisoner, and although I had learned to write I could not; as creature of the sound and the voice of the word that arrives in an instant and is going to visit perhaps other nests of silence. I had taken it for granted that writing is the concern of a few men, unless there is a writing from ear to ear. Talking, on the other hand, was natural to me and, like all things that are done according to nature, it had its eclipses, its interruptions. The word itself is discontinuous, but it only becomes sensitive when it has to be formed and then it is no longer a thing of nature, but that which a few men strive to do and which they call thinking.

But I have never thought, one must resolve it. And now, I realize that all my movements have been natural, invisibly drawn like the tides, I know that much, pulled by an invisible sun, by a moon barely denoted, white, the moon born white on a bluish sky continuation of the sea; the navigator lonesome moon, destitute queen who reigns more as a goddess of a lost world. Queen turned goddess of the dead, of those condemned to silence and the cold. Savior of those without a homeland.

Mother of souls..sank into me when they became disembodied. And I suffered their untold sorrows, of those who had had no name. All their non-being and that which they had ceased to feel and had let go outside of themselves. But not all the souls had bear the burden of destiny that weighed on them, nor assembled the pains of the entrails in their care; nor have they been the invisible guide who swiftly summons thought and delivers a verdict on life's secret steps. When separating themselves from their bodies, they fall like a blind man who suddenly restored, without the help of any other senses. And the bodies they left hurt and their history they do not know what to do about, [a history] full of interruptions and parentheses, like a cloth made carelessly. And the pain they did not use up, and the possible love barely glimpsed in an instant of infinite weakness: they roam and flit like birds. Without abode in the country of the dead, too weak to cross its lintel, helpless as at the moment of birth, they came to me. And I did not realize at the beginning, so I had to bear the reproaches of my strange sorrow, not similar to anyone's when someone closed to me or linked to me by some tie died

Strange, irreducible agony neither appeased nor comforted. And while they sang the ritual psalmody in which they enumerated the virtues which oh! not always told a truthful account, the poor anima palpitated blindly, without recognizing herself. And at the most she feels the ambiguous succor of the animal they caress for a moment before being returned to her corner to suffer alone her pain as a beast strange to everything. Those reliefs that the living bestow to stay free on this side of life, warding off the approaching threshold of death, the escorting of the disembodied soul for a few instants even, and in the end lending it a hole–the maternal cave that the earth itself provides. For before death, the living close and oppose the resistance of their impenetrable time, they become hostile enemies. Thus one day, death will penetrate them also from the outside, and not like the sea that floods and carries us far away.

I have carried them, yes, all my dead over me, feeling their weight, that awkwardness of their new state; I kept them while they could not depart. And I knew the others' sorrows alien to my condition, so much so that sometimes I could not discern what error, what weakness instigated them– or what truth. I sank into myself, making myself dark, filling myself with death and the living fled from my side. And then, I would get up and feel my anonymous soul that sustained those half awakened souls already burning with a light that emanates from the soul and begins to burn in its own fire, which starts to reduce itself to its indestructible life.

I had a dream, I do not know if it was a dream, I think so: a serpent advancing towards me: it was not bad nor did bring maybe a drop of poison. But it was a snake although it was almost white, white and grieving which wanted to live with me and I was afraid that nobody would come to visit me anymore. A man abruptly chopped it in two and I saw his soul, small, weak, whitish, that trembled like someone suddenly naked and sad; nobody was going to come and pick it up. I found myself saying: "soul of the serpent, you are sad without your body, come with me and I will take you in my soul," at the same time, a kind of white disc appeared to me holding many souls, which my soul carried by my heart. And I almost regretted my words, my offer because I feared not being able to deal with these two burdens, even though I was weak and small, and its poison had passed to me and I was bad at times. But compassion was stronger than my fear of turning bad so, without any words, I leaned forward, and it ascended to join the other souls. Awaken, I remembered from time to time and scrutinized my own movements, my thoughts; but I did not notice anything alien.

At that time, I began to regard in a different way from time to time, sometimes asleep, sometimes awake. I saw a tree, it is what first happened to me; a tree that I constantly saw between the columns of the temple: a sea pine, tall, with a divided slopping top, erect and alone among a group of cypresses surrounding it without taking away its protagonist role in such symbolic forest. And I saw it without looking at it, in a distinct medium not the air, but rather a more transparent and fluid milieu; it seemed the proper environs of vision, visibility's locale where things never reveal themselves to us. And the difference was as if I had only seen it in bulk hitherto. It was not more real because of that, it was simply true. It was the only and unique tree, it was real and there; this is the hardest thing to put into words. If I could have thought it, I would have thought about it, but I had to settle for seeing it from time to time. Another night, I saw while asleep, but not in dreams, in that space where things are entirely what they are, in a clarity without any remnant of opacity, [I saw] the pure white moon, self-absorbed; its light did not radiate or have any phosphorescence, it did not shine or sparkle, just the moon with its soft light. But I am not even putting that into words because I have never been able to think. Repose and movement are relative things, states. And although there is action in movement or at least activity and passivity, things endure their repose and their movement, therefore they are not fully visible. Well, how may one see what is suffering when it is subject of alteration, depleted at rest, and expanded in movement? While in that visibility environs things neither move nor rest, they do not suffer any state, they simply are. They breathe in the light, in a light that does not vibrate, nor it is dead.

That white moon poured its clarity. And a white sphere I do not know of what substance, because matter did not exist, corresponded with it. Then, when I woke up, I looked at the sky and in front of me the moon was in the same position, equally white. But no, no; I had not invented anything. The white sphere was undoubtedly thought, and that of being in permanent unity, which can only be seen when ... but no, I do not know about it, just a nothing.

Then, I saw a human scene that had happened a long time ago and perpetuated by a story in verse. I understood that the poet had envisioned it like that; it was a different way of seeing, because it was a historical event which represents another kind of movement. I saw it as i were under water. And in the water there were areas of different light and density so the real image gave rise to several fragmentary images that vanished. Some were always repeated; others were a matter of an instant. How many strange rhythms!

I always felt faraway things, those which arise in other times and in other spaces. Events that occur in some place different from ours, instants of reality that are consumed here in durations akin to deserts. And so I have crossed several of them, which point out the true times of my life and have been marking my age.

One of those deserts was the one of dreams. One night, the star appeared to me, one I had seen so many times reigning in the sky, alone, before the sunrise. It, the love that puts an end to the night and illuminates its first steps. I knew I was tied to it. And I saw it in the lucidity of certain dreams, under the shadow of the rings of Cronos, obscured by them. So my life, love crossed by time, divided by time. It was my horoscope that I never wanted to be ascertained. And I began to understand: it was not an event of mine alone.

Time covers the things of the earth and of themselves, only love surpasses it. Love crossed by time which crosses it. The solitary star opening the day illuminates the birth of the night as a threshold and a law. The shadow of Cronos' rings divides it, hurts it. Because it is not only a shadow, it is wounded; Time penetrates love and thus love always engenders.

For a while I was locked up. It was the time when I was a statue. Someone called me Aphrodite Hermetica; my beauty, according to him, was not visible to all; it only showed at certain times. And one day they found me naked, drowsy at the edge of the foam, they confused me with her [Aphrodite]; strange thing; but I did not wrap myself in my violet cloak and when I collected my hair soaked in the thick, bitter water, it was gray.

Did I depend on my soul? No, I did not; now I see that. Very soon it was snatched away from me and taken away. Now that it assists me almost visible, I know.

And now I see myself like that, as I was: an almost pure presence for anyone who came looking for me. Later, I did not understand not being me, myself, the sought after it. But without understanding hardly anything, there continued to sprout from me an inexhaustible and increasingly pure presence. It was something that came out of me, while I was behind and locked in my wounded darkness; such is the spring in which all drink and refresh themselves and become pure and soft. And no one enters into the depth where the hidden spring lymph flows. Hence, it also must be what is behind a voice heard in the distance. Apparently, it had always been so, since I was very young.

The crying girl buried alive. Antigone alive in his impenetrable grave. And her weep is water; a wound's weeping no one notices, over which nobody tends but to drink; life itself in its first manifestation; water.

A wise man, I heard, had said all things are water. I do not think that is so. I do not know about that nor know what things are or if there are any things. In all things there is water, yes. And some of them are injured so that they spring and become mothers of life. Others are undone by fire in water.

For life was sea and then it was abducted; life was stolen and imprisoned first. And there are those who restore it and those who do not.

And it always springs from a wound. It is love. There is a life, love imprisoned in everything, but there are those who hold it: afraid, if alive, of dying.

One day when I was more alone than ever, sunk as I was in my darkness - my clarity rejected - I felt the birth of music, the nascent music. It was the day I began to die, I heard the old song of water within me and I saw the ghost of water in that kind of vision that began then. I began to sing between my teeth to obey in the absolute darkness not known hitherto, the old song of the water not yet born, confused with the moan from which it was born; the moaning of the mother who gives birth again and again to end being born herself, intermingled with the wail of what is born, the parturient life. I felt cradled by this weeping that was also singing so far away and in me, because it was never mine at all. Would I have no owner either?

Music has no owner. Well, those who go to it never have it. They have been first possessed by her, then initiated. I did not know that a person could be like that, like music which possesses while it penetrates and separates from its source, also in a wound. Music is open only in some places unexpectedly, when the soul wanders alone, feels faint without owner. In this loneliness no one appears, as no one appeared either when I settled in my ultimate solitude; not even the beloved without a name. Someone I fell in love with in the night, on a lonely night, on an unique night, until dawn. He never appeared again. No one else could find me anymore.

And I stayed at the edge of dawn. He, the beloved without a name, led me to it, to the very edge of dawn. And there he was shivering cold. A smell of violets enveloped me; it always followed me as an impalpable trace. It vanished for a long time, but it would come back and even someone noticed it once and approached me, someone approached me when nobody was looking for me any longer. It was as if he recognized me. But he was perfectly opaque to me. This did not matter either. He was a man of earth color and gave me confidence. He had made a war and wanted to wash it off there in the fountain. I left him alone for a long time and then we talked until dawn. I do not remember what I said. And I was left uneasy and this avid man drank, so thirsty in all his pores; he imbibed my words, and seemed to take them with him, because he did not know how to write either.

I did not talk anymore, I think. Then came that child who one day, when he stopped being blond, left. Then only the innocent goat was a friend as an undiscovered constellation.

Assisted by my old soul, by my first soul at last regained, and for so long lost. She, the lost one, finally came back to me. And then I understood that she had been the one in love. I had gone through life just as a transient, far from myself. And from her came the words without an owner which everyone drank without leaving me nothing in return. I was the voice of my old soul. And as she consummated her love, there, where I could not see her, I began to initiate myself through the pain of abandonment. That's why nobody could love me while I was coming out of love. And I did not love myself either. Only one night until dawn. And there I stayed waiting. I would wake with the dawn, if I ever slept. And would think he had arrived, I, she, he....

The sun was rising, and the day was falling like a verdict on me. No, not yet.

I came to breathe in time, I breathed the time until I entered its heart. Insensibly, I entered into its heart the inside of matter. The matter ... I had always felt dust as the residue of time; time stopped to become sensitive. But in the hardest matter, I had felt the hidden beat of time. The time that descends, extends, and quiets without ever disappearing from everything we see. Time only tamed in stone, asleep in marble. Everything breathes.

There is no body, there is no matter completely separate from time. And everything which is destroyed will end up in its heart.

Because matter is only matter because it lacks a heart of its own. And life unwraps where something begins to beat from within itself, to breathe with its own time, where a hole is carved, a temporary cavern created by a small heart, a core. But there is a pulse in everything; the night uncovers it.

They called me the pale one; I hardly felt my body and my gray, green, blue eyes must have seemed blind, especially when I was looking at my hands that always seemed a mystery to me.

I could never hold up my dark hair that weighed so much on me. I was so odd that I passed as invisible.

I chose the darkness as my part. I wanted to be like the shadows which give birth to the clarity that makes obscurity succumb, vanish.

An unbroken absence, the gap from someone, has filled my life more than any other event. A flat absence when I was young and widened in the endless afternoons in which I preferred to sink in some solitary corner, refusing to see or be seen by anyone. Thus, I stayed away from girls of my age, until no one remembered me for the holidays. My youth with no application shrunk, like a river absorbed by the sand. I suddenly had not the right age. I was nobody now.

Then I began to count endlessly and to draw lines in the hope that they would find themselves and form a figure. I noticed the distances, the positions of some stars that I knew while also going through the changes of time and place without wanting to see them. And I began to feel some resentment towards time because it arrived before me, and did not allow me to set those distances, perform those calculations that so slowly began to emerge in my mind. I was shut out of time in and in between realm. Every geometric figure attracted me, and every number, as if they were small visible pieces of a country I could enter. The constant emptiness merged with a sort of whiteness with a subtler air where the accuracy of the numbers revealed itself. And I was not moved by anything of the earth or of myself that I could not relate to that map of the stars and the numbers. I was hoping that mathematics would come to life: the life in which that confusion that is so unacceptable to me were deciphered, that sketch that I found myself to be. And the opacity.

I finally entered into something: cavern, nest, heart. In dreams without images, in wakefulness without conscience. First, there was silence and a vacuum greater than the horizon. The images disappeared in that immobility, as if the image is dependent on a certain kind of movement and a semi-infernal time. As just one more step in this fall of time, presences would be without their image in their pure suffering. This hell of the suffering with neither a face nor a shape and I know it; it is under the stillness and also in the threshold of birth.

And silence further deepened and expanded within. Thus the pure vibrations of the heart of the stars begin to be felt, of the plants and of the beasts and of the sacred heart of matter, which is inert only because it lends itself to being tamed to turn even into non-being to be of service. And also the original time falls and descends rescued from each thing. The sea of life contains vibrations without limit and a primal heart. It is a chalice where each vibration is transformed, and matter is redeemed in its servitude, time is turned into instant, as if that unknown God, they told me about, would claim it irresistibly, an abyss where each vibration, every beat, become life. Chalice and abyss where a moment stops being just a grain of sand; turning into seed, fire, light. Event which does not pass.

I looked at the sea long afternoons until I realized, because I had stared at it confusedly, that someone was waiting and calling quietly. Someone who would come, a man perhaps, from the depths of the waters. I always got along well with fishermen and with those who had crossed the sea so many times that they felt at home there, and had even forgotten to lay their feet on the land ground. Someone would come over the waters, and when the clarity of the first dawn merged with the sea leaving the earth dark, I came out of my dreams violently believing that someone could come in that silence in which the earth withdraws, erases itself. Before the light of the aurora. Before the dawn I woke up. With the rose color of the dawn the earth rises, the world of blood, of fire, of the dryness of desire and opaque things. The blood already appeared in that barely white light, a few drops of celestial blood diluted in the dawn's light and the day along with history unfolded, for the man from earth son of that celestial wound. While the one who would wake me up would fall from the light, born of the light in the depths of the waters. Just an instant would make the air vibrate. A bird extended its huge wings, stopping for a moment, suspended, an unknown bird that I saw again. But I came out of my dream because of the sound of its wings, before the daybreak and its light.

And I saw it coming from the horizon at last, walking on the waters, on a rough sea which curled up in circles around itself. My seashores sunk into the sand deep like roots while my arms faltered. I went to meet him without being able to let go. At that moment I knew I was chained. I cannot say whether it left, vanished or sank. I found myself in another time and that circle in the sea seemed the imprint of an unattainable future that would be never be for my present with the unique denied and offered clarity that appears in some dreams. And at the same time, that dawn woke me up, the dawn that only visits me in dreams.

And in this way, I lived in the secret background and beyond the door where all the galleries where I descend with my lamp end; then I realize I lost it and I am lost too. A hurtful clarity emerges without my knowing its visible birthing source. Light of a sunrise that appears only when I lost light. And there are crystal rocks in the night, mountains, hidden rivers and air thick like that of a bridal chamber, when an awaited child is born, unknown inside and beyond it. There, no, I do not know where.

One day, one afternoon, after many days without sun, I felt more than I saw on the beach. Like a wide wound, shining in the sun in the middle of a white water, with more life than that of the sea. A water that came from the bottom of the seas. And when I got to where I thought I was, I was not there anymore, and I only found one footprint in the shape of a fish. It was a drawn fish that stayed there a long time, because the water that covered it in the tide, left it with more life. It was my secret, that I never revealed to no one and I distracted visitors so that they would not visit that part of the seashore. Then, a day of solar eclipse, a strong wind swirled the sand and lifted it to the black sky. And where the fish was, only a few lines remained, perhaps a word, which then the water erased too, leaving a shifting hollow, as if created by an invisible animal.

And so I have been staying in the seashore. Abandoned from the word, crying endlessly as if crying rose from the sea, without no other sign of life than the beating of the heart and the throbbing of time in my temples, in the indestructible night of life. Night myself.

Appendix III

Manifiesto a los universitarios madrileños[1]
Madrid, 1º de febrero de 1956

Desde el corazón de la Universidad española, los estudiantes de las Facultades y Escuelas Especiales de Madrid, abajo firmantes, en la convicción de que ejercen un auténtico derecho y deber al buscar el medio de salir de la grave situación universitaria actual, invitan a sus compañeros de todos los Centros Superiores de España a que suscriban la presente petición, elevada a las autoridades nacionales:
«Al Gobierno de la Nación, a los Ministros de Educación Nacional y Secretario General del Movimiento.»
En la conciencia de la inmensa mayoría de los estudiantes españoles está la imposibilidad de mantener por más tiempo la actual situación de humillante inercia en la cual, al no darse solución adecuada a ninguno de los esenciales problemas profesionales, económicos, religiosos, culturales, deportivos, de comunicación, convivencia y representación, se vienen malogrando fatalmente, año tras año, las mejores posibilidades de la juventud dificultándose su inserción eficaz y armónica en la sociedad y comunicándose, por un progresivo contagio, el radical malestar universitario a toda la vida nacional que arrastra agravándolos todos los problemas antes silenciados.
Nosotros, los estudiantes españoles, queremos afrontar esta situación de una manera clara y definitiva. Queremos lograr una respuesta capaz de satisfacer los legítimos intereses y aspiraciones de miles de jóvenes universitarios, condición indispensable para una convivencia civil digna y estable entre los ciudadanos de nuestro país.
El estudiante se encuentra, a su llegada a la Universidad y a las Escuelas Especiales, con una carrera que consiste en ir salvando, con medios escasos y difíciles de conseguir, una serie de obstáculos al final de los cuales se presenta el hoy más grave de todos: ¿qué hacer con el título académico?

---

[1] http://www.filosofia.org/his/h1956b01.htm.

Cuando las Residencias de Estudiantes y Colegios Mayores son escasos y caros, y muchos nos vemos reducidos a pensiones de precio creciente donde la vida de estudio y convivencia universitaria es casi imposible, cuando los libros de texto son deficientes y costosos, cuando los precios de matrículas y seguros suben continuamente, el estudiante se ve falto de medios suficientes de asistencia universitaria y todas las cargas recaen sobre los agobiados presupuestos de las familias, que no ven compensación a tales sacrificios. Así España, para su mal, permanece en vivo contraste clasista –en éste como en tantos otros aspectos– con la realidad universitaria europea, donde el Estado asume buena parte de tales cargas facilitando el acceso de todas las clases sociales a los Estudios Superiores.

La situación material y vocacional del universitario español es de indigencia, su perspectiva intelectual es mediocre –¡cuántos catedráticos y maestros eminentes apartados por motivos ideológicos y personalistas!– y su porvenir profesional totalmente incierto por la escasez de salidas y especializaciones y por la intervención de excluyentes criterios extraprofesionales, precisamente cuando las necesidades del país reclaman todo lo contrario: aportación de nuevas capacidades y esfuerzos.

Las causas de este desolador panorama, del que ningún buen fruto puede esperarse, son múltiples y hunden sus raíces en todo el clima material y espiritual de nuestra actual sociedad, pero vienen a resumirse y anudarse en una: la organización que hoy se atribuye cada día de un modo más ilusorio al monopolio del pensamiento, de la expresión y de la vida corporativa de la vida universitaria en el aspecto profesional, social, cultural e internacional, posee una estructura artificiosa que o no permite o tergiversa la auténtica manifestación y representación de los universitarios.

Existe un hondo divorcio entre la Universidad teórica, según la versión oficial, y la Universidad real formada por los estudiantes de carne y hueso, hombres de aquí y de ahora con sus circunstancias, opiniones y deseos. Este divorcio explica muy bien la esterilidad y los fracasos cosechados en el terreno intelectual, deportivo y sindical, fracasos que nos humillan en todo contacto internacional ante los estudiantes de otros países.

Al ambiente de desencanto como españoles que quisieran ser eficaces, colaborar y servir inteligente y críticamente a la empresa del bien común y ven ahogado este noble propósito, hay que unir ya la amargura que provoca la emigración creciente de cientos y miles de nuestros mejores graduados. Estos hechos sólo pueden perturbar hondamente en el futuro la ya nada fácil ni justa, en otros aspectos, vida social de la Nación. Porque el camino hasta hoy seguido es el de la ineficacia, la intolerancia, la dispersión y la anarquía.

Precisamente para evitar esta terrible amenaza, conscientes de nuestra responsabilidad y con espíritu constructivo, proponemos volver la vista a la Universidad real y pedimos con el mayor calor y energía un cambio de perspectiva para el bien de España.

Petición

Que se convoque un Congreso Nacional de Estudiantes, con plenas garantías para dar una estructura representativa a la organización corporativa de los mismos. Estas garantías, sin las cuales el Congreso sería una nueva ficción en perjuicio de la Universidad y del País, son:

1º. Que en el Congreso Nacional de Estudiantes tomen parte todos los estudiantes de Centros Superiores de Enseñanza de España, por medio de sus representantes, designados por libre elección, garantizada por el control de los Claustros de Profesores. Y que estos representantes se constituyan automáticamente, una vez elegidos, en cada Distrito Universitario, en comisiones para la organización del Congreso.

2º. Que las elecciones se celebren entre el 1 y el 15 de marzo de 1956 y el Congreso tenga lugar en Madrid del 9 al 15 de abril de 1956.

3º. Que los representantes elegidos, reunidos en el Congreso Nacional, nombren a sus presidentes de Comisiones y que los acuerdos y conclusiones se aprueben por mayoría.

4º. Que por los Ministerios correspondientes se alleguen los medios de toda índole precisos para la preparación y el desarrollo del Congreso, así como para evitar toda clase de obstáculos que pudieran interponerse a su plena efectividad.

Madrid, 1º de febrero de 1956.

Historical Sciences

Sebastian Haumann, Martin Knoll, Detlev Mares (eds.)
Concepts of Urban-Environmental History

2020, 294 p., pb., ill.
29,99 € (DE), 978-3-8376-4375-6
E-Book:
PDF: 26,99 € (DE), ISBN 978-3-8394-4375-0

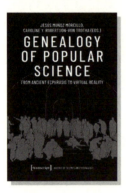

Jesús Muñoz Morcillo, Caroline Y. Robertson-von Trotha (eds.)
Genealogy of Popular Science
From Ancient Ecphrasis to Virtual Reality

2020, 586 p., pb., col. ill.
49,00 € (DE), 978-3-8376-4835-5
E-Book:
PDF: 48,99 € (DE), ISBN 978-3-8394-4835-9

Monika Ankele, Benoît Majerus (eds.)
Material Cultures of Psychiatry

2020, 416 p., pb., col. ill.
40,00 € (DE), 978-3-8376-4788-4
E-Book: available as free open access publication
PDF: ISBN 978-3-8394-4788-8

All print, e-book and open access versions of the titles in our list
are available in our online shop www.transcript-verlag.de/en!

Historical Sciences

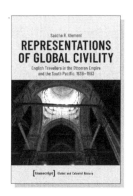

Sascha R. Klement
Representations of Global Civility
English Travellers in the Ottoman Empire
and the South Pacific, 1636–1863

May 2021, 270 p., pb.
45,00 € (DE), 978-3-8376-5583-4
E-Book:
PDF: 44,99 € (DE), ISBN 978-3-8394-5583-8

Berthold Over, Gesa zur Nieden (eds.)
Operatic Pasticcios in 18th-Century Europe
Contexts, Materials and Aesthetics

May 2021, 798 p., pb., col. ill.
60,00 € (DE), 978-3-8376-4885-0
E-Book:
PDF: 59,99 € (DE), ISBN 978-3-8394-4885-4

Federico Buccellati, Sebastian Hageneuer,
Sylva van der Heyden, Felix Levenson (eds.)
**Size Matters – Understanding Monumentality
Across Ancient Civilizations**

2019, 350 p., pb., col. ill.
44,99 € (DE), 978-3-8376-4538-5
E-Book: available as free open access publication
PDF: ISBN 978-3-8394-4538-9

All print, e-book and open access versions of the titles in our list
are available in our online shop www.transcript-verlag.de/en!